sical progression: Lonnie Johnson to B. B. King CREDITS: LONNIE JOHNSON PHOTO BY VAL
OTO BY DICK WATERMAN

# THE ORIGINAL GUI
## and THE POWER (

*The Legendar*

# Lonnie Joh
## Music and Civil

# THE ORIGINAL GUITAR HERO
# and THE POWER OF MUSIC

*The Legendary*
# Lonnie Johnson
## Music and Civil Rights

*Number 8 in the North Texas Lives of Musicians Series*

Dean Alger

University of North Texas Press
Denton, Texas

10  9  8  7  6  5  4  3  2  1

Permissions:
University of North Texas Press
1155 Union Circle #311336
Denton, TX  76203-5017

The paper used in this book meets the minimum requirements of the American National
Standard for Permanence of Paper for Printed Library Materials, z39.48.1984. Binding materials have been chosen for durability.

Library of Congress Cataloging-in-Publication Data

Alger, Dean, author.
The original guitar hero and the power of music : the legendary Lonnie
Johnson, music, and civil rights / Dean Alger.
    pages cm. --  (North Texas lives of musicians series ; number 8)
Includes bibliographical references and index.
ISBN 978-1-57441-546-9 (cloth : alk. paper) -- ISBN 978-1-57441-556-8
(ebook)        1894
1. Johnson, Lonnie, 1899-1970. 2. African American
guitarists--Biography. 3. Blues musicians--United States--Biography. 4.
African American musicians--Biography. 5. African Americans--Civil
rights 6. Music and race--United States. I. Title. II. Series: North
Texas lives of musicians series ; no. 8.
ML419.J625A44 2014
782.421643092--dc23
[B]
                                    2013050120

*The Original Guitar Hero and the Power of Music* is Number 8 in the North Texas Lives
of Musicians Series

The electronic edition of this book was made possible by the support of the Vick Family
Foundation.

## To B. B. King

who took the guitar virtuosity and impassioned singing,
the profound musical feeling, and the deep dignity of Lonnie Johnson, developed
his own superb style, and brought this great music to the world, eventually
becoming the universally beloved "Ambassador of the Blues"

∽∞∾

and to

*Bernie Strassberg and Roberta Barrett*

who understood the greatness of Lonnie's music,
transcended societal barriers and backgrounds,
and were there for him as friends and foundations
(and they're marvelous *characters*, as well!)

∽∞∾

". . . *I knew that some day, somehow, somebody would find me.*"
— LONNIE J, 1960

Well, the fact that *I* rediscovered you in the 21st Century
has enriched my life, Lonnie; I hope that this book
will be the pathway to discovery of you by many others.

— DEAN ALGER, 2013

∽∞∾

# Contents

# List of Illustrations

# Preface

Blues music has long moved me, and jazz and all that it signifies has intrigued me. Starting in the 1990s, I more deeply explored the history of the blues and jazz, reading widely and listening intensively.

But as I read more and more I had concerns about the fact that a number of books on jazz and blues were written in a way that discouraged reading by a broader audience than core specialists. I hope that the way I've written this book exemplifies a better approach, one that's more accessible, yet with ample serious substance.

Frankly, I was shocked by the responses to the book by a series of editors (and literary agents); if this book gets the reception suggested by early reviews, I hope it will help move more editors and agents to deepen their understanding of figures like Lonnie Johnson, and to think in terms beyond a simple, standard old musician biography, including the importance of incorporating broader perspectives.

Blues and jazz are great art forms of major cultural and societal importance, and a wider range of people deserves accessible, significant books on them. I was determined to write *this* book in a manner that could reach more people, *and* to include ample material, analysis and insight of value to specialists. I hope the evidence, logic and wider musical perspectives in this book add significant elements to the appreciation and discussion of popular music, and that the broader societal theme adds to our understanding of the development of American society.

As a "child" of the '60s I saw "The Power of Music" strikingly demonstrated in my youth; so it was natural to see that concept as highly relevant to the present book.

Early in the process of finishing the manuscript and starting to find a publisher for the book, I sent materials to a senior editor for music at a major press, who rejected the book for this primary reason: "Lonnie

Johnson is not *central* enough to blues history to merit a separate book." Well, this book offers compelling proof she was very *wrong*—in more ways than one: The legendary Lonnie J was one of the most important artists in the history of the blues; *and* he was prime founding father of lead and solo guitar in jazz, *and* his influence (in *singing,* as well) was pervasive in popular music of the twentieth century.

Among the reading noted above was a fine, well-written book by Francis Davis, *The History of the Blues.* The book had dedications to drummer Fred Below "and to Lonnie Johnson, subject of one of the great *un*written biographies." I seem to have taken that as a challenge.

As I read more on him, I learned of pioneering guitar duets Lonnie did with Eddie Lang. Loving acoustic guitar and being a humble guitarist, I bought, *Eddie Lang and Lonnie Johnson: Blue Guitars, Volumes I and II,* with the duets they recorded and more. I was entranced. A book on this great musician was needed. So I began a six-year quest to research and write this book, then four additional years of feedback and endless refinement of the book, and of efforts to find an editor and publisher with the understanding, depth and commitment to publish it.

In an article in the December 1939 *Down Beat,* jazz guitar legend Charlie Christian wrote: "Guitar players have long needed a champion, someone to explain to the world that a humble guitarist is something more than a robot pluckin' a gadget to keep the rhythm going." I've sought to do just that in this book, with the keynote and foundation of that explanation in the section headed "The Guitar" early in chapter 4.

I talked with Dick Boak, Director of Artist and Public Relations at Martin Guitars, about Lonnie's importance and the significance of the guitar. We considered a collaboration between the Martin company, the world's greatest makers of steel string acoustic guitars, and this book, but unfortunately couldn't collaborate due to other major projects. The author's favorite guitar is a Martin J-40.

I also enjoyed discussing Lonnie with Howard Kramer, Curatorial Director of the Rock & Roll Hall of Fame. Unfortunately, the Hall of Fame has failed to induct Lonnie Johnson into its Early Influences section. This book provides overwhelming evidence of Lonnie's huge influence on the development of Rock & Roll. I hope it starts a letter-writing campaign to encourage the Hall of Fame to "do the right thing" and induct the great Lonnie Johnson!

This book's release in Spring 2014 is a good time for prominent note of **Lonnie Johnson: February 8, 2014 was the 120th anniversary of his birth in that original music city, New Orleans.**

# Acknowledgments

ADDITIONAL DEDICATION: To the memory of my **cousin Dan Porter** who understood the nature of blues and jazz earlier than I did and introduced me to them.

I was fortunate to have assistance from able people as I went through the process. I hope those people and others with deep interest in him will be pleased to see Lonnie Johnson finally presented *whole*—as well as correcting some inaccuracies that have been passed on from one article and encyclopedia entry to the next.

In a message to me early in work on the book, Lawrence Cohn said, "Lonnie Johnson's musical importance is monumental." This book provides compelling confirmation of that assessment. Also, given the importance of Lonnie Johnson and the broader approach of the book, Larry saw the possibility that this book could "shape up to be one of the most important books ever done in American Vernacular Music." I hope the book lives up to that foreseen potential.

Cohn, former Vice President of Columbia/Epic Records, Grammy-winning producer of *Robert Johnson: The Complete Recordings*, editor of the superb book, *Nothing But the Blues*, was a profound inspiration and guide for me over virtually the entire period I worked on this book. As the Lonnie Johnson photo on the cover of Cohn's book illustrates, he understood the importance of Lonnie Johnson long before I did. Larry was especially helpful at several crucial points. I've treasured our talks about this and other music.

I also richly enjoyed my visit to Cohn's house, with his remarkable collection of historic photos, posters, other memorabilia, and recordings and test pressings in blues, jazz and more. His collection is an American cultural treasure.

In a later stage of the work, Grammy-winning record producer and respected blues writer Richard Shurman did a careful, detailed review of the full manuscript and offered many suggestions and comments in a most constructive way. And he did so in expeditious manner, knowing the time issue. His deep understanding of the subject and his profound insights significantly contributed to making this book what it needed to be; and the e-mail exchanges along the way were an edifying pleasure.

My interview and long visit in New York with Chris Albertson, and later communications, provided important information and insight. His endeavors in blues and jazz, as record producer, writer, broadcaster, and now blogger, have been extraordinary contributions to our culture. Getting to know him was another of those special treats in this process.

Late in the process professor (and musician) Steven C. Tracy read the book at a critical time (despite intense time demands of his own) and offered thoughts that were profoundly important in preserving the nature and significance of this book. He, along with Cohn and Shurman, were heroes for this process.

Earlier, Chris Smith of Great Britain read the complete manuscript and gave me a thorough review and critique. With his great knowledge of blues and other music, especially including Lonnie Johnson's work, and of other relevant subjects, he understood the multiple dimensions of the book and provided many helpful recommendations.

Alan Balfour offered encouragement through the entire process, sent articles and recordings, and made helpful suggestions. For this and other people's projects, he has been one of those unsung heroes who has contributed so much to blues writing.

Thanks to Rick Bates who has contributed information and encouragement to this project for years and has been operationally helpful on multiple fronts; and it's been a pleasure to talk about all this with him. He has been a great contributor to purveying America's profound music. Thanks also to his partner and wife Nancy Meyer for her fine work.

Special thanks go to musicians who gave their time for interviews, etc. First and foremost, B. B. King and Buddy Guy gave me very helpful interviews—and some great quotes—as well as inspiration. The late Henry Townsend was another very valuable information source. Pete Seeger provided some reflections, as did Robert Lockwood, Jr. My interview with superb jazz guitarist and guitar teacher Jack Wilkins added more enlightenment—conducted during a break in his New Birdland Jazz club gig (in Manhattan) with Larry Coryell. Jack's dazzling playing that night was one of my finest musical experiences.

Thanks to Lewis Porter and Ed Berger of the Institute of Jazz Studies, Rutgers University, for inviting me to air my research and thoughts in their Jazz Research Roundtable series and for encouragement of the project. Prof. Porter was a continuing inspiration and information resource (and is a fine keyboards player). Thanks to IJS grad student Sean Lorre for RA work.

Superb Minneapolis musician and friend "Papa John" Kolstad gave me guidance in some musical analysis. His continuing encouragement of this book project was appreciated. Thanks also to guitar virtuoso and expert analyst of guitar work, Lenny Carlson, for guidance in analyzing some of Lonnie's most important recordings.

Others who read parts of the manuscript and provided valuable feedback, helped with information, etc.: Bruce Boyd Raeburn, Curator of the Hogan Jazz Archive at Tulane University, New Orleans, read the chapter on "New Orleans Music" and made helpful suggestions. Thanks to guitar experts Andy Cohen, Neil Harpe, Jas Obrecht and James Sallis. Thanks to: Howard Rye, Paul Oliver, Jim O'Neil, Joe Mosbrook, Jeff Harris, Bob Eagle, Eric LeBlanc, Bob Koester (President of Delmark Records and The Jazz Record Mart in Chicago), Michael Fitzgerald, Barry Mazor, William Anderson (of the Cleveland Public Library), Andy Balterman and Brian Powers (of the Cincinnati Public Library), Deborah Gillaspie (formerly of the Chicago Jazz Archive in the University of Chicago Library), staff at the Williams Research Center in the Historic New Orleans Collection, Richard Flohil, Bob Groom, Paul Garon, Chris Barber. Thanks to St. Louis musician Leroy Pierson, who, in encouragement of this book effort, generously gave me an old 78 record of Lonnie's "St. Louis Cyclone Blues," as well as assistance on St. Louis music history; and thanks for information to Ron Edwards, fine St. Louis bottleneck guitarist and blues radio host.

Thanks to Susan Henry, Carla Foley, and John Ohr of the St. Anthony Park branch, St. Paul Public Library system, for their thoughtful help—and for offering a wonderful library service, housed in that architectural gem of a Carnegie Library. Thanks to Sam Ryan of the Hamline-Midway branch, as well.

Speaking of librarians, thanks for research help to Deborah Kelly-Milburn, special online research librarian for The Harvard College Library—and dear friend.

As noted in the Dedication, special thanks go to Bernie Strassberg and Roberta Barrett who were there for Lonnie and who gave me vital information and perspective for this book.

Of course, any remaining errors, mistakes in interpretation, etc., are the responsibility of the author.

No "literary agent" played a significant role in the development of this book or in getting it to a publisher; that fact and the narrow-minded orientations, failure of due diligence, and lack of understanding I experienced from them are troubling for our culture. The same was the case with a series of editors in this field, as noted in the Preface.

To her credit, UNT Press Managing Editor Karen DeVinney responded well and promptly to my initial letter, expeditiously read the full manuscript (unlike most other editors), saw the basic significance of the book, and started the process. Marketing Manager Paula Oates worked diligently to get the word out on the book. An anonymous reviewer for UNT Press offered useful suggestions.

My brother Ardon Alger and sister-in-law Nancy Mintie cheered me on in the project, and added some financial help when most needed; the later stages of this book were prepared on the Ardon Alger Honorary iMac.

Thanks again to cousin Dan Porter (no relation to Lewis). At a difficult point in the process of doing the book, he offered financial assistance, despite very modest resources. Sadly, late in the process, cousin Dan passed away.

Otherwise, my family did not help when I was in serious need in a late stage of this project. Frankly, three members of my generation of the extended family were selfish, self-indulgent, and betrayed the values our Granddad Holloway gave to us.

Thanks to Dr. Michael Freischel (also known as "the Do Wop Dentist") for encouragement in the project and for special consideration.

Thanks to Rena Dundovic for various assistance, including expertly putting together the DVD "mock-up" of the opening scene for the prospective movie of Lonnie J's life.

I again appreciated the encouragement from my friends, the notorious Williams Brothers of the Minneapolis area: Brent (a thoughtful guy who has a fine musical sensibility and is my favorite tennis buddy) and his wife Barb (special friend and music lover) and Todd (with whom I enjoy sharing music, and who serves as my Special Spiritual Guru).

Finally, thanks for the continuing encouragement and wisdom of my Soul Brother, Dr. Michael Milburn.

*Dean Alger*
*St. Paul, Minnesota*
*October 2013*

# 1

# The Legendary Lonnie Johnson— One of the Most Important Musicians of the 20th Century

## MUSICIANS AND PROGRESS ON CIVIL RIGHTS

Although he's not well known today, Lonnie Johnson was one of the century's most important musicians. His story is of major musical and cultural significance; and it's a fascinating and inspiring tale in its personal elements.

> *"When you mention guitar, the first thing I think of is Lonnie Johnson."*
> —B. B. KING.[1]

In *The Guitar Players,* James Sallis put Johnson in proper company: "Lonnie Johnson probably should be as well known as Bessie Smith or Louis Armstrong; his artistry is at that level. . . . His touch, the expressiveness he achieved on the instrument, was a revelation in his time and still affords a rich and rare harvest to guitarists."[2]

Former Rolling Stones bass player Bill Wyman (a serious student of blues history), in his well-presented book *Bill Wyman's Blues Odyssey,* pointed out Lonnie's pioneering significance: "He was a guitar legend before we knew what they were. You can trace his playing style in a direct line through T-Bone Walker and B. B. King to Eric Clapton."[3] The legendary Lonnie J was the Original Guitar Hero.[4]

A particular element of Lonnie's virtuosity, which Sallis alluded to, is of profound importance in guitar history: Lonnie was the principal early figure in developing the full *expressive* capacity of the guitar (other than specialty use of a "slide"), which has been of huge significance in the development of blues and Rock music especially, as well as in Country music and the guitar in jazz.

**A Note on the Nature of this Book:** Since no full biography of this important musician has been published, I present ample biographical information on Lonnie Johnson, a fair amount of it not previously reported. However, I want to emphasize that this book is not just a standard biography. In fact, this book is *more* about describing and analyzing Lonnie's work, assessing his influence on other musicians, and his general importance for twentieth century music. Second, it is about using Lonnie's musical output as a vehicle for discussing the evolution of *the guitar* in popular music and how artistry on the guitar developed—and ultimately, how the guitar became the dominant instrument in popular music and a cultural icon.

There is an important further dimension of Lonnie's impact in conjunction with other musicians, over several decades: Because of their public prominence and because of how they presented and conducted themselves, Johnson and other great Black musicians—and some White ones—had a very important effect on the self-image of African-Americans and their image in the broader White-dominated society; and they contributed significantly to the gradual, agonizing progress on Civil Rights. This vital subject is introduced in this chapter and discussed at further points in the book; and my own vision on this is more fully discussed in Appendix II. Another more limited theme is about the nature of blues and jazz in modern society and their relation to modern art, with Lonnie as a strong contributor; this adds perspective on the significance and impact of the music in and for the century. These themes are profoundly interwoven, in our history, in Lonnie's life, and in the book.

I've presented the material in a way that a seriously interested but wider audience than specialists with technical music training will find engaging and very readable. In this chapter, I introduce the extraordinary Lonnie Johnson to a somewhat broader audience who may have heard little about him. Because of Lonnie's importance for the music of the twentieth century and his fascinating story, a wider audience than the core specialists should have readable access to this material. But the book also includes ample material and analysis of value to those specialists.

## The Legendary Lonnie J

Alonzo "Lonnie" Johnson was born into a musical family in New Orleans in 1894.[5] He was a major early influence on many of the greatest figures in blues history, and he readily spanned blues and jazz. He played on three of the Louis Armstrong "Hot Five" recordings that were landmarks in the history of jazz. Regarding Lonnie's playing with Satchmo on one of those recordings, "Hotter Than That," the distinguished music writer and composer Gunther Schuller said: "Johnson's swinging, rhythmic backing and his remarkable two-bar exchanges with Armstrong are certainly one of the highlights of classic jazz."[6] He also played on four early Duke Ellington tunes, including one of Duke's most celebrated early works titled, "The Mooche." Ellington said: "Lonnie Johnson helped bring about one of my giant steps, milestones established by men [who were] sound of ear and skilled to thrill through the climate they created with their music magic. I have always felt indebted to him because his guitar added a new luster to my orchestral attempts on the records we made in 1928."[7]

As jazz writer Martin Williams said, "Charlie Christian was not, as some commentators have contended, the first important jazz guitar soloist. Anyone who has heard Lonnie Johnson, with Louis Armstrong, Duke Ellington or on his own, will know that he was not."[8] In fact: "As the inventor of the guitar solo, Lonnie created an approach to that instrument which revolutionized the history of jazz, blues and popular music in general," Gerard Herzhaft said in the *Encyclopedia of the Blues*.[9]

Indeed, with all that, Lonnie Johnson was a prime precursor to the Rock guitar heroes. For two examples, in his autobiography, Chuck Berry cites Lonnie's influence; and a member of Buddy Holly's band reported Lonnie's influence on Holly.[10] Lonnie had significant influence on key Country guitarists like Chet Atkins, as well.

With all that and more, Lonnie Johnson was the leading original force in moving the guitar to be the dominant instrument of the second half of the twentieth century through today.

Further, Lonnie's *singing* influenced major figures in twentieth century music, B. B. King being one of the most famous examples. The other most famous example was Elvis, who covered Lonnie's big 1948 R&B ballad hit, "Tomorrow Night," at Sun Records at the beginning of his recording career; listening to the Elvis version of "Tomorrow Night," one can hear a significant effect of Lonnie's vocal work on Elvis's singing style (discussed later in detail). Even most specialists don't fully understand the caliber and influence of Lonnie Johnson's singing.

Lonnie's poorly understood excellence as a singer is potently demonstrated in four of the first six songs on *The* Ultimate *Best of Lonnie Johnson* CD, prepared by the author as a companion to this book. (Available by non-traditional means; see the author's website: *www.deanalger.com*.) Grammy-winning record producer Richard Shurman has said of this album, "The CD is wonderful. It's very well compiled and balanced and showcases Lonnie's greatness beyond question."

Still further, Lonnie, in his singing combined with his guitar-playing, was the first musician to present the smoother, more sophisticated "urban blues" (in contrast to the old Country Blues) which were a prime force leading to Rhythm & Blues and then to Rock & Roll.

Another notable impact: Lonnie and Bob Dylan crossed paths in the early '60s in places like Gerdes Folk City in Greenwich Village, New York. In his memoir, *Chronicles*, Dylan said:

> Besides my devotion to a new vocal technique, something else would go along with helping me re-create my songs . . . I played guitar in the casual Carter Family flat-picking style . . . The style had been practical, but now I was going to . . . replace it with something more active with more definition of presence.
>
> This style had been shown to me in the early '60s by Lonnie Johnson. Lonnie was a great jazz and blues artist from the '30s [*sic*] who

was still playing in the '60s. . . . Lonnie took me aside one night and showed me a style of playing based on an odd rather than even numbered system, saying "this might help you." He had me play chords and he demonstrated how to do it . . . It's a highly controlled system of playing and relates to the notes of a scale, how they combine numerically, how they form melodies out of triplets and are axiomatic to the rhythm and the chord changes. I never used the style. . . . But now all of a sudden it came back to me, and I realized that this way of playing would revitalize my world. I understood the rules and critical elements because Lonnie had showed them to me so crystal clear. [11]

Elsewhere Dylan said of Lonnie, "I must say he greatly influenced me."[12]

The multiple dimensions of Lonnie Johnson's work are how effective he was at performing as a lead player and singer, *and* fitting in well with a big jazz band like Ellington's and smaller blues and jazz groups, *and* being an outstanding accompanist who was able to adapt to a wide range of singers' styles. His fine accompanist work ranged from backing the relatively crude country blues singer "Texas" Alexander, who didn't "keep time" accurately, to backing powerful blues singer Bessie Smith, who didn't tolerate other musicians "stealing" her spotlight, to doing masterful duets with other guitarists and with a piano master and singer like Otis Spann. Only T-Bone Walker even approached such versatile virtuosity. As B. B. King said:

Lonnie Johnson was one of the greatest influences in my life. . . . because he recorded with Duke Ellington . . . , Louis Armstrong, he recorded with many people of various styles of music and he fit in. He was that link in the chain between whatever musical style there might be. . . . God almighty I loved him. So, I wanted to be like him. I still do.[13]

But stunningly, Lonnie Johnson has not been inducted into the "Early Influences" section of the Rock & Roll Hall of Fame. That is a big hole in the Hall's presentation of the history and origins of the music that dominated the music scene—and the broader culture—over the second half of the twentieth century through today. This book and coordinated projects will, hopefully, lead to rectifying that great gap in the Rock & Roll Hall of Fame.

This then, is a man whose story must be fully told as a vital part of the development of American musical art. But, as was lamented by B. B. King, "it hurt me . . . that Lonnie never got the critical acknowledgement he deserved." Interviews I did with blues guitar stars Buddy Guy and Hubert Sumlin (lead guitarist for the Howlin' Wolf band) yielded the same thought.[14]

Further, Lonnie Johnson's fascinating, dramatic life ranged from losing most of his family in the influenza pandemic of 1918 to fame and musical prominence in blues and jazz in the later 1920s to working in steel mills and as a janitor at various times to a musical comeback in the blues and folk revival of the 1960s. And that considerably shortens the story and lessens the twists and turns of his life. Aspects of Lonnie's life also represent significant elements in the broader American experience and the mosaic of the American character.

## A Glimpse of the Person

Lonnie Johnson's life was an extraordinary saga of superb musical work, recording with many of the giants of jazz and blues, and developing relative fame in the later 1920s. But there were also times when he had to work at "blue collar" jobs. In chapter 2 we explore Lonnie's beginnings in the "Original Music City," New Orleans, and his personal origins in a family of musicians. Additionally, among many other stories, there is the compelling tale of his final years, spent primarily in Toronto. Those years were highlighted by his determination to overcome the effects of a horrible auto accident and three strokes and his dramatic appearance in a final concert at age 76, with up-and-coming blues guitarist Buddy Guy accompanying him.

A glimpse of the kind of person Lonnie Johnson was and how his music could affect people is provided by a story related by his friend Bernie Strassberg, with whom Lonnie stayed when he was in New York City in the '60s. This tale illustrates the *personal* dimension of the Power of Music; an introduction to the broader societal dimension of The Power of Music follows.

For me, one of the most memorable occasions when you can say music could soothe the soul and affect a person involved my youngest son, Mitch, around '62 or '63. Mitch had a friend who he said was kind of strange. He said, "Dad, this kid never smiles. He has a real hard life at home. I know his father is very old, and he beats him up; and this guy, he's stoic, he never shows any emotion at all." Then my son brought this kid over to our house. Lonnie was sleeping, then he came downstairs to the living room. Seeing the kid [and sensing the situation] he got out his acoustic guitar and sat on the sofa and started passionately singing this song, "Red River Blues." And this kid, who had shown no emotion to my son Mitch all the time he had known him, the tears just started pouring down. (I'm crying just thinking about it.) I looked at my wife and she looked at me, I looked at my son, Lonnie hugged my son . . . I mean, this kid from New York City encountering that music from this old blues guy singing . . . That's just the power of what his music could do.[15]

Through the rest of this book I explore Lonnie's musical work and significance, including a musical tendency and some developments that were not so musically effective that also explain part of why this giant of twentieth century music did not achieve the fame his artistic importance merits. I also relate as much of his life story as is obtainable at this late date.

Here, let me relate two anecdotes that lend interesting perspective—and a little humor—to the story of this extraordinary musician. Firstly, while Lonnie was aware of his musical significance, he had a decent dose of modesty. In Paul Oliver's *Conversation with the Blues*, from interviews Oliver did in 1960 with major blues musicians, Lonnie says: "My brother [James 'Steady Roll' Johnson], he played piano *and* violin *and* guitar. He was better than me"[16]—this from the remarkable instrumentalist so highly praised by the musicians and writers noted earlier, who also played all three instruments and more. (It reminds me of those passages when Sherlock Holmes talks of his *smarter* brother.)

On early records he also played banjo and even kazoo and the now largely forgotten harmonium. Amusingly, British blues writer Chris

Smith sent me this observation: "On the evidence of his two recordings with it, Lonnie was an awful kazoo player. Somehow it's good to know he was human—he wasn't brilliant on *every* instrument!"[17]

An article in *Billboard* magazine on home recordings released on CD in 2000 began by saying: "Was there ever a blues performer who got a rawer deal from history than Lonnie Johnson?"[18] No, there wasn't. Hopefully, this book and related projects will finally give this musical master his due.

Next I build a foundation for understanding the broader societal impact of Lonnie and other musicians, along with the nature of the music itself. Lonnie Johnson's life and music did not take place in a vacuum, as with Louis Armstrong, Duke Ellington and other top Black musicians; they were unavoidably involved in the struggle of African-Americans and developments leading to progress on Civil Rights. A more complete discussion of this vital subject is presented in Appendix II; I urge the reader to take in that striking, inspirational material on developments that were so significant for American history and further demonstrate the broader Power of Music.

## Blues, Jazz, and the Power of Music

Regarding the nature of the blues and jazz and their broader human and societal significance, jazz writer Martin Williams wrote of a couple of prominent White musicians and posed a vital question. He noted how famous jazz clarinetist Benny Goodman wanted to learn to play like New Orleans "colored Creole" Jimmie Noone and "staked his career on" playing music primarily from African-American sources. And Williams asked why Mick Jagger from London would want to sing like some old Black bluesman from Mississippi or Chicago. He wondered: "What drew Benny and Mick to make such music?" And: "Both men obviously express something deeply, abidingly important for their followers. What is it? Why do we all . . . find such meaning in the musical culture of Afro-Americans? . . . I can't answer my question."[19] As noted jazz writer and performer Ted Gioia put it: "Why has this music resonated so profoundly in the American consciousness?"[20] The following two sections, plus later material, answer the questions of Williams and Gioia, for African-Americans and for the wider society.

Blues and jazz have been of seminal importance in the music of the last century, and in the broader American culture and society. The United States Congress proclaimed 2003 "The Year of the Blues" and there were related events, culminating in films shown on U. S. public television that commemorated the blues and their significance. In 2001, to much media attention, public TV ran a ten-part documentary film by Ken Burns on the history of jazz.

The blues and jazz arose from the most humble and oppressed of people; and yet this deep, moving, innovative music had such profound impact.

Blues songs are often about human relationships and everyday troubles and triumphs. But as Black bluesman Memphis Slim once said, sometimes they would sing verses that were actually veiled, often metaphorical, versions of "cussing out the bossman. . . ."[21]

Further, as jazz writer Gary Giddins and others have said, "jazz incarnates liberty."[22] With the improvisation and the essential spirit of the music, jazz does embody the genuine spirit of liberty. In related manner, the blues musicians who traveled around the country in the first half of the twentieth century sang about their freedom to move around and escape the neo-slavery of share-cropping, levee work, and so on, and they embodied the desire of many of their brothers and sisters to leave and be free of the brutal, racist conditions in the South. Lonnie Johnson's powerful protest song about forced levee work, "Broken Levee Blues," is an especially good example of that spirit and orientation (more on that in chapter 5).

There is a wonderful anecdote that takes us to the heart of the power of the main stream of this profound African-American music over its history. This anecdote involves Paul Robeson and Negro Spirituals and is especially striking in that the observation came from a music critic in Vienna, Austria, after Robeson gave a concert there, thus illustrating the internationally recognized power of the music:

> . . . Viennese music critic Siegfried Geyer, knowing of Paul's minimal formal voice training, fully expected to hear [amateurish sounds.

But:] "When this man began to sing one of those Negro spirituals filled with the deepest melancholy—when slow and full came the first words 'Wade in the water'—the hall suddenly grew hushed and still. We were listening to [vocal] tones of purity seldom heard, and what followed—one spiritual after another—confirmed the phenomenon which the Negro singer represents: a voice which is no mere function of the larynx, but of which the motive force is the soul."[23]

Lonnie Johnson's powerful, soulful *singing*, as well as his exceptionally expressive guitar work, demonstrate that deep "motive force of the soul," from "Broken Levee Blues" of 1928 to "Backwater Blues" of 1948 to "Mr. Blues Walks" of 1965.

The stunning power and beauty of this music was recognized early on by classical music composer Antonin Dvorak, who came to America in 1892; he wrote his masterwork, Symphony no. 9, "From the New World," drawing on his experience in the U.S. He said: "I am now satisfied that the future music of this country must be founded upon what are called the negro melodies. In the negro melodies of America I discovered all that is needed for a great and noble school of music. They are pathetic, tender, passionate, melancholy, solemn, religious, bold, merry. . . ."[24]

That the profound, powerful music that developed from those origins came from the most oppressed people makes it an ultimate artistic expression of the triumph of the human spirit.

Albert Murray articulated a key human function of the music: The blues "deal with the most fundamental of all existential imperatives, affirmation, [that is,] reaffirmation and continuity in the face of adversity."[25] Blues writer Paul Garon added further perspective, in effect completing Albert Murray's thought: "As the poetic voice of a people distinctively victimized by the whole gamut of the repressive forces of [society], the blues long ago found itself in the service of human emancipation by virtue of the particular manner in which it deals with such repression."[26]

From the jazz side, Dizzy Gillespie added a further dimension: "Our music really exemplifies a perfect balance between discipline and freedom."[27]

As far back as Plato the power of music was recognized: "The introduction of novel fashions in music . . . [can affect] the whole fabric of society, whose . . . conventions are unsettled by any revolution in that quarter." But he also said that, "rhythm and harmony sink deep into the recesses of the soul and take strongest hold there."[28]

## "Somebody Plus": The Impact of Lonnie Johnson and Fellow Musicians on African-Americans' Image and Progress Towards Civil Rights

*"When the time came for Lonnie to [perform] at any place, everyone respected him as a real renowned guy. He wasn't just anybody, he was somebody* plus."[29]

—Henry Townsend

Beginning in the 1920s, Duke Ellington, Louis Armstrong, Lonnie Johnson, and some other leading African-American musicians gave a big boost to the image-enhancement of the race and helped move progress on civil rights. The nature of the music and the experience of making it were also part of the impact. I introduce this broader societal theme here, touch on it further throughout the book, and explore it in more detail in Appendix II.

Tragically, the societal standing and *self-image* of the "Negro" in America for the first half of the twentieth century and more was deeply troubled. Listen to the great African-American singer, actor, lecturer, and activist Paul Robeson. He spoke at first of those magnificent "Negro Spirituals," but the basic point also applies to the blues (with partial origins in the Spirituals) and jazz:

These songs are to Negro culture what the works of the great poets are to English culture. They are the soul of the race made manifest . . . But the suffering he has undergone has left an indelible mark on the Negro's soul, and at the present stage he suffers from an inferiority complex. . . .[30]

A telling exemplification of how the racist system actively beat down the self-identity of Black folks on a daily basis comes in an anecdote related by Alan Lomax in his book on his blues-hunting experiences,

*The Land Where the Blues Began.* Lomax had "discovered" the early great bluesman Son House on a cotton plantation in Mississippi in the early 1940s, and, while listening to House and some fellow musicians play, he ran afoul of the plantation manager, who took Lomax to the local sheriff. Starting to explain about how they had "the finest blues combination I've heard," he was asked their names and then said: "Well, Mister House is the . . .". Then, as Lomax relates in the book: "I knew I'd made a mistake before the words were out of my mouth. The sheriff's red face turned beet color. His eyes narrowed to pinpoints. 'You call a nigger *Mister*,' he snapped. 'I don't believe you're from Texas [or] Washington either. You're a fake. You're probably an agitator. . . .'"[31] To address Son House as "Mister" House violated the race code; that came dangerously close to recognizing this man's adult humanity.

It's interesting to consider the title of Lonnie Johnson's very first recording in that light: "Mr. Johnson's Blues"—recorded a full sixteen years before the Lomax-Son House incident. Lonnie addressed others in that respectful form and expected to be referred to as "Mr. Johnson."

Samuel Floyd's work on "The Power of Black Music" discussed the "black cultural apostasy that resulted from modernism," which came with the new (twentieth) century. (For more on modernism and its relation to art, music, society, and this book, see the "Interlude" section in chapter two.) Floyd also noted: "Another . . . response to—or perhaps even a cause of—this apostasy was the determination of elite and middle-class African-Americans to 'elevate the race' by producing within it the artistic and intellectual resources and excellence that would prove them to be the intellectual and social equals of white Americans." And many Blacks felt they should and could do so "not by denying the value of their racial heritage, but by reaffirming and asserting it."[32] Lonnie Johnson's role in that is discussed in the following and later in the book.

The 1920s was the time of the "Harlem Renaissance," that burgeoning of Black arts, culture and intellectual life, as well as a time when many African-Americans were starting to more aggressively assert their rights. Their people had earned the right to full citizenship and equality in society, they felt, by fighting and dying for the United States in World War I, though in segregated manner, and due to the increasingly significant achievements of their musicians and artists, writers and intellectuals, educators and scientists. It's noteworthy that the first book of poems by that icon of the Harlem Renaissance, Langston Hughes, was *The Weary Blues*.

A principal way to elevate the race was through the profound music, which, more than any other form of Black achievement, reached throughout American society starting in the 1920s. Through the '50s African-Americans were shut out of upper positions in business, the professions, and even in sports (mostly). Only in music were Blacks able to command a national stage, though still facing much discrimination. Music was the one area in which an African-American could, in a broad public arena, show a face of their race that contradicted the discriminatory notions held by most Americans. As Ted Gioia summarized, "In America, music was the first sphere of social interaction in which racial barriers were challenged and overturned."[33]

Through the '20s, '30s and '40s, the migration of Blacks out of the brutal, racist conditions in the South to better job possibilities and (theoretically) more benign settings in northern cities like Chicago, called "The Great Migration," was a major sociological development in America. With that came changes in orientations and aspirations, which affected and were affected by the blues and jazz. As Paul Oliver said, Blacks newly arrived in Chicago and other cities wanted "both a reminder of their home background and reassurance in their new and unfamiliar environment. They wanted to feel in touch with their friends and at the same time be urban and sophisticated. Lonnie Johnson was the kind of singer [and guitarist] who met their needs."[34]

As Giles Oakley wrote, Lonnie's "whole musical style and manner spoke of urbane sophistication. . . . "[35] Bill Wyman of the Rolling Stones said Lonnie was "a superb guitarist and a sharp dresser who oozed urban sophistication."[36] Lonnie, like Duke Ellington and some other great Black musical artists, provided a compelling image that said, "we are sophisticated people and the greatest of artists." It bolstered Blacks' pride of race and gave significant added impetus to the movement among African-Americans to demand equal rights. Bert Williams, Paul Robeson and Bill "Bojangles" Robinson added to this in the '10s, '20s and '30s (as did James Reese Europe in the teens, at least around

New York). The creativity, elegance, dignity, and striking public presence of people like Duke Ellington and Lonnie Johnson gave such "a sense of *possibility*" for Black folks, as Ralph Ellison astutely put it."[37] Camille Forbes stated it well:

> The reconstruction of blackness entailed an assertion of a new representation, which required . . . the creation of a "presentable" image and the shedding of the past—the "Old Negro," defined in opposition to the new. In order to create a presentable image, blacks had to invalidate the dominant society's notion of the race as childlike, ignorant, and immoral by supplanting it with the reality of blacks as mature, intelligent, and principled. They would do that by displaying exceptional Negroes. . . . [38]

Lonnie Johnson was doing this by 1926, with recordings out and prominent appearances (before Ellington was widely noted—see chapter 4) during that crucial period of the reconsideration of African-Americans' self-concept,[39] the Harlem Renaissance. It's also notable that Lonnie's celebrated guitar duet recordings with Eddie Lang in 1928 and 1929 were, as blues writer Chris Smith has pointed out, "the first significant interracial partnership in jazz."[40] (Jelly Roll Morton, a mixed-race Creole from New Orleans, made recordings with a White band, the New Orleans Rhythm Kings, in 1923. But those recordings were a guest appearance and Jelly was more Creole than Black; bassist Milt Hinton called him "half white."[41] The French in his background is clear in his mother's photo.[42] Creoles are discussed in chapter two. The Johnson-Lang guitar duets solely involved two equal partners, one Black and one White.)

**Radio and the Transcending of Racial Barriers** The 1920s also saw the rise of radio as a mass medium of communication. Duke Ellington's band broadcast over the CBS radio network from the famous Cotton Club, starting in December 1929. These broadcasts made the Ellington band famous and exposed a wide public to his creative jazz compositions and his brilliant soloists like Johnny Hodges. Lonnie had his own New York City radio show in the early '30s.

The number of homes with radio sets grew at a rapid rate in the second half of the 1920s; and as music historian John Edward Hasse wrote, "Radio transformed American life, creating instantaneous common experiences through the vast nation. . . ."[43] Radio had a revolutionary trait: Its broadcasts refused to conform to the boundaries of a racially segregated society. As top communications scholar George Gerbner articulated it: "New media of communication provide new ways of selecting, composing and sharing perspectives. New institutions of communication create new publics across boundaries of time, space and status."[44]

Thus, starting in the late 1920s, jazz from African-Americans reached large numbers of White listeners via radio and entranced them, though some Americans also got a taste of the music in concerts, clubs, and elsewhere. Then the Great Depression made radio the primary form of popular entertainment, since it was free and most folks had radios by the 1930s. Starting in the early 1940s, blues was being sent from stations in Memphis, Helena, Arkansas, etc. (In New York City there was a program called "The Spell of the Blues" that was aired at different times and days on stations WPCH and WMCA as early as fall 1929.)[45]

As the years went on, White audiences for the music expanded and future music stars were influenced. Peter Guralnick said of a young Elvis Presley in 1952–1954, "if he had never left his apartment, just listening to the radio would have been a big step toward completing his musical education." Elvis heard "Red, Hot and Blue," the radio show of DJ Dewey Phillips on WHBQ in Memphis, which played blues by Muddy Waters, Elmore James, etc., as well as other types of music. On WDIA Elvis heard the young B. B. King, Black gospel quartets, and so on.

WHBQ or WDIA is also, no doubt, where Elvis first heard Lonnie Johnson's big hit from 1948, "Tomorrow Night," which Elvis covered at the beginning of his recording career in 1954 and from which he borrowed what became a signature part of his vocal technique (analyzed in chapter 7). Indeed, after hearing it on the radio, "Charlie's Record Shop in Memphis was where Elvis first played [for his girlfriend] the original of *one of the songs he sang all the time*, Lonnie Johnson's 'Tomorrow Night'," as Guralnick reported[46] (emphasis added).

But the influence could also move in the opposite racial direction—again, radio not respecting the boundaries of segregation. Starting in the late 1920s many Black folks, including many southern Black musicians, liked the records of Country music founding father, Jimmie Rodgers, for example. Moving it forward a generation, Chuck Berry heard Black jazz, blues and boogie woogie by Fats Waller, Louis Armstrong, Lonnie Johnson and others from an East St. Louis radio station. But Chuck also said: "The beautiful harmony of the country music that KMOK radio station played was almost irresistible."[47]

As jazz increasingly dominated American music and captivated much of Europe from the late 1920s through the mid-1940s, Duke Ellington and Louis Armstrong especially became widely popular and transcended racial boundaries. In the summer of 1933, Duke and band did a European tour. "The press interest on both sides of the Atlantic was phenomenal. *Time* magazine dispatched a reporter to accompany the Ellington men on the [ocean] liner. In England the band was feted, and at a party given by [newspaper baron] Lord Beaverbrook, the Prince of Wales famously sat in on the drums." Jazz in general and Duke and band in specific were getting increasing praise from the realm of classical music, as well. Boston Symphony conductor Serge Koussevitzky said: "Jazz is an important contribution to modern musical literature. It has an epochal significance—it is not superficial, it is fundamental." British composer Constant Lambert wrote: "I know of nothing in Ravel so dexterous in treatment as the varied solos in the middle of [Ellington's] ebullient 'Hot and Bothered,' and nothing in Stravinsky more dynamic than the final section." One of those "solos in the middle" of "Hot and Bothered," playing counterpoint, was the guitar work of Lonnie Johnson.

By the 1930s Louis Armstrong, with his increasing connection with all types of audiences and his marvelous humanity, appealed well beyond racial lines. As jazz writer Gary Giddins has written, "By 1936, when Bing Crosby brought him to Hollywood to appear in *Pennies from Heaven*, Armstrong's popularity was immense, and . . . he used his renown to shatter racial obstacles while spreading the gospel of jazz." Marc Miller described the tremendous standing and influence of Louis Armstrong:

> A central figure in the culture of his times, Armstrong's impact extended well beyond the field of music. His talent as a musician . . . [and] on

stage allowed him to become a major player in a changing entertainment world. . . . New media allowed Armstrong to reach audiences throughout America and much of the world. . . . The force of his creativity and personality left its mark on dance, theater, the visual arts, fashion, poetry, and literature. Armstrong's story also touched the social and political currents of his time.[48]

Armstrong, like Ellington, was receiving praise from significant figures in classical music. In 1938 noted composer and music writer Virgil Thompson said that Louis was "a master of musical art . . . His style of improvisation . . . combined the highest reaches of instrumental virtuosity with the most tensely disciplined melodic structure and the most spontaneous emotional expression. . . ." Gunther Schuller has discussed how this recognition began with Armstrong's later recordings of his "Hot Five" and "Hot Seven" bands, especially starting around the time Lonnie Johnson played on three of those landmark records in late 1927 (as is discussed in chapter 4).

**KEY POINT:** *All this helped further legitimate for the general public the music and its brilliant Black creators as important artistic forces and contributors to American culture.*

In the '20s, '30s and early '40s there were other major figures in jazz and other genres of popular music who transcended racial barriers and enhanced understanding. Those included the great, entertaining pianist and songwriter Fats Waller, singer Ethel Waters, and lovely singer and actress Lena Horne. Notable events like the 1938 "From Spirituals to Swing" concert and Marian Anderson's 1939 performance before 75,000 people at the Lincoln Memorial further contributed to the movement. So did popular White Big Band leaders of the later 1930s and 1940s, then Norman Granz and his Jazz at the Philharmonic in the '40s and '50s, who took stands against racism. As the subtitle of his biography put it, Granz was "the man who used jazz for justice."[49]

The unique stature and impact of Louis Armstrong, as a striking part of the story of the power of music in this realm, was illustrated in a marvelous and delightful way that I can't resist noting here. During a mid-'50s tour under U.S. State Department auspices, Armstrong and band performed in East Berlin. After the performances, they found East Berlin under communist control dreary, so Louis said to some band members, "Let's go to West Berlin." Bass player Arvel Shaw continues this story of the international power of the music:

> Couldn't do that with papers from Russians in East Berlin and from the U.S. Louis said, "Let's go anyway." So we got on the bus to go through the Berlin Wall at Checkpoint Charlie. We got to the East German side and the Russian soldiers and East German police had their guns out. One of the guards looked at us and said, "Louis Armstrong!" He called out all the guards, got Louis' autograph, and waved us all on. And when we got to the American side, a six foot seven sergeant from Texas—oh, he was fierce!—said, "How'd you get through here? Where are your papers?" And he got out handcuffs. Sergeant then looks and says, "Satchmo—this is Satchmo!" He called the guards and they got autographs and waved us on. Every night we went back and forth. When the American ambassador heard, he said: "How'd you do that? *I* can't do that!"[50]

An anecdote from the early years of Rock & Roll adds to this story of the power of music—in that crucial stage of American society regarding race relations, the mid-1950s. The Supreme Court decision in *Brown vs. the Board of Education of Topeka* was handed down in 1954; in December '55 Rosa Parks sparked the Montgomery bus boycott and the prime active phase of the Civil Rights movement by refusing to give up her bus seat, and so on.

Pioneering White "rockabilly" figure, Carl Perkins, from Tiptonville, Tennessee, remembered a talk with Chuck Berry (both influenced by Lonnie Johnson):

> There was no [segregation] in music. When you walked up to an old 1954 or 1955 Wurlitzer jukebox it [didn't say] "Blue Suede Shoes, Carl Perkins, White," [or] "Blueberry Hill, Fats Domino, Black." There was no difference. Kids danced to Little Richard, Chuck Berry, Elvis, Carl. Chuck Berry said to me one time, he said, 'You know Carl, we just might be doing as much with our music as our leaders in Washington to break down barriers." He was right.[51]

One could argue they were doing *more* than those Washington leaders, in reality. Craig Werner's book title was so right: *A Change is Gonna Come: Music, Race and the Soul of America*.

Peter Guralnick, in *Sweet Soul Music: Rhythm and Blues and the Southern Dream of Freedom*, spoke of Rhythm & Blues and Soul music "that . . . came to its full flowering, along with Motown, in the 1960s, . . . [A] growing legion of young White admirers picked up on Rhythm and Blues on the radio. . . . In the beginning, like Rock 'n' Roll, it was an expression of rebellion. . . . Once it emerged from the underground, it accompanied the Civil Rights Movement almost step by step."[52] (See chapter 7 for Lonnie's role in Rhythm & Blues— and the beginnings of Rock.)

A series of White musicians, in jazz, country and other musical genres, starting with Bing Crosby, Jimmie Rodgers and Jack Teagarden in the '20s, also made significant contributions to progress on racial tolerance (discussed in more detail later in the book and in Appendix II). Part of that impact was the interactions, mutual respect, and pure joy in making music together felt by those Black and White musicians. A notable *start* of those interactions came in Lonnie Johnson's home music and social environment of New Orleans; that is discussed in the next chapter.

**A CRUCIAL POINT:** Starting in the 1920s, the impact of those great musicians grew with each succeeding generation of young people, as they increasingly embraced Black music and style as "cool" and significant for their lives; their exposure to the music and style and to Black folks as fellow Americans kept broadening and made them less and less inclined to buy into the racist system. Examples of Lonnie's impact of this sort on young folks are noted at several points through the book; and illustrations of the societal dynamic involved are related in the section on Lonnie's label, King Records, in chapter 7 and regarding developments in the South at the end of the chapter. And (to draw on my political science training in my *other* field), "opinion leaders" at the national to local levels influence the perspectives of "regular folks." When a *number* of high profile, greatly respected and liked White people such as Bing Crosby, Artie Shaw, Frank Sinatra, Leonard Bernstein,

Edward R. Murrow, and others figuratively or literally embraced top Black musicians, expressed admiration for them, recognized their creative work as significant contributions to American culture, and called them "my friend," this had increasing impact. In its fall 1990 special issue, *LIFE* magazine named Bernstein and Murrow among the "100 most important Americans of the 20th century"; Louis Armstrong was so named, as well. (See Appendix II for evidence on the impact of all this on public opinion.)

Lonnie Johnson's "urbane sophistication" and virtuoso guitar playing and singing made a significant contribution to the image enhancement of the race. Lonnie, like Duke Ellington, always carried himself with great dignity, as fortunately preserved on the American Folk Blues Festival DVDs.[53] He spread that model widely: "I worked from Coast to Coast on the TOBA circuit [Theater Owners' Booking Association, Black theater venues] and the RKO circuit and I played in everything that was playable, every theater there was. . . ."[54] As John Lee Hooker said of Lonnie later on: "He was a hero to everybody. When he lived in Canada I'd go see him play, and everybody loved that man. He was so friendly . . . Everybody loved him—black and white."[55]

Blues guitarist and pianist Henry Townsend was in St. Louis in the 1920s during the first stage of Lonnie's professional music career and followed him later. In an interview with me, Townsend added to the evidence on Lonnie's societal impact. He said, "When the time came for Lonnie to do a job at any place, everyone respected him as a real renowned guy. He wasn't just anybody, he was somebody *plus*." After Lonnie's initial years in St. Louis, when he would come back to St. Louis or Chicago to play, "he was a real crowd drawer. Everyone wanted to get to Lonnie Johnson and talk with Lonnie Johnson; he was the first name you were going to hear if you're talking about music." Townsend also noted how professionally Lonnie acted and how people admired the way he presented himself in public, with class and dignity.[56]

In an interview I conducted with B. B. King, he confirmed all this regarding Lonnie Johnson. He noted Lonnie's musical importance and influence on him, then BB related his thoughts on Lonnie: "He seemed to be a modest man, he seemed not to be 'bragadocious'—and was a real nice person. I had never seen a picture of him where he didn't look presentable, as a man you'd welcome into your home for a visit. He made me want to be more like him." Question: "Was he kind of a model, then?" Answer: "Yes, of course! Yes, sir, he was a model. I'd feel ashamed to be doing anything weird around him. That's how much I respected him."

The blues was not just entertainment to African-Americans. It came from the core and history of the Black experience in America, and its music hauntingly and powerfully expressed the circumstances and feelings that came from that experience. As the great Black migration took African-Americans out of the South and their brutally repressive past and into the hope and haltingly increased economic well-being of Northern and Western cities, the brilliance and sophistication of a Lonnie Johnson also contributed significantly to enhancement of the image of the race and to progress toward realization of Jefferson's ideal that "all men are created equal."

This chapter presented an introduction to Lonnie Johnson and his musical importance in a manner that is readable for non-specialists. Also, in laying the foundation for this book, I've set out some main elements of the important broader societal theme of musicians and progress on Civil Rights, including some other key figures in the full context of Lonnie Johnson's experience.

In the musically seminal city of New Orleans around the beginning of the century we see the beginnings of the impact of music and great musicians on race relations and the possibilities for transcending the bitter fruits of racism in that transforming musical city. Lonnie Johnson's brilliant career and fascinating life began in New Orleans, where jazz itself began life. I take up that story in chapter two, which begins the chronological review of Lonnie Johnson's musical life and profound, widespread musical influence, plus review of his personal story.

# 2

# New Orleans Music

## The Original Music City

Seemingly from every direction in the city, the clarion call of cornets and siren song of clarinets, the sliding, punchy blare of trombones and pounding beat of drums, the strum of guitars and thrum and ricky-tick of banjos poured forth.

In New Orleans from the 1890s through the teens of the twentieth century, music wasn't just appreciated and plentiful in entertainment venues, it was a pervasive presence; it colored and gave verve and rhythm to daily activities and was woven into the very fabric of life. Danny Barker, jazz guitarist born there in 1909, reported that "the city was full of the sounds of music" in those years.[1]

As jazz historian James Lincoln Collier points out, "By 1890, New Orleans was a city filled with a rich diversity of musical forms"—from multiple opera houses to symphonies and chamber music groups to a sizable number of "orchestras," bands, duos and trios playing a wide variety of popular music. An interesting illustration of this is found in volume one of the historic Jelly Roll Morton recordings made with Alan Lomax in 1938 for the Library of Congress. One of the prime "Founding Fathers of Jazz," Jelly demonstrates how, in New Orleans, an old French quadrille was transformed into the early ragtime, then jazz piece, "Tiger Rag." He also plays his version of Verdi's "Miserere." Research has found that the city had actually "been drenched in music and dancing for nearly two centuries," with its French and some Spanish history and unique mix of people and races. It's also worth noting that early on the city's culture produced the first American to become internationally rec-ognized as both a pianist and composer in the realm of classical music: Louis Moreau Gottschalk, who was born in New Orleans in May 1829. Gottschalk's compositions also "represent one of the first attempts to introduce native popular and folk music into art music," most notably in "Bamboula," "Ballade Creole" and "Chanson Negre."[2]

Amusingly, in his landmark book, *Music in New Orleans*, Henry Kmen reported the observation of a "Yankee" visitor in those early days: ". . . New Orleanians managed during a single winter to 'execute about as much dancing, music, laughing and dissipation as would serve any reasonably disposed, . . . sober citizens for three or four years'."[3]

New Orleans occupies a unique place near the mouth of a river that served as a central channel of commerce and human travel both within America and into the country from foreign lands: the mighty Mississippi. This meant a constant influx of a wide variety of people who carried an extraordinary array of cultural ways and ideas, including music. That included the influence of Caribbean culture. The result was a rich stew of people and aesthetics. The great clarinetist from the city, Barney Bigard, expressed it well at the beginning of his autobiography: "New Orleans was one hell of a town. . . . There is something about the place that grabs you. It's such a mixture, a melting pot of peoples and races: artists, sailors, writers, whores, poets, pimps and just about every kind of person you can think of. It's like a 'gathering place of lost souls.'"[4]

Still another part of the mix was noted by Geoffrey Ward and Ken Burns: "The city's musical heritage grew steadily richer. Brass bands cap-tivated the whole country after the Civil War . . . and the New Orleans 'mania' for them, noted before the war, intensified afterwards."[5] Later, the Spanish-American War of 1898 added more such band instruments to the Crescent City scene. (New Orleans got that nickname because the main part of the city sprawls along a crescent in the Mississippi River.) Cuba was just a few hundred miles from New Orleans, which served as prime embarkation and return point for American soldiers.

Then there were the famous funeral marches led by powerful brass bands. Since before jazz began, many people of New Orleans, especially Blacks, were members of fraternal organizations. And when a mem-ber died, the organization would engage one (or more) of those bands, which routinely wound their mournful and soulful way through the city's streets playing "Nearer My God to Thee" for all to hear, making a musical trail to the cemetery "to give the poor fellow his last ride." Then, for the return, they'd step up the pace and swing into such upbeat musical fare as "Oh, Didn't He Ramble" and "When the Saints Go Marchin' In," with many people along the route joining in via the "second line." Those bands, playing in parades, funeral marches, and for other occasions, were among the precursors of jazz. For a taste of the atmosphere of those days, read David Fulmer's wonderfully evocative novels.[6]

In light of all that, it isn't surprising that an extraordinary series of great musicians came from New Orleans, especially from the 1890s to about 1920. Those musicians included prime "Founding Father of Jazz," Joe "King" Oliver, his student, that towering figure of twentieth century music, Louis Armstrong, the soprano sax and clarinet genius Sidney Bechet, and so on. Another musical giant, who spanned jazz and blues, to whom we return shortly, was Lonnie Johnson. The Original Music City, indeed.

**The Blues in New Orleans**  The "Mississippi Delta" cultural and sociological area covers territory roughly from Jackson, Mississippi, to the northern end of the state, and from the Mississippi River east through Highway 61 to roughly the middle of the state. This is often said to be the area where that powerful musical expression of deep soul and human experience, the blues, originated—"The Land Where the Blues Began," as the title of Alan Lomax's book put it. But given the location of New Orleans just a couple hundred miles down America's great water artery from the heart of the Delta, it's not surprising that the blues made an early appearance in New Orleans. In fact, the Crescent City may have been an, or even *the*, original incubator of the blues.

The blues were a musical factor in New Orleans very early on, especially among Blacks in that area. Buddy Bolden, an African-American born in 1877, is generally credited as leader of the first band to play jazz. As jazz historians and ear-witness testimony report, Bolden's specialty was the blues, which he would play with great power, supported by his five or six other band members. Sam Charters wrote: "When [Bolden's] band improvised a blues in public, at a dance in Globe Hall in the summer of . . . 1895, he became famous as the man '. . . who invented the hot blues'," i.e., the first jazz. The best research now indicates that 1895 is probably two or three years too early; but certainly by 1897 or 1898 Bolden was playing that music.[7] "Bunk" Johnson, a Black man born in 1889, was another of the early major cornet-playing jazz guys from the New Orleans area. He reports, "when I was a kid, I'd go to the barrel house and play along with them piano players . . . We used to play nuthin' but the blues."[8] Further, that great character and even greater musical force, Jelly Roll Morton, a Creole born in New Orleans in 1890, reported, "I heard the blues when I was knee-high to a duck . . . *When I first started going to school* I heard some of the blues piano players [doing tunes like] 'Make Me a Pallet on the Floor'. . . ." (emphasis added). Jelly Roll also talked of how, "when [he] was quite small" he heard older men playing and singing such blues songs as "See See Rider"; and he famously spoke of Mamie Desdoumes playing the blues on piano "in those early days."[9]

It seems clear, especially from the testimony of Jelly, that the blues was being *widely* played, primarily by Blacks, by 1896 or 1897; and that means it had to have first made its appearance in New Orleans by 1894 at the latest and probably earlier. Those blues may not have been in the strict 12-bar form that later came to be the prime form of the music; but the essential spirit of the music, the presence of those "blue" notes and "bent" notes, and the deep soulful feel was surely there, whether in eight, twelve or sixteen bars, or some musically irregular variant thereof. (Some specialists get hung up on the 12-bar form; but this constriction of thought and notion of the blues misses significant parts of the early history of the music.) The testimony of all the figures quoted above came years later after the blues had become famous in the 1920s and beyond; they were well aware of what the blues was. So it is highly likely that the music they identified included the essential elements of the blues, and their identification was not a vague, early misuse of the term. Further, many blues historians recognize that principal direct antecedents of the blues were chants developed by cotton field workers ("field hollers") and by levee and dockworkers loading ships. As the most important port in the South in the 1890s, New Orleans was a prime place for dockworkers to develop and sing chants of that sort.

Joe "King" Oliver was born in 1885 and was the greatest New Orleans cornet player and band leader after Buddy Bolden. It is telling that when the first recordings with his Creole Jazz Band were made in 1923, over a third of the songs were the blues; they were simply continuing the tradition begun in the city in the 1890s. William Russell and Stephen Smith added this note to the reprint of the early classic book, *Jazzmen* by Ramsey and Smith, based on interviews in the 1930s with remaining original jazz musicians: In discussing "some of the popular dance tunes of early New Orleans" they note, "then there were always the blues. . . ." Indeed, a pioneering New Orleans jazz clarinet player was Louis "Big Eye" Nelson/Delisle, a "Creole of color" born in 1885 who played with several of the best early New Orleans bands. He said, "Blues is what cause the fellows to start jazzing."[10]

Despite all that, there has been surprisingly little recognition given to the fact that the blues was a powerful presence in New Orleans from the early 1890s on. Most blues writers have focused on the Mississippi Delta as the origin of the blues (some also suggest multiple areas of origination, like Texas, Georgia and the Carolinas) and they have missed this.

## New Orleans: Unusual Realm of Race Relations

New Orleans also had a rather unusual history in the course of race relations. There was a predominantly French cast to the city, since it was established by the French in 1718; the Spanish controlled the city from 1763 to about 1800, when it was returned to France before the Louisiana Purchase in 1803. The combination of the French and Spanish control, the extremely varied human composition, and the cosmopolitan nature of the city lessened the intensity and harshness of the racial situation through most of the nineteenth century.

Another significant reason for the more benign conditions regarding race was the unique people of New Orleans called "Creoles." Many were primarily French in origin, but with some admixture of one or more other race or ethnic origins; others were "Creoles of color" who were part French with a substantial part Black. As Ross Russell relates in the autobiography of New Orleans bass player Pops Foster: "They spoke French and prided themselves on being co-heirs of French culture . . . In the free and easy atmosphere of [pre-Civil War] New Orleans, Creoles were considered every bit as good as white folks."[11] Even the "Creoles of color," but especially the Creoles, often held good jobs, had education, and many had formal musical training. But it was also true that many Creoles, who lived in the "Downtown" area of the city, saw themselves as a higher class of people than the pure Blacks in "Uptown." Jelly Roll Morton (born "Lamothe"[12]), for example, heatedly maintained he was not a Black.

Still, slavery was a factor. Indeed, given the city's location for shipping on the Gulf and Mississippi River, it was a major location for slave auctions. One manifestation of the slave presence was the Congo Square music and dance sessions on Sundays. Sundays were the "days off" for slaves and, from 1817 to the Civil War they would congregate in a lot that came to be called "Congo Square" (part of what is now Louis Armstrong Park, just across Rampart Street from the French Quarter). There they would drum on various home-made percussion instruments creating striking patterns of multiple rhythms ("polyrhythms," in formal terms), and, with any other instruments available, they would generate a powerful, rather hypnotic music. Large numbers of African-Americans would dance to the music; in later years, White tourists would observe in fascination.

After the end of the Reconstruction regime in the South following the Civil War and the departure of federal troops and administrators in 1877, the status of African-Americans deteriorated. In New Orleans, however, Blacks' rights and roles were slower to deteriorate. To an unusual degree, New Orleans was a place where people of different ethnic backgrounds and races mixed together—in all kinds of pursuits in that wide-open, live-life-to-the-fullest city. As jazz guitarist Danny Barker said, there had been "a whole lot of integrating going on" in the city.[13] Pops Foster reported: "The white and colored musicians around New Orleans all knew each other and there wasn't any Jim Crow between them. They really didn't care what color you were, and I played with a lot of them."[14] Well, Foster was a little optimistic, especially after 1894.

A post-Reconstruction racist reaction developed. Then an 1894 Louisiana law imposed strong Jim Crow discriminatory rules, but many

Creoles at first sought to maintain their relatively privileged status. As early clarinet player George Lewis (a Black) complained about top Spanish-Creole band leader Manuel Manetta, "I . . . never played with him, because there was prejudice. . . . Some of those Creole bands wouldn't hire a man whose hair wasn't silky." With the 1894 law, anyone who had *any* African blood was discriminated against. The Creoles, especially the Creoles of color, were driven out of their positions of influence, better jobs and ultimately much of their economic well-being. But they retained their profound appreciation and performance of music. With less access to the "better class" of venues, they were increasingly thrown in with the Blacks, playing for whatever gigs they could get. This resulted in a melding of the two musical traditions and was a significant contributor to the development of jazz—and more sophisticated blues. Indeed, "the emerging New Orleans style, already enriched by elements from so many diverse musical cultures, further benefited from the marriage of the two schools: the clean, pure, limpid [and smooth, lyrical] playing of the Creoles and the rough, more dynamic [and soulfully expressed] style of the Afro-Americans."[15]

A significant part of the Creole attitude toward Black musicians may not have been direct racial prejudice. Rather, it was probably a combination of how much the Creoles, with their identification with French culture, valued education, speaking well, and general sophistication, along with how much they valued formal musical training. This climate in New Orleans among musicians was probably part of why Lonnie Johnson always sought to speak English well, although Lonnie didn't get formal education and it showed in some of his language. He was explicit in noting how he strived for such language use and urbane personal conduct.

Another side to the impact of music on African-Americans came from a kind of transformation resulting from regular Black folks parading in sharp uniforms and playing stirring music in the street bands, in that famous New Orleans manner. This effect was especially significant for a Black boy who went on to immense impact on twentieth-century music, Louis Armstrong: "And when neighborhood bandsmen took to the streets for Sunday parades, the transforming effect of music became visible to him. Handymen, porters, cigar makers—even laborers, like his father—became grand figures in braided uniforms, marching under elaborate banners, and playing shiny instruments. People who didn't have much to smile about on weekdays smiled when they saw and heard them on Sundays."[16] Guitarist Danny Barker added: "Most kids in New Orleans had a great interest in jazz music because it was all around . . . Kids today, they're all interested in the football teams, like the Dallas Cowboys, or the baseball teams, like the New York Yankees, and so on. But in New Orleans back then, the kids were interested in the bands. Whose band was great? The trumpet players became famous . . . You heard about them having success . . . , and that inspired you to learn to play an instrument."[17]

Especially for a Black kid in New Orleans at the end of the 1800s or early 1900s, those people with the fine uniforms making beautiful sounds and proudly playing in dance halls or parades, which had folks appreciating such great musical expression, were persons to emulate; it was part of the musical and social environment in New Orleans. It was also a good way to transcend the frustrations, pains and limitations of everyday life for an African-American.

But the inspiration of those bands wasn't confined to Blacks. As Creole clarinetist Barney Bigard wrote: "On Saturdays we used to play ball in the street and we would hear a parade coming. That's really [the origin of] my first interest in music: as a kid watching the brass bands. We'd hear the parade coming and that was the end of the game. We would try to follow the band as far as our folks would let us. . . ."[18]

## The Guitar in New Orleans

Despite the fame of the drums in Congo Square and of brass instruments in the classic New Orleans period, observer Benjamin Latrobe noted in 1819 that a stringed instrument, which was a descendant of an African instrument, played a prominent part in the music creation in Congo Square. An 1886 article by G. W. Cable, drawing on earlier reports, said: "But the grand instrument was the banjo," which added interesting embellishment to the rhythm; and the musicians sang a European-style melody in French-Creole language. As jazz historian Marshall Stearns pointed out, a very significant musical melding was happening:

"A few European instruments and a European melody . . . exist in the middle of this predominantly African performance. The blending of European and West African music is well under way. . . ." (Various jazz histories state that there was music-making in the square as late as the 1880s, but recent research found that the Congo Square musical gatherings were gone by then.)[19]

Speaking of such string instruments and Blacks in New Orleans, notes in the Pops Foster memoir are also significant. He was born in 1892 outside of New Orleans and was one of the first two great bass players in jazz from the area. His family moved to New Orleans in 1902 and he was musically active in in the city fairly soon thereafter. Foster reported in his autobiography that, "None of the white bands had any violin, guitar, mandolin or string bass. Only the colored played them . . . I never heard of any white guitar players around New Orleans." This may be slightly overstated, but the main tendency is correct.[20]

Foster also reported: "[Many] saloons had two sides, one for whites and one for colored. The colored had so much fun on their side dancing, singing, and guitar playing, that you couldn't get in for [all] the whites. It was the same way at Lincoln Park for the colored; you couldn't tell who it was for, there were so many whites there."[21] Foster singled out *guitar playing* as a key instrument in many saloons. Accounts of early New Orleans jazz have focused on the cornet and other horns, drums, and the piano in the Storyville, but from Foster's observations—in about twenty places in his memoirs Foster notes guitarists or bands with guitarists—the guitar was much more prominent in the area than has generally been suggested; most jazz writings have missed this. The Lee Collins autobiography mentions a series of guitarists in New Orleans from 1910 into the 1920s; and Johnny St. Cyr, who was born in New Orleans in 1890 and played banjo and guitar with Jelly Roll Morton and Louis Armstrong, notes a series of guitarists in interviews held in the Hogan Jazz Archive.[22] Wellman Braud, the other great early bassist from New Orleans (b. 1891), was asked, "Did they use banjoes when you were down here [in New Orleans] much?" He said: "No. Guitar. Only after I left here [did] the banjoes get popular, I think about 1917 or 1918, because all the bands up north were using banjo."[23] The banjo surged in popularity from about 1917 through about 1928—after its substantial use in the 1800s, in prominent association with minstrel shows. The fading of its popularity, with the guitar becoming the dominating string instrument by the later 1920s, was a trend in which Lonnie Johnson played a major role. Interestingly, this also caused "a further distancing from the minstrel trappings of black banjo-picker, allowing jazz to develop an even stronger urban identity."[24]

## String Instruments and the Development of African-American Music

Before the emergence of the guitar as a leading instrument in popular music, other string instruments played a vital role in the development of the music of African-Americans—and in Lonnie Johnson's musical development and subsequent impact on blues, jazz, and beyond.

From their origins in Africa, Black folks in America had carried experience with and an affinity for string instruments, from the one-string *riti* (something like a crude fiddle) to the five string *halam* (a predecessor to the banjo). In slavery times and immediately after, the fiddle and banjo were used by African-Americans in various parts of America. A number of notices of escaped slaves in early news sheets of the 1700s mentioned slaves' abilities to play the fiddle. Thomas Jefferson himself, in his *Notes on the State of Virginia* of 1803, said, "The instrument proper to [Blacks] is the banjor, which they brought hither from Africa."[25]

The violin holds a gloried place in the European classical music tradition; indeed, the first violin player in an orchestra is designated the "Concert Master" in America ("leader of the orchestra" in Europe). The violin is a principal lead instrument. It is also a uniquely expressive instrument, with an ability to make sounds like vocal expressions and cries using vibrato and sliding notes. (The great nineteenth-century classical violinist Paganini was famous for such effects on his violin, which dazzled and moved many audiences.)

Pops Foster pointed out that, "For a long time the violin was the top instrument around New Orleans"; in fact, in the earlier years, "the violin was usually the leader" of bands. An example was violinist Armand Piron, who led the Peerless and Superior Orchestras.[26]

There is another dimension of the adoption of the violin by Blacks, a dimension related to the effort to "improve" themselves and to enhance the presentation of themselves in American society that was discussed in chapter one. William McFeely wrote of Frederick Douglass that he played "the violin, that emblem of European culture," and his son Joseph became an accomplished violinist. Reading about early Black musicians, it is striking how many started on the violin, even ones like Freddie Keppard and Dave Nelson who became jazz trumpeters. Indeed, as leading jazz scholar Lewis Porter said about patterns in interviews of early New Orleans area musicians, "the oldest interviewees quite frequently first played in or were impressed by three- or four-piece string bands," including violin, guitar, etc.[27]

(For an interesting sampling of violin music among Blacks playing the blues, mostly during the 1920s and 1930s, see, *Violin, Sing the Blues for Me: African-American Fiddlers, 1926–1949*, an Old Hat Records CD.)

The cornet/trumpet came to dominance in jazz bands at the end of the nineteenth century and through the early years of the twentieth century, boosted by the great early cornet players Buddy Bolden, Manual Perez, Buddy Petit, Joe Oliver, and Freddie Keppard of New Orleans.

As things developed, however, the guitar steadily gained in use in the late 1800s; and by the 1890s, the guitar was fairly widely used.[28] Mandolins were also popular. There were a few relatively outstanding guitarists in the 1890s and the early years of the new century; but the guitar was primarily a rhythm instrument in New Orleans and elsewhere.

Then along came Lonnie Johnson. The violin was the instrument he began on. He applied some of the violin's musical capacities to the guitar, and then took the guitar to new heights in American music.

Lonnie Johnson grew up immersed in the two styles of music-making in New Orleans in the 1890s: The powerful, bluesy, soulful, impassioned, note-bending music of great vitality that Blacks in the "Uptown" area played, and the sophisticated, smooth, lyrical, well-trained Creole "Downtown" music that was influenced by European classical, march and dance music. And from the general environment of the original music city, Lonnie (like Louis Armstrong in a somewhat different way) drew deeply on that rich musical gumbo and took the melding of those musical forms to the greatest artistic heights.

That was reflected well in a comment by B. B. King in my interview with him. B. B. didn't know exactly where Lonnie originally came from. When I told him Lonnie was born and raised in New Orleans, B. B.'s immediate response was, "Oh, that's where he got that great combination of blues *and* a lyrical jazzy feel in his music!"

## Personal and Musical Beginnings for Lonnie

Lonnie Johnson's birth in the extraordinary musical and cultural environment of New Orleans came at a truly historic, genesis-like and transitional time for popular music, when the blues was in its infancy and just before jazz was born.

In that setting, Alonzo "Lonnie" Johnson developed his first instrumental skills in the Crescent City. He was born to George and Angieline Johnson. The unusual spelling of his mother's name is what he wrote on his application for Social Security; in fact, he spelled it with a capital "L" in the middle—AngieLine—although the handwriting is not ideally clear, and Lonnie's lack of formal education made some of his English prose erratic. It's also interesting to note in that application that in the place for middle name, Lonnie wrote "No," then crossed it out. That seems to indicate that he didn't have a middle name, though someone apparently told him that he should leave the space blank.

In one of many mysteries regarding Lonnie and relevant dates, on his Chicago Federation of Musicians "Membership Record Card," filed in 1944, 1889 is given as the year of birth, presumably supplied by Lonnie, since the signature is in Lonnie's handwriting. Some blues and jazz writers think this is the correct birth year; but the best available evidence, including statements Lonnie made three different times to three different people in circumstances that made the statements highly credible, indicates he was born on February 8, 1894. The year 1894 is most consonant with other elements of his history, as the following details.[29]

Frustratingly, it proved extremely difficult to nail down Lonnie and his family in census and state or local birth records. Census records can be inaccurate on individuals, especially as recorded back in 1900 or 1910; the census enumerator had to get the information from others in the house or neighbors or plantation personnel if the person or family was not home when the enumerator came by. And birth records for Black persons in the South in those years are often incomplete. Speaking of records and frustration, Lonnie told someone close to him late in life that all the family history had been written down in the family Bible, but that the Bible was lost in a flood. There were two major floods on the Mississippi River in 1912 and 1913, and there was flooding from a 1915 hurricane, so that is probably when the family Bible was lost; but since both parents survived the 1918 flu epidemic, it might have happened during the famous 1927 Mississippi flood.[30]

The few previous publications indicating exactly where Lonnie was born say he "was born on Franklin Street near Rampart" in New Orleans.[31] (One source said "between" Franklin and Rampart.) There is a problem with such statements, however, in fact, several problems, which called for some detective work. If one looks at a current New Orleans map, Franklin Street doesn't exist. But looking at a map of the French Quarter and "The District," better known as Storyville, from the early 1900s one finds a Franklin Street; later it was renamed Crozat Street, a section of only a couple of blocks. But Franklin Street did not cross Rampart Street; rather, they were parallel. And a little road called Basin Street, one of the most famous street names in music history, was between them. Evidently, previous writers did not check current or old maps. Now there is a Franklin *Avenue*, which does cross Rampart, but those written sources say "Street." (Franklin *Avenue*—which may be why Franklin Street got renamed—is a little northeast of the French Quarter.)

There is a more crucial problem with that stated location of Lonnie's birthplace: Lonnie himself told Roberta Barrett (nee Richards), his booking agent and close friend in his last five years, that he was actually "born on Wall Street in New Orleans." Looking at a current map of the city, one can find no Wall Street anywhere in the main part of New Orleans. But a late 1800s atlas of the City of New Orleans[32] shows there was, indeed, a Wall Street (the street name was changed to an extension of Prytania in the mid-1920s). That map also shows how very close to the river the Johnson house was, so Lonnie's statement about losing the family Bible in

1886 map of section of New Orleans showing the former Wall Street (now Prytania) where Lonnie was born. SECOND PAIRED PHOTO: Two duplex houses from the 1890s just off the former Wall Street, probably like the house of Lonnie's earliest years. PHOTOS BY DEAN ALGER, 2005.

a flood makes sense. When I visited that stretch of Prytania/Wall Street in June 2005, there were some houses still there that the locals assured me were there in the 1890s, and they were 1890s style. The accompanying photo is one I shot of two of those houses, both humble duplexes. It is likely that the Johnson house in the 1890s was like one of these.

This little neighborhood was located well west-southwest of the French Quarter in a section that, back then, was marvelously called "Black Pearl." (Today, it's the southern part of the section called Carrollton, just west of Audubon Park.) According to Louisiana history specialists in the Tulane University Library, around 1900 this was an African-American section of town (it still is, mostly, along Prytania/Wall Street west of Broadway); and it was at least somewhat known for producing creative people. Indeed, this immediate neighborhood was also where, less than two decades later, the great gospel singer Mahalia Jackson (born 1911) started singing in a little Baptist church, which is still there: Mount Moriah Missionary Baptist Church, located a couple of lots above the old Wall Street on Millaudon Street.

Lonnie told Roberta Barrett he was raised a Baptist. Besides the church Mahalia started in, there is another Baptist church on the next block to the east, the side of which is on Wall Street/Prytania Street, with the front on Alvin Street. Both churches were there by the later 1890s, so it's likely one was the church of Lonnie's family. I found an elder for the second church and she looked at their records, but found no listings for an Alonzo "Lonnie" Johnson. So, by process of elimination, it seems likely that Lonnie Johnson and Mahalia Jackson started out in the same quaint little Mount Moriah Baptist Church in the Black Pearl section of New Orleans (see photo).

## "The Whole Entire Family Was Musicians"

"Dear old New Orleans, it's known as the land of dreams,
It's my old home town, dear old New Orleans."
—from Lonnie Johnson's, "New Orleans Blues"

Beyond the remarkable musical environment of New Orleans, Lonnie's family provided extra-rich specific soil for the flowering of this

Mount Moriah Baptist Church, just off old Wall Street, New Orleans; probable church of Lonnie Johnson's family (and church of Mahalia Jackson's family). PHOTO BY DEAN ALGER, 2005.

musical figure. As he put it in an interview, "the whole, entire family was musicians." Lonnie's father played violin and evidently other instruments, his mother apparently played piano, and his five brothers and at least two of his six sisters seriously played music. As he said in an interview, "There was music all around us, and in my family you'd better play something, even if you just banged on a tin can."[33]

In a 1963 interview, Lonnie gave us insight into his family origins; he also revealed how his father influenced the kind of a person he became:

My father taught me everything I know. He gave me schooling, he gave me everything I got. I don't know how the inside of a school looks, and I can read anything that's on paper. I can talk to anybody on any subject they like talking about, and any time I get spare time, I sit down and read and read and read. So when I say something, I have the correct pronunciation of my words, not flat and rude . . .[34]

This indicates that Lonnie's father was literate and had some decent education, which was unusual for Southern Blacks at that time. British jazz and blues writer Val Wilmer reported, in introducing an article based on her interview with Lonnie: "He converses knowledgeably on any number of subjects." The last two sentences in the previous quote illustrate Lonnie's strong desire to present himself as sophisticated and as a model for his race, as has been noted. The statement above, along with testimony from two friends later in life about how strongly he felt about his mother, also show a man who had family origins of great importance, and from which he gained good values and deep guidance in life. A favorite song of his in later years was "My Mother's Eyes," which he would sing with special emotion and would sometimes dedicate to his mother.[35]

Lonnie's father not only introduced him and his brothers and sisters to music and taught them to play instruments, he had some of them playing with him in a little string band. They played for weddings and other occasions. But it wasn't the blues; they played schottisches (a European music often danced to) and waltzes and such music. Like many other early blues and jazz players, they played the sort of music their audience wanted or the particular engagement required. String bands, with violin, guitar and mandolin or bass, were widespread in the Black music world at the end of the nineteenth and in the early twentieth centuries.

Additionally, his father took Lonnie and a brother, almost certainly James, and played for tips at selected spots around New Orleans. As Pops Foster related it: "All around the New Orleans area we had street corner players. They used guitar and mandolin and played for coins on street corners . . . Lonnie Johnson and his daddy and brother used to go all over New Orleans playing on street corners. Lonnie played guitar, and his daddy and brother played violin." Foster is not specific as to what years he saw them playing around the city, but it's likely that this was either around 1908–1909, when Lonnie was 14–15, or maybe in 1913–1914, after his time in the Raceland area (discussed below). Since Foster spoke of Lonnie playing "with his daddy," suggesting a quite young Lonnie, and since the rest of the available evidence indicates Lonnie was playing on his own or with his brother James by the mid-1910s, those dates seem right. Interestingly, Pops went on to say: "Lonnie was the only guy we had around New Orleans who could play jazz guitar [i.e., lead guitar, rather than just rhythm]. He was great on guitar. Django Reinhardt was a great player. They'd really take off on a number. Lonnie was tough to follow."[36] This is testimony on how early it was that Lonnie had developed superb playing skills, since Foster had to have been talking about the years, 1914–1917. And that is another reason for my claim, later on, that Lonnie was the true founding father of lead jazz guitar.

In an interview with Paul Oliver, Johnson said, "Then I bought my guitar . . . in 1917." Some have interpreted this to mean he got his first guitar in 1917. If that's what he meant, he got the date wrong (he got the year wrong in some other specifics in later interviews, such as when he made his first recordings); as the previous paragraph made clear, Lonnie was obviously playing guitar well before 1917. In an interview with Moe Asch of Folkways records, Lonnie said he started playing with his father's string band when he was fourteen, which would be in 1908. That makes sense; and it also reinforces the conclusion about when Pops Foster saw him "playing with his daddy" on New Orleans street corners.[37] (He is much more likely to remember accurately how old he was when he started playing with his dad's band than what calendar year it was.) Playing all over New Orleans, on the streets and in various types of other music jobs, Lonnie further soaked up the music pervading the Crescent City.

Besides the Johnson family string band, in his later teens and early twenties Lonnie and his older brother James played in cafés around the city, with Lonnie playing violin or guitar. Again, mostly it wasn't the blues they played: "We played anything they wanted to hear—ragtime melodies, sweet songs, waltzes, that kind of thing. A lot of people liked opera, so we did some of that, too." Lonnie also played in the (in)famous bordellos of "the District," better known as Storyville, in the 1910s. A couple of publications say 1910–1917 for those Storyville gigs, though the source of those dates isn't clear; it was likely between 1914 and early 1917. Lonnie apparently played solo guitar. But also: Tom Anderson was the leading figure in Storyville and Tom Anderson's Annex often used a string trio; it's likely Lonnie played there some of the time, probably with his brother and a third musician.[38]

Interestingly, for the man who became a very good and prominent blues, jazz and ballad *singer* in the 1920s, and later became a great one, in those early years around New Orleans Lonnie didn't even consider singing. "I just didn't think about it," he said, "because me and my brother was doing all right with our instruments, and those joints we played in didn't particularly want any vocals."[39]

The violin was Lonnie's first primary instrument, which, again, is a natural lead and strikingly expressive instrument. Now remember that the guitar, in the earlier years of music in New Orleans and elsewhere, was primarily a rhythm instrument, one offering chords for the harmonic structure of the music and providing or helping with the beat. As guitarist Charlie Bocage of the major musical family of New Orleans put it in an interview: "In those days, solos were not required of banjos and guitars. . . . I played rhythm guitar."[40]

But with his rich family musical milieu and Lonnie's great talent, just a little later he took that *expressive* capacity of the violin, including ways to make the instrument give voice to human feelings, and conveyed other aesthetic sound effects, *and he transferred it to the guitar*. A little later he began developing the interplay of voice and guitar, which became such a prime element of the blues. In later decades, that expressive capacity on the guitar became central to Country, Rock and much of popular music in the twentieth century. Lonnie was the principal original figure in the development of expressive artistry on the guitar (beyond the specialist use of a metal tube or glass bottleneck for "slide" guitar).

## Rural Louisiana and "Rooster" Johnson; Later Playing in New Orleans

Lonnie always said he was born and spent his early years in New Orleans. But he spent some time, apparently about two years, in more rural Louisiana. In a 1959 interview, jazz trumpeter Punch Miller from Louisiana told how he and Lonnie "worked all up and down Bayou Lafourche, with guitar and trumpet, and made our living at it when we were young kids." He also said: "In Raceland [a main town in the parish], we would play on Saturday all afternoon and evening on a big store gallery. We'd put our hat down and the people would drop money in it . . . ; and when we got through, we would have enough to last the next week" (usually amounting to about $15). Further, sometimes they would play a little guitar, bass and trumpet for White folks on Sunday night, and got paid about $2.00 apiece. In a 1971 conversation with the director of the Hogan Jazz Archive, Punch told him, "Johnson lived in Raceland for two or three years."[41] Raceland and Bayou Lafourche are in Lafourche Parish in the extreme southern end of Louisiana in a finger of solid land amidst the swamps about 40 miles southwest of New Orleans (now connected by federal highway 90).

Unfortunately, Punch Miller was not specific about dates in that interview. He said this happened "when we were young kids," but wasn't specific about their ages either. Since Punch was born in 1894 in Raceland and was 65 at the time of the main interview, "young kids" probably means mid-teens. Given Lonnie's birth year of 1894, and since other sources indicate Lonnie was back in New Orleans playing in cafés and elsewhere in the mid-1910s, the best estimate of his years in that rural part of Louisiana are from early 1910 through early 1912. That would make Lonnie and Punch both 16 to just-turned 18-years-old at the time, which makes sense. In an interview with Paul Oliver, Lonnie said he was "home in New Orleans in 1914."[42] But note: That phrase does not specifically say he *returned* to New Orleans in that particular year, and his memory for dates, other than his birth year, was inaccurate at times. If anything, that comment seems to reinforce the previous note that he had been *out* of the city, i.e., in the Raceland area, but was back in New Orleans *about* 1914, in fact, probably sometime in spring or summer 1912.

Again, it was difficult to find a listing for Lonnie and family in census reports early in the century. One entry from the 1910 census for the Raceland area was tantalizing, but the specifics don't jibe with what else we know about Lonnie. Especially in light of Lonnie and the rest of the family moving around playing music, it wouldn't be surprising if the enumerator missed them.

One other interesting—and fun—tidbit came from the Punch Miller interview: Punch said that in those Raceland/Lafourche Parish days, "all of them called Lonnie Johnson 'Rooster'."[43] Stumbling on that nickname was a new one for this writer; it is not mentioned in any other publications on Lonnie. It's interesting that Lonnie never mentioned anything about his rural Louisiana experience to interviewers. There are at least two good explanations for this. As introduced in chapter one, Lonnie Johnson, from at least 1926 on, presented himself as an urban, urbane and sophisticated person, unlike various country blues guys. He always said, "I play *City* Blues, not Country Blues." So, it's not surprising that he would not talk much about his experience in rural Louisiana. Second, given the near total family tragedy in 1918, it's not surprising that he did not want to talk much about the early years. In any case, it is a fun bit of background to know of a youthful Lonnie "Rooster" Johnson. It also gives an interesting twist to one of his most noted later songs, "Crowing Rooster Blues." And, while Lonnie sought to present an urbane and sophisticated image through his adult life, his early nickname "Rooster" was not without relevance through his later life, since he always had a striking appeal for and interest in the ladies.

Lonnie was playing music from around 1912 to 1917 in New Orleans. Beyond the cafés, he worked "Frank Pineri's place on Iberville and Burgundy" for a considerable period in what is basically the west corner of the French Quarter (a block from Rampart and Canal Streets). In that club, it was "strictly blues all the way," and much of it he played on violin, according to Lonnie, but added some piano and guitar work, as well. Notably, he also "worked at the Iroquois Theater for a long time," probably from 1915 or 1916 through spring 1917, before he left for overseas.[44]

The Iroquois Theater, which began operations in 1911 or 1912 and was located on South Rampart Street at the edge of the French Quarter, was part of an important development in Black music and entertainment during the 1910s involving "a widespread proliferation of independent African-American vaudeville houses." In the climate of deepening racism in the Jim Crow era, these theaters gave Black communities entertainment from members of their race, as well as a place to commune with their "own people." One other thing needs to be noted about places like the Iroquois. A theater setting may seem like it would not lend itself to the exciting interplay between musician and audience that one found in jazz clubs, juke joints and the like. But, "Contemporaneous black press reports suggest that early African-American theater settings fairly *thrived* on interaction between performers and audience . . . In terms of participatory 'feedback,' the new black vaudeville theater audiences were not unlike the 'shouting,' dance-in-the-aisle congregations of store-front Baptist churches."[45]

That vaudeville theater and active audience participation and community scene reached a height in the 1920s and 1930s; it was especially evident in large theaters for African-Americans in major cities.

New Orleans was a unique, stirring place, with unconventional and experimental inclinations and a freedom of life and art, especially in the first years of the new (twentieth) century. And with its location on the Gulf and at the mouth of the Mississippi, with the influx of people carrying new ideas and trends, it was a natural place for development of music that manifested and "spoke" to a now rapidly changing society and what came to be called "modernism."

## Interlude: The Changing Modern World, Music, and Modern Art

As American society and European societies moved through the first decades of the twentieth century, visual artists and musical figures, novelists, observers of society and social scientists sensed, felt, drew and wrote about fundamental changes in the human condition in the "more advanced" societies. The machine age and industrialism, urbanization, the development of huge, powerful corporations and big government, and new products of science and industry changed the nature of people's lives and communities, often through impersonal mechanisms. The sheer cacophony and confusion of city life was especially notable in this.

Correspondingly, the ideas and social causes of alienation were being investigated by European and American thinkers. As American political theorist Sheldon Wolin summarized, those investigations especially focused on "the attempt to restate the value of community, that is, of the need for human beings to dwell in more intimate relationships with each other, to enjoy more affective [emotional] ties, to experience some closer solidarity than the nature of urbanized and industrialized society seemed willing to grant."[46]

At the same time, a "modernist" movement in the arts and literature developed in accordance with all that, which sought to both express the nature of those new circumstances of human existence and to depict and comment on the often frustrating, frenzied and disorienting experience involved.

With post-Impressionist Cezanne as an original inspiration, Picasso, Braque, Brancusi and other visual artists radically recast painting and sculpture. Stravinsky, Debussy and others from the classical music realm dramatically recast that musical art. And increasingly, jazz was recognized as creative expression in the same vein. In fact, those other artistic realms were variously influenced by and connected with jazz (and the blues at its foundation). Thus, the painter Mondrian and the sculptor Brancusi were avid listeners to jazz; Mondrian's last and perhaps most noted work was *Broadway Boogie Woogie*. Matisse produced an illustrated book simply titled *Jazz*—though it wasn't so musical, mostly using jazz as a symbol of "vitality and vernacular" in modern life, as Appel points out. Stravinsky wrote "Ragtime," "Piano-Rag-Music," and "Three Pieces for Clarinet Solo," the latter of which was inspired by an early performance of the jazz master Sidney Bechet in Europe; Ravel and Debussy were also affected by jazz.[47]

It is also interesting that, at a critical juncture in the development of his art (1912–1913), Picasso produced a series of works with the guitar as central iconic image. That's not so surprising since Picasso's home country, Spain, was the culture most responsible for giving us the modern guitar, and Picasso played a little guitar himself. (See the discussion in chapter five regarding the reference to one of those Picasso paintings, used in the title of one of the landmark Lonnie J-Eddie Lang guitar duet recordings.) Those Picasso paintings were probably inspired, in part, by the fact that Spain's Francisco Tarrega, a principal pioneer of virtuoso classical guitar playing, had recently passed away, and his masterful student, Miguel Llobet, was at his height in 1912. Flamenco guitar was also growing, led in 1912 and thereafter by Ramon Montoya, and had its origins in Andalusia (southern Spain) where Picasso came from.

A major exhibit at New York's Museum of Modern Art in 2011 displayed a number of these Picasso works. The *New York Times* story on the exhibit took note of the societal setting for the "modernist revolution." Further illustrating the prominence of the guitar in twentieth century society, that Picasso exhibit had a companion exhibit: "Guitar Heroes: Legendary Craftsmen [of guitars] from Italy to New York." The guitar was a major icon of twentieth century music, art and culture.

Jazz music was indeed seen as symbolic of fundamental changes people were experiencing. The already prominent classical music conductor Leopold Stokowski visited the famous Cotton Club in New York in the mid-1930s to hear Ellington's band and praised Duke. On jazz, Stokowski said:

> Jazz has come to stay because it is an expression of the . . . breathless, energetic, superactive times in which we are living . . . Already its new vigor, its new vitality is beginning to manifest itself . . . America's contribution to the music of the past will have the same revivifying effect as the injection of new, and in the larger sense, vulgar blood into dying aristocracy. Music will then be vulgarized in the best sense of the word, and enter more and more into the daily lives of people. The Negro musicians of America are playing a great part in this change. They have an open mind and unbiased outlook. They are not hampered by conventions or traditions, and with their new ideas, their constant experiment, they are causing new blood to flow into the veins of music . . . They are the pathfinders into new realms.[48]

Walter Isaacson summarized well the startling scientific and artistic developments of this extraordinary time:

> A pinnacle of the modernist revolution came in 1922, the year Einstein's Nobel Prize was announced. James Joyce's *Ulysses* was published that year, as was T. S. Eliot's "The Waste Land." There was a midnight dinner party in May at the Majestic Hotel in Paris for the opening of "Renard," composed by Stravinsky and performed by Diaghilev's "Ballets Russes." Stravinsky and Diaghilev were both there, as was Picasso. So too were both Joyce and Proust, who "were destroying 19th century literary certainties as surely as Einstein was revolutionizing physics."[49]

Cultural historian Warren Sussman noted the impact of all this in America: "By 1922, an exceptional and ever-growing number of Americans came to believe in a series of changes in the structure of their world, natural, technological, social, personal, and moral."[50]

As the century proceeded, there were two other roughly related senses of the impact of modern experience that were crucial to the appeal of jazz and especially the blues. With those huge, impersonal, powerful, remote, and often greedy (in the case of corporate) organizations, there was an increasing sense that something in the human spirit was being lost, inundated, battered and even betrayed. Second, especially in contrast to the simpler and more direct experiences of smaller towns and rural areas where people knew many of the folks in their localities, there was an increasing sense of a loss of genuine, honest expression and feeling, and of a lost depth of human connections, as Professor Wolin noted. The modernist American writer John Dos Passos talked of how "both government and business had corrupted discourse, and the individual seemed equally swamped by goods and words."[51]

As a result, many people developed a hunger for genuine human expression and interactions, for reconnecting with a broader spirit, and for feeling in touch with the human soul. As another writer said, "Modernist literature . . . experimented with new forms . . . out of the conviction that old forms did not capture something important in life, a 'spirit,' and force . . . existing somewhere below or above consciousness but beyond the purviews of traditional art which concerned itself too much with surface."[52]

Jazz writer and performer Ted Gioia understood all this, explaining it from a slightly different angle: "By the dawn of [the twentieth century], the social cohesiveness of the communities that gave birth to the nation was already on the wane. American life had already begun its inevitable collapse into the hyper-individualism, the fluidity, the cultural tumult so characteristic of modern times." And, drawing especially on blues and jazz, he suggested: "Perhaps the *outsider* was best capable of giving expression to what was destined to become the mainstream reality, to the emotional landscape of a world in which no ties held fast, no ground remained firm underfoot, no certainties stood unquestioned."[53] (Emphasis in original.) Christine Stansell's *American Moderns:*

*Bohemian New York and the Creation of a New Century* discusses this is detail (though oddly, she largely misses the jazz and blues elements).[54]

The blues, as performed by the masters of the genre, came from the depths of human experience and expressed human feelings in powerful ways. Thus, the blues, and jazz, with the blues as a prime foundation, effectively "spoke" to the modernist orientation. Houston Baker's *Modernism and the Harlem Renaissance* profoundly discusses this and more. [55] The blues struck a nerve and began to spread through American music and culture. Nat Shapiro's *Annotated Index of American Popular Songs for 1920–1929* reports over 200 songs with blues titles, including work by "the names of virtually every top Tin Pan Alley songwriter" (though some were not truly blues). A European fascination with African art and African-American music in the first three decades of the century also illustrates this.

Another striking demonstration of the wide impact of the blues was its impact on Country music, especially its beginnings. Of the song tracks (1927–1933) on the RCA best of Jimmie Rodgers, "father of Country music," CD, half are the blues. Jimmie was born in Meridian, Mississippi, and in his youth he learned banjo playing and songs from Blacks in town and along the railroad tracks. (See the end of Appendix II for more on Rodgers.) Other important early country musicians recorded the blues, from the 1927 Dock Boggs side "Country Blues" to Frank Hutchison's "Cannonball Blues" (1929); and later that great country music figure, Hank Williams, recorded such tunes as "Long Gone Lonesome Blues." As Bill Malone reports in his major history of Country music, *Country Music U.S.A.*: "Blues singing remained popular among country singers, but only part of it came from the Rodgers tradition; much of [it] . . . came directly from black singers."[56]

That note on Country music brings up a fascinating point of historical perspective. In the period discussed here, the 1890s through the 1920s, there was an astonishing outpouring of new and fundamentally altered musical art forms: The blues, jazz, and Country music all were born and developed their basic modern forms; and Stravinsky, et al., radically recast classical music. The dramatic developments in society discussed above were a major factor; as Bob Dylan put it much later, "the times they [were] a-changin'." But also, it was a time before television or even radio (until the last part of that period), and people had to rely more on themselves to create music. Indeed, a "piano in the parlor" was widespread throughout American society in the 1890s through the 1910s, and inexpensive guitars and like string instruments were available from Sears and Roebuck or local stores.

Those concerns and feelings deepened, right through the end of the century and into the twenty-first century. That is why the blues continues to resonate profoundly, and it is why B. B. King, having taken the blues form to a high level of moving expression and art, was so universally and deeply appreciated by the end of the century, and became the "Ambassador of the Blues."

Jazz, with its fast rhythms and multiple instruments doing different things simultaneously seemed to represent the modern age; indeed, early commentaries called the music a "cacophony." With the wailing horns and the new sound effects drawn from them, jazz at the same time articulated a powerful artistic expression of the feelings evoked, and it offered unique ways to comment on this crazy new world. Duke Ellington's compositions were especially striking exemplifications of jazz music as modern art, as early as "The Mooche" of 1928, featuring Lonnie Johnson, and "Mood Indigo" of 1930. The stunning, soaring, expressive achievements of Louis Armstrong's trumpet also exemplified this. From Ellington's much heralded 1933 tour of England, a columnist specially commented on "Mood Indigo" and imagined that Wagner "would have hailed this music as [one of] the most significant phases of modern musical art"; this was much quoted in the American press after the Ellington band got back from the tour of Britain. *Sound Wave* magazine of Britain, during the tour, said Ellington's band had instilled "impressionism" into the art of dance music. Speaking of the American press, after the tour of Britain, the *Memphis Scimitar* said Duke had earned the title, "the negro Stravinsky;" and a Dallas paper called him "the African Stravinsky." That both newspapers were in the South is striking.[57]

It's interesting and noteworthy that the year after that 1922 "culmination of the modernist revolution," Joe "King" Oliver and his Creole Jazz Band, with a young second cornet player recently up from New Orleans named Louis Armstrong, made the important recordings that were arguably the prime force that started jazz music on the road to powerful, innovative artistic expression affecting the general society, as the direct precursor to the landmark recordings of Armstrong and his Hot Five. As Dan Morgenstern wrote, "1923 was a watershed year in jazz recording," with Bessie Smith and Jelly Roll Morton also making their first recordings.[58] The following year, 1924, popular "symphonic jazz" maestro Paul Whiteman, in a New York concert accompanied by big publicity, introduced the unique new work by Gershwin titled, "Rhapsody in Blue." In fact, the concert was called "An Experiment in Modern Music." Gershwin's piece was nominally classical music ("Rhapsody . . ."), but jazz and blues were central elements. In 1925, Louis Armstrong and Lonnie Johnson made their first recordings as featured performers—and the rest was musical and cultural history.

With a master like Louis Armstrong also drawing on that key foundation of jazz, the blues, he, along with pure blues masters like Bessie Smith through B. B. King, musically and lyrically expressed the profound feelings of this modern experience. This music also served as a vehicle that people variously used to reconnect with and effectively express more profound, human elements of their nature.

Speaking of that, one other factor in Western society and the social psychology that had developed as of the early twentieth century should be noted. In his discussion of the stage of "the rise of industrial America," at the end of the nineteenth century and moving into the twentieth century, historian Page Smith pointed out that "*control* remained the major preoccupation of middle and upper middle class families." (Emphasis added.) This included many African-American families striving to be accepted as full partners in society.[59] Such intense personal control and regimentation began to engender a reaction in American society, with a first culmination in the 1920s—which appropriately came to be called "The Jazz Age." As Court Carney wrote in his exploration of how early jazz got Americans' attention and began to change the culture:

> The shift from Victorianism to modernism formed the context in which Americans reacted to jazz music. In general, Victorianism created a dichotomy separating controlled human instincts from natural impulses, and modernism strove to reunite these two forces. The refashioning of traditional musical forms into something more modern—both

rhythmically and harmonically—characterized the larger cultural role jazz performance played. . . ."[60]

Indeed, the blues and jazz were liberating forces that fundamentally changed popular music in America; and they led to broader changes in people's behavior and in the culture.

I return to this music and modern art subject at various points and late in the book to specifically assess Lonnie Johnson's music in those regards. As a first stage of that assessment, let me cite the early French jazz writer, critic and record producer Hugues Panassie, who wrote in light of the societal considerations just discussed. With insight (though maybe with some overstatement) he said: "Inspiration without culture [meaning developed, advanced "civilized" society and its formal arts] can produce beautiful works; culture without inspiration is incapable of doing so . . . In music, primitive man generally has greater talent than civilized man. An excess of culture atrophies inspiration, and men crammed with culture tend too much to play tricks, to replace inspiration by lush technique under which one finds music stripped of real vitality."[61]

What makes the musical art of Lonnie Johnson so powerful is the fact that he, like Louis Armstrong, was a technical virtuoso *and* could employ the highest "inspiration" and deepest human feelings of pathos and joy. Their music rose up from the vitality of the African-American experience, slicing through the deadening inundation of the modern world, using the unique aesthetics of blues and jazz for intense expression.

In his masterful early guitar instrumentals like "Playing with the Strings" and "Away Down in the Alley Blues," in his historic guitar duets with Eddie Lang, and in his landmark recordings with the Louis Armstrong and Duke Ellington bands, all from the late 1920s, Lonnie Johnson demonstrated supreme technical mastery and fine thematic coherence, while also maintaining the rhythm and vitality of African-American music. And he powerfully purveyed and conveyed the passion and depth of human expression in his blues songs, from his first hit record, "Mr. Johnson's Blues/"Falling Rain Blues" (1926) to "Don't Ever Love" (1960) and "Mr. Blues Walks" in 1965. Indeed, the latter two recordings truly soar with the "inspiration" to which Panassie referred.

## "1917 Uncle Sam Called Me" and the Influenza Blues

Now we come to another mystery of the saga of Lonnie J. In many blues and jazz encyclopedias and other publications with entries on Lonnie's music and life, some variation of the following line is included, though usually without the qualifier on lack of information on the name: "In 1917 he traveled to London with a musical revue whose name is lost to history."[62] Although jazz and blues writers have tried for years to discover the specifics of that "musical revue" and the exact dates Lonnie was in London, nobody has been able to nail them down. In interviews Lonnie made reference to his visit to London or "overseas" during World War I; yet he never supplied details, and the (few) interviewers usually didn't probe enough. British jazz and blues researcher Howard Rye searched records in London, but could not find direct evidence of Lonnie's arrival in ships' manifests or of his appearances in theater records. The only source to give specifics is an old article by Mark Thomas from a British jazz journal from 1945, which includes a little interview material (the source of the interview material isn't clear). He said: "In 1917 Lonnie joined a theatre company to go to London. For two years he played and sang between acts of a comedy routine by the R.K.O. team, Glenn and Jenkins." A statement by Lonnie in a 1960 interview with Paul Oliver suggests the validity of that information (without proving it): Lonnie said he toured the RKO theater circuit in America "with the team of Glenn and Jenkins" just a couple of years later, and his part in the act was as just described.[63]

Interestingly, Lonnie left a clue in a patriotic song, which blues and jazz writers have missed. Somewhat oddly, the song title is "Victim of Love"; it was recorded in December 1944 (it's available on the RCA-Bluebird CD, *Lonnie Johnson, He's a Jelly Roll Baker*). The song is basically about women being proud of their men who went to the war—and how they are missed (the "victim of love" part, evidently). Early in the song he talks about "fighting the Japs." But in the middle he says this: "*1917 Uncle Sam called me*, left only my mother and dad. [Repeat line.] And to fight for freedom, it's the best thing we ever had." Especially coming from a bluesman who, unlike many of the old Country blues guys, was famous for songs that had coherent lyrics that told a story in a logical sequence of verses, the "1917 Uncle Sam called me" line makes no sense in a song about women and their men folk in WW*II*, unless it is autobiographical. Lonnie seemed to be saying he served (in his own way) in the previous world war, as he urged people on in the present one. (See the beginning of chapter 6 for further evidence on Lonnie's apparent service.)

Adding to the perspective, a music writer noted that "a New Orleans musician playing in London during the first World War was not unusual . . . ; there are accounts of other well-known jazz musicians [using the term "jazz" loosely] who also appeared in the war-torn city at this time, no doubt as a direct result of the US involvement in the war."[64]

The entry for Lonnie Johnson in the Louisiana Blues Hall of Fame probably has it right: He "worked with a theatrical company touring overseas to entertain troops." The most famous case of such musical entertainment of American troops in WWI was James Reese Europe and his orchestra on the continent. It is probable that Lonnie was in London (and possibly elsewhere in Europe) roughly from the summer of 1917 until the summer or fall of 1919, returning to New Orleans at that time. A request for information in US Army records on Lonnie's apparent service came up empty; but they said a fire some years ago destroyed a number of records from that time.

**The Influenza Blues** What Lonnie did make clear was that when he returned to New Orleans from London, he discovered the great tragedy in his life. The flu pandemic of 1918 through early 1919 had wiped out almost all his family; only his brother James and, evidently, his mother and father survived. I say "evidently" because almost all previous writings on Lonnie say he lost the entire family except brother James. For a good example, a 1963 article by Steve Voce in the British *Jazz Journal* offered this quote, supposedly from Lonnie himself, thus adding to the confusion (although I couldn't identify the original source of the quote or interview): "The flu epidemic of 1917 killed all of my people except me and my brother James. . . ." A series of other articles, starting in 1945 (if not before), implicitly indicated the same by saying, "an influenza epidemic took all thirteen of Lonnie's immediate family."[65] Since he made clear that there had been five sisters and six brothers, that suggests the parents were victims too. But in an interview with Lonnie recorded by Moe Asch of Folkways Records, conducted during a 1967 recording session, Lonnie says: "I'm the only one left—me and my mother [brother James had died some years earlier]. My mother is 94 now . . . ;" and he goes on to supply specifics of her actions in his Philadelphia house during that period. (Note: The Folkways/Smithsonian CD includes four and a half minutes of the interview, but that section does not include the statements on his mother.)[66] In an unpublished segment of a 1960 interview Paul Oliver conducted with Lonnie, he says, "I joined my father in Beaumont, Texas, where he had a restaurant" (in 1929, in my reconstruction, though he wasn't clear about the year). Then, Lonnie said his father died in 1934.[67] This is the only mention of his father I could find after the New Orleans years.

My best conclusion on all of this: In 1918 the flu pandemic caused the death of all of Lonnie's brothers and sisters except Lonnie and older brother James. (Henry Townsend, who knew both brothers in St. Louis in the 1920s, confirmed for me that James was the older brother—about two or three years older, he said.[68]) Unfortunately, we were unable to find actual listings of the family in death certificates. It is my inference that those two were the oldest siblings and they were out of the house at that point. The parents were spared, however. In any case, losing most of the family to the flu epidemic was certainly an impetus to play and sing the blues! (And his parents may have left New Orleans around that time to avoid the epidemic.)

Evidently, Lonnie returned from London in the second half of 1919. With all his brothers and sisters except James lost in the epidemic, and with the corresponding deep sadness now attached to his home town, Lonnie and his brother went up the Mississippi River to take the next step in his life, like so many Black folks in general and blues- and jazzmen in specific. Lonnie is quoted in one place putting this in the following perspective: "With no one at home [which may mean his parents had moved from New Orleans], I came north with Louis Armstrong to make my living as a musician."[69] We can't take this literally; it is a general statement that the two great New Orleans musicians, who knew each other, left while still young and headed north in similar fashion and during the same period. Armstrong went north to Chicago in August 1922 when Joe "King" Oliver sent for him to play in Oliver's band in the Windy City. About his own case, Lonnie said, "When a thing like that happens you don't want to stay around. It keeps on your mind. So I left New Orleans. . . ."[70] Evidently he left the Crescent City in late 1919 or early 1920.

He and older brother James went up that great "river of song," the Mississippi, and settled in St. Louis. It was to be a fateful move for Lonnie—and for music in the twentieth century.

# 3

# St. Louis Blues

## ST. LOUIS, THE FORGOTTEN MAJOR MUSIC CITY, AND THE BLUES

As New Orleans is located near the mouth of the Mississippi River, at a key juncture for travel, St. Louis is the major river city midway up the Mississippi, and in the period of rapid American expansion in the late 1800s and early 1900s, it was the Gateway City to the West. By 1910, it was the fourth largest city in the nation.

New Orleans, with its unique cultural heritage, provided the genesis of the startling new music, jazz, as well as being an early source and site of the development of the blues. Chicago, Memphis, and New York have been the other American cities most celebrated for being central to the development of blues (Chicago and Memphis) and jazz (Chicago and New York). All too forgotten or ignored is the very significant role St. Louis played in the history of blues and jazz—and, with Chuck Berry, in the genesis of Rock & Roll. Those developments and other evidence offer strong reasons to conclude that the main early corridor of the blues was the Mississippi River, from New Orleans along the Mississippi Delta area up to Memphis and St. Louis. Kevin Belford has given us a book beautifully illustrated by himself on the St. Louis musical heritage, *Devil at the Confluence*, which focuses on the blues, but does a fine job of setting the general historic music scene for the Gateway City. As he points out: "St. Louis' advantage was its unique location for the merging of the old and new, the urban and the rural, the north and the south."[1]

Blacks were a significant presence in St. Louis from early on. By 1870, the city had the third largest aggregation of African-Americans of any city in America. The significance of St. Louis for African-American music is well symbolized by the fact that the most famous early blues song was "St. Louis Blues," W. C. Handy's landmark contribution to bringing the blues out to the wider public; that song remains one of the most notable and popular blues and jazz songs ever recorded. (It is also interesting that the first significant recording made by the Duke Ellington band was "East St. Louis Toodle-Oo.") Further, W. C. Handy tells us, from his own experience, that some of the earliest songs of a basic blues nature were in evidence in St. Louis: In 1892 he "heard shabby guitarists picking out a tune called 'East St. Louis'" that was blues-like, with a series of "one-line verses, and they would sing it all night." Some knowledgeable interpreters perceive this as two-line verses that came out roughly like an eight-bar blues number. St. Louis blues pianist James "Stump" Johnson, born in 1902, said, "the levee at St. Louis was known throughout the country as the origination of blues." It wasn't "known throughout the country," but this statement didn't come out of nowhere; it came from the passed-on stories Johnson heard from older musicians regarding the long history of blues and proto-blues in St. Louis. The levee along the Mississippi was certainly territory for such music to start its development, as I noted earlier. Handy was not specific in describing exactly where in St. Louis he heard the singers in 1892, other than saying "while sleeping on the cobblestones," but the general context in that part of his book suggests it was at or near the levee.[2]

For years St. Louis had a thriving "sporting-life" district (gambling, bawdy houses, etc.) and a very lively, robust music scene among Blacks. For the St. Louis population as a whole, there were actually two such sporting districts: the premier one along a section of the parallel Market and Chestnut Streets, where there was also some mixing of the races, and a second one frequented by Blacks along Morgan Street (now called Delmar Boulevard), about eight blocks north of Market; the area was known as "Deep Morgan," as you can hear in some old blues songs. Deep Morgan was an extremely lively area with everything from a vaudeville theater to bordellos; in some parts, it was pretty much anything goes and could be violent. Bluesman Henry Brown, born in 1906, told of a "real old-time blues piano player" known only as "Blackmouth" who, in the early 1920s, would "stomp 'em down to the bricks there on Deep Morgan" in the saloons, etc.; "he was some blues player, oh man!" That description, "real old-time blues" player, noted from the early '20s, also strongly suggests that "Blackmouth" was playing the blues before 1900—still more evidence that the notion that the blues did not appear until after 1900 is wrong.[3]

A fascinating sidelight to the story of the blues in St. Louis is the fact that two of the most famous American songs from the general folk and blues idioms had their genesis in incidents in the city. "Frankie and Johnny" was inspired by the 1899 shooting of Allen (not Johnny) Britt by Frankie Baker. More prominently and interestingly, the memorable and powerful song variously called "Stack O' Lee," "Stagolee" or, mostly later, "Stagger Lee" arose from an altercation between Lee Shelton, also called "Stack Lee," and Billy Lyons in December 1895 in the Bill Curtis Saloon in the heart of Deep Morgan. As Cecil Brown relates in his fascinating book (though with some factual flaws) on the song and the saga, *Stagolee Shot Billy*:

> Everybody knew the saloon's reputation for crime. Murders had taken place in the rowdy atmosphere. Billy Lyons didn't have to read the newspapers to know that the saloon was the "envy of all its competitors and the terror of the police," or that the newspaper owner and moralist Joseph Pulitzer regarded it as one of the "worst dens in the city . . . patronized by the lower-class of river men and other darkies of the same social status."

Stack Lee was a well-known fancy-dressing pimp; and when he and Billy Lyons got into it, as most of the versions of the song have it, Lee did indeed have on a fine Stetson hat. Apparently, the two began arguing over politics! Brown describes the details (with some loose borrowing from a novelistic source), but summarizing: After some increasingly angry back and forth, Lyons grabbed Lee's Stetson, who then demanded it back, and when that didn't happen, Stack Lee shot Billy Lyons in the stomach, and then just walked out of the saloon; Lyons later died.[4]

This widely performed and recorded song had meaning and impact on several levels. Besides the great music and the dramatic story (with hints of the old Wild West), there were two more important levels of meaning. "Stack (O') Lee," as transmuted by oral, folk means, came to symbolize low-status Black people fighting back against an oppressive social system. The song emerged sometime following the 1895 incident—and around the time of the 1896 *Plessy vs. Ferguson* Supreme Court decision that legitimized segregation and the deepening discrimination of that time. In illustration of the song's place among humble status Blacks, in 1910 early folk song collector John Lomax received the first copy of "Stagalee" to be put in print, and it was accompanied by a note from the person who wrote it down: "The song is sung by the Negroes on the levee [on the Mississippi] while they are loading and unloading the river freighters. . . ."[5] A second, more stark, relative of the first meaning was that Stack O'Lee, or Stagger Lee, came to be the epitome of what writers and sociologists came to call the "Bad Nigger"—a raw, outlaw form of total protest against the racist society's impact on Black folks. The most noted version of this latter form is the significant work of literature by Richard Wright, *Native Son*.

The other interesting perspective on this is that Lonnie Johnson was increasingly developing himself to present to the public—Blacks and Whites both—precisely the opposite persona, that is, a dignified, urbane, sophisticated person and a superb musical artist, who consistently sought what can be called constructive engagement between the races. Ultimately, that approach by Lonnie, Duke Ellington, and others had a big impact on the American system—though with a great deal of pain along the way. Lonnie's self-presentation was developed further during his experience on the Mississippi riverboats, as is reviewed shortly.

The central role St. Louis played in the development of ragtime music has been amply written about. Scott Joplin was the leading figure in this new musical form, and Tom Turpin's Rosebud Bar on Market Street was home base for the development of ragtime, that marriage of European musical form and notation with African-American syncopation. It was a major precursor to jazz. Ragtime began to develop sometime in the early 1890s. During the 1893 World's Columbian Exhibition in Chicago, "pianists from all over the central United States converged on the amusement thoroughfare called the Midway, as well as the huge Chicago red-light district," at least some of whom played early ragtime or direct precursors to that music.[6] In 1897 came the first publication of a "Rag," and Joplin's famous "Maple Leaf Rag" was published in 1899. Ragtime took America by storm from the end of the nineteenth century through roughly the first fifteen years of the twentieth century.

Here I should add some perspective on the significance of ragtime and a song and performance strain offshoot in the development of the music of African-Americans. Researchers on early Black music, Lynn Abbott and Doug Seroff, give us important understanding of the role of ragtime and the vocal and performance music called "coon songs." This perspective also relates to the discussion of "the changing modern world, music, and modern art" in chapter 2. They report:

> Ragtime released a pent-up reservoir of modernism in African American culture, providing an antidote to "Ethiopian minstrelsy," which had stifled the development of race entertainment for most of the nineteenth century. Just as the century drew to a close, the lid blew off, unleashing a torrent of creativity that swept thousands of Black writers, performers, musicians, and entrepreneurs into the professional ranks. . . .
>
> . . . In the course of this development, audiences [White, as well as Black] were charmed into accepting a much broader panorama of Black stage arts and music.

That "Ethopian minstrelsy," i.e., the famous minstrel shows, was the presentation of typically denigrating stereotypes and caricatures of African-Americans by White performers in blackface; later Black performers offered their own minstrelsy, sometimes mocking those caricatures. Ragtime started changing the pure musical calculus. But an offshoot of ragtime, used for vocal music and performance, took off from that minstrelsy base and produced the "coon songs." That term is now racially offensive, but Abbot and Seroff, in their book, *Ragged But Right*, enlighten us on this whole process. Many of the lyrics for the "coon songs" were, at least on their surface, racially denigrative, but they became a stage and device that moved the development of Black music to the tremendously important next phase:

Commercially published coon songs spilled into turn-of-the-century Black vernacular culture, where they seem to have served a transitional function. Two-way traffic between the grass roots and the Black professional stage, intensified by the popularity of ragtime coon songs, cleared the way for the "original blues."[7]

Back to St. Louis and the development of its music: "By the turn of the century blues was beginning to emerge as an element in published ragtime. The first scored twelve-bar blues was published in St. Louis in 1904 as the 'A' section of a ragtime tune named 'One O' Them Things'" (by Chapman and Smith). By 1916, the blues appears to have exceeded ragtime in popularity in St. Louis, especially among Black folks; and by 1920 the blues was dominating nightlife music in the city.[8] In light of the ragtime piano background, it's also appropriate that, by the early to mid-1920s, St. Louis had a number of excellent bluesy pianists such as Roosevelt Sykes. Several of them played both piano and guitar, like Peetie Wheatstraw and Henry Townsend—and Lonnie and brother James "Steady Roll" Johnson. St. Louis blues musician and historian of today, Leroy Pierson, has also pointed out that the playing of *both* of the only two instruments that could produce a full scale of notes and rich, dense chords, namely, piano and guitar, "provided . . . a depth of understanding and musical empathy unknown in most quarters."[9]

An interesting perspective on the blues in the two cities we've considered came from the great jazz drummer Zutty Singleton, originally from the New Orleans area, and his wife Marge: "The blues, the real blues, were played in St. Louis, different from New Orleans blues. In very low dives, among cut-throats and gamblers, there was always some guy who could play the blues on the old broken-down piano. Blues that would break your heart. During the race riot in East St. Louis [in 1917] and directly afterwards you really heard blues." That's a fascinating comment in itself![10] They may have somewhat overstated the difference, but the point is that St. Louis blues was even deeper, more gritty, more drawn from the depths of the soul than the New Orleans variety had tended to be.

## Music on the Mississippi

Not long after Lonnie Johnson had settled in St. Louis in late 1919 or early 1920, he began playing on one of the famous Mississippi river-boats owned by the Streckfus family, the *St. Paul*, which was so named because it chugged all the way up the river to St. Paul, Minnesota. Soon he was playing with the "Jazz-O-Maniacs" of bandleader Charlie Creath (pronounced "Creth"). It's not surprising that Lonnie would hook up with Creath, because in 1919 and 1920 Creath's companion band leader, Fate Marable, had established an excellent band playing on other Streckfus riverboats, and that band had significant New Orleans musicians like Johnny St. Cyr on banjo, "Baby" Dodds on drums, and a young Louis Armstrong, all of whom knew Lonnie. As best we can tell (though the evidence is thin, and Lonnie overstated the amount of time he spent with Creath), Lonnie played on the riverboats from roughly the summer months of 1920 through the summer or fall of 1922, primarily with the Creath band on the *St. Paul*. He probably did some playing with the band in 1924 and 1925, as well. He typically played violin.[11]

One source also says Lonnie "played briefly in St. Louis with Nat Robinson and Will Marion Cook's Concert Orchestra in 1921," but I haven't been able to verify that.[12] (Will Marion Cook, a highly trained musician, was a very significant figure in the development of African American music in the early years of the century.)

Those magnificent old riverboats and their excursions up and down the Mississippi were grand things.

The riverboats also had symbolic and nostalgic effects; the latter related to the world that was lost with those modernist developments discussed earlier. As Professor Kenney spelled it out in his book on the riverboats and "jazz on the river":

> People liked to take to the river in steamboats whose form . . . evoked a slower, less technologically advanced, and supposedly more elegant and graceful time. . . . [They were] symbolic vessels [that] stim-ulated enchanting visions of graceful harmony with the forces of nature. . . . Americans liked to . . . enjoy reveries in which the vessels resembled wedding cakes, Victorian mansions . . . and even

The *St. Paul* Mississippi riverboat, on which Lonnie Johnson played with Charlie Creath band.
PHOTO COURTESY OF JOSEPH MERRICK JONES STEAMBOAT COLLECTION, LOUISIANA RESEARCH COLLECTION, TULANE UNIVERSITY.

swans paddling through peacefully calm, glassy waters, that wedded past with present and North with South. For most White people, riverboats stirred nostalgic longings for gentle voyages into an earlier era. . . .[13]

Black folks were allowed to ride only on Monday nights; later an excursion steamer from another company provided more rides for them. The Streckfus company said it wanted to "attract the best class" of people and families.

The special joy of these excursions was hearing music played superbly as the steamboat glided down the river, and to be able to dance to the music in the beautiful main halls. Now it must be noted that, contrary to the impression of many who know of those riverboat cruises, jazz was only one type of music played (and deep blues was not played at all). In fact, jazz was mostly *not* played until 1919 and thereafter, and even then in strictly modified form. The policy was to please the passengers, which "meant performing a diversity of musical styles with an emphasis on playing the popular songs of the day and playing them well," with tempos that were easy to dance to. Into the 1920s, improvisation was mostly discouraged, though in 1919 on the *St. Paul* there was a first effort to adapt New Orleans jazz to the "repertoire, tempi, and sensibilities of stock dance arrangements."

Fate Marable and Charlie Creath were very well-trained, excellent musicians; and they and the Streckfus folks required that their musicians be able to read music, be disciplined in playing the music properly, and present themselves well in dress, grooming and demeanor.[14]

Lonnie Johnson was already a superb musician, and he was evidently able to read music well. But he certainly got more experience playing with those fine bands; he also deepened his personal orientation towards presenting himself in a dignified, well-dressed manner. And he made more contacts in the music and general entertainment world.

## Riding the Vaudeville Circuit

During the general time Lonnie played on the riverboats, he probably also played in some St. Louis clubs. With the people he got to know doing both, from his later New Orleans club and theater performances, and with the continued development of his musical and entertainment abilities, he also performed on the RKO theater circuit, starting as early as fall 1920 or 1921. He did performance tours of the Theater Owners Booking Association (TOBA), the circuit of theaters for Black folks, as well.

Lonnie told British blues writer Paul Oliver: "I worked from Coast to Coast on the RKO circuit and I played everything that was playable, every theater there was and every place they could make into a theater or call a theater." On the TOBA circuit, he started in the Standard Theater in Philadelphia, with a band, and then the show went on the road: "I played the TOBA from end to end. Just about every place they had from New York to Texas." He would do five, even six, shows a day. On the RKO circuit, he primarily worked with the dance and comedy team of Glenn and Jenkins. Of those vaudeville performers and his work with them, Lonnie said: "They were the greatest. They had an act, they were street sweepers with brooms, and they'd dance while they were sweeping the streets. And in between their act, I'd sing and play 'til they made their changes [of clothes and scene], and then I'd work with 'em, and then I'd go off." (In a 1960 interview with Paul Oliver, he said he worked with Glenn and Jenkins for four years.[15] In his interview with Moe Asch, he said, "I worked with them, I'd guess, two or three years."[16] That seems more accurate.)

At one point, the circuit took Lonnie to his home territory in New Orleans, where he played the Lyric Theater—with "classic" blues singers Clara and Mamie Smith.[17] The Lyric Theater of New Orleans (at the corner of Iberville and Burgundy) was reconstituted in 1919 to serve as a theater for African-Americans. It was owned by two White businessmen, but all operations at the theater were conducted by Blacks. They promoted it as "America's Largest and Finest Colored Theater" of the time; it had around 2,000 seats.

There was an interesting special type of show there, which also occurred in several other theaters in larger cities through the South like Atlanta. This was a show which, along with sales of blues and jazz records to Whites *as well as* Blacks, also had implications for the broader theme of this book on the race issue. The shows had the delightfully revealing name, the "Midnight Frolics." These were late-night shows in the Black theaters for Whites, who could come, enjoy the more exciting and soulful music, "let their hair down," and have a looser, rousing good time. It also provided more exposure by Whites to this great Black music and to the remarkable spirit of those folks. As a result, these shows also helped to slowly eat away at the terrible racial divide.[18]

## From Blues to Blue Collar Work; Marriage (?)

Those theater tours probably ended sometime in 1924. Johnson then took jobs outside the music world for 12 to 15 months. From Lonnie's rather vague testimony, it appears he worked in a steel mill, or "steel foundry," in East St. Louis; the foundries, along with stockyards, provided a substantial amount of employment in the city. East St. Louis was also a major hub for railroads at the time. I was unable to find him in city directories in either city, but it is probable that he was living in East St. Louis at this point; that is what veteran bluesman Henry Townsend told me.[19] East St. Louis had a substantial African-American population (as it still does). During this time he surely continued to play in various local clubs and for parties and other special occasions, as he had done in New Orleans. In 1925, Lonnie may have worked as a carpenter and/or as cook; Lonnie said in a later interview he had those skills available as fallback trades.[20]

In late 1924 or the first half of 1925 in St. Louis, Lonnie romantically linked up with blues singer Mary Smith. She was an attractive woman with a lovely smile,[21] originally from Mississippi. She worked in St. Louis clubs with Lonnie a number of times. Mary made some recordings on her own in 1929–1932, and a few in 1934–36. She did not make any recordings with Lonnie, which seems odd, at first glance. But the dates of her recordings, in conjunction with the following information, suggest why that didn't happen.

Most blues writers report that they married in 1925 in St. Louis or in East St. Louis, which is across the state line and river in Illinois; indeed, Mary took the Johnson last name. Unfortunately, when I checked public records in the St. Louis Public Library, and also submitted a formal request to the appropriate Illinois state agency for the East St. Louis site, no marriage record was found in either place. (Of course, searching records for a Johnson and a Mary Smith is almost a guarantee of frustration!) In fact, Lonnie proved to be a very difficult man on whom to obtain public records. The best answer on this question and the reason I couldn't find public records on the marriage was supplied by Robert Koester. Koester is president of Delmark Records and the famous Jazz Record Mart in Chicago; but he started his involvement with records in St. Louis, and he recorded Mary Johnson in 1955. In an interview with me, Koester said, "You know, Mary Johnson was Lonnie's common law wife."[22]

In the interview with Moe Asch in 1967, Lonnie said something that, on two levels, explains why blues and jazz researchers have struggled to find out these particulars, especially from his personal life. Interestingly and appropriately, Asch started the interview by saying to him, "You're something of a mystery. Has anyone written up your life?" With an editorial comment on some writers' and publishers' tendencies Lonnie amusingly said, "No; some writers started to, but they looked to me to tell about the hardships in my life and not the good things." Then came the revealing comment—or rather, the *non*-revealing comment: "Some parts of a man's private life he keeps to himself, he don't tell it to the public."[23] In our celebrity tell-all age, with the media invading people's private lives in the most appalling detail, this may seem like something from another time—or another planet. But on the other hand, in this sleeze-saturated age, I'm sure there are many people who will respond to that statement with an "A-men!" for the sanity displayed. Nevertheless, Lonnie's reluctance to go into detail does limit even a reasonably sober-minded writer in his ability to tell Lonnie's full story. An even more startling example of that privacy orientation is noted in the following.

*Blues Who's Who* by Sheldon Harris is a respected source of collected biographical information for the blues—though it was published some years ago. Harris reported that the two were married and that they had six children. But in the few later interviews with Lonnie, he usually said nothing about the marriage to Mary or those six children. The single exception came from the memory of a jazz writer, Verum Clapp, in an article written upon Lonnie's death in 1970. Clapp said, "One time Lonnie turned to me and said, 'I've got six beautiful daughters and the Lord has spared me'."[24] (This is probably the source for the Sheldon Harris statement.) But startlingly, in Lonnie's interview with Moe Asch, after Lonnie talks fondly about his mother, Asch asks Lonnie if she had any grandchildren (i.e., Lonnie's children or some from his brother who survived the flu epidemic). Lonnie responds that his daughter Brenda, by his 1960s partner Susie, "is her only grandchild." (Susie and Lonnie were not formally married.) What about those "six children" Harris reports?

I was not able to find names or anything else about those children—with one notable exception; a key factor in that exception leads to a conclusion about why Lonnie would not talk about the one child, at least. (Susie and Brenda told me that Lonnie said he'd had some children with Mary, but he didn't state how many, and they knew nothing else about those children.[25])

Here, I need to jump ahead in time. *Blues Who's Who* and other sources report that the marriage lasted from 1925 until 1932. But for a variety of reasons discussed in subsequent pages and chapters, I now doubt that the marriage actually lasted that long. Lonnie's musical prominence began in 1926 and reached its height in 1928–1930. Throughout those five years, like most top musicians, Lonnie was often on the road playing concerts and clubs, as well as recording in Chicago, Memphis, New York, and elsewhere. When a musician at that level is regularly traveling like that, they are away most of the time from their established partner, at a time when they are youthful and with active appetites, *and* there are many attractive women who are seeking to connect with the music star. This is a recipe for going astray. One particularly significant example of Lonnie on the loose has been documented. In his definitive biography of Bessie Smith, Chris Albertson reports it this way: "While touring with [Bessie's] 'Midnight Steppers' show [in fall 1929] she carried on an affair with one of her performers . . . Lonnie Johnson. 'It was a constant thing to see Lonnie coming in and out of Bessie's stateroom' . . . ," recalled Bessie's niece Ruby Walker, who was on the tour. In a later interview, Lonnie acknowledged the affair, saying, "She was sweet on me, but we never got too serious. . . ."[26] Note that this was in 1929, and the marriage between Lonnie and Mary supposedly lasted until 1932. Obviously, there were marriage issues. That Bessie found Lonnie attractive is not surprising. Lonnie Johnson, in the later 1920s and all the way into the early 1960s, was a charming, urbane, attractive man who was also a master artist; and he was "at the top of his game" in the late '20s. Bessie would have been among legions of women to find Lonnie of interest (though that's about the *only* way Bessie Smith could be compared with other women!).

What all that suggests is that the marriage broke up in significant part due to Lonnie's wandering eyes. We can't know what Mary's story was here, but it was Lonnie who was the music star at the time. My educated guess is that the marriage ended badly, with hard feelings. Given Lonnie's refusal to talk about it, it's possible there was also some bad faith behavior on Mary's side; or possibly, Lonnie, who was fundamentally a very decent, moral man, may simply have been chagrined later on at some of what he did and just shoved it to the back of his mind so he didn't have to deal with it. If they did have the children Harris reported and Lonnie apparently mentioned, I would also guess that the child or children stayed with Mary. That, along with the fact that Lonnie was constantly on the road, getting lots of attention through 1931, may have led to an enduring disconnect with the kid(s). But given the fact that the two were really together for only four years or so, possibly less (see the next paragraph), if they had six children, at least two had to be twins!

Several writers have said that Lonnie and Mary moved to New York City in 1927 (one said 1929), where Lonnie's increasingly active and prominent music career was centered. I now doubt that happened because of some things Lonnie said in an unpublished section of a 1960 interview. His discussion in that interview also raises further questions about the state and duration of the marriage. That material is discussed in chapter 5.[27] I can't establish this definitively, but in short, my conclusion is that Lonnie went directly from St. Louis to Dallas, Texas, possibly with Mary for the first year or more, though probably not. In the interview he said, "I left from there and went to Texas." Where "there" was is not clear from the discussion; but from the context and chronology of things, it was surely St. Louis. Mary probably stayed in St. Louis while Lonnie went to Texas for his good, extended music gigs, and he got back to St. Louis whenever he could. What is clear is that, in that 1960 interview, he made no mention or even gave a hint of Mary in talking about his time in Texas.

Anyway, my best guess is that the marriage was seriously faltering by the first half of 1929; and after the tour with Bessie Smith in fall 1929, it was effectively ended. In his excellent and insightful book on blues history, *The Devil's Music*, Giles Oakley offers his own take on the marriage. He thinks it lasted, formally at least, until 1932, when Mary moved back with her mother in St. Louis. Some of Mary's own songs, as well as Lonnie's, impressionistically suggest what was happening.[28]

Songs Lonnie recorded on June 11, 1929, present tantalizing circumstantial "evidence" for that timetable of the fading marriage. The six sides cut that day included, "You Can't Give a Woman Everything She Needs," "From Now on Make Your Whoopee at Home," and "Baby Please Don't Leave Home No More." The song title sentiments need not be taken as simple direct references, but rather as a basic concern about the marriage, rendered in various blues song forms and phrasings. A song *after* the probable break-up is even more suggestive, especially in conjunction with the second side cut in June: After "From Now on Make Your Whoopee at Home" in June 1929, Lonnie recorded "She's Making Whoopee in Hell Tonight" on January 7, 1930. The lyrics include pretty harsh sentiments in general, and this line in specific, directed at a partner: "You'll be makin' whoopee with the Devil in Hell tonight." This is speculative; but with one as articulate in his lyrics as Lonnie and as inclined to tell a story in his songs, rather than just throw together random lines from the big blues bucket of common phrases, those tentative conclusions are plausible. Mary Johnson's songs also impressionistically suggest the marriage problems, although the most focused songs don't help with the chronology of the marriage because they were recorded in 1932. The closest to a direct reference came in "Mary Johnson Blues": "I once was a married woman, sorry the day I ever was; [repeat]; I was a young girl at home and I did not know the world."[29]

Now, there is one (apparent) child about whom there is some information: *Blues Who's Who* did mention that child, Clarence, who actually made a few recordings. But little has been known about him. In my own field research in St. Louis, some local musicians provided material. In fact, blues musician and historian Leroy Pierson gave me a photo taken by fine St. Louis bottleneck guitarist, Ron Edwards, which is displayed below. Clarence is the one sitting with the Gibson guitar leaning against him; the White guy is Leroy Pierson; the fellow on the right is major St. Louis bluesman Henry Townsend; the other guy is Fred Grant. Leroy and Henry both told me that Clarence, who long lived in East St. Louis, claimed to be the son of Lonnie. They both said they believed that was true, and they said Clarence played superb guitar, very much in Lonnie's style. (The bad news: Other sources only mention six *daughters*?)

So why would Lonnie not want to talk about Clarence, or even acknowledge that child and his mother's grandchild? Well, Leroy Pierson and Henry Townsend told me that, for a long time, Clarence had a serious drinking problem. And, he got in trouble with the law more than once, and spent time in prison—more than once, if I got the story straight. Lonnie may have "wandered" in all too human and personal terms, but he was always a dignified and otherwise proper man. My guess is that he felt that Clarence had, more than once, betrayed the

Lonnie's probable son Clarence Johnson, Leroy Pierson, Fred Grant, and Henry Townsend (left to right), May 9, 1991, during "Guitar Masters" at "Mississippi Nights" event in St. Louis. PHOTO TAKEN BY AND COURTESY OF ST. LOUIS BOTTLENECK GUITARIST, RON EDWARDS.

image of a dignified, responsible member of society that Lonnie sought to offer, and he gradually just ceased to recognize the existence of the son. But that's just a guess.

Now I have to relate a delightful story that developed in my St. Louis research on Lonnie and Clarence. Henry Townsend was a principal source of information on Lonnie for this and the next chapter. He fully understood Lonnie's importance and wanted this book project to come out; he, like B. B. King, thought Lonnie had not received his due. Henry came to St. Louis at age 9 or 10 shortly before Lonnie arrived. When I first interviewed him in summer 2004 he was 95 years old and still very sharp. (He also emphatically stated that he would not tell me anything that he did not know directly; he was scornful of other old blues guys who would just pass on rumor and speculation—or just make up stories, as some did. As far I as can determine, he did just as he said.) I asked him about Clarence; Leroy had already told me about him. Henry told me what he knew about him. He hadn't seen Clarence in a good while, but as far as he knew, Clarence was still alive and in East St. Louis. As he ruminated out loud about how I might connect with Clarence, I said, "well, if you've got an address, I'll just go over and see if I can catch him." Henry muttered about how tough a place East St. Louis had become, and he suggested it wasn't a place for someone like me to be wandering around alone (meaning it was overwhelmingly Black and some White guy looking semi-professional and semi-benign might be in a dangerous situation). He then got himself a bit worked up, and pretty soon he said, "Well, I'll just go over there with you; you won't have trouble that way." Here was a 95-year-old man, in a wheel-chair, who was going to hop in the van and be my body guard and guide over in tough East St. Louis! It was a wonderful moment. Henry Townsend was a bluesman with steel in his spine to the end. But after a while, he realized this probably wasn't the best plan. A little later, after I had returned to Minnesota, Leroy contacted me and told me he found that Clarence had actually died a while earlier. What a shame I couldn't get to him sooner, or that those St. Louis guys didn't do a thorough interview with Clarence to extract whatever information he could give about himself and Lonnie!

## Katy Red's and the Blues; Winning a Singing Contest and a Recording Contract

Increasingly through 1925, Lonnie was playing in various clubs in St. Louis and, especially, in and around East St. Louis. It is likely that Lonnie played in a club in St. Louis called Jazzland, where a number of excellent jazz and some blues musicians played. Jazzland was located at 23rd and Market Street, adjacent to the famous Booker T. Washington Theater. It was formerly the Rosebud Bar, which was Ground Zero of the playing and continuing development of ragtime piano. Speaking of 1925 and 1926 primarily, Henry Townsend said Lonnie also played in the Revere Club in St. Louis; but more frequently, "any place in East St. Louis that was major, he played there."[30]

The most notable of those East St. Louis clubs was called Katy Red's; it was *the* place for the best bluesmen of the area to play—and for any such musicians visiting from out of town. From all the testimony, it was one of those special clubs in various locations around the nation where the very best Black musicians would get loose and produce the most incredible soulful, blazing blues and/or jazz. As Henry Brown told Paul Oliver, "We get over to ole Katy Red's . . . and we'd break 'em on down over there in those days." He noted that the great blues and Boogie Woogie piano player Roosevelt Sykes was there frequently, among other top blues guys.[31]

Another who played there was guitarist Teddy Roosevelt Darby. It was not an accident that he had those first two names. In 1901 President Teddy Roosevelt invited the Negro leader Booker T. Washington to dine with him in the White House. No president had invited a Black person to dine there before. Many Southerners and others were upset; one prominent figure called it "the most damnable outrage." As a result, as Edmund Morris wrote, "Ever since his dinner for Booker T. Washington, southern Blacks had called him 'our President' and compared him to Lincoln." In 1903, Roosevelt also took actions demonstrating concern for Black citizens. Those actions included his response to a vicious, racist campaign by Mississippi's James Vardaman and an increase in lynching with a public letter that said, "All thoughtful men must feel the gravest alarm over the growth of lynching in this country. . . ." All this demonstrates the power of symbolic actions by prominent figures, various versions of which are a key part of the broader societal theme of this book. Another interesting symbolic development with Roosevelt, which also illustrates how Black music and performing styles reached through American culture from early on, came at a 1901 Christmas party at the White House: President Teddy, "beaming like a boy, performed a variety of buck-and-wing steps to loud applause." "Buck-and-wing" steps were a prime Black entertainers' dance often performed in vaudeville and Black theaters. Another interesting illustration of Blacks' response to Teddy Roosevelt is the fact that the great African-American pathfinder in baseball, Jackie Robinson (born in 1919), was given the middle name of Roosevelt in honor of President Teddy.[32]

Lonnie and his brother James "Steady Roll" Johnson often played together at Katy Red's in 1925–1926. Steady Roll, like Lonnie, could play piano, guitar, banjo, and violin. The two brothers would each play a different instrument, then switch off. Blues singer and vaudeville performer Victoria Spivey met and recorded with Lonnie in 1926 in St. Louis. Years later she reflected on that time: "How many people know that Lonnie Johnson was considered the greatest violin player for blues in this world? I have great memories of him sitting on top of the piano playing violin with brother James at Katy Red's. . . . Dollar, five dollar, and ten dollar bills would be flying as tips."[33]

Henry Townsend said Steady Roll was an extraordinarily talented musician. Lonnie himself said, "My brother, he played piano and violin and guitar. He was better than me . . . ; Lord sakes yes, he was better than me!" Looking at the testimony and listening to their recordings (see chapter 4), my sense is that Steady Roll was probably a little better than Lonnie on piano and very good on guitar, though not as good as his brother. Townsend: "When Lonnie and Steady Roll played together in those clubs it was always a smash!" But Townsend also said that, unlike Lonnie, Steady Roll didn't have a lot of ambition, and he found a nice well-off lady in the region whom he linked up with, so he was content to just stay in the St. Louis/East St. Louis area. (A few times Steady Roll did venture out of the area for recording or music gigs; that included backing Ethel Waters on one tour.)

Lonnie and Steady Roll also played in Alton, Illinois, just north of St. Louis, and in the Waterfront Club (which wasn't on the waterfront) in Newport, Illinois, in the St. Louis area. In 1960, Townsend said Steady Roll had stayed at the Waterfront Club pretty steady (so to speak) for the next 29 years (from 1926 on).[34]

Lonnie evidently continued to play the RKO and TOBA theater circuits. In my research this was confirmed with a fun, unexpected twist. I was working in the Schomberg Center for Research in Black Culture, a special library collection that is part of the New York City Public Library system located in Harlem. In a reference book titled, *A Century of Musicals in Black and White: An Encyclopedia of Musical Stage Works By, About, or Involving African Americans*, I found this entry: "**Ebony Vampires** (1925–1926). Touring vaudeville revue in at least two eds. [i.e., 2 separate tours with many but not all of the same performers]. Cast of both eds. featured Watts & Mills . . . and Alonzo Johnson."

It's probable this was our Lonnie, but it's not certain. Some reports of an "Alonzo Johnson" on the vaudeville circuit seem unlikely to be Lonnie J due to the timing of what's reported, so there may have been another "Alonzo Johnson."[35]

So, why the vampire theme? My initial reaction to this was that it must have something to do with the Dracula story. But I was later informed by knowledgeable blues and popular music writer Elijah Wald that "they are actually vampires, as in Theda Bara (early film star), 'I'm a Jazz Vampire,' and so forth. The word was generally shortened to 'vamp,' but in either case, it meant a temptress, like the 'ebony' show-girls who were presumably the main draw of this revue."

**First Recordings** Lonnie first appeared on record with Charlie Creath's band on a 78 side made on November 2, 1925, for the OKeh label; it had the wonderful title, "Won't Don't Blues." (The other side of the 78 was a recording of the Creath band without Lonnie.) Lonnie played violin on the record, as he had in Creath's band on the riverboats. In the band were fellow New Orleans musicians Pops Foster and Zutty Singleton, who also played on the riverboats. Since OKeh was using the original "acoustic" recording method, the sound quality of the record-ing is poor and one really can't hear much of Lonnie's violin playing.

More noteworthy is the fact that Lonnie is doing the *singing* on the record. Lonnie's instrumental abilities were already advanced, as his recordings over the ensuing year strikingly demonstrate, but his singing on this recording was still developing. Remember what he said about the question of his singing in clubs in New Orleans before 1917: "I just didn't think about it," he said, "because me and my brother was doing all right with our instruments, and those joints we played in didn't par-ticularly want any vocals." Thus, he developed his vocal work in this St. Louis period. Big Bill Broonzy said he "came to St. Louis in 1921" and met Lonnie and his brother sometime soon thereafter. Broonzy's comment on the multiple musical talents of Lonnie, including his sing-ing, was striking: "Lonnie was playing the violin, guitar, bass, mandolin, banjo and all the things that you could make music on, and he was good on either one he picked up; and he could sing too, just as good."[36] That suggests Lonnie's singing was developing pretty rapidly in the early '20s.

For the Creath 78, the acoustic recording technology also forced Lonnie to basically shout into the recording horn, thus distorting the caliber of singing he was capable of at that early stage. As was noted in a chronicle of the development of the recording industry, in the recording studio "the change [from acoustical to electrical recording] was drastic and abrupt . . . The microphone was capable of capturing the sound of even the softest pianissimo on the violin, so it was no longer necessary to crowd studio musicians together in front of the horn . . . It was as though the window of a hot, stuffy room were opened for the first time." The author exaggerates the quality of the early microphones, but compared to the old acoustic method, the change was dramatic.[37] This recording also suggests Lonnie had again played with Creath's band around St. Louis in 1925, other than on the riverboats.

Meanwhile, in fall 1925 came the sequence of events that dramatically changed Lonnie's life. A blues-singing contest was held in the Booker T. Washington Theater in St. Louis, apparently on Thursday evenings. Music contests were actually a regular feature of the theater for years. In the few interviews with him, Lonnie said he won the contest either eight weeks in a row or eighteen weeks in a row, the larger figure tending to be his later memory. This contest was conducted by Jesse Johnson, a key figure in Black music in the city in the 1920s, who also served as a talent scout for record labels. Apparently, as a result of Lonnie winning the blues-singing contest, he got a recording contract with OKeh Records. Two days after the recording session with the Creath band, on November 4, 1925, in St. Louis, Lonnie Johnson made his first records as the featured musician.

In the magnificent, ornate old St. Louis Public Library (designed by the great American architect Cass Gilbert, who designed the Supreme Court building and the masterful Minnesota state capitol building), I searched the *St. Louis Argus* newspaper for African-Americans, to see if I could document just how long the contest went and other details. In the Friday, October 23, 1925, issue I found an advertisement for the "Booker Washington Theatre, 23rd and Market" ("General Admission: 30 cents"), which showed that Bessie Smith was appearing there for the week of October 26. The Booker T did indeed bring the greatest

Black music stars. In a line at the bottom of the ad it said, "BLUES SINGING CONTEST—STARTING SOON. I found that line in the ad for a couple of days after that. Looking through the news stories and ads for the rest of October through most of November, I could not find a mention of the outcome of the contest. I couldn't establish the length of that particular contest.

Mark Miller looked in earlier issues of the *Argus* and found a blues-singing contest from November 1923 through February 1924, and, though his description is a bit fuzzy, he found that Lonnie wasn't among the "initial 31 entrants," but somehow he "qualified for the finals in mid-February" (and it did run for 18 weeks). The *Argus* reported Irene Scruggs as the winner of that contest. But that was earlier. In a reference note, Miller said, "there are no reports in the *Argus* of a similar contest in winter 1924–1925."[38] But that's the *wrong period* for leading into the Lonnie recording. Further, as just noted there was an October 23, 1925, announcement of another such contest; and those contests were a continuing thing at the Booker T. Thus, it's very likely that the *late October–early November 1925* contest did occur. Given the timing of Lonnie's OKeh recording, it may have been only a one-week or ten-day contest; or Jesse Johnson may simply have seen an exceptional musician during the contest (and in the previous contest). The fact that it probably wasn't followed up in the *Argus* is not so surprising:

The African-American oriented *Argus* was, ironically, not a good place to read about the blues. As Bill Greensmith reports in his introduction to the Henry Townsend memoir: "Published weekly, the *Argus* was operated by middle-class Blacks who viewed blues music and its musicians with disdain. To these arbiters of taste, jazz was on the borderline of respectability; blues most definitely was disreputable. Outside of advertisements, the [major bluesmen's names] fail to appear in the pages of the *Argus*. . . ."[39] Henry Townsend said the same to me.

Ultimately, the length of the contest is not important. Lonnie sang and played violin and (apparently) won; and as Lonnie put it in his interview with Moe Asch, "I sang and played violin at the same time, and I were doing a very good job of it! That's not easy, you know!" Indeed, it's not. Most importantly, Jesse Johnson, who was probably responsible for setting up the blues contest *as* a lead-in to a recording contract, saw and heard a uniquely talented performer, and he set up the OKeh recording session. I return to the results of that recording session at the beginning of the next chapter.

## The Booker T. Washington Theater: Musical and Cultural Heart of the St. Louis Black Community

From about 1910 well into the 1930s, "the world of American entertainment [and the presentation of musical art were] forever changed by a widespread proliferation of independent African-American vaudeville houses . . . sponsoring Black entertainment for Black audiences."[40] This came in the context of the "Jim Crow" segregationist actions in the first decades of the century, where African-Americans were either not allowed in theaters at all or were treated badly and relegated to an upper balcony.

A few of those independent theaters in major cities stood out as the premier arenas for presentation of African-American music, theater, variety shows, and so on. One of those leading theaters was the Booker T. Washington Theater in St. Louis (named, of course, for the famous educator and Principal of the Tuskegee Institute). In New York, in the later 1910s through the 1920s, the Lafayette became the premier theater until supplanted by the subsequently famous Apollo; the Lincoln Theater was a second significant Black theater in the Big Apple. Other top Black theaters were the Howard Theater in Washington, D.C., the Royal in Baltimore, the Earle in Philadelphia, the Grand Theater in Chicago, and the 81 Theater in Atlanta; the very fine Regal Theater was added in Chicago in 1928. These palaces of African-American performance art and entertainment brought the greatest African-American musicians, dancers, and other entertainers to "their people."

We must remember that this was a time before television or radio, until the latter became a factor in the second half of the 1920s. It was a time when, from previous years, people were used to getting out of their houses and apartments and going to a central place of entertainment and artistic expression, a place that was a gathering place, a place to be seen, and a place to convene and commune with fellow members of the African-American community. This was a central, shared experience, as well as a celebration of the arts and entertainment of Black folks. In a society where Black people were segregated, put down, and suffered economically, a grand theater like the Booker T. Washington, presenting strikingly dressed and proud African-American entertainers and great artists like Louis Armstrong, Bessie Smith, and Lonnie Johnson in "their" theater, was an affirmation of the creative leading lights of the people. The audience celebrated and genuinely reveled in the prominence and success of those great musicians who were recognized more broadly in America, as well as appreciating the artistic brilliance and powerful human expression of the performers.

Chapter 1 discussed the general setting of this, but let us note here that music was centrally important in the African-American community at the beginning of the twentieth century and continued to be over the ensuing decades. As author and musician Ben Sidran has written: "Music is not only conspicuous within, but *crucial to*, Black culture . . . Thus, the investigation of Black music is also the investigation of the Black mind, the Black social orientation, and the Black culture." He also noted music's great role as a socializing element in Black culture.[41]

Remember, as well, that these independent Black theaters were not places where the audience passively sat back and had music directed *at* them; rather, the experience was dynamically and dramatically participatory and interactive for audience and performers, and everyone expected it to be.

The Booker T. Washington was in a central location in St. Louis on Market Street and 23rd Street, just west of the grand Union Station (which is still there). Market Street was a main avenue of the downtown area, as it still is. The Theater operated from about 1912 to 1930 and apparently had over 1,000 seats (accounts differ as to its size); Henry Townsend remembered it, many years later, as "the huge Booker Washington Theater." It certainly was huge in the Black community. As Townsend said, "Everybody who was anybody [in the Black entertainment world] played there," including Bessie Smith, Ma Rainey, Ethel Waters, Bill "Bojangles" Robinson—and Lonnie Johnson. The Booker T. Washington was also part of the Theater Owners Booking Association circuit, T.O.B.A. That acronym, the performers sardonically said, stood

78 record, *Mr. Johnson's Blues*, with stick-on label from De Luxe Music Shoppe of Jesse Johnson, St. Louis. IMAGE COURTESY OF TOM KELLY OF ST. LOUIS.

for "Tough on Black Artists" or, more colorfully, "Tough on Black Asses," because some of the accommodations in TOBA theaters (but not the Booker T) were very modest and the circuit worked them hard.

Regarding Lonnie Johnson, as Henry Townsend said in my interview with him: "Lonnie would fill up the huge Booker Washington Theater anytime he came" in the later 1920s.[42]

The Booker Washington Theater had two other significant musical associations. The owner was Charles Turpin, who was the first Black elected to local government office in the city, and whose brother was Thomas Turpin of the Rosebud Café and Ragtime. Charles also owned the Jazzland club.

The second musical association of significance for the Booker Washington in the 1920s was the store just across a narrow side street from it: the De Luxe Music Shoppe of African-American Jesse Johnson (no relation to Lonnie). The store was a prime place for musicians to hang out and to meet others in music. I've included a photo of an original 78 record of Lonnie's first hit, "Mr. Johnson's Blues," with the label of Jesse Johnson's music shop affixed. (Thanks to St. Louis 78 records collector Tom Kelly for the image.) Jesse Johnson also became a principal early finder and promoter of Black musical talent, channeling them to record companies like Victor, OKeh, Brunswick, and Paramount.[43]

## November 1925

On November 12, 1925, Louis Armstrong went into a recording studio with jazz musicians Kid Ory, Johnny Dodds, Johnny St. Cyr, and Lil Hardin Armstrong. These were the first recordings by Louis Armstrong's "Hot Five" group; like Lonnie's, they were made under the OKeh label. Jazz historians consider this the beginning of a transformation by Louis Armstrong of the jazz art form—and ultimately, of much of American popular music for the century. The original New Orleans jazz style was ensemble band music, with each musician contributing to the music and none being the primary featured attraction who dominated the music-making; sometimes a musician would solo for two to four bars, but it was primarily collaborative group music. With the Hot Five recordings beginning on that November day, Louis Armstrong's virtuoso work as a soloist was the central factor in changing the direction of jazz. As Armstrong scholar Michael Cogswell points out: "Although jazz may have evolved into a soloist's art without him, there is little doubt that his innovations in the 1920s established a new standard that other musicians were then obligated to meet . . . With the Hot Five, Louis created chorus-length solos of unprecedented virtuosity and stunning inventiveness."[44]

With Lonnie Johnson's first two recordings, made eight days before that first Armstrong-Hot Five recording session, he began the process of doing the same thing for the guitar in jazz, in blues, and beyond.

In the next chapter we turn to the release of those first two recordings, which led to Lonnie's ascent to the heights of musical achievement and his transformation of the guitar as a solo instrument in popular music.

# 4

# Playing with the Strings, Part I

*"Lonnie Johnson was one of the transcendent people who influenced everybody."*[1]

—RY COODER

## 1926 and the Launch of Lonnie Johnson, Recording Artist

In early January 1926 the OKeh label released the 78 record of the new recording artist Lonnie Johnson, playing guitar and singing "Mr. Johnson's Blues" on the "A" side, and on the "B" side playing violin and singing "Falling Rain Blues," both accompanied by John Arnold on piano. The record was a hit. OKeh Records had Lonnie make 26 more record "sides" that year. The final side Lonnie made in 1926, in August 14, was his first solo guitar instrumental, "To Do This, You Got to Know How." It was such an appropriate title; Lonnie was already showing that he "knew how" to play the guitar better than anyone else in popular music, and was putting that extraordinary technical skill in the service of a rich and creative musical sensibility.

After some historical perspective, I begin by discussing the guitar in music. Chapters 4 and 5 are especially focused on the recordings. It was Lonnie Johnson's records during this time that had a huge impact on 20th century music.

1926 was the first of three years of tremendous creative development and ferment in music and more broadly in society. The following timeline lists some key developments that put things in historical perspective.

## 1926–1928: A Musical-Cultural Explosion

In 1926 through 1928 there was an extraordinary musical-cultural explosion, bringing the developments discussed in the Interlude in chapter 2 to a broader culmination, and bringing to the nation—and the world—a remarkable series of musical works. This included the formal establishment of a new musical genre. Just listing some of the more significant developments in music and beyond makes for a dazzling review:

### 1926

**Lonnie Johnson's** recordings during the year were striking, from release of his first record to his first guitar duet (with his brother) to his excellent first solo instrumental.

The first set of **Jelly Roll Morton's** "Red Hot Peppers" recordings were made, which were among the most important in early jazz history.

**Louis Armstrong's** historic "Hot Five" recordings were released and having an impact; in fact, with his trumpet solos, they were laying the groundwork for much of the jazz art form's subsequent history. And with Armstrong's *singing*, including his "scat" singing on "Heebie Jeebies," he began to profoundly influence all of popular music in the century.

The first significant recording by **Duke Ellington and band** came out, "East St. Louis Toodle-Oo."

**Fats Waller** made his first band recordings with the Fletcher Henderson group, as well as his first record as a soloist (playing "St. Louis Blues" on the Victor studio organ).

**Paul Robeson** recorded the great Negro Spiritual, "Deep River," and performed his first major concert in New York's Town Hall.

**Blind Lemon Jefferson** made his first recordings, which were very influential and opened the doors for many other "*country* blues" artists to be recorded; along with Lonnie Johnson's more sophisticated, "*city* blues," it allowed the blues genre to be well documented and boosted the impact of the blues on twentieth century music. Later in the year, excellent finger-picking Ragtime and blues guitar player **Blind Blake** also recorded for the first time.

The **Savoy Ballroom** was opened in New York City's Harlem section, covering a full city block. It became a premier palace of music and dance in America, with two top bands typically working the huge ballroom, playing for hundreds of dancers—and from the beginning it was racially integrated.

(In 1925, **Bessie Smith** had recorded the all-time classic, "St. Louis Blues," accompanied by Louis Armstrong, arguably her most celebrated recording.)

(In 1925, while Europe was in the heat of fascination with African art, music and "primitive culture," and also with the music of Black people coming out of America, the musical, *La Revue Negre* introduced beautiful, athletic African-American Josephine Baker as an exotic dancer-performer in Paris; she became a huge hit.)

**Jimmie Rodgers** is first heard on radio, leading to the establishment of the uniquely American Country music genre.

**Bing Crosby** made his first record, singing with Paul Whiteman's popular orchestra.

**NBC** formed the first radio network, bringing the means to broadcast music and other cultural fare to a nationwide audience.

### And for the future:

**Chuck Berry**, **John Coltrane** and **Miles Davis** were born. (**B. B. King** was born in September 1925, and jazz piano virtuoso **Oscar Peterson** was born in August 1925.)

### Other cultural developments:

**Fritz Lang's** landmark movie with a modernistic theme, *Metropolis*, came out.

African-American **Langston Hughes** published his first collection of poems, *The Weary Blues*, part of his significant contributions to the Harlem Renaissance.

(In 1925, the African-American professor at Howard University, **Dr. Alain Locke**, published the book that was seminal to the Harlem Renaissance, *The New Negro*. It included pieces by the leading lights of Black writing, poetry, other arts, and intellectual life. The book sought to show that there was flowering of creative production amongst African-Americans, all demonstrating the rise of Blacks, and that they were ready to take their fair place as co-equal members of American society and as superb contributors to its culture.)

The **Surrealist** arts movement was formalized with the establishment of an official group in Brussels.

**Ernest Hemingway's** first great novel, *The Sun Also Rises*, was published.

(**F. Scott Fitzgerald's** *The Great Gatsby* and Kafka's *The Trial* were published in 1925.)

(**Art Deco** style was formally introduced at the "Exposition Internationale des Arts Decoratifs et Industriels Modernes" in Paris in 1925.)

### Intellectual, Scientific & Industrial Developments:

**Pan American Airways**, the first great airline, began service.

American astronomer **Edwin Hubble** began classifying galaxies in the universe beyond our own Milky Way. In 1927 he discovered that those galaxies are receding from the Milky Way, and the further they are from this galaxy, the faster they are receding, which had huge implications for the study of physics and the universe.

(In 1925, the British philosopher and mathematician **Alfred North Whitehead** published Science and the Modern World, which critiqued the impacts and implications of what he saw as the reigning idea of "Scientific Materialism" and raised questions about whether that abstract scientific method was causing its practitioners to lose contact with the concrete reality of nature and to submerge due consideration of human values. It was a debate that was of central relevance to the century.)

## 1927

### *Music:*

**Louis Armstrong's Hot Five** recordings took jazz development even further, and they included three recordings **with Lonnie Johnson** on guitar, led by "Hotter Than That," one of the highlights of classic jazz.

In early December, **Duke Ellington's band** began their historic residency at Harlem's Cotton Club. Shortly thereafter, he brought in the great clarinet artist Barney Bigard, and in March 1928 he brought in the alto sax player Johnny Hodges. Duke then developed the band and sound that was among the most important developments in all of music for the century. After they were at the Cotton Club for a while, segments of their performances were broadcast over the new NBC radio network, which made them increasingly famous and brought jazz to a wide national audience.

In December, the musical *Show Boat* opened in Broadway. As one history said: "It was immediately obvious that 'Show Boat' was different [from the usual Broadway fare] . . . The opening scene replaced the traditional line of high-kicking chorus girls with a chorale of Black riverbank stevedores angrily declaiming, 'Niggers all work on de Mississippi, Niggers all work while de White folks play.'" Stage scholar Miles Kreuger: "The history of American musical theater is divided into two eras: everything before *Show Boat* and everything after *Show Boat*."[2] (But the Kreuger assessment misses the important, superb predecessors of *Show Boat* developed in Black New York theaters, *Shuffle Along* of 1921 being the most important precursor.)

In November, **Jimmie Rodgers** made the landmark recording that launched his career, "Blue Yodel (T for Texas)," and, along with the next item, laid the foundation for effective formal establishment of the Country music genre. (In 1930 Rodgers recorded "Blue Yodel #9" with Louis Armstrong backing him on trumpet.)

Laying down the other cornerstone in the foundation of the emerging Country music genre—and also pointing to the future of folk music—the **Carter Family** made their first recordings in Bristol, Tennessee, in August.

**Andres Segovia** made his first commercial recordings, solidifying his role in making the guitar a major solo instrument in classical music.

### Other Cultural Developments:

The first significant "talking" motion picture, *The Jazz Singer* with **Al Jolson,** was released.

Seminal creator in modern dance, **Martha Graham**, performed her work "Revolt" with her small dance troupe; "Revolt" forcefully struck, even startled, its audiences with its stark depiction of human injustice. (She formed the group in 1926.)

*Elmer Gantry* by **Sinclair Lewis** was published.

### Intellectual, Scientific & Industrial Developments:

Physicist **Werner Heisenberg** published the landmark scientific paper that has reverberated ever since, which announced the "uncertainty principle." Many would say it was also a metaphor for the age.

**Charles Lindbergh** became the first person to cross the Atlantic Ocean nonstop flying solo; he became a huge national hero and a significant symbol of the age.

**Martin Heidegger** published his masterwork, *Being and Time*, a major contribution to philosophy (unfathomable for normal people). *Its title is an excellent three-word summation of key musical, personal, and societal developments of the times—and of themes discussed in this book.*

## 1928

### Music:

In a February session, **Lonnie Johnson** recorded solo guitar instrumental masterpieces, "Playing with the Strings," "Away Down in the Alley Blues," and "Blues in G."

In November, **Lonnie Johnson** and White jazz/popular guitarist **Eddie Lang** (appearing as "Blind Willie Dunn") recorded the first two of their 10 historic guitar duets that have inspired and amazed guitarists and others ever since, one being the classic, "Have to Change Keys to Play These Blues."

In June, **Louis Armstrong and band**, with virtuoso pianist **Earl Hines**, recorded one of the greatest masterpieces of classic jazz, "West End Blues," which opens with an awe-inspiring trumpet solo by Armstrong.

In October, the **Ellington band** recorded one of their greatest early works, "The Mooche"; one of the featured artists was **Lonnie Johnson** on guitar.

**Blind Willie McTell** recorded his classic "Statesboro Blues" (though it was little noted at the time). Much later the song was powerfully covered by the Allman Brothers Band in one of the best ever "live" Rock albums, saturated with the blues.

**Mississippi John Hurt** recorded his first version of "Stack O' Lee Blues," with **Lonnie Johnson** helping in the studio (though, again, the recording was little noted at the time).

*The Three Penny Opera* by guitar-playing German playwright **Bertolt Brecht** and modernist German composer **Kurt Weil** opened in August. Its edgy, jazz-influenced songs included "Mack the Knife." At the suggestion of leading record producer George Avakian, Louis Armstrong recorded the tune in the 1950s and it became hugely popular in America.

In May, the **Carter Family** recorded their landmark song, "Wildwood Flower," and other classics of Country music.

**Ravel's** powerful **"Bolero"** premiered in Paris in November; it became tremendously popular worldwide. Ravel believed that music comes "from the deepest pockets of the soul."

### Other Cultural Developments:

**Will Rogers**, comedian and folksy but sometimes penetrating political satirist, was at the height of his great national popularity. On January 4, over NBC's national radio network, he gave a much-noted satirical "report on the state of the nation." His approach appealed to traditional style, old fashioned, down home virtues and values, and to the hunger for simple, honest, "straight talk"—and thus, was a manifestation of the modernist issues discussed in the Interlude section of chapter 2.

The Amos 'n Andy radio show debuted, with White comedians Freeman Gosden and Charles Correll performing in neo-minstrel manner, talking like stereotyped African-Americans (in two contrasting roles, one industrious, the other the standard, much-lampooned shuffling shirker). The show became very popular—even among many Blacks.

**Salvador Dali** and **Luis Bunuel** finish their noted surrealist film, *Un Chien Andalou* (released in 1929).

**D. H. Lawrence's** daring novel, *Lady Chatterley's Lover* was published.

**Brancusi's** futuristic but elegantly simple, abstract bronze sculpture *Bird in Space* so confused U.S. customs agents that they held it up from entering the country, thinking it must be some unknown industrial equipment being smuggled in—which caused an international stir (at least in the arts and cultural world).

### Intellectual, Scientific & Industrial Developments

**Columbia Broadcasting System (CBS)** was founded, the second national radio network.

**Penicillin** was discovered.

(In 1929, **Freud** published the first chapter of *Civilization and Its Discontents*; the full book was published the following year.)

## The Guitar

In the second half of the twentieth century, the guitar became the dominant instrument in popular music. This section explores that extraordinarily appealing, versatile, and evocative instrument to set the scene for the tale of how Lonnie Johnson played a prime, pioneering role in moving the guitar to that status. It also explores key elements of his profound influence on many of the leading guitarists in twentieth-century popular music.

While the piano and violin received more attention in previous centuries, the guitar was recognized long ago as an extraordinary instrument by towering figures in classical music. Beethoven said, "The guitar is an orchestra in itself." He apparently said this after attending a concert by the Italian guitar virtuoso Mauro Giuliani in Vienna. (It's fascinating that Beethoven's famous "Immortal Beloved" was Antonie Brentano, and part of her inspiration for him was that she was an accomplished guitarist.)[3] Schubert said, "The guitar is a wonderful instrument understood by few."[4] In the first third of the nineteenth century, however, there was a vogue of interest in the guitar in Europe, with virtuoso guitar players and composers for guitar like the Spaniard Fernando Sor and Mauro Giuliani. That ultimate violin virtuoso of the nineteenth century, Paganini, also played the guitar at a high level. He wrote exquisite guitar-violin duos (listen to the album, *Itzhak Perlman and John Williams: Duos for Violin and Guitar*, on Columbia). It is said that he wrote those pieces after staying for a while with an aristocratic lady of Florence, whose guitar playing (among other things) inspired him. An earlier version of the guitar became significant by the sixteenth century; in the mid-1500s England's King Henry VIII had 21 guitars among his large collection of musical instruments.[5]

Writer on the guitar, Tony Bacon, said, "No other instrument combines in such a portable package such inherent harmonic, melodic, and rhythmic potential."[6] The Spanish composer Manuel de Falla said the guitar is "the instrument most complete and richest in its harmonic and polyphonic possibilities."[7] The acoustic guitar, especially premier models from the great steel string makers like C. F. Martin and other top "luthiers," are beautiful works of the craftsman's art, with the rich wood grain finish, the ebony fingerboard, the mother of pearl inlay, etc. (For interesting discussion of the craft of making great guitars, see the Bibliography section "About Guitars," especially the Brookes, St. John, and beautiful *Martin Guitars* books.) The richness of the sound a good player can get from such instruments is like nothing else, for my aesthetic sense. Musician Stephen Stills eloquently expressed the glories of the best Martins (which Lonnie played at times and praised):

> Like the Stradivarius violins . . . , Martin guitars—especially those created between 1900 and 1945—are masterpieces of carefully chosen woods and handcrafted elegance . . .
>
> They have a crystalline high end that resonates with the purity of a waterfall in a mountain stream. The mid-range produces overtones that can fill a theater with no amplification. The bass is so rich it can overwhelm a microphone and is best enjoyed live. Press your ear against the side of one, right above the waist, so that your head is in direct contact with the wood, and you'll think you are in a cathedral.[8]

The unequaled magic of the acoustic guitar, even at the height of the electric Rock era, was strikingly demonstrated in the famous riff beginning the Led Zeppelin song, "Stairway to Heaven"—as also shown in the *Eric Clapton Unplugged* CD and video from the MTV program. More poetically, Segovia said a fine acoustic guitar can "echo the song in man's soul."[9]

The guitar also has the capacity for "sustain"—the note keeps going as the strings continue to vibrate, adding a significant dimension to the music. Then electric guitars took that capacity to a new level. Further, as music writer Robert Palmer pointed out: "The acoustic guitar's flexibility in terms of tuning made it the ideal instrumental vehicle for the nontempered, microtonal melodic language of the blues, in which key intervals [of the harmonic scale] such as the third, fifth, and seventh are not *flatted*, as a black key flats the tone of the adjacent white key on a piano, but *flattened*, with the degree of the flattening bearing a direct relationship to the emotional intensity" of the musical performance. It is that characteristic of the guitar, employed so effectively in the foundation of so much of twentieth-century music, the blues, which has also made the guitar central to Rock and Country music—along with the following.

That leads to the next key characteristic of the guitar: its *expressive* capacity. Alluded to by Segovia, this characteristic is well stated by Robert Palmer; he does so in the course of identifying the key artistic features of the playing of premier guitar heroes of Rock history:

> Since the 1960s, rock and roll fanatics have been, ipso facto, guitar fanatics [think of the popularity of "air guitar"]. Their ideal of rock and

roll heaven might be Eric Clapton's blues feel, melodic invention, and tonal purity; Jimi Hendrix's vocalizing of the instrument's expressive capabilities in the course of turning its sound into an elemental force; the tonal elegance, long-lined lyricism, and coherent thematic development of Duane Allman's marathon improvisations . . .

And he notes Keith Richards' electric guitar work, with the pounding rhythm of the Rolling Stones, and the screaming lead lines of heavy metal.[10] (Richards superbly demonstrated the unique sound of the steel string *acoustic*, as well, in such recordings as "No Expectations"; you can *see* and hear it well on the Stones' video from '68, *Rock and Roll Circus*.)

Then came the full power and effects of electric guitars. Particular electric guitars became prime icons and symbols of popular music and culture. Principal examples are Gibson's ES-335-355 series, used by B. B. King and Chuck Berry, Gibson's Les Paul, used by Jimmy Page of Led Zeppelin and Duane Allman, and the Fender Stratocaster, used by Eric Clapton, Buddy Guy, Stevie Ray Vaughan and John Mayer. Thus, it's not surprising that the symbols used for the two biggest events in Rock music history, Woodstock and Live Aid, employed guitar imagery (an acoustic guitar in the former case, and the neck and headstock of a Fender Strat, in the latter case). The fact that the acoustic guitar and some electric guitars had the curvy shape of a woman, and that the neck and headstock of most guitars were widely seen as phallic-like, also made the guitar a big time sex symbol. That didn't stop women, from Bonnie Raitt to Joan Jett, from making it their own. All that made for a unique mystique among musical instruments.

And so, the guitar became a cultural icon. Besides the 2011 New York Metropolitan Museum of Art exhibit, "Guitar Heroes," on great guitar makers (noted in chapter 2), in 2000 Boston's Museum of Fine Arts had an exhibit called, "Dangerous Curves: The Art of the Guitar." And in 2014 a Metropolitan Museum of Art exhibit was "Early American Guitars: The Instruments of C. F. Martin," with a companion book, *Inventing the American Guitar*.

Now, note again what Palmer said of three of the greatest guitar heroes of Rock. He cited Clapton's "blues feel, melodic invention, and tonal purity," Jimi Hendrix's "vocalizing of the instrument's expressive capabilities," and the "tonal elegance, long-lined lyricism, and coherent thematic development" of Duane Allman's improvisations. *That also serves as a superb summation of the enormous impact of Lonnie Johnson on twentieth century music; each of those elements of guitar-playing artistry were first developed by Lonnie Johnson, much more so than anyone else—and he did so fully 40 years before those Rock stars.* This chapter and chapter 5 especially discuss and analyze those developments. Later chapters discuss how Lonnie augmented those innovations, on electric guitar—despite some questioning of his guitar work with electrics. (Robert Palmer titles the chapter focused on the guitar in *Rock & Roll: An Unruly History,* "The Church of the Sonic Guitar." In that case, Lonnie Johnson was popular guitar's St. Peter.)

Speaking of Lonnie's development of the hugely important *expressive* capabilities of the guitar, let me add a note on the origins of that musical approach, which returns us to Lonnie's New Orleans background. In an article on "the nineteenth-century origins of jazz," noted jazz scholar Lawrence Gushee drew on the thoughts of early New Orleans composer W. T. Francis and wrote: "Francis . . . suggests two favorite themes in discussions of the nineteenth century origins of jazz. I will call one the 'French Opera hypothesis' and the other the 'Spanish tinge hypothesis.'" Again, the Spanish controlled New Orleans for thirty-seven years until about 1800, and added the "Spanish tinge" to New Orleans musical culture. As Gushee said, those two musical traditions significantly involved "a love of lyrical expressiveness in music."[11] Besides Lonnie's violin background, a key part of the musical tradition in New Orleans was that lyrical expressiveness, which Lonnie drew on and transferred to the guitar in an unparalleled manner. Building on all that, Lonnie produced the highest level of what classical guitarist Julian Bream called "tonal nuance," with exquisite touch, tone and vibrato. Prime examples are reviewed late in this chapter; and listen to tracks 2 (acoustic) and 5 (electric) on the companion CD.[12]

St. Louis blues guitarist, pianist and singer Henry Townsend said in the late 1980s, after watching the development of popular music for the previous 65 years: "Lonnie Johnson was quite an influence on guitar players all over the world. He hasn't been talked about, in my opinion, as much as he deserves to be. Lonnie was what you'd call the guy that paved the way. . . . The man was great at the time, and there wasn't anybody that exceeded him."[13]

## Setting the Scene: "Classic" Blues Singers and the Impact of Records

Before reviewing Lonnie's recordings of 1926 to 1931, let me do a little more setting of the scene. The release and big sales of "Crazy Blues" by Mamie Smith in November 1920 woke up the record companies to a big market among African-Americans and others for blues records.[14] This opened the gates. From 1920 through most of 1925, labels like Columbia, OKeh, Paramount, etc., followed the Mamie movement and recorded other women blues singers, from Alberta Hunter, Ida Cox and Ma Rainey to the other Smiths: Clara, Trixie and, most famously, Bessie. Those women blues singers of the early '20s have often been called the "classic" blues singers. I don't see what makes them "classic" blues singers, other than that the record labels, in their limited vision, happened to record those ladies a few years before other blues musicians. Since those women singers mostly came out of the vaudeville theater circuits, calling them the "vaudeville blues singers" makes more sense. Or, following Tony Russell, we can simply say this early 1920s period was the second of the "nine ages of the Blues," which happened to focus on recording women blues singers. (The first age was the birth of the blues and its initial conveyance to a wider public, with special help from W. C. Handy.)[15]

By late 1925, however, the labels were realizing that there were blues-*men* who might just have good record sales potential. (On the jazz side, the 1923 recordings of Joe "King" Oliver's Creole Jazz Band with the young Louis Armstrong, which had been dazzling people in Chicago, started in motion increasingly substantial recordings of African-American jazzmen.) The discovery and first recording of the instrumental brilliance and quality singing of Lonnie Johnson in November 1925, with the January release of the record to a great response, opened the door to a broader set of blues musicians to be recorded. A little later in 1926 came the first recording of the "*country* blues" singer and guitarist, "Blind Lemon" Jefferson, probably recorded in March and released in

April or May; it became a hit. That, in turn, opened the door for the recording of other *country* blues guys and gals.

(I should note that, while Lonnie Johnson, along with Blind Lemon Jefferson, was the most important pioneer in recorded blues after the vaudeville blueswomen to record, he was not the first blues player to record; neither was he the first fairly accomplished popular guitarist to record solo. In an e-mail to me, guitar-playing expert Jas Obrecht suggested Nick Lucas could, technically, be seen as the Original Guitar Hero because he recorded two guitar instrumentals before Lonnie and had prominence as a guitarist for a few years starting in 1922. But "Original Guitar Hero" has a meaning in our culture, and Lucas doesn't qualify; he didn't have wide and lasting influence as a guitarist and he was nowhere near the level of virtuoso that Lonnie was.[16])

## Records and the Changing Dynamic of the Development of Blues and Jazz

In the early years of blues and jazz, the leading players tended to have an impact in their local regions; most musicians from elsewhere in the nation did not have substantial exposure to them.[17] An example was Charley Patton, whom many blues writers see as something of a founder of the blues genre; but his influence was principally in the Mississippi Delta region (and in truth, Patton did not first record until mid-1929, three and a half years after Lonnie did). Because those musicians operated primarily in their own areas, there was a tendency to have different styles of blues in different regions, like the "Delta Blues" of Mississippi versus the "Piedmont Blues" of North Carolina and surrounding areas.

The increasingly wide spread of records and those old Victrola wind-up or plug-in record players began a process whereby records had a wider and wider influence; this gradually resulted in some standardizing of the blues form of music, as well. The sizable sales of records and the artistry of Bessie Smith and some of the other women vaudeville blues singers began to spread blues music more widely. Then, with the 1926 records of Lonnie Johnson and Blind Lemon Jefferson leading the way, the blues began to have a wider and wider impact on American music in general.

Beyond the sheer fact of the national spread of recordings, Lonnie Johnson in specific transcended regional styles in blues or jazz; this added to his wide appeal and influence. Lonnie explained it to British blues and jazz writer Val Wilmer, and he added a note on what his blues tended to be about: "I sing *city* blues. . . . My style of singing has nothing to do with the part of the country I came from. It comes from my soul within." And as to what he draws on and writes about: "My blues is built on human beings . . . , see how they live, see their heartaches and the shifts they go through with love affairs and things like that."[18]

A close student of Lonnie's recordings, Lenny Carlson, articulated the point well: "He had an ability to observe and capture the struggles and triumphs in the daily lives of Black people in the lyrics to his songs. . . . His smooth, refined voice and delivery endeared him to an ever-widening audience that bought each new record with great anticipation."[19]

Writer Bill Greensmith pointed out the impacts of the first couple of years of Lonnie's recordings, starting in St. Louis: "Doubtless encouraged by their discovery in 1925 of the urbane and influential guitarist Lonnie Johnson, record companies began to focus further attention upon St. Louis artists."[20] Those artists included pianist Roosevelt Sykes, pianist, guitarist and singer Henry Townsend, and pianist Henry Brown first recorded in 1929, and pianist and singer Peetie Wheatstraw, pianist and singer Walter Davis, and guitarist Charley Jordan, recorded in 1930.

## Lonnie Johnson Recordings—1926

As noted at the beginning of this chapter, Lonnie Johnson launched his recording career with a bang, with his double-sided hit 78, the "A" side being "Mr. Johnson's Blues." This is track 8 on *The* Ultimate *Best of Lonnie Johnson* CD. The one verse of lyrics in this first recorded song wound up being a striking epitaph for Lonnie's career: "I want all you people, to listen to my song. (Repeat.) Remember me, after the day I'm gone." Through the later 1920s, many people did listen to his song(s), and he had great impact; but unfortunately, after he was gone he was forgotten by most everyone but specialists. I hope this book and related projects finally put him in his rightful place in the top rank of the pantheon of the century's musical greats.

In "Mr. Johnson's Blues" we already hear characteristic Lonnie licks on the guitar; indeed, the tune starts with catchy, memorable guitar lines, with a coherent structure and theme, serving as a kind of overture to the singing of the verse. We also hear a light-fingered, skipping quality to his guitar-playing, which was a main characteristic of his guitar work through his career, especially on acoustic guitar. That quality leaves the listener with an upbeat feeling; it also has something of a dance feel to it—unsurprisingly, since dance was so big a factor in New Orleans. After the one verse, the tune is a fine guitar workout displaying Lonnie's already superb technique and excellent harmonic sense.

Lenny Carlson has authoritatively transcribed fifteen of Lonnie's better songs and describes and analyzes them. He offers a bit of technical analysis of "Mr. Johnson's Blues" and uses it to make an important general point (in English, after the first sentence of technical talk): "In measure 32 he uses the note 'B' as a melodic target point to outline a D6 chord at the third beat. This is an example of his flair for creating interesting and beautiful melodies. Lonnie Johnson's popularity with the listening public and his pervasive influence over other guitarists were based on such melodies, which he composed and improvised with remarkable ease and consistency."[21] We hear some of the other guitar techniques Lonnie used thereafter in this first recording. Starting in his solo introduction (before the piano comes in) Lonnie uses double stops. That is, he presses down two of the strings with his left hand and strums those two strings with his right hand for special harmonic effects; this is often done in the midst of his inventive melodic single string playing. In later recordings during general flights of melodic invention Lonnie used double and triple stops to exquisite harmonic effect and to add accents and further dimensions of tonal color. A particularly good example was his masterpiece solo guitar instrumental of February 1928, "Away Down in the Alley Blues," which is discussed towards the end of this chapter.

The "B" side of that first record, "Falling Rain Blues" (track 9 on the CD) demonstrates both Lonnie's instrumental origins, with use of the violin as his instrument, and, with the song's first notes, shows how the violin can play some very expressive, crying blues. That is especially evident on the extended bridge after the third verse, which offers us the creative melodic variations that became a trademark of Lonnie's style and were so influential. His superb harmonic sense is even more evident in this "B" side recording; and he adds to all that a rather unique shuddering effect with his bow and violin that offers another technique for expressing the blues feel via the violin. That violin technique works especially well with these compelling lyrics.

It should be added that Lonnie's violin playing on "Falling Rain Blues" and his and brother Steady Roll's violin playing on about ten other 1926 sides are "the only contemporaneous non-Creole examples of New Orleans fiddle styles from the early 20th century" on record, as was pointed out to me by Bruce Boyd Raeburn, Curator of the Hogan Jazz Archive at Tulane University.[22]

Unfortunately, the original, crude acoustic recording does not do justice to his violin playing on "Falling Rain Blues," which makes for a less than enjoyable sonic experience. That's probably why this tune is not found on the various Lonnie Johnson compilations, which is a shame, given its significance. *The* Ultimate *Best of Lonnie Johnson* CD that I compiled as a companion this book finally rectifies that omission with a new, digital remastering of "Falling Rain Blues."

The singing on this tune displays a good feel for rhythm and syncopation, the latter from his New Orleans and St. Louis jazz backgrounds, and the phrasing is good. But the sheer vocal quality and expressive facility in his singing is merely pretty good, with a little too much thin, nasally sound. This shows that his vocal ability and style were still developing.

The lyrics and basic music, however, show a good songwriter was already beginning to find his voice. After use of the storm idea in the first verse, the second adds nicely to the blues story, with its punch line enunciating the keynote; and the music is well suited to the lyrics:

The storm is risin', the rains begin to fall
The storm is risin', the rains begin to fall
I'm all alone by myself, no one to love me at all.

My blues at midnight, and don't leave me until day
My blues at midnight, and don't leave me until day
I got no sweet woman, to drive my blues away.

Then the "A" lines of the third verse in this 12-bar blues offer a positively poetic phrase, which also points to an interesting and musically consequential impact of Lonnie's recordings.

Here let me note the nature of the standard 12-bar, three-line, "AAB" form of the blues: There is an "A" line that is repeated, followed by a "B" line that serves as the punch line or resolution, usually rhymed with the "A" line. But also, the singing of the lyrics in a typical 12-bar blues does not take the full four-bar line; there is "space" at the end of the lyrics offering room for instrumental "responses" to or musical embellishment of the words. A virtuoso like Lonnie Johnson used that space for evocative playing that sharply enhanced the musical expression.

The "A" line in the third verse of "Falling Rain Blues" is, "Blues, falling like showers of rain"—which perfectly fit the music. This line has been heard, in the same words or in slight variation, in some other blues songs; it was also used, much later, as the title of a film on the blues, which used Lonnie's music. As far as blues expert Chris Smith and I can tell, this was the first appearance of that line on record.[23]

**Influence on Robert Johnson** Perhaps the most famous example of use of a variation of the line is from that bluesman who later was shrouded in myth and mystery more than any other character in blues history, Robert Johnson. The second line of his most haunting song, "Hell Hound on my Trail," is "Blues falling down like hail," which is repeated three times. It is probable that Robert borrowed the line from Lonnie and slightly altered it. Certainly, Lonnie Johnson had a significant influence on Robert Johnson's music in general. Henry Townsend played with Robert in St. Louis, probably in 1934 or 1935. In our 2004 interview he said, "I knew Robert was playing a lot of Lonnie's stuff." Blues writer Mark Humphrey reported:

Via record, [Lonnie] Johnson's [city blues] reached listeners in such remote rural environs as Robinsonville, Mississippi. It was there that Robert Johnson patiently studied Lonnie Johnson's OKeh 78s, blending their smoothly urban guitar licks and vocals with sounds gleaned from such local role models as Eddie "Son" House and Willie Brown. . . .[24]

In an interview for *Living Blues*, Johnny Shines, who travelled with Robert Johnson, said: "Robert often talked about Lonnie Johnson. He admired his music so much that he would tell people that . . . he was related to Lonnie Johnson."[25]

Francis Davis wrote with insight about this in his superb history of the blues, dealing with the construction of songs with coherent lyrics, as well as Lonnie's general influence on Robert:

> Among the outlandish claims made for [Robert] Johnson is that he was the first blues performer to develop coherent themes in his songs—to think of them as songs or records, rather than as tossed-together blues verses. But so had Skip James and Blind Lemon Jefferson. . . . And so did Lonnie Johnson, whom Robert Johnson idolized to the point of virtually imitating his delivery (slightly careworn even when he was young) on songs like "Malted Milk" and "Drunken Hearted Man". . . . Though commonly acknowledged to have been Robert Johnson's primary model as a guitarist, [Lonnie] Johnson . . . is rarely mentioned as an influence on the younger [man's] lyrics, though Robert probably learned a good deal from studying such sustained narratives as "Blues for Murder Only" and "She's Making Whoopee in Hell Tonight," songs of Lonnie's [that are] full of playfully misanthropic imagery which the younger Johnson took to crazed extremes in his own songs.[26]

As Peter Guralnick has also pointed out, "clearly Robert Johnson pays stylistic tribute to [Lonnie] in one of his most idiosyncratic masterpieces, 'Me and the Devil,' which takes off brilliantly from Lonnie's own 'Blue Ghost Blues'."[27] Robert's "Malted Milk" also takes off from Lonnie's "Blue Ghost Blues." The "Malted Milk" line, "My doorknob keeps on turnin', there must be spooks around my bed," borrows directly from verse two in "Blue Ghost Blues": "my doorknob turning round and round"—and the general words about ghosts/spooks. The line, "blues, fallin' like showers of rain," was borrowed by another Delta Blues legend, Charley Patton, in a principal song, "Pony Blues."

(This is speculation, but Robert Johnson's 1937 title, "I'm A Steady Rollin' Man," *might* have been influenced by Lonnie's brother, "Steady Roll" Johnson.)[28]

At Lonnie's second, two-part recording session, on January 19 and 20, 1926, he recorded nine more sides. The first song I want to look at is an early, little-known gem: "Sun to Sun Blues." This was his fifth recorded side, with Lonnie on guitar and brother Steady Roll playing some fine piano. At the beginning and in the middle, Lonnie and Steady Roll give us guitar-piano duets that are very well coordinated and offer the complementary harmonic and tone capacities of those two instruments in ways that wonderfully enhance the music. The main melody and variations are musically very appealing and memorable, and they perfectly suit the lyrics. The "A" line lyrics spell out a line that became very popular and was used in many blues songs thereafter, but with a twist with the opening word in the first line; the repeat line used the phrase that became standard: "Love, it will shine in my door some day"; then, "The sun, it will shine in my door some day . . ."[29] The second verse contains some of those evocative images that give the best of the blues such power and resonate so well with people: "The blues all 'round my bed, and 'round the foot of my door; [repeat]; When I find my sweet lover, I won't have the blues no more." (It's interesting that B. B. King, who was profoundly influenced by Lonnie, titled his autobiography *Blues All Around Me*, although I'm not saying that B. B. directly borrowed the phrase.)

On these and the rest of the sides made in 1926, except for his first guitar solo, Lonnie and his brother Steady Roll played together, often switching instruments. On two of the sides, "No Good Blues" and "Newport Blues," Steady Roll is listed as the featured performer. On the 1926 recordings, Lonnie plays violin on eight of them, plus guitar, banjo, piano, harmonium, and even kazoo. Steady Roll played violin, piano, guitar and banjo. On this tune, Steady Roll played violin and sang well—despite having to shout into the acoustic recording horn—on the fine tune with very good lyrics, "No Good Blues." In that tune we hear an example of Lonnie's ability on banjo; the recording ends with a superbly interwoven, unique violin-banjo duet by the brothers Johnson. Thus, those 1926 sides demonstrate Lonnie's multi-instrumental abilities, as Big Bill Broonzy pointed out about Lonnie's playing in St. Louis.

It's worth repeating the amusing comment sent to me by blues researcher-writer Chris Smith, however: "On the evidence of his two recordings with it, Lonnie was an awful kazoo player. Somehow it's good to know he was human—he wasn't brilliant on *every* instrument!" He played kazoo on "Newport Blues" with brother Steady Roll as featured performer singing and playing banjo. The song title is surely from their playing at the Waterfront Club in Newport, on the Illinois side of the river in the St. Louis area; most likely, it was formally or informally composed at the club one evening. Steady Roll's singing on this side is good, with a bit more robust and deeper blues feel than brother Lonnie at this stage. Lonnie's initial kazoo playing is a kind of a "mee, mee mee, mee mee mee" thing on a descending line; the rest of the playing sounds roughly like a young cat being strangled and complaining in syncopated time. On "Five O' Clock Blues," from the January 20 session like "Newport Blues," Lonnie plays fine, crying blues violin for the first half of the tune. Later in the song Lonnie encores on kazoo, and this time his kazoo playing sounds like a very old cat being strangled, but who barely has the energy to complain. Fortunately, that was his first and last encore on kazoo. Of course, the funniest and most ironic part of the accurate Chris Smith comment is that it's a simple toy of an instrument, the kazoo, on which Lonnie's skills fail; meanwhile, he's masterful on difficult instruments like guitar, banjo, and piano!

The next notable recording also came from the January 20, 1926, session and was a precursor of historic things to come: "Nile of Genago." (Some blues writers have wondered what "Nile of Genago" means; I turned up no answer to that question.) This recording is notable because Lonnie and brother Steady Roll perform Lonnie's first guitar duet, which is also the first guitar duet ever recorded in popular music, to my knowledge. It was the precursor to the historic Lonnie Johnson-Eddie Lang duets, which I discuss in the next chapter. The duet on "Nile of Genago" has strong hints of nineteenth-century popular melodies, something Lonnie not only had experience with in the New Orleans café and club gigs with his brother, but also on the Mississippi River boats. The recording sounds to me like Steady Roll is laying down the foundation bass and harmonic parts, while Lonnie, with that skipping quality and creative melodic sense, plays the lead over the top. Those specific elements were also precursors to the Johnson-Lang collaboration. Especially with Lonnie's lead work, there is a coherent thematic development, and the two of them build an excellent "architectural" structure for the song as a whole. This is an enjoyable piece in itself, and is also a pioneering work.

The final side recorded in the January sessions should also be noted. It is a uniquely interesting piece titled, "Johnson's Trio Stomp"—even though it wasn't played by a trio, with only Lonnie on violin and Steady Roll on piano. Use of the word "Stomp" in the title is not an accident—in two ways. "Stomp" was the name given to an early variety of jazz tunes; and Steady Roll's piano playing on this recording has some of the character of Jelly Roll Morton's playing—who advertised himself as "the originator of jazz and stomps." (There is a wonderful promotional photo of Jelly, dressed in very natty manner, which has that advertising label on the bottom left.[30] In an interview with Paul Oliver, Lonnie said: "Jelly Roll Morton, I knew him in St. Louis. We were playing on the excursion out of St. Louis."[31] I couldn't directly verify that claim; but Martin Williams reported that Jelly Roll was in St. Louis and working on the riverboats around that time.)[32] Steady Roll provides a romping, rolling piano foundation, and Lonnie's violin sails and skitters over the top sounding rather like a bluesy version of an ol' country music fiddle break-down. That is an unsurprising conjunction of music, since Black and White fiddlers played with and learned from each other in the South in the first decades of the century. Later, in December 1927 in Memphis, Lonnie recorded another pair of sides with that feel, playing violin, with Nap Hayes on guitar and Matthew Prater on mandolin, on "Memphis Stomp" and "Violin Blues." (Illustrating that ol' country music connection, those two recordings were actually released in the OKeh Hillbilly series instead of the Race Records series.) "Johnson Trio Stomp" is taken at a rapid tempo; but interestingly, at about 2:40 into the recording, Steady Roll takes a piano solo that sounds more like a bit of a classical music. On this side we get a hint of the caliber of Steady Roll's ability on piano.

An interesting event in February illustrated the increasingly note-worthy impact of blues and jazz and Lonnie's rapidly growing prom-inence: On February 27, 1926, OKeh Records sponsored a huge jazz and blues concert at the Coliseum North Annex in Chicago, in cooperation with the Black musicians' union. It was called the "OKeh Race Record Artists Night" and included Joe "King" Oliver, Clarence Williams, Louis Armstrong, Kansas City jazz band leader Benny Moten (mentor of Count Basie), Lonnie Johnson, vaudeville blues singers like Alberta Hunter, and others. Two interesting ads in the January 30 and February 13 issues of the *Chicago Defender*, the major newspaper for Blacks, announced the event. It's noteworthy that, at such an early date, Lonnie was featured with his photo in the January 30 ad, just a month or so after release of his first recordings. It is a strong indication of how well his early records sold. The same goes for Louis Armstrong and his Hot Five.

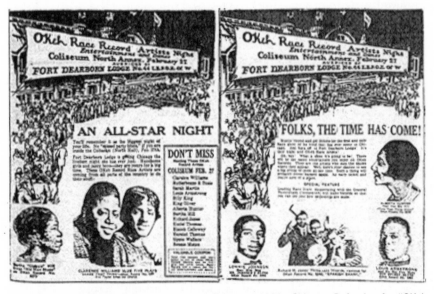

Pair of newspaper ads from January and February 1926, *Chicago Defender*, for "OKeh Race Record Artists Night," with images of Lonnie Johnson (lower left) and Louis Armstrong (lower right) in the January 30 version, which is on the right. SOURCE: RESEARCH IN CHICAGO'S HAROLD WASHINGTON PUBLIC LIBRARY, THE *CHICAGO DEFENDERS* ON MICROFILM.

In the recordings made on August 13, Lonnie displays his skills on piano. Those sides are: "You Drove a Good Man Away," "Ball and Chain Blues," and three others in succession. One of those others, "There's No Use of Lovin'," has Lonnie's best, bluesy piano playing, with dense, rich chords, rippling treble punctuations of the melody, and a rumbling, continuous bass. It includes a fun spoken intro and interjections during Lonnie's playing by brother Steady Roll. At the beginning he says, in the manner of a grand, vaudevillian introduction of a featured entertainer, "Mr. Lonnie Johnson, Lord, at the piano"—the last letter pronounced and lingered on as a very broad "O". Then, after Lonnie plays and sings the first verse, Steady Roll says in that vaudevillian voice: "Oh, it sho is good! Ah, do that thing Lonnie! Mr. Lonnie Johnson, the man with nine different feelin's, and he puts it in the same place every time." And before Lonnie's final piano run, Steady Roll says, "You don't have to worry, he's gonna play it again." These brothers were having *fun* in the studio. Steady Roll was also showing some older brother pride in how accomplished a musician his little brother Lonnie had become, and they were demonstrating what a great relationship these two had.

Because of Lonnie's use of what is now a little-known instrument, I have to add a brief mention of "Oh! Doctor the Blues," which is one of two sides on which Lonnie plays the harmonium. This tune is the better of the two in lyrics and music. The song is taken at a slow tempo, which works best with the harmonium, with its slow response and the instrument's wonderful sound quality—sort of halfway between a small pipe organ and a calliope. I'm not aware of a digitally remastered version of this recording. That's a shame because it has a very interesting sound quality to it and offers some great sonic color and texture for a recording. The lyrics are almost like a good and fun parody of standard blues lyrics. The first verse: "Oh doctor, doctor, tell me the time of day. [Repeat.] All I want's a good drink of whiskey, to drive my blues away." Second verse: "Some people say, that it's women, wine and song. [Repeat.] But it's the blues, that can lead a good man wrong."

Finally, there is the important first Lonnie Johnson solo guitar instrumental, with that oh-so-appropriate title, "To Do This You Got to Know How," recorded on August 14, 1926. This recording is effectively the announcement that an unparalleled musical talent on the guitar had now presented himself to the world. Remarkably quick fingers, a superb harmonic sense, an exceptional melodic creativity, and a note-bending bluesy feel in perfect complement to the surrounding music, are all on display in this significant record. There was no other blues guitarist who could match this virtuoso guitar work at the time. The first *Country* Blues singer and guitarist who was recorded, Blind Lemon Jefferson, was a powerful force in the blues and had strongly evocative guitar playing and singing abilities, but he was not the versatile, virtuoso guitar player that Lonnie Johnson was. B. B. King put it well in relation to Lonnie J: "My blessing [was that] I was old enough to have felt first-hand the old country blues. Singers like Blind Lemon Jefferson formed the backbone of the music. And I got to see how those blues were modified and modernized by artists like Lonnie Johnson."[33] Blind Blake was a fairly advanced guitarist, but he played pretty straight, if intricately finger-picked, ragtime and blues. Lonnie was more creative in melodic invention, had a richer harmonic sense, and displayed more sheer technical virtuosity. The only guitarist in popular music who was even in Lonnie's league in the later '20s was the jazz/popular guitarist, Eddie Lang (more on him in the next chapter).

## RECORDINGS—1927

With his musical developments in 1927, we begin to review the period of Lonnie Johnson's greatest impact; the years 1927 to 1931 were years of epic creativity and achievement.

The most notable development for Lonnie in 1927 actually came at the end of the year; but due to its significance, I'll start there. Louis Armstrong's "Hot Five" and "Hot Seven" recordings are among the most important and fundamental classics in jazz, in fact, in all of American music history. Emphasizing a featured soloist, rather than the original pure ensemble band music of New Orleans, they laid down principal foundations of jazz for the ensuing decades. All the Hot Five musicians except pianist/wife Lil Hardin Armstrong were from New Orleans. For three special recordings on December 10 and 13, Armstrong made the addition of his old friend from New Orleans, Lonnie Johnson. They were special recordings, indeed.

The most celebrated side had the perfect jazz title—not to mention double entendre—"Hotter Than That." Louis Armstrong continues the development of his historic power and expressiveness on the trumpet. Two special features stand out in this recording. Louis continues the scat singing that he first put on record in the 1926 track, "Heebie Jeebies." ("Scat singing" is using nonsense syllables in a kind of punchy, rhythmic sound via the voice; the scat singer mimics a horn solo, often using slurs and other instrumental techniques.) Rather like a cadenza, in formal terms, the band lays out for a two-part interlude of Louis's scat singing, with Lonnie on guitar: First, Louis sings those scat lines while Lonnie manages to both keep the feel of rhythm guitar accompaniment *and simultaneously* offers creative counterpoint lines and accents. In the second part of the interlude, the expression is highlighted, with extra punch, as a series of solo Armstrong scat wails, followed by Johnson's perfectly attuned, punctuated guitar work in a call and response dialogue—Lonnie's guitar sometimes echoes or saucily mimics the scat musical line and sometimes comments on the wail/line. As Gunther Schuller writes in *Early Jazz*, "Lonnie Johnson's swinging, rhythmic backing and his remarkable two-bar exchanges with Armstrong are certainly one of the highlights of classic jazz."[34] These two masters brought out the best in each other. Adding to this great recording, Johnny Dodds plays a soulful, bluesy clarinet solo, evoking the original New Orleans jazz environment, a feel that's furthered when Kid Ory, in some of his best work in the Hot Five, adds some classic New Orleans tailgate trombone.

After listening to that recording with me, the fine Minneapolis musician "Papa John" Kolstad offered this interesting perspective: "It's like Louis is calling out the guitar player to see if he can stand up to the traditional jazz instruments [in more than a background rhythmic role]. Lonnie brilliantly passes the test. I think this was Louis's tribute to the playing of Lonnie Johnson and a mark of his respect for this unique guitarist."

Another superb side was laid down three days earlier: "I'm Not Rough." This tune has a distinctive, powerful and memorable melody, and an evocative, folk-bluesy lyrical theme: "I ain't rough and I don't fight, but the woman that's got me got to treat me right, 'cause I'm crazy 'bout my lovin'. . . ." (Non-specialist readers of this book will probably enjoy this tune even more than "Hotter Than That" because of the clear melody, the lyrics, and the more accessible music in general.) The musical lines emphasize the theme of the lyrics; the music soars in perfect accord with those lyrics. With constant swing and momentum, these great musicians build crescendos that give punch and emotion to the message. Armstrong's trumpet technique punches out accents, dynamically flows through the melodic theme lines, and uses slides, slurs and bent notes to dramatically demonstrate how the blues is a prime foundation of jazz. Lonnie Johnson's playing starts with guitar tremolos, which add intensity and texture to the music. Then his guitar-voice exchanges with Armstrong both complement and stimulate each other; and he offers a ringing and intense but smoothly flowing guitar solo in the middle that, along with his work on "Hotter Than That," added a new dimension to the Hot Five recordings.

(Let me also mention that a sparklingly good new version of "I'm Not Rough" was recorded as part of an excellent 2008 album aptly titled, *Rediscovering Lonnie Johnson*. The songs are performed by the Philadelphia-based group, Blues Anatomy, with guest guitarist Jef Lee Johnson. The group captures the spirit of the original, but plays it with their own particular style and verve. That track has become one of my favorites of recent years. The rest of the album is very good, including a powerful, moving rendition of Lonnie's "Broken Levee Blues." Jef Lee Johnson also bravely and ably tackles Lonnie's solo guitar masterpiece, "Playing with the Strings," discussed toward the end of this chapter. These recordings show how fresh and relevant Lonnie's songs can still be.)

A second Hot Five side with Lonnie was made in the "Hotter Than That" session, "Savoy Blues," which is a very accessible recording for non-specialists. This is track 10 on *The* Ultimate *Best of Lonnie Johnson* CD. This recording is of particular interest because Johnny St. Cyr switched from banjo on the other two sides to playing guitar on this one, thus making for a kind of guitar duet amidst the rest of the band. Now, St. Cyr of New Orleans had strong enough standing to play rhythm banjo or guitar on Armstrong's Hot Five recordings *and* on the Jelly Roll Morton "Red Hot Peppers" sessions in 1926, which were also of huge importance. But on "Savoy Blues" Lonnie's guitar playing is on a profoundly higher level than that of St. Cyr. Noted blues researcher-writer Tony Russell put it in interesting perspective: "To hear these three sides is to hear the turning of a page. St. Cyr was a well-respected musician, and not an old man [only 37] . . . Johnson was only a few years younger . . . , but in approach, technique and even temperament he belonged to another era, a Model T to St. Cyr's horse and buggy."[35]

**"Savoy Blues" and Broader Societal Meaning** In October 1931, a young White freshman at the University of Texas, Charlie Black, saw Louis Armstrong perform:

> Armstrong began to play. Charlie [said later]: "He was the first genius I'd ever seen. It is impossible to overstate the significance of a sixteen year old Southern boy seeing genius for the first time in the face of a Black person. Louis opened my eyes and put to me a choice. 'Black people,' the saying went, 'are OK in their place.' But what was the place of such a man—and the people from which he sprung?"[36]

Charlie Black went on to become a noted law professor at Yale University and was one of the lawyers in the landmark Civil Rights case, *Brown v. Board of Education of Topeka, Kansas*.

After that Supreme Court ruling, a banquet honoring the NAACP lawyers was held in 1955 in the famous Savoy Ballroom, including Charles L. Black. With his wife, Black went home after the banquet and put "Savoy Blues" on the record player and listened. Here's why: "In the trumpet on that record . . . I thought I heard something said . . . gently, without stridency or self-pity: 'We are wronged, grievously . . . Is anyone listening? Is there anyone to come and help us?' . . . That is what I heard in his horn . . . in 'Savoy Blues'."

As Brian Harker wrote, "Black's very personal response to 'Savoy Blues' bespeaks an intimacy, a pathos, and a subtlety of expression in Armstrong's performance that one does not always associate with 1920s jazz." Harker then asserted that how Louis played on that recording "marks a clear departure from his previous work." Harker suggested an interest in "sweet jazz" and "societal respectability" was probably part of this. *But,* "it is striking that he chose to make the change not in popular songs . . . , but in the blues."[37]

As just discussed, Lonnie Johnson played a significant part in the performance on "Savoy Blues" and spurred on the full band. And I would argue that Lonnie's profound grasp of the blues and unparalleled expressive capacity on the guitar significantly enhanced Armstrong's expressive playing and beautifully bolstered his already deep blues feel in this recording, in which all those years later lawyer Black found such an extraordinary impressionistic cry of outrage against discrimination and call for something to be done for Civil Rights.

**Ultimate Musical Analysis and Perspective** Gunther Schuller offered the following significant reflections on those landmark Louis Armstrong-Hot Five recordings: "The beauties of this music were those of any great, compelling musical experience: expressive fervor, intense artistic commitment, and an intuitive sense for structural logic, combined with superior instrumental skill. By whatever definition of art—be it abstract, sophisticated, virtuosic, emotionally expressive, structurally perfect—Armstrong's music qualified." Schuller added specific reference to Armstrong's legendary solo at the beginning of his 1928 record, "West End Blues," which left other trumpeters (and musicians in general) awestruck for decades to come, but he used the specific reference for an important general point: "Like any profoundly creative innovation, 'West End Blues' summarized the past and predicted the future."[38]

In my judgment, those words and assessments also apply to Lonnie Johnson's dazzling guitar work during the same period, from the first recordings in November 1925, with releases and first impacts in 1926, through 1928 and 1929. Thus, the pinnacle of Armstrong's Hot Fives came with "West End Blues," recorded in June 1928. Lonnie made superb contributions to the three late 1927 Hot Five recordings. Then he matched Louis's tremendous, creative trumpet work with equally historic and stunningly virtuoso guitar playing on "Playing with the Strings" and "Away Down in the Alley Blues" in February 1928, in the landmark guitar duets with Eddie Lang from November 1928 through October 1929, and so on (all of which were preceded by earlier work like "Woke Up This Morning with the Blues in My Fingers").

Another way that Lonnie's work profoundly affected music must be noted—and it is a corrective to the claim in some books that gives credit to Leroy Carr and Scrapper Blackwell of Indianapolis for launching the more smooth, sophisticated, "urban blues." For one of several examples, in his exhaustive book on the railroad in folk songs, *Long Steel Rail*, Norm Cohen said of Carr and Blackwell: When they recorded their first sides in June 1928, "they were inaugurating a major change in the nature of recorded blues music. Smoother, more urbane than most of the country blues that preceded them, more polished . . . , their style was immediately emulated by other artists."[39] Starting with their first and biggest hit, "How Long, How Long Blues" of June '28, pianist Carr and guitarist Blackwell did indeed make some superb and very popular smoothly urban blues, in contrast to the rougher and frequently less lyrically coherent "country blues" recordings that often included country images.

But Carr and Blackwell were certainly *not* the "inaugurators" of the smoother, more urbane and urban blues—which led to one of the two principal strains of blues in Chicago that had a huge impact on American music, subsequently leading to Rhythm & Blues and ultimately to Rock & Roll. (The other principal strain of Chicago blues came from country blues musicians originally from the Mississippi Delta and other regions who developed a more electric guitar- and band-based music in those Chicago clubs. Their music, led by Muddy Waters in the 1950s and 1960s, still drew on the essence of the old Country Blues.)

It was Lonnie Johnson, in contrast to Blind Lemon Jefferson and others in 1926–1928, who, well before Carr and Blackwell's first recording, produced more sophisticated, urban-style instrumental and vocal work. This was evident in recordings from the brothers' guitar duet on "Nile of Genago" and the jazzy "Johnson's Trio Stomp" in January 1926. It was also evident in the more urban lyrics in recordings like "St. Louis Cyclone Blues" of October 1927. Guitarist and writer Dan Lambert offers a particularly telling illustration: "Even while accompanying a straight-ahead country blues singer like Texas Alexander, Lonnie managed to take the song uptown. . . . Take, for example, Alexander's 1927 recording of 'Cornbread Blues.' Johnson's playing during the vocal accompaniment sounds like a not so erratic Blind Lemon, staying with a I-IV-V harmony [standard chord sequence] and weaving intricate lines around the vocal. . . . [And then on an instrumental break, he] begins with the traditional harmonic scheme, [but he does so] playing block chords with sophisticated voicings, not unlike a piano player." Lambert sums up well: "With . . . his always-smooth delivery, Lonnie was able to accompany a singer like Texas Alexander and lend an overall sound of sophistication . . . without destroying Alexander's country roots. Lonnie took the blues sound and the jazz sound, put them together and made it work."[40]

There is still another way Lonnie changed popular music—with some notable help, in this case. Through 1926, Lonnie was playing banjo and other instruments, as well as guitar. But by 1927 he was focusing almost totally on the guitar. It is not coincidental that another notable development was occurring in 1928 and 1929, especially in jazz. As I mentioned earlier, the banjo had long been used by Blacks; it was prominently used in the minstrel shows of the late nineteenth century and early twentieth century, and then in vaudeville. Then, after the rapid rise of jazz on the national scene following the 1917 recordings of the Original Dixieland Jazz Band, banjos were used in many jazz bands from 1917 to about 1928. This is most prominently demonstrated by Johnny St. Cyr's banjo presence on the Jelly Roll Morton "Red Hot Peppers" sessions and on Louis Armstrong's Hot Five recordings. More broadly, the banjo presence is seen in many photos from the period that are shown in the striking visual archive of jazz bands, *Black Beauty, White Heat*, by Driggs and Lewine.[41] The banjo had a more penetrating sound, allowing it to be heard over the band, which boosted its use.

However, the powerful, virtuoso guitar work of Lonnie Johnson as featured on increasingly popular recordings and tours in 1926–1928 and prominent in the Armstrong-Hot Five records of 1927 and recordings with Duke Ellington in 1928, led to the guitar taking a dominant position. Along with two other factors, all that led to the decline of the banjo in jazz. This can be literally seen in the post-1928 photos in *Black Beauty, White Heat*. The second factor in the rise of the guitar was the other original guitar master in jazz and popular music in general, Eddie Lang. Lang's playing from 1924 to 1929 with the "Mound City Blue

Blowers" (where Eddie switched from banjo to guitar) to important recordings with Bix Beiderbecke and crew, to playing with the famous Paul Whiteman orchestra, to Eddie's guitar duets with Lonnie, also had a significant impact on the movement to guitars. A third factor: Some larger guitars with more volume became available, like Gibson's notable L5 archtop (brought out in 1924 or 1925 and the direct successor to the fairly large L4). This allowed the guitar to be more effectively heard in a band and auditorium setting. From 1926 into 1928, Lonnie used that "big, concert-sized guitar that Gibson was marketing at that time," the L5 model, and helped Gibson promote it, according to Henry Townsend.[42] So did Eddie Lang.

In spring 1927 Lonnie recorded two songs inspired by the Great Mississippi River Flood of later 1926 through the first half of 1927, the most destructive flood of the century. On April 25, along with four other tunes, Lonnie recorded "South Bound Water." Lonnie's recording came just four days after the major break in the levees at Mounds Landing and Greenville, Mississippi.[43] A lilting melody at a slow pace, with mellow pluckings of the bass string marking time, gives the feel of the river flowing along. Lonnie's guitar also provides a series of riffs on the treble strings for accents that enhance the music. Later, he increases the intensity to portray the impact of the flood. The lyrics offer a coherent narrative of the flood and its impact. The second verse well captures the nature of the song: "Through the dreadful night I stood, no place to lay my head. (Repeat.) Water up to my knees, and the water had taken my bed." And, as with so many Lonnie J songs, the music is perfectly suited to the lyrics. A downside to this recording was that, at times, Lonnie's vocal quality was not so good, with a somewhat harsh, thin edge to his tone detracting from the vocalizing of some key words.

The other Great Mississippi Flood song he cut in '27 was his cover of Bessie Smith's popular "Back-Water Blues," which he recorded on May 3; the precise rendering of the title for Lonnie's version was "Back Water Blues." This was released as the "B" side of the 78 with "South Bound Water."[44] He was accompanied by John Erby on piano. Lonnie's singing is mostly more resonant than on "South Bound Water," with effective use of syncopation and soulfully bent and extended notes in his vocals. His excellent guitar work alternates sharply picked but rich-toned single string notes, often ascending evocatively, with percussive chord strums. He sometimes adds three-string strums ("triple stops") for special harmonic touches. And all the while he keeps a propulsive rhythm going. In his acoustic guitar stylings here we can also hear the kernel of the unique and masterful electric guitar accompaniment that he developed for his 1948 recording of the tune, which is discussed in chapter 7.

In April Lonnie also recorded six tunes with vaudeville blues singer Victoria Spivey. Since they recorded their most notable sides in 1928, I discuss all their recordings in the next chapter.

In sessions on successive days in August (11 and 12), Lonnie laid down an interesting novelty number and then a classic blues tune with a classic title, which was also autobiographical. The novelty tune was "Mean Old Bedbug Blues"—a novelty, but it also spoke to something suffered by many poorer folks. (Chris Smith tells me that this song "started a small craze for blues about insect pests."[45]) The opening "A" lines identify the nasty little culprit, then the "B" line offers a whimsical perspective designed to help people laugh at their tiny but frustrating pests: "Man, a bedbug is evil, he don't mean me no good. [Repeat] He thinks he's a woodpecker, and he takes me for a chunk of wood." This is sung in a mockingly mournful manner, with some of that typical Lonnie guitar work in accompaniment. Illustrating his widespread influence, classic Country singer Ernest Tubb recorded the tune in 1936, and folk-cowboy musician Ramblin' Jack Elliott recorded it (in England) in 1957.[46]

The other noteworthy side from August 12 was "Roaming Rambler Blues" (which was used as the title of a later journal article on him)[47]; it's track 11 on the companion CD. Either this version or Lonnie's 1942 recording of the tune is a favorite recording of B. B. King.[48] Lonnie's singing on his 1927 recording is particularly resonant, with a mellow feel. My ears tell me that Lonnie was the influenced one here, since he seems to have drawn on the resonant, mellow, soulful singing Texas Alexander offered on sides on which Lonnie accompanied him that same day. The song had quintessential Lonnie J guitar work; and he embellished each vocal line at the end with elegantly finger-picked descending lines, with a harmonic jump up the scale at the end, employing his exquisite touch and tone. This was one of Lonnie's characteristic guitar techniques. And as guitar expert Jas Obrecht observed: "His crisp rhythms revealed a vast chord vocabulary, and he had a fabulous way of ending songs with elegant chord climbs."[49]

The particular guitar riff he used in "Roaming Rambler Blues" became a signature Lonnie guitar pattern. Lonnie was validly criticized for using standard riffs over and over in later years, and the pattern in this tune was frequently used thereafter; but it was good, fresh music in this 1927 recording.

"St. Louis Cyclone Blues," was recorded in New York on October 3, 1927. The OKeh label put out an advertisement promoting the record (and other Lonnie sides) with a photo that interestingly but inaccurately showed Lonnie playing his violin, despite the fact that he had been focused on the guitar for months before the recording and played that instrument on this side. The ad copy is illustrative of the stereotyped and hyped promo writing for "race records" in the late '20s: "Lonnie Johnson is weighted with misery . . . hear him sing the horrors of 'St. Louis Cyclone Blues'. The wind goes wailing through the song like a gale of madness."

Here, Lonnie's guitar is just for basic accompaniment and a few accents. This song is about the lyrics, and the words are one of the best examples of how Lonnie could provide a coherent full narrative that effectively and vividly told the story, in this case of how he and others in St. Louis experienced the cyclone tearing through the city. Note that this is expressed in a way that *all* St. Louis residents could relate to; it was not just about the Black experience. Thus:

> I was sitting in my kitchen, lookin' way out across the sky. (Repeat)
> I thought the world was ending; I started in to cry.
>
> The wind was howling [howling wind sound effect added here],
>     the buildings beginning to fall. (Repeat)
> I seen that mean ol' twister comin', just like a cannonball.
>
> The world was black as midnight, I never heard such a noise
>     before. (Repeat)

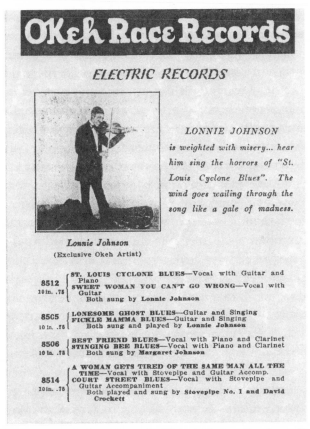

Ad for OKeh Race Records—Lonnie Johnson for "St. Louis Cyclone Blues" and other recordings, with only known photo of Lonnie playing violin. FROM AN OKEH RECORD COMPANY CATALOGUE SUPPLEMENT; IMAGE COURTESY OF GAYLE DEAN WARDLOW.

Sound like a million lions, when they turn loose their roar.

Oh, people was screamin', and runnin' every which-a-way.

(Repeat, with a spoken: "Lord have mercy on our poor people"
    at the end)

I fell down on my knees, I started in to pray.

The shack where we were livin', it really rocked but never fell
    ("Lord have mercy" . . .) (Repeat)

How the cyclone spared us, nobody but the Lord can tell.

Lonnie's influence on *lyrics* is evident in a 1937 side recorded by blues-man Kokomo Arnold. The tune title is taken from the "B" line of "St. Louis Cyclone Blues": "Mean Old Twister," and the first half of his third line is taken from that same source, with the second half taken from the "A" line of the fourth verse: "Now that mean old twister's coming, poor people running ev'ry which-a-way." Lightnin' Hopkins also performed and recorded the song, mostly using Lonnie's lyrics.

"Blue Ghost Blues" from November 9 is a song I'll talk more about in chapter 7, since he recorded a more striking version in 1938. But as already noted, Robert Johnson took off from this tune for his song, "Me and the Devil Blues," including his guitar styling, especially noticeable in the intro. Further, as writer and guitarist Elijah Wald has pointed out, Robert Johnson "learned the guitar part to 'Life Saver Blues' [recorded in the same session] virtually note for note, missing a couple of the faster passages but managing all the jazzy diminished chords and making a respectable attempt at Lonnie's superb vibrato, and used this arrangement for . . . 'Malted Milk' and 'Drunken Hearted Man.'"[50]

Three other sides recorded in April, May and October of that year are noteworthy not only for the exceptional guitar playing on them, but also because they were *not issued* back then. Lonnie's first solo guitar instrumental cut in August 1926, "To Do This, You Got to Know How," displayed his early virtuoso playing; it was new and extraordinary, and was released. But then, in April 1927, Lonnie cut "Steppin' on the Blues," with piano accompaniment, but featuring Lonnie's guitar instrumental. It was good enough (along with the striking title) that the best of Lonnie Johnson's earlier recordings that Columbia put out on CD in their notable "Roots & Blues" series used "Steppin' on the Blues" as the CD title and included that track. But in 1927, it went *unissued*. In May he cut another solo guitar instrumental which was a further advance from "To Do This . . . ," namely, the wonderfully titled, "Woke Up This Morning with the Blues in My Fingers." But this side also went unissued. Still further, in October Lonnie recorded a guitar instrumental, using a 32-measure song form and extended chord progression, with the cool title, "6/88 Glide"—so named because his six-string guitar was accompanied by the 88 keys of Porter Grainger's piano playing. It had a very interesting, engaging and memorable pattern of guitar riffs and held together well as a coherent whole. But it also went unissued. What was going on?! Before I answer that, let me take a moment to look at the extraordinary side, "Woke Up This Morning . . . ."

That recording is a striking demonstration of how far Lonnie's instrumental virtuosity had developed. James B. Dalton, after close study of Lonnie's playing, has written an astute, more technical analysis of his guitar work on "Woke Up . . . ," from which I quote key passages here (I rearranged the order of a couple of passages). Dalton specifically analyzes "Woke Up . . . , but many of his points apply to Lonnie's playing in general:

> Lonnie Johnson's right hand technique was at times fingerstyle and at times pickstyle. Neither of these techniques seemed to limit him in any way. Notice, on the fingerstyle pieces, how freely he was able to syncopate the lead over a steady bass . . . His accompaniment figures [on the bass strings] are played by his right thumb, while the fingers execute the lead or add chord tones. . . . His supple lead lines betray a remarkably developed left hand [making chords, etc., on the neck]. I believe he used all four fingers of his left hand with equal dexterity. . . . His left hand technique seems quite different from that of his contemporaries and may be related in some way to his experience as a violinist.
>
> Johnson's harmonic language provides us with a number of examples of his debt to New Orleans. For instance, few other blues guitarists have utilized diminished chords to the same extent that he has. . . . His use of diminished chords in turnarounds [at the end of a verse as a transition to the next verse], endings and intros were distinctive. . . . A rather more sophisticated use of diminished chords occurs in "Woke Up This Morning with the Blues in My Fingers." In this instrumental solo, Lonnie uses the diminished chords, ascending and descending chromatically, as a way of clearly delineating the form of the piece.[51]

Speaking of Lonnie's employment of those diminished chords, often used in descending lines, as guitar expert Dan Lambert has pointed out, "he used them not so much as passing chords, but as coloration devices, much the same way Django Reinhardt [a few years later] created diminished and augmented chords."[52]

Here, let me remind the reader of the prime artistic features of the playing of the top guitar heroes of Rock that Robert Palmer spelled out: Clapton's "blues feel, melodic invention, and tonal purity," Hendrix's "vocalizing of the instrument's expressive capabilities," and the "tonal elegance, long-lined lyricism, and coherent thematic development" of Duane Allman's improvisations. Those features of popular guitar artistry are evident in their original form in Lonnie's playing on "Woke Up This Morning. . . ." In a good, digitally remastered rendering of this tune, the "tonal purity" and "tonal elegance" are especially evident. The one flaw I hear in "Woke Up . . ." is a less than perfectly consistent flow and structure of the music; in a few places there is a choppy jump to another phrase or riff. All those Palmer-identified guitar qualities were even more stunningly evident on the instrumentals he recorded on February 21, 1928, to which I turn after the following paragraph.

So, why weren't those superb, unprecedented guitar instrumentals released? Well first, at that point in the history of recordings, I think people mostly expected singing and lyrics, with the exception of piano rags, some jazz recordings, and a few other things. Lonnie's recordings had been very popular, in general, and his great guitar work was recognized. But remember how Lenny Carlson assessed Lonnie's popularity in this period: "He had an ability to observe and capture the struggles and triumphs in the daily lives of Black [and other] people in the lyrics to his songs. . . . His smooth, refined voice and delivery endeared him to an ever-widening audience. . . ." This is what the record company wanted. While Lonnie was a fairly new recording phenomenon in 1926, he slipped in a guitar instrumental; but for the next year and a half, the label was focused on the songs with lyrics that people responded to best. But then, in December 1927, Lonnie made those three recordings with the increasingly popular and influential Louis Armstrong and his Hot Five. The impact of those recordings was big enough, and Lonnie's reputation and popularity continued to increase, so that by early 1928, OKeh Records was ready to go with some more instrumentals.

## February 21, 1928—A Banner Day in Guitar History: Masterpiece Guitar Instrumentals

On February 21, 1928, Lonnie recorded four sides for OKeh Records in a studio in Memphis. The first side he recorded that day had the oh-so-apt title, "Playing With the Strings"—borrowed for the title of these two chapters. This is track 12 on *The* Ultimate *Best of Lonnie Johnson* CD. Beyond the obvious reference to the guitar strings, the title is apt in the sense that his guitar work here has a playful nature, it is very upbeat and lively, and one just *feels* Lonnie's fingers dancing over the strings. Listening to this whole recording, I get the sense of experimental music creation, and of a unique musician just bursting with talent and creative ideas that he proceeds to pour forth in a free-wheeling manner; and that makes the piece constantly interesting and often surprising. Dan Lambert has summarized the structure of the piece, including the fact that in this improvised composition, some of the "surprises" are due to the way Lonnie plays fast and loose with standard musical form:

> The basic structure is an intro, seven choruses of varying length, a bridge, three more choruses, and the bridge again to wrap it up. The choruses range from roughly eight measures to roughly thirty—[I say] "roughly" because Lonnie frequently ignores the bar lines, changing chords at will. . . . These irregular measures, the general rushing of the cut time, the quick, upper-register melodies and descending chords, all add up to give this tune a hot, zany feel.

Lambert then offers some detailed technical analysis, which I'll leave for pursuit in the original source by those who have the training. But after that, he sums up well:

> Lonnie Johnson here has taken the abandon of primitive country bluesmen, insofar as meter is concerned, adding the melodic variation and harmonic sophistication of a jazzman and playing it all over a hot 1928 rhythm. It's a tune that stylistically bridges the gap between blues and jazz . . .[53]

Lenny Carlson's analysis found that Lonnie placed a capo at the third fret for this tune, which "gives a higher, more metallic clarity to the melodic figures." I'd say it a little differently: That position with the capo allowed his single notes especially to ring out with clarity. This is a blessing for us today because it also helped the 1928 technology to record the performance unusually well; and with digital remastering, we hear this virtuoso playing remarkably well. Also, the term "metallic" conveys a kind of hard, sharp sound; but that's misleading because, even with that capo pushing the playing to a higher register, Lonnie managed to produce a very rich, sumptuous tone, helped by his unparalleled touch.

"Playing With The Strings" received more attention, but "Away Down in the Alley Blues" was an even better composition and display of unequaled guitar virtuosity. This track—number 2 on the companion CD—exemplifies Lonnie's talent for very sophisticated guitar work, with exceptionally quick fingers and a bluesy feel, and yet the music was very accessible to a broader public. Of special importance is the masterful thematic coherence. In the midst of all that, he also keeps an underlying propulsive beat going, and regularly adds exquisite harmonic touches. His guitar work on these recordings exemplifies how Lonnie enlarged the language of the guitar for jazz and blues. Lenny Carlson summarizes well: **"This is a virtuoso improvisation based on the 12-bar blues progression . . . ; and like the classic 'West End Blues' of Louis Armstrong, it represents the pinnacle of musical thought and solo technique on a particular instrument at that point in history."**[54]

The two other guitar instrumentals Lonnie recorded on that February day were "Stompin' 'Em Along Slow" and "Blues in G." "Stompin' 'Em Along Slow" doesn't have quite the thematic coherence of "Away Down . . .", and there is a falter or two along the way, but it manifests many of the other qualities already noted. "Blues in G" is another genuine gem that belongs in the royal crown of virtuoso popular guitar music. It has a different musical character than the other three, with a very distinctive, memorable and delightful main melody line, repeatedly used, which again helps make for a superb thematic coherence. And it has even richer harmonic dimensions than the other three, as well as the extraordinary touch, tone and vibrato in Lonnie's playing.

**Influence on B. B. King and Beyond** That touch, tone, and vibrato in "Blues in G" was like no one else could play; and in "Away Down in the Alley Blues" their presence was simply sublime, beautifully displayed right to the final subtly ringing note. Such touch, especially with Lonnie's exquisite *vibrato*, along with bluesy bent notes, added so much to the *expressive* capacity of the guitar; Lonnie made his guitar *sing*. Eric Clapton talked about this technique in a remarkable film of a concert tour made by Martin Scorsese (for some reason it's hard to find).[55] Clapton said:

> There were a couple of people that had something that I didn't hear anywhere else really taken to its fullest development, which is the finger vibrato. . . . T-Bone [Walker, for example,] would play a lot of phrasing, but he wouldn't really end up on a note and make it . . . [here Clapton hits a nice-toned note on his guitar and gives it a soulful vibrato] give it that *vibrato* thing. That's what it was. It's almost like a *voice*. . . . And the great players had it. B.B. King is the best; he has the kind of vibrato that you would *die* for.

In the film Clapton talks about various early blues guys and how they influenced him. But startlingly, Clapton manifests no awareness of Lonnie's seminal role in the expressive use of the vibrato (as well as the touch and bluesy bent notes) in popular guitar music, and how he was the prime original source of that B. B. King vibrato that was so influential for Eric.

Those special guitar-playing effects had tremendous influence over the ensuing decades. The most notable specific influence was, indeed, on that ultimate icon of the blues later in the century, B. B. King, who, in turn, influenced so many twentieth-century blues, Rock and even jazz guitarists. The prime origins of the famous touch, tone and vibrato B. B. King has gotten on his guitar are found in the playing of Lonnie Johnson, and they are displayed in particularly high relief in "Away Down in the Alley Blues."

But Lonnie's influence on B. B. King went beyond specific guitar technique to more general musical effects, including singing. As B. B. told me in my interview with him: "My Great Aunt Mima [short for Jemima] bought records, and when I went to see her, I wanted to play her machine [her Victrola record player]. I listened to records by Lonnie Johnson, Blind Lemon Jefferson, and others—including Jimmie

Rodgers. And I just found that Lonnie Johnson sounded better to me than anything else."[56] This was more strikingly demonstrated in another interview when B. B. was asked the classic question, "If you had to go to an island with only one record, what would that be?" B. B. replied, "I guess it would be Lonnie Johnson's 'Roamin' and Ramblin' Blues'" (either "Roamin' Rambler Blues" of 1927 or "Rambler's Blues," the 1942 version; unfortunately, he didn't specify which).[57]

**Segovia** Andres Segovia (born February 21, 1893, in Linares, Andalusia, Spain) is widely credited with being the single most important figure of the twentieth century in establishing the guitar as a major solo instrument in classical music. Segovia made his first commercial recordings on May 2, 1927, which, after tours of South America and Europe, were key factors in the early establishment of the guitar's prominence in the classical world. Nine months later, with Lonnie Johnson's performance in "Away Down in the Alley Blues" and some other recordings strikingly displaying his development of the "expressive capabilities" of the guitar, the "tonal purity and elegance," the "melodic invention and blues feel," and the "long-lined lyricism and coherent thematic development," Lonnie provided the ultimate demonstration of the unique solo capacities of the guitar in popular music. With that and the extraordinary guitar-trumpet exchanges with Louis Armstrong in the 1927 Hot Five recordings of "Hotter Than That," "I'm Not Rough," and "Savoy Blues" he took the first major steps in making the guitar the premier instrument in and for all of popular music. And in one of those interesting coincidences of history, the two most important guitarists of the century, Segovia in classical music and Lonnie Johnson in popular music, were born less than a year apart.

# 5

# Playing with the Strings, Part 2

*"Me, hearing what I heard Lonnie play, I know even today, a lot of it
I can't play. And I don't hear anybody else playin' some of the things he
played. The man was way ahead of his time."*[1]

—B. B. King

In a special 2003 issue of *Rolling Stone* magazine, the editors
compiled their "100 Greatest Guitarists" list. (There is much that is
debatable in that list, including the lack of any specified criteria or param-
eters for who was considered; but the following comments are appropriate.) In ranking B. B. King as the third greatest guitarist, they said, "[he]
has become such a beloved figure, it's easy to forget how revolutionary
his guitar work was. From the opening notes of his 1951 breakthrough
hit 'Three O'Clock Blues,' you can hear his original and passionate style,
juicing the country blues with electric fire and jazz polish."[2] That was
well stated. Indeed, B. B. King is universally considered one of the great
guitarists of the century in all of popular music. Thus, the observation
by him in the epigraph above is a remarkable testament to the level of
guitar virtuosity Lonnie Johnson had attained by the late 1920s.

B. B. King's comment is also, in effect, a powerful criticism of
the astonishing absence of Lonnie from the *Rolling Stone* "Greatest
Guitarists" list; despite the inclusion of older blues guys like Robert
Johnson, T-Bone Walker, and Lightnin' Hopkins, the editors didn't
really know their guitar history. Lightnin' Hopkins was not remotely
close to being in Lonnie's league, let alone his equal or better. (His fairly
broad basic musical influence, rather than pure greatness of guitar virtuosity, must have been the principal reason for his inclusion.) As for

Robert Johnson, whom they ranked fifth greatest, Lonnie was actually the prime inspiration for the more sophisticated dimensions of Robert's guitar playing. And as blues and popular music writer (and guitarist) Elijah Wald wrote, "Lonnie Johnson's fastest, most complex guitar solos would have been far beyond Robert's technical abilities. . . ."[3] (T-Bone Walker, at number 47, was ranked too low.) The striking irony is that Lonnie Johnson had a profound direct or indirect influence on at least seven of the top eight in that ranking: Jimi Hendrix, Duane Allman, B. B. King, Eric Clapton, Robert Johnson, Chuck Berry, and Ry Cooder. (The direct influence was clear and strong for B. B. King, Robert Johnson, Chuck Berry, and Ry Cooder, and the indirect influence on Clapton, Hendrix, and Allman is also strong, as discussed in the previous chapter and further in later chapters.) As reviewed in chapter 4, it was Lonnie who originally laid the foundations of the main, noteworthy features of most of their guitar artistry. All of those Rock and blues guitar heroes could validly say about Lonnie Johnson what jazz trumpet great Dizzy Gillespie said of himself in relation to Louis Armstrong: "No him, no me."

(For the December 8, 2011, issue, *Rolling Stone* produced another "100 Greatest Guitarists of All Time" list. It had the same weaknesses as the 2003 version; and this time the "panel" of musicians and writers were to choose their "favorites," whatever that meant for greatness in guitar work. The substantial changes in the rankings also demonstrate the far less than systematic methods employed. For example, in 2011, B. B. King's ranking went from third to sixth; Duane Allman's ranking went from second to ninth; Pete Townshend's went from fiftieth to tenth; and so on.)

## Some Time in Texas; Two Great Songs; With Duke Ellington; Victoria and Lonnie and a Little Hokum

In his few interviews, Lonnie's statements on where he was during given periods were sometimes vague and contradictory, and his memory often led him to exaggerate the length of time he worked in various clubs, lived in certain areas, and worked with various musicians. One clearly verifiable example: In a 1960 interview he said the OKeh recording contract he won at the Booker T. Washington Theater in St. Louis was "for eleven years"; it was actually for less than seven years.[4] The period of later 1927 into the 1930s is particularly fraught with difficulties. What follows is my best reconstruction based on the information available.

First, remember that Lonnie and Mary Johnson almost certainly did *not* move to New York City in the summer of 1927, but stayed in St. Louis, and Lonnie went to Texas for extended engagements starting in June or July of 1927.

Let me spell out my logic (particularly for specialists), since this is hard to sort out. The keystone of my inferences is this statement by Lonnie in material from a 1960 interview with Paul Oliver, material that has not previously been transcribed or published. Here Lonnie is referring to the famous 12-string guitar he used in the duets with Eddie Lang: "I bought that 12-string guitar in San Antonio during the time I was playing at the Chinese Tea Garden."[5] Since we know he used that 12-string at least by the time of the first of the Johnson-Lang duets, which occurred on November 17, 1928, clearly he had to have been in San Antonio working in that extended engagement before November 1928. While Lonnie was faulty in remembering what he did in what years, he was quite likely to have remembered what he was doing when he bought the most significant instrument of his life, and in the audio he is very clear and precise in that statement.

As a result, here is my sense of the chronology (I go into the San Antonio stage a little later in this chapter): He went from St. Louis to Dallas, in June or July 1927 after his April and May recording sessions in St. Louis. In the Oliver interview he says he played at the Ella B. Moore Theater there: "They had different artists come in, blues singers and things, and we had a stage show." He said he was well paid for that gig. He stated his contract was for two years,[6] but this is probably another exaggeration about the duration of an engagement. My best guess—it is an inference based on the rest of the circumstances I know about—is that it was a one-year contract. During that time, in March, he went briefly to San Antonio for a recording session with Texas Alexander and then for his own session four days later. He probably made contacts while there that later resulted in his long gig in San Antonio—and that fateful guitar purchase.

Some previous writers say Lonnie entered a blues singing contest at the Ella Moore Theater while in Dallas and came in second to local favorite, Lillian Glinn.[7] But in the interview with Paul Oliver, he said he'd never heard Glinn sing, so that casts doubt on the contest anecdote, though it doesn't definitively disprove the claim.

Some insight into other jobs Lonnie did—and general confirmation of my chronology—comes in a tale from the youth of jazz sax and clarinet player Buddy Tate. This source says he was born in 1913, another source says 1914, and he says he was about fourteen or fifteen years old at the time, which indicates a likely year of 1928, probably in the spring; he was already playing around the area with a band:

> Lonnie Johnson was a big man, you know, he had hits one after another. Between my home and Dallas . . . there is a place called . . . McKinney, and my aunt ran a dance hall there. Lonnie Johnson was playing a dance there and concert, and when he got there that afternoon . . . from Dallas his band didn't show.
>
>     . . . My aunt . . . called us. . . . To play with Lonnie Johnson! You *know* we were all excited . . . He says, "I'll only do about three or four numbers and then you play for the crowd." They were all lined up all around the corner. So we went and did some blues, and then he turned it over to us to play some dance music, and he loved it . . . .[8]

When they finished, Lonnie gave each of them fifty dollars, which astounded and encouraged these young guys. Tate turned professional three or four years later and became an outstanding jazz musician, playing in the Count Basie band, among others. This (including how Lonnie shared the money) is one of the stories showing how Lonnie would encourage young musicians.

On March 13 in San Antonio, Lonnie made the first recording of one of his best songs: "Crowing Rooster Blues." (He recorded three other sides in that session, one of which was another gem, which is discussed just below.) In "Crowing Rooster Blues," Lonnie's guitar serves as simple accompaniment to his singing. But in my judgment, especially in comparison with some later vocal performances, his singing here offered only pretty good vocal tone; Lonnie was still wrestling with consistently producing excellent vocal tone and singing style. The biggest problems came in his upper register, where his vocal quality tended to thin out and become more nasal, a problem many singers have.

In this and other songs throughout his career he often made a basic singing mistake that showed his lack of formal vocal training: He tended to end a musical line on a hard consonant and try to hold it, instead of continuing the vowel sound until the last second, then ending on the consonant; this makes it nearly impossible to produce good, sustained tone quality. (This is one of the things this author learned while singing in a very good college choir, directed by a former student of the great American choral conductor, Robert Shaw.)

Evidently my own judgment on these examples of Lonnie's singing is, however, somewhat at odds with other musicians of the time and at odds with the public. His records sold very well and, from his first recordings in November 1925 to August 1932 he cut about 130 sides, more than any other blues musician of the time. Also, as noted in the previous chapter, his urban/urbane singing style appealed widely. Indeed, in an interview held in the Hogan Jazz Archive, blues pianist Little Brother Montgomery said: "Lonnie Johnson was the [male] blues singer I liked. He was tops at the time," though that comment probably applied as much to his late '30s and early '40s records.[9] Lonnie's singing also had a major influence on blues musicians Robert Nighthawk and Johnny Young, among others.[10]

There is a specific moral of the story presented in the first verse of "Crowing Rooster Blues," and then the second and third verses offer the more general moral of paying appropriate (and savvy) attention to your woman so she doesn't wander. The first verse: "What makes a rooster, crow ev'ry morning 'fore day? (Repeat.) To let the pimps and ramblers know, that the workin' man is on his way." (Later recordings of this tune added a second verse on the subject that reinforced and made more explicit that moral of the story.) The second 1928 verse tells guys to pay appropriate attention to their woman. And the third verse adds this advice: "If you buy your woman pretty silk things, don't buy them all in one time. (Repeat.) She will get ramblin' in her brains, and some travelin' man on her mind."

That last line is one that, in one variation or another, has been used in other blues songs. The most noted case is the use Robert Johnson makes of slight variants of both the "A" and "B" lines from that verse in his June 1937 recording, "I'm a Steady Rollin' Man." The last two lines of that Robert Johnson song are: "You can't give your sweet woman, everything she wants in one time. Well boys, she get rambling in her brains, uhmmm some other man on her mind." The fact that Robert used the unusual "*in* one time," as Lonnie did, instead of the more common "at one time," is further reason to conclude that he borrowed it from Lonnie J.

The great Mississippi River flood of 1927 inspired a series of songs; Bessie Smith's "Back-Water Blues" was the most famous of them. "Broken Levee Blues," also recorded on March 13, 1928, is Lonnie's second original song in response to the big flood and its impacts; it's track 18 on the companion CD. It is one of his best songs. The blues melody is memorable and very expressive. The track opens with strongly and distinctly picked single-string notes, with deep tone, in a two-part ascending line, then moves in a richly articulated descending line that ends with a little jump up to a higher note, which is played with Lonnie's fine vibrato. That opening, while simple in form, is almost like a brief overture to this gem of a song that is like a mini-folk opera of the vast flood and its terrible human impacts. Lonnie continues his guitar work with that inimitable Lonnie Johnson touch, tone, and rhythm on the guitar, and with his usual exquisite sense of harmonics; these techniques not only augment the pure music and add texture to the song, but often impressionistically complement and enhance the meaning of the lyrics. Indeed, he repeatedly uses two- and three-string higher note treble percussive strums to convey the stress involved; then he uses such strums in descending lines, as accents and to aesthetically give the feeling of everything sinking under the massive flood of water.

The lyrics of "Broken Levee Blues" compellingly convey the natural disaster and its human impact, as in the first verse:

I want to go back to Helena, the high water's got me barred.
  (Repeat)
I woke up early this morning, high water all in my back yard.

Lonnie's singing on "Broken Levee Blues" (mostly avoiding his upper range) had better vocal tone, with richer resonance, and more nuance in expressive technique, as well as superb phrasing and dynamics; on this recording he starts to demonstrate the significant vocal mastery he fully developed by the 1940s. He also makes effective use of syncopation in his singing, as he often did. On the last word of the repeated "A" line, "barred," Lonnie even uses some vocal vibrato to add to the feel of the difficult situation. (Vocal vibrato was unusual for Lonnie, despite his use of vibrato in his guitar playing.)

There is a deeper dimension to this song, which is in accord with the broader societal theme in this book. The song's lyrics express striking protest about the means by which the levees along the Mississippi were maintained, a system which a few years later was called a new form of "Mississippi Slavery" by Roy Wilkins of the NAACP.[11] As David Evans reported in his analysis of the series of songs inspired by the Great Mississippi Flood: "In many places, Black men who tried to leave the area, even those who were simply passing through, were arrested by White police and National Guard troops and forced to work on the levees." They were "forced to work in extremely dangerous conditions to save and rebuild the world that the White folks had made and ruled. . . ."[12] Lonnie's second and last verses convey the issue well:

They want me to work on the levee, I have to leave my home.
They want me to work on the levee, then I had to leave my home.
I was so scared the levee might break, Lord and I may drown.
The police say, "Work, fight or go to jail." I say, I ain't totin' no sack."
Police say, "Work, fight or go to jail." I say, "I ain't totin' no sack."
And I ain't buildin' no levee; the planks is on the ground, and I
    ain't drivin' no nails.

The music and Lonnie's vocal delivery give verve and punch to those lyrics. This powerful Mississippi River flood song is not as widely known and lauded as Bessie's. It should be.

Four days before the recording session for "Crowing Rooster Blues" and "Broken Levee Blues," Lonnie was in the recording studio in San Antonio serving as accompanist for Country blues singer Alger "Texas"

Alexander. In a busy pair of sessions that day and the next the two of them cut eleven sides; among them were two outstanding recordings, "No More Women Blues" and "Deep Sea Blues." Here I must note that "Texas" Alexander, like some other Country blues musicians, sometimes did not "keep time" accurately, so he was difficult to follow. Lonnie expressed it well, after an interviewer says that Alexander "must have been a very difficult singer to accompany": "Oh yes! He'd either jump a bar, or five bars, anything. You just have to be a fast thinker to play for Texas Alexander. When you get out of there you've done nine days work in one! He would jump keys, anything; you just had to watch him. . . ."[13] But with Lonnie's consummate skill and his sensitivity as an accompanist, the recordings came out well.

Lonnie's guitar accompaniment for Alexander in "Deep Sea Blues" is a good illustration of what Dan Lambert said: "With . . . his always-smooth delivery, Lonnie was able to accompany a country blues singer like Texas Alexander and lend an overall sound of sophistica- tion . . . without destroying Alexander's country roots."[14] His accom- paniment begins with a beautifully intricate intro, with fine harmonic touches; he then proceeds to offer the memorable melody in a deeply felt and nuanced manner in support of Alexander's vocals. "Texas" sings in an excellent Country blues voice, with a mellow, soulful feel. All of the above also applies to that other recording of the day, "No More Women Blues"; Lonnie ends the tune with a nice little flourish on the guitar.

Later, Lonnie had an even more interesting recording session with Texas Alexander, one that set the scene and served as a warm-up for the historic guitar duet sessions that began two days later. On November 15, 1928, Lonnie entered the recording studio in New York along with Eddie Lang to accompany Alexander for another pair of sides. The more interesting of the two, in my judgment, is "Work Ox Blues," track 13 on the companion CD. What impressive support these two guitar mas- ters provided! The melody is at least as good as "Deep Sea Blues," and Texas again sings with that rich, soulful Country blues voice. It's inter- esting that Lonnie and Eddie were already working so well together in this recording. Starting with an intro that perfectly prefaces their subse- quent duets, Lonnie and Eddie play a very fine, well-coordinated open- ing sequence to set the scene for Alexander's singing. What makes this particularly interesting aesthetically is Alexander's excellent vocal tone, used in a plain, straightforward Country blues delivery, *in combination with* the duet of sophisticated, intricately woven, and rich-toned guitar work that forms the musical context for the singing. Lonnie and Eddie are given feature time when Alexander yields to their duet artistry for a chorus after the first verse. That segment is an even more striking preface to their subsequent duets; but there are also a couple of points where they aren't perfectly coordinated, which is an interesting window on the beginning development of those historic duet recordings. Thereafter, the trio continues the collaboration, with Lonnie adding occasional guitar flourishes. This recording has not gotten much attention. That's too bad because it is something special that many music-lovers, not just blues specialists, would really enjoy.

Evidently, some time in summer 1928, Lonnie went to San Antonio to work at the Chinese Tea Garden—"that's when I *really* made some money!" He worked there "a long time," he said, and then said it was for three years. But again we need to use a standard Lonnie Johnson Time Discount Factor on his chronology; indeed, a specific date he adds a little later contradicts his expressed chronology when one adds up the years, and so does other information presented early in chapter 7. My estimate is that he worked there for about one year. He also said he lived in San Antonio for quite a while thereafter; but for several reasons, it can't have been very long. Then, in the Paul Oliver interview, he said that, after being in San Antonio for a while: "I couldn't keep my feet still, so I just started traveling. And I went to Houston [and worked] a little club there (I can't remember the name) for a couple of weeks. Then I went to Beaumont, Texas, and I joined my father there; he had a restaurant on Forsythe Street." A little later he specifically said his father "died in 1934"[15] (which is one of the things that makes clear he couldn't have worked at the Chinese Tea Garden for three years and then lived another three years in San Antonio). That his father had a restaurant suggests another pair of inferences: It seems probable that his father earned his living doing the same thing in New Orleans; and perhaps that is where Lonnie learned his trade as a cook, which he said he could fall back on whenever he wasn't able to make enough money in music.

Speaking of family, Lonnie offers not a word or even a hint of his common-law wife Mary during his review of those times in Dallas, San Antonio, and elsewhere in Texas. Since this was about 1928–1929, again, this raises profound doubts about the actual length of his marriage to Mary. He also makes no mention of his mother when he talks about joining his father. Because his mother was so dear to him, it seems likely that his parents had divorced or separated by that time. He then said he "went east." This was probably in early fall 1929. By October, Lonnie was on a show tour out of New York with Bessie Smith, as I discuss later.

One of the most notable developments in his eventful year of 1928 was the three recordings Lonnie made on October 1 with the Duke Ellington band: "The Mooche," "Hot and Bothered," and "Move Over."

Lonnie made more records than any other blues musician of the time (though, again, Lonnie worked in both blues and jazz). Evidently, such popularity with Blacks led Duke's savvy manager Irving Mills to recruit him for special sides with Ellington's band. "The Mooche," among the compositions with a "jungle" motif made for Harlem's famous Cotton Club, was an early Ellington masterwork. It also exemplified orchestral jazz as modern art (as discussed in chapter 2). It seems to me that "The Mooche" is a prime popular music counterpart to Stravinsky's *The Rite of Spring*. The tune includes one of the memorable musical themes in jazz history. The Ellington band played in their usual rich, innovative manner, with striking modern art accents and musical impressions. Lonnie's guest guitar work came in two successive parts. First, with perfectly attuned and placed rhythmic accents, using percussive but rich-toned strums, Lonnie complements Barney Bigard's impressive, haunting, and soulful clarinet lead part in the lower register. That was directly followed by accompaniment of Baby Cox's scat vocal with skipping, intricate, climbing, and descending lines that perfectly complemented her vocal and made for a unique guitar-voice duet. Lonnie's ability to produce a second superb complementary counterpoint with a completely different approach and feel immediately following the first accompaniment demonstrates his versatility and ability to adapt. On "Hot and Bothered" (a variation on the old New Orleans standard, "Tiger Rag"), the way Lonnie's guitar work melded with the band showed how well he worked in a jazz band setting. This was an up-tempo, pure late '20s jazz-style tune. Lonnie's feature contribution came a little past the middle of the tune; he played a solo with inventive, rollicking guitar lines, with superb rhythm and syncopation, and with rich and interesting tone and harmonic accents.

Lonnie's part in "The Mooche" and his improvised lines in "Hot and Bothered" showed why Duke praised him so, as noted early in chapter 1. "The Mooche" and "Hot and Bothered" were the most significant of the recordings; but Lonnie also made a fine contribution to "Move Over," recorded in that same session, and in November, he made another side with Duke's band, "Misty Morning."

Ten days after the main Ellington session, on October 10, 1928, Lonnie went into the recording studio again to play with a group using the colorful name (pun intended), "The Chocolate Dandies." This wasn't a regular group; rather, it was the name for groups of varied composition recording under the direction of jazz alto sax players and arrangers Don Redman and/or Benny Carter. The four sides Lonnie played on were made with Redman's notable regular group, "McKinney's Cotton Pickers." (That name made them sound like a crude Country blues band, but they were actually an accomplished jazz band.) Lonnie had brief solos on a relatively jaunty, uptempo version of "Stardust" (avoiding the usual slow-and-schmaltzy approach) and on the slower "Paducah"; his solo on the latter was the more interesting, with his characteristic skipping lead work complemented by some nice harmonic touches and rhythmic accents.

Two days after the Chocolate Dandies session, Lonnie was back in the studio in a quite different—and delightful—collaboration. Victoria Spivey was a very attractive vaudeville-blues singer, originally from Dallas[16]. Born in 1906, she first recorded in May 1926 in St. Louis (again, where she crossed paths with Lonnie). She had a long career as a singer and general entertainer. In the 1920s she made a striking presentation in her recorded singing and in her club and theater appearances. She and Lonnie made an excellent male-female recording duo—in more ways than one. In their first session together, in April 1927, Victoria and Lonnie had recorded six sides, including "Steady Grind" and "Idle Hours." Lonnie's playing on each was pure accompaniment (along with pianist John Erby) for Victoria's good vaudeville-woman's blues singing. Those sides and the recordings they made the following year also draw on the style of such premier Black vaudeville performers as Butterbeans and Susie, who, for so many years before and after that recording, were famous figures in Black entertainment.

A good deal more interesting was "New Black Snake Blues," with Lonnie singing a duet with Victoria, as well as playing guitar in support. It was recorded on October 13, 1928. This was a redo of Victoria's first recording, "Black Snake Blues," cut in May 1926. There is a dramatic difference between the two recordings. Victoria's singing on the earlier version is rather crude and more like a Country blues performance. But by the October 1928 session, with Lonnie Johnson helping in the studio and performing vocal and guitar parts, this is a polished, engaging performance by Spivey; Victoria's singing was much smoother, more pleasingly soulful, and more nuanced. The voices of Victoria and Lonnie complement each other very well, though they mostly alternate singing verses, rather than singing a direct duet. That tune, like the following one, had parts 1 and 2, covering both sides of the 78. The melody is, essentially, one Lonnie used for a number of songs thereafter. They recorded a similarly accomplished, moving performance on "You Done Lost Your Good Thing Now."

The resonance and broader significance of that latter song, as employed in public concerts by a master like B. B. King, are excellently illustrated in this description of a B. B. King performance at Harlem's famous Apollo Theater:

> . . . he moves on into one of his most popular numbers, "You Done Lost Your Good Thing Now," and is instantly transformed from a performer on the stage into a down-hearted man pouring out his pain to a woman who has walked all over his heart . . . Squeals of delight at recognition of this common human plight issue from the audience as he . . . builds up to a tortured confession. Women shout out, "No! No! Don't *do* it B. B.! . . ."[17]

Scenes like that prompted Lawrence Levine and Charles Keil to suggest that much of what appears on the surface to be mere popular entertainment actually has a ritual significance:

. . . that such Black performers . . . share the expressive role occupied by the preacher. The kind of blues gathering described has definite sacred overtones in that it combines the elements of charisma, catharsis, and solidarity [like a] church service does: Common problems are enunciated, understood, shared, and frequently the seeds of a solution to them are suggested.[18]

An ultimate example of that latter phenomenon is B. B. King's remarkable album, *Live at the Regal,* considered by many to be the greatest live blues album ever made. He demonstrates all those qualities, and, in the cadences of a preacher, he literally dispenses advice and "solutions" to men and women to *keep* their good thing going with their partners.

Now, from the profound to the humorously profane: A Lonnie and Victoria recording of October 17, 1928, was a special novelty tune, which also helped launch a little trend in fun-saturated and somewhat salacious tunes that came to be called "Hokum." Blues writer Mark Humphrey defined and explained the term well: "'Hokum' (i.e., nonsense, derived from hokus-pokus) . . . was hip Jazz Age jive. . . . Though rooted in ragtime and minstrelsy antecedents, hokum evokes the Roaring Twenties, a time when Prohibition was [flouted] and sexual mores loosened."[19]

The fun tune Victoria and Lonnie cut was titled "Toothache Blues," with Victoria offering playful, well-toned, and slightly salacious singing; it's track 14 on the CD. On the surface it's about Victoria's vocal character visiting the dentist. But the way the "dental" needs and activities are cleverly described and the accompanying moans issued, they leave little doubt something much more personal is being alluded to. The fun starts with early jazz pianist and songwriter Clarence Williams playing a piano intro that sounds straight out of vaudeville. Then Victoria, in a young, coquettish voice, gives out a combination whimper/moan (sounding quite sexy), and "dentist" Lonnie says, "What's the matter, darlin'?" Victoria describes her toothache troubles, interspersed with a series of moans, and Lonnie, in a very assuring, authoritative voice, tells her she needs "a quick-fillin' dentist." Lonnie then sings, "Don't get nervous honey, when I LAAAY you in my chair." Victoria goes "ummmm!" Victoria adds other pure hokum lines like, "I feel a funny little somethin' easing into my cavity" (pronounced "caaa-vi-ty"). Well, you get the idea. These two were having a whole lot of fun, with a naughty undercurrent, while making the record!

"Furniture Man Blues," recorded the next day with Clarence Williams again on piano, was a roughly similar romp (also with a salacious metaphorical dimension). In this case, it was like a little playlet, in form about Victoria losing her furniture because she couldn't make the payments and Lonnie being there to collect the goods (on a literal level, something a number of their music fans could relate to).

Even more in the Hokum vein was another duet, this time with early jazz songwriter and musician Spencer Williams singing a duet with Lonnie, "It Feels So Good," Parts 1 and 2, recorded in February 1929. A year later Lonnie made another side with an appropriate Hokum title, "Dirty Dozen," with Spencer Williams again doing sardonic harmony vocals with Lonnie. This one's a fun romp of a record. Also notable on this side was the fact that the piano accompaniment was provided by the great New York "Stride"/jazz pianist James P. Johnson.

I should also mention Lonnie's first recording of what was already something of an old classic, a tune we might call a blues ballad, "Careless Love," cut on November 16, 1928. This is indeed an old classic: The legendary father of jazz, Buddy Bolden, would often play "Careless Love Blues" back around 1900.[20] In a way, it was the first foray on records into emotive (some say schmaltzy) ballad-singing that Lonnie got more into during his later years. Lonnie's singing on this tune is, again, merely OK for a top performer; at times the tone is not so good, and the phrasing and vocal expression are not very imaginative, nor does the singing convey the meaning of the song in a very moving way. Since the day before this recording he and Eddie Lang had done the masterful accompaniment to Texas Alexander's "Work Ox Blues," and the day after the "Careless Love" session Lonnie and Eddie recorded the first two of their great guitar duets, obviously Lonnie's singing ability was lagging behind his guitar work at this stage.

Lonnie accompanied other women blues singers, as well, including the startlingly young Helen Humes in April 1927 when Helen was just shy of her fourteenth birthday! Sounding more like 24 than almost 14, she sang "Black Cat Blues" and "A Worried Woman's

Blues," with Lonnie's usual sensitive backing. Helen went on to sing with the Count Basie band. He also accompanied Bertha "Chippie" Hill in December 1927.

Speaking of accompanying women blues singers, on October 31, 1930, Lonnie recorded two sides for Columbia, singing duets with vaudeville blues vocalist Clara Smith. (He recorded under the name "Tommy Jordan," since he was under contract to OKeh.) These sides, "You're Getting Old on Your Job" and "What Makes You Act Like That?," are absolutely delightful. They have a vaudeville feel, and Lonnie and Clara exchange verses and responses, with spoken and sung ad lib comments and jabs, and Lonnie adds excellent guitar accents and embellishments. "You're getting old on the job" may not be the most enjoyable lyrics for those over 50, but the exchanges are just light-hearted jiving, and Clara and Lonnie are having such a good time, you can't really take the lyrics seriously. Their voices blend and complement each other very well—though at the end they aren't perfectly coordinated; they obviously didn't do a lot of rehearsing for this recording. The second song ecologically recycles the melody. It's sung in an even more playful spirit, though tapping into that basic question in human relations of why a partner or friend *acts like that* sometimes; it is even more enjoyable. In addition to the spoken and sung banter back and forth in line with the song's theme, after a verse or two Lonnie plays a characteristic solo on guitar, with flair, and in effect lets his guitar speak for him: indeed, in the middle of the instrumental solo he says, "*That's* what makes you act like that!" Later, in response to Clara's turn going on about what makes him act like that, Lonnie says, "Now get a load of *this*!," and adds another scintillating guitar solo in the spirit of the theme and the back and forth. Clara urges him on during the solo by saying, "Ah, boot that thing, boy!," and then utters, "uhmm, uhmmm!" As John Henry Vanco has written, "and Johnson predictably provided the best guitar accompaniment Smith would ever have."[21] These were so enjoyable one wonders why more sides weren't made. Perhaps there were contract issues; and of course, the Depression was on. In summary, Lonnie's versatility and sensitivity made him a superb accompanist, which he demonstrated on still more recordings not specifically reviewed in this book.

## The Historic Johnson-Lang Duets

The ten guitar duets Lonnie and Eddie Lang recorded were landmarks in guitar history. As British blues and popular music writer Tony Russell has written: "It is difficult to overestimate the importance of this handful of discs."[22] They were also sociological landmarks as the first full partner interracial recordings.

For these sides, Eddie used the name of "Blind Willie Dunn." Jazz and blues writers have wondered why he did so, rather than use his real name—which, actually, wasn't his real name. Salvatore Massaro was his original name, which he changed to Eddie Lang in the early '20s, probably because of prejudice against Italian-Americans during that time—and to simply broaden his appeal. Interestingly, one story has it that Eddie got the Blind Willie Dunn name from "a blind youth from whom Lang bought his newspapers, whose name he used with permission, and to whom he gave the session fees when his name was used," as the tale was recounted in an online discussion among blues writers.[23] I don't know whether that is correct; it sure makes a good and plausible story, though (Lang was that kind of guy).

So, why did Eddie feel the need to use another name for the records? Many blues and jazz writers have thought it was due to the

Lonnie Johnson and Eddie Lang about the time of their historic duets. LANG PHOTO IS OF UNKNOWN ORIGIN; photo of Johnson is a cropped version of the photo on the book cover, FROM MICHAEL OCHS ARCHIVES/GETTY IMAGES.

racism of the time. That conclusion makes sense, given the circum-stances of that era. But when we remember that Eddie Lang was exceed-ingly well known by that time, and Lonnie was quite well known, and that they were the only two popular guitarists in existence who could possibly play the material they produced, using that name to disguise who Eddie was becomes less plausible. (There has also been a sugges-tion that Eddie used that name to hide his recording with a Black man because Eddie's prime musical partner and old Philly friend, violinist Joe Venuti, was racist. But beyond what was just noted, the fact that Eddie recorded "Knockin' a Jug" in March 1929 with Louis Armstrong and His Orchestra using his own name casts further doubt on that notion, though Eddie's name was not on the record label itself.) Lenny Carlson offers a different reason: "Blind Willie Dunn" was used "due to other contractual obligations."[24] In English that means that Eddie was under a recording contract to a different label (artists using a different name to record for another label was fairly common; Lonnie himself did so, as has been noted). But there is a problem with that conclusion: Lonnie and Eddie, er, "Blind Willie," recorded their duets for OKeh Records. Eddie Lang, under that name, recorded solo and guitar-piano sides for OKeh through late September 1927; his guitar-violin duets with Joe Venuti were also recorded for OKeh through May 1927; and "Eddie Lang and His Orchestra" recorded for OKeh Records May through October 1929. So, that contractual obligation reason seems invalid.

Here's my take on this: First, Eddie was well aware of Lonnie's great-ness as a guitarist. Second, Eddie was recording with this *Black* blues- and jazzman, and a number of Black blues and jazz musicians liked to use colorful names; further, several popular "Blind" blues guys had recorded by that time, including Blind Willie McTell and Blind Blake. So, Eddie may have just decided it would be appropriate and fun to use a colorful bluesman-sounding name—and that boy at the newsstand had a perfect name, so he borrowed it. The tunes they recorded were the blues, after all, starting with "Have to Change Keys to Play These Blues." This interpretation is circumstantially supported by the fact that Eddie and Lonnie recorded two sides in April 1929 with original jazz cornet great Joe "King" Oliver, J. C. Johnson on piano, and Hoagy Carmichael on percussion and scat vocal, and they used the wonderful and playful band name of "Blind Willie Dunn and His Gin Bottle Four." (Given Hoagy's proclivities, he probably joined with Eddie in coming up with that band name.) Thus, my conclusion is that Eddie was just being blues-appropriate and playful, and the joke is on all us blues and jazz writers who have spent years avidly debating this great mystery!

In a 1963 interview, Lonnie said of Eddie Lang, "I met him in Philadelphia." He didn't say when this first meeting took place or under what circumstances he was in the city. He went on to say, "We just decided to make some records together so that was it."[25] This contradicts the speculation of some writers that it was the OKeh recording director who had the idea to bring Johnson and Lang together. While we have to be careful about reading too much into that not-so-specific memory, it suggests they probably met in late 1927 while Lonnie was in the general region for recordings and some appearances in October and November, or sometime in fall 1928 for the same purposes, before Lonnie and Eddie backed Texas Alexander on November 15 and did the first duet recordings on November 17.

There was an agreement as to the basic structure of what they were going to play on each of these recordings, but much of what they did was improvised. Lonnie said, "We rehearsed [the tunes] in the morning, recorded in the evening. Only one rehearsal, that's all." (Unfortunately, the latter isn't specific and detailed.) On Eddie's primary role, Lonnie said: "Eddie could lay down rhythm and bass parts just like a piano."[26]

"Have to Change Keys to Play These Blues," track 15 on the CD, is the better known of the first two of their duets, recorded on November 17, 1928. This recording proceeds at a rather stately tempo. The title is correct: The song begins in the key of D major, then changes ("modulates") to G major, then goes back to D, and finishes in G. The song shows how the two guitarists took the basic music and bent notes and slurs of the blues and added sophisticated and intricate jazz-style interweavings of Eddie's solid rhythm and harmonic framework with Lonnie's lead guitar playing. Those elements made a whole that was, indeed, much more than the sum of its parts. Eddie occasionally takes the lead, as in the fourth chorus here (sounding, frankly, a bit plodding and less imaginative *compared with* Lonnie, though with Eddie's usual rich and sophisticated harmonic sense). Usually it is Lonnie in the lead, however, managing to combine a light, jazzy skipping quality with rich tone and a bluesy feel, as his inventive melodic lines and harmonic accents soar above Eddie's foundation. They are so attuned to each other in the interplay of their two guitars that they are like a pair of superb long-time dance partners whose two bodies move as one.

Lenny Carlson's expert analysis and transcriptions of fifteen of Lonnie's recordings include an astute assessment of "Have to Change Keys. . . ." That analysis also speaks more generally to the roles each played in all the duets.

Indeed, Carlson starts by making the point I have made about Lonnie's greater abilities, saying "Lang . . . was considered the top guitarist in jazz at the time. . . . However, as a melodic improviser, he was nowhere near Johnson's equal." Carlson's analysis adds:

> Lang's rhythm guitar work and ensemble instincts [from playing with a series of significant bands] were the perfect foil for the rhapsodic inventiveness of Johnson. Lang's counterlines and bass figures were crisp and articulate, his chord voicings made musical sense in context, and his passing harmonies propelled the music forward most effectively. Though he could not match Johnson's facility as a single note [lead guitar] player, Lang made interesting and rather complete statements.

Carlson then made an observation about a tendency in the solo playing of the supremely talented Lonnie J that is correct and should be noted. This tendency is even heard a couple of times in that masterpiece, "Away Down in the Alley Blues":

> On Johnson's solo recordings, he tended to rush, especially in faster songs or passages. This is very common for a player of his technical facility, and of course such acceleration can be exciting for the listener. But in some instances, the original "groove" or rhythmic feeling of the music is altered, not always for the better. Lang's presence in the duets had a stabilizing effect on the tempo and feel, allowing Johnson to fire away with intensity and confidence.[27]

All of that and the rest of the discussion of these duets illustrate how Lonnie Johnson, much more than Eddie Lang, was the leading creator of the virtuoso jazz guitar *lead* work.

The other side recorded at that first duets session was "Two Tone Stomp." It was a worthy addition, but is not quite as strikingly innovative, nor is the over all structure of the piece as coherent or creative as "Have to Change Keys." . . . Also, as was occasionally the case with Eddie's rhythm guitar work in bands or other duets (such as on his "Stringing the Blues" duet with Joe Venuti), his rhythm guitar work comes off as a bit choppy at times, and it's not as harmonically interesting as his partner's playing in that recording session.

On May 8, 9, and 16, 1929, Lang and Johnson cut four more sides, all of which were superb work; they were also varied in nature. The first two released sides were "A Handful of Riffs" and "Bullfrog Moan." In contrast to "Have to Change Keys . . . ," "A Handful of Riffs" is a very lively, up tempo tune, and Lonnie provides rolling, ornately finger-picked lead lines in a series of distinct, repeated forms (a "handful of riffs") over Eddie's usual rich harmonic structure and rock-solid rhythm. At times the two seem positively telepathic in knowing the next move the other will make in this dual improvisation, as they play superb complementary notes and harmonies. All that is done while both, in their respective roles, drive the song with a propulsive beat. Calt, Mann and Miller offered this additional analysis:

> Although it takes a conventional 12-bar blues progression in D [Lonnie's favorite key], its spontaneity and supple rhythms (qualities virtually absent in early jazz guitar-playing) give it a true jazz character. Spinning an improvisatory melody line, Johnson toys with the beat in a different fashion on each verse, changing the tempo after the seventh verse and launching a perfect series of pulled-off triplets.[28]

(The *Larousse Music Encyclopedia* defines triplets as "a group of three notes played in the duration allowed by the time signature for two notes of the same denomination."[29] For example, that would be three eighth notes where two eighth notes (or one quarter note) would normally be heard; thus, one hears three faster notes in the context of the rest of the music, which enhances the musical excitement.) Lenny Carlson marvelously sums up the nature of the performance and the experience of recording "A Handful of Riffs":

> [This recording] could be titled, 'The Joy of Guitar,' and it encompasses some of the finest melody and rhythm playing Lonnie and Eddie Lang ever did. . . . [In that fast tempo,] Johnson builds ideas, creating and resolving melodic and rhythmic tension all the way through 14 wild and wooly choruses. The second one . . . is so bouncy and melodious that it startles the listener. It is very much the kind of solo chorus that western swing guitarists played 20 or 30 years later, and one might hear music like this coming from younger players like Doc Watson as well. Lonnie Johnson's influence has indeed been enormous.

Carlson added a point from late in the song, the twelfth chorus, starting with the pickup from the previous chorus: This "is a classic example of rhythmic syncopation. The strategically displaced two-note figure here has become a standard jazz device . . . ; but Johnson employed it with extraordinary drive and purpose"—and thus was inventing still more of the vocabulary of popular guitar. [30]

"Bullfrog Moan" has a very different character and sound. Eddie starts the tune with deep harmonic strums on lower strings to create the aural impressionistic feel of a bullfrog sound, and then Lonnie leaps in with his usual innovative lead guitar work, with bent strings for a blues feel and accents that punctuate so well Eddie's rich musical foundation. In this case, the sound of his string work is so perfectly collaborative with Eddie's chords, lines and musical texture that together they produce a sumptuous, complex sound that is unlike any of the other duet sides. The very rich guitar tone, bent strings and other effects by Lonnie further show his historic development of the expressive capacities of the guitar; and all that results in a gorgeous, impressionist aesthetic overall.

Lenny Carlson says this tune "was a novelty outing, not a virtuoso piece by Johnson-Lang standards."[31] I disagree, and this illustrates a fault of some observers with a high level of technical training: They get so fixated on technical analysis of particulars of the playing that the result is a musical version of losing sight of the forest for the trees. The overall aesthetic of this tune is sublime and musically moving; that they used the idea of a bullfrog to stimulate their sonic creativity does not make it simply a novelty to dismiss as lesser music. In chapter 8 I review Lonnie's 1948 recording of "Backwater Blues," a side that most blues writers and critics have missed because, like "Bullfrog Moan," it doesn't have the blazing speed and intricate, fancy finger-work. But in that recording, like "Bullfrog Moan" to a somewhat lesser degree, Lonnie created an exquisite aural impressionist painting that is a genuinely great work of musical art.

The other May recordings were released as the two sides of a 78, which seems appropriate, given their titles: "Guitar Blues" and "Blue Guitars." "Blue Guitars" was something of reference to the famous Picasso painting often called the "Blue Guitar" work (technically: "The Old Guitarist," 1903 in his "blue period"); in fact, the later LP album of the recordings used an image of Picasso's painting on the cover— speaking of my music and modern art theme. "Guitar Blues" has similarities to "Handful of Riffs," including the fact that Lonnie, in at least one part, uses essentially the same riff, and the fact that it's taken at a fast tempo. But that doesn't diminish the piece, which is played at the same high level as "Handful. . . ."

Lonnie's playing on "Guitar Blues" illustrates still more ways he was both musically ahead of his time and so profoundly and widely influential. Lenny Carlson's analysis spells it out. First, in the fourth chorus of "Guitar Blues" (actually starting with the pickup in the previous measure) Lonnie's playing "is quite a study in concept and execution. It takes great strength and concentration to carry out such an intense and extended melodic idea." And particularly notable was that, in "emphasizing the #5, E#/F, in the general context of the dominant A7 chord, the Root, Lonnie suggested an augmented figure, which was a modern sound for the time; this showed he had a melodic [and harmonic] sense ahead of his time." Second and further demonstrating Lonnie's wide influence: "The wonderful rhythmic displacement of the simple melodic idea in the eighth chorus has become standard. It can be heard in the music of most swing and bebop guitar players who came later."[32]

"Blue Guitars," on the other hand, is taken at a stately pace, rather like "Have to Change Keys . . . ," and it displays the same superb duet coordination. The rich foundation supplied by Eddie and the intricately interwoven guitar work by the two of them is again a sophisticated but accessible treat for the ears.

On October 9, 1929, Lonnie and Eddie were back in the studio for what turned out to be the final duet recordings. In all the duets, Johnson used a specially tuned, custom-made 12-string guitar; some experts also say it had just single strings for the upper two positions. This guitar can be seen in the classic 1929 photo portrait that's shown on the cover of this book, with Lonnie sitting and dressed very stylishly, this exceptional instrument leaning against him with his hands on the neck. (Some blues and jazz writers think this is the most elegant portrait ever taken of a bluesman, which is appropriate, given Lonnie's dignified, urbane nature.) There has been debate for years about what kind of guitar this was, with several possibilities suggested. I discussed this with several top specialists. At one point in our discussions guitar expert Neil Harpe e-mailed and said: "What that guitar was is one of the Great Mysteries of Western Civilization!" (But see below for a new finding that sheds light on the Great Guitar Mystery.)

The artistry that guitar enabled the virtuoso Lonnie J to create is most strikingly heard on my favorite of the duets, "Midnight Call Blues," track 16 on the CD. At the beginning of the recording he creates a fascinating zither-like sound, giving a wonderful, exotic feel, ringing above Eddie's rhythmic and harmonic foundation, rising to musical heights and elegantly descending. Then, in the third chorus, the musical feel changes, as Eddie takes a one chorus lead, playing a simple but deep-toned bluesy line, while Lonnie strums chord backings that, on that 12-string, are so rich it strikes the ear like a combination harp-zither-guitar. They finish out the song with the usual brighter sounding, sophisticated, inventive lead lines by Lonnie, all combining in a beautiful thematic coherence. I can't think of anything else that sounds quite like this glorious music.

As the title suggests, "Hot Fingers" was a fast tune designed to show off the remarkably agile and quick fingers of this duo. It is constantly engaging and attention-getting, Lonnie's speedy and creative virtuosity is on impressive display, and the overall thematic coherence is outstanding. He also offers a consistent set of accents with interesting bent string effects that add strikingly to the tune. "Blue Room Blues" is played at a slow tempo, with a smoothly flowing character; this one feels like Lonnie drew on his time floating down the Mississippi River on those excursion boats, playing tunes while people elegantly danced. Again, the guitar tone and playing style both players achieve is rich and expressive. Lonnie produces extraordinary sounds from his unique 12-string guitar on this tune, rather like he did on "Midnight Call Blues." Finally, "Deep Minor Rhythm" continues the fine duet playing, though it isn't quite as unique and interesting as most of the other sides.

Specialists in blues and jazz and various guitar greats sing the praises of these duets. But the music was and is accessible to the more general music-loving public. I demonstrated that—to myself first—when I played "Have to Change Keys . . ." and "Midnight Call Blues" for a class I taught on the blues in the College of Continuing Education at the University of Minnesota. (The course was conducted during the time that special films on the blues, organized by Martin Scorsese, were broadcast on American public television in fall 2003.) These folks were older than standard university students, with ages ranging from their twenties to their sixties, and they were in the class simply because they wanted to know more about the blues. None had a substantial knowledge of the music before the class, so they effectively served as stand-ins for people in the general public who appreciate good popular music and want to understand it better. When I played those two duets, the students' mouths literally dropped and they had looks that were a combination of "What's this?!" and sheer delight. One, right at the end of the second recording, burst out with, "I never knew there was such a thing! Wow!" I saw other avidly nodding heads. (To say the instructor was pleased would be a considerable understatement.)

This guitar collaboration was indeed something special. As Lonnie later said of Eddie, "He was the finest guitarist I had ever heard in 1928 and 1929." Lonnie also said creating those duets was his "greatest musical experience."[33] That says a lot coming from the man who made landmark recordings with Louis Armstrong and Duke Ellington, solo guitar masterpieces, and so on. Eddie died too young (in 1933 at age 31) for someone to capture his own later reflections, but the fact that he deferred to Lonnie to play the lead guitar parts the great majority of the time in these duets speaks volumes about what Eddie thought of Lonnie's playing.

The magic of these duets has been seminal in guitar history. Music writer Tony Russell, in a chapter and book with perfectly apt titles, "The Guitar Breaks Through" in *Masters of Jazz Guitar*, offered this observation, adding an interesting further perspective: "That two musicians as prodigally yet matchingly gifted as Johnson and Lang should have been near contemporaries is one of those happy accidents that make the history of jazz such a tantalizing affair."[34] (That this Black man and this White man were so "prodigally yet *matchingly* gifted" and produced such perfectly blended music was also symbolically special for American society, a subject I return to at the end of the book.) Of those duets, Lonnie said: "I valued those records more than anything in the world. . . ."[35]

But also, in assessing these two original greatest guitarists in popular music, it is worth noting that "a recurrent criticism has been that Lang did not *swing*, and his playing does seem stiff by today's standards," as James Sallis wrote. I would agree, as did jazz guitarist Marty Grosz (though he didn't think it was as great a problem as some others thought). Nobody ever suggested Lonnie J was wanting in the swing department, however. Again, as Gunther Schuller said of Lonnie's work with Louis Armstrong and the Hot Five on "Hotter Than That": "Johnson's swinging, rhythmic backing and his remarkable two-bar exchanges with Armstrong are certainly one of the highlights of classic jazz."[36]

For those who are not so conversant with jazz history, maybe a definition would be helpful here: "Swing" is a key rhythmic element in jazz that makes the music—and the body in response—move in that special jazz way. Danny Barker, major rhythm guitarist from New Orleans, "suggested that Armstrong's greatest achievement was to jettison the jaunty . . . [original] two-beat rhythm of New Orleans in favor of the evenly distributed four-four beat that is the basis of swing." Gunther Schuller (after noting the difficulty of defining "swing") said there are two characteristics of swing jazz music not generally found in classical or other music: "a specific type of accentuation and inflection with which notes are played, and the continuity—the forward-propelling directionality—with which notes are linked together."[37] The famous Duke Ellington song title, which amounts to the Jazz National Anthem, said it best: "It Don't Mean a Thing If It Ain't Got That Swing." But just *listening* to the better recordings of that tune offers the best "definition."

In summary, in light of Lonnie's superior melodic improvisations and other playing, it is clear that those several jazz books that call Eddie Lang the greatest early guitarist and *the* creator of jazz guitar are simply wrong. Also, some jazz writers and players have recognized that Lonnie had a significant influence on Eddie's own playing. Marty Grosz made an interesting observation along those lines, specifically focused on Eddie's own solo guitar record, "There'll Be Some Changes Made." Starting with reference to Eddie Lang/Salvatore Massaro's Italian ethnic origins, Grosz offered this wonderfully stated assessment: The tune "is a trip from Naples to Lonnie Johnsonville . . . in two and a half minutes." And as Steve Calt wrote in the notes to a collection of Lang recordings, "Johnson's contagious effect on Lang's tone, timing, accenting and choice of registers . . . clearly emerges on 'Melody Man's Dream' and 'Perfect'."[38]

Now, let me add the "new" findings that solve much (though not all) of the Great 12-string Guitar Mystery. In segments of the interview Paul Oliver conducted with Lonnie in 1960 that have not previously been transcribed and published Lonnie says: "I bought that 12-string guitar in San Antonio during the time I was playing at the Chinese Tea Garden. . . . They only make 12-string guitars in San Antonio. The Mexicans and the Spanish, that's all they use . . ."[39] Especially since the discussion by Lonnie surrounding that passage was all about Mexican and Spanish guitars and their makers, this seems to essentially confirm the statement by Mark Humphrey in Lawrence Cohn's *Nothing But the Blues* that the guitar "was made expressly for him by a luthier in [or from] Mexico."[40]

Lonnie also talked about how much he liked the guitar and how he played it:

> I got more enjoyment out of the 12-string instrument than the Gibson I play now; 'cause at the time I was playing with my hands [instead of using a pick]. I'd just use all five fingers in playing. . . . It's sweeter; the sound came out more perfect. And I had my own way of tuning the instrument.

The latter comment led to further informational good news. There has long been debate among writers and scholars on blues and jazz as to what his tuning was like, which sounded nonstandard. The following offers answers from Lonnie himself to at least part of the question about tuning. His statement also seems to contradict what several experts of the last two decades thought was Lonnie's tuning (see below); and it contradicts assumptions that Lonnie used only single strings at the upper two positions (the normal high E string and the second B string), although he was not ideally clear about all that. Here is Lonnie's statement, with some explanatory interjections in brackets, for which I had advisory assistance from guitar expert Andy Cohen:

> The first two [i.e., pair of] strings is the E strings, and those was tuned correctly [apparently meaning in standard manner for the upper/treble string pairs, i.e., in unison]. The G string . . . [he skipped the second B strings, and didn't finish the sentence. Then he said:] They were *all* double. [The preceding most likely means the second/B string pair was also in unison.] One G string was lower and one was a tone higher than the other. [This apparently means the pair were an octave apart—standard for 12 string guitars—as in the following:] The D string [pair] was the same. The A string was natural—octaves. And the bass string, the E-6, was natural, but it had a G string next to it; with the lower pitch, it made the sound of an organ.

Cohen thinks the second of the low string pair was a D, rather than a G, because "a G string would have to be tuned awfully slack to pair with a low E." But Lonnie said it was a G string. Could use of the normally higher G string, tuned way down like that, have enabled him to get the "sound of an organ," which is most evident in the ending note of "Midnight Call Blues"?[41] After listening again to the "Midnight Call Blues" end note, Cohen says he can't see how a G string could make that sound due to the required slack tuning. There's still some mystery here.

More on Lonnie's tuning, in general: He didn't always use the same tuning, but the following observations by technical experts should be registered. Guitar virtuoso and teacher Stefan Grossman summarized: "I hear his arrangements played in dropped D tuning (D A D G B E, from low to high strings on the guitar) [that is, dropping the standard low

E string down to a D tuning]. But Woody Mann and Lenny Carlson hear many tunes played with the guitar tuned, D G D G B E." James B. Dalton agrees with the latter tuning for "a great number of Johnson's pieces."[42] I can't resolve this question any further.

(What happened to that guitar? In the Oliver interview Lonnie said, "I wore out that 12-string." How I wish we could find that guitar to use in what should be Lonnie's installation in the Rock & Roll Hall of Fame!)

## Touring with Bessie; Lonnie and Common Folks; Other Events of '28–'32

By 1928, if not before, Lonnie had become, in effect, a staff guitarist for OKeh Records. He served as something of an "A&R" (artists and repertoire) man who advised the label on songs to record and helped musicians new to the recording studio with that process. Thus, those impressive solo guitar instrumentals Lonnie recorded in Memphis in February 1928 occurred during a field trip Lonnie made with OKeh recording people, with Lonnie helping out with the musicians in the recording studio and doing accompaniment work. For example, during the Memphis sessions, Lonnie played additional guitar with "Mooch" Richardson on some recordings (and at times was the sole guitar); particularly notable among those recordings were his complementary guitar work and especially his accents and embellishments on "Burying Ground Blues." This was further example of his able work as an accompanist on many recordings in the late 1920s and early 1930s.

Another example of Lonnie's service as OKeh recording advisor: In December 1928 Lonnie was helping in the studio for the first recordings of Mississippi John Hurt, who was a Country blues player and singer, but whose intricate finger-picking and slide guitar work were well above those of most other Country blues musicians. It's worth noting, in light of the musicians and progress on civil rights theme, that Hurt was recommended to OKeh Recording Director Tommy Rockwell by a White fiddle player named Willie Narmour, with whom John had played, and who was also from around Avalon, Mississippi, Hurt's home. This was still another example of how the music was strong enough to bring

Whites and Blacks together across that awful racial chasm, even back in the late '20s in the Deep South.

Mississippi John said of the recording session: "Me and Lonnie was in the recordin' room there. I had just written this [song] 'Candy Man.' I'd written it in pencil, and I forgot some of the verses, so they typed them on the chart. So I was practicin' on it while they were gone. Lonnie says, 'Ain't that a little too high?' Gotta let it down, son'." Lonnie also showed Mississippi John around the Big City of New York; John fondly remembered Lonnie's help for the rest of his life.[43]

Starting in fall 1929 and continuing into early 1930, Lonnie toured with the "Empress of the Blues," Bessie Smith in her "Midnight Steppers" show. The show played at a string of theaters in the North (like the Royal Theater in Baltimore and the Elmore Theater in Pittsburgh in October 1929) and in the South (such as the 81 Theater in Atlanta in early February 1930)[44]. Like Lonnie, Bessie was born in 1894; they were both thirty-five, still youthful and very vigorous. With Lonnie's instrumental virtuosity, deep blues feel, and superb ability to accompany a singer, yet not overshadow her, and with Bessie's power and ability to convey the deepest blues sense and her magnetic attraction for audiences, those performances must have been dazzling. Lonnie was a star of Black music himself by late summer 1928—though not quite on Bessie's level of fame. What a shame we couldn't have gotten some live recordings of those two in full musical cry at one of those great Black theaters, like the important "81" theater in Atlanta! It's also too bad, and a bit surprising, that they didn't make any studio recordings together.

There were popular recordings by Lonnie from 1926 through 1929, his 1927 appearances with Louis Armstrong in the Hot Five recordings, recordings with the famous and admired Ellington band in October 1928, prominent concert and club appearances, touring with Bessie Smith, and the historic Johnson-Lang duets. With all that making him a music star and a hero to his race, Lonnie could have become full of himself, arrogant, operating in a more rarified realm. But, St. Louis bluesman Henry Townsend told me that Lonnie "stayed a common man; he didn't let nobody put him on a pedestal, where he'd look down on people. He really connected well with regular people." And as registered earlier, B. B. King reinforced that point, especially reflecting on the evening he met Lonnie later in life, by saying, "He seemed to be a modest man, he seemed not to be 'bragadocious', and was a real nice person."[45]

As mentioned, Lonnie and Eddie Lang also made two recordings in May 1929 with that wonderfully named group, "Blind Willie Dunn and his Gin Bottle Four," brought together just for those recordings. With Joe "King" Oliver on cornet, they had one of the original giants of New Orleans jazz and mentor of Louis Armstrong. J. C. Johnson was the pianist, and that notable songwriter, character and musical raconteur, Hoagy Carmichael, composer of "Stardust," filled out the lineup. The two sides were "Jet Black Blues" and "Blue Blood Blues." In both tunes, Lonnie and Eddie continued their well-woven duet work, including the rich harmonic framework by Lang and well-placed special harmonic touches and accents by Johnson, along with his usual fine single-string lead lines. I find the slow tempo "Jet Black Blues" to be a bit more coherent and consistent work, so I'll say a word on that tune. After a rich-toned intro by the two guitarists, though it feels slightly plodding at times, Oliver plays fairly simple but well-timed cornet lines that seem to partly draw on old New Orleans march music. His cornet playing adds a bit of a majestic touch in how the notes ring out above the two guitars and the piano—although, in truth, his tone is not really full and rich, probably manifesting the beginning of his sad decline due to mouth and other problems. Still, this piece has a good ensemble sound, and it includes a mid-way piano solo by J. C. Johnson that's initially rippling, with a prominent descending line, then adds a brief hint of ragtime, and ends with playing that's reminiscent of Fats Waller; Hoagy adds some pure-essence-of-late '20s style mellow scat lines, as well as simple percussion.

Two months earlier Lonnie did a reunion recording with Louis Armstrong and band, including several New Orleans musicians: "Mahogany Hall Stomp" (Mahogany Hall was a premier bordello in Storyville). Louis was in fine form, and Lonnie played well with the jazz band and contributed a brief but rolling, rollicking, and deeply rhythmic guitar solo.

*Blues Who's Who* says Lonnie had his own radio show that began in 1929 and lasted until sometime in 1930; it was called *Lonnie Johnson, Recording Guitarist*, and aired on WPAP/WOV Radio in New York City.[46] That unparalleled discoverer of jazz and blues musicians, John Hammond, mentioned to Lawrence Cohn that he had heard the radio show. (Hammond was 20 in 1930, already into jazz and blues records, and listening to such music on New York City radio.) Some research in a New York newspaper for Blacks through 1930 did not turn up a listing for this; it appears that the radio show was on in 1931 and/or 1932.[47]

The titles and lyrics of some of Lonnie's songs raise a different question that should be addressed. Lonnie, like Mississippi John Hurt, was a gentle soul, and yet, like Mississippi John, Lonnie produced a series of songs that had some harsh, even violent titles and lyrics. Three examples are "She's Making Whoopee in Hell Tonight," recorded in January 1930, "Another Woman Booked Out and Bound to Go" (January 1930), and "Got the Blues for Murder Only" (November 1930). Lyrics for the first tune include: "Baby you been gone all day, set to make whoopee tonight, (repeat) I'm going to take my razor and cut your late hours, I will be servin' you right." And: "The undertaker's been here and gone, I give him your height and size, (repeat) You'll be makin' whoopee with the devil, in Hell tomorrow night." And so on. "Another Woman Booked Out and Bound to Go" includes the B line, "If I catch you makin' whoopee on me, then you don't mind dyin'." That's pretty harsh, violent stuff! (Though it should be noted that the nature of the *singing* is best characterized as mellow-sorrowful.) What's a nice fellow like Lonnie Johnson doing with lyrics like that?!

This issue has been discussed and debated by blues researcher-writers, but without conclusive consensus. I don't have a definitive answer, but here is my best take on it: In the first half of the century, Black folks in the South, and to varying extents elsewhere, lived with the pervasive threat of violence. The most stark, horrific form in which it came was lynching. Between 1880 and 1930, 3,220 Black people were reported lynched, incidents that were witnessed by thousands of Black folks, which was half the point; and the incidents were rather widely reported in newspapers, thus scaring many more. Many times that number suffered serious beatings and other violence and intimidation. When human beings live in such an environment, year after year, it would be surprising if it did not enter their psyches and their various modes of expression. Adam Gussow, in an informative exploration of violence, the Black experience in the South, and the blues, found, "Blues song was lyricized complaint as countervailing representation, a way of contesting both violence-enforced silence and the compliant Sambo-grin that Black men were expected to present in public."[48] Further, living in such an environment, with all the psychic steam built up from that experience, it would be human nature for the state of mind and developed common language tendencies to be transmuted into various relationships among Blacks themselves, including those between men and women. But also, references to violence, even in words that seem at first to indicate specific, tangible acts of violence, would be used metaphorically or just be expressive letting-off of steam, as in the case of many blues songs.

Lonnie Johnson made records that needed to appeal to the Black sub-culture, and most of his records were produced in the general blues context, so it's not surprising that he would feel it appropriate to use such language in some tunes. *But,* Lonnie also had experience of an ultimate horror of racial violence in New Orleans when he was very young. In 1900, when Lonnie was six years old, an incident with Black man Robert Charles at the center led to a race riot in the city with intense violence. No doubt his parents conveyed their worry over the racial environment and extreme danger at the time. Further, he got to St. Louis/East St. Louis somewhat over two years after what some call the worst race riot in American history, which occurred in East St. Louis in July 1917. One hundred or more Blacks were killed, many in especially brutal manner (Google "East St. Louis-race riot" if you want more). And part of what started the riot was White workers' resentment of recently arrived Blacks getting jobs at the American Steel Company foundry in East St. Louis—which was probably the "steel foundry" Lonnie worked in during 1924–1925. Lonnie had reason to have images of severe violence in his head.

## The Dazzling "Uncle Ned"

*"Lonnie Johnson was an absolutely terrifying guitar player. There's no explanation for the way he played. Stefan Grossman [guitar virtuoso from the 1970s on] was trying to figure out how Lonnie was playing his solos, and Stefan had gotten the tape and was playing it at half speed. Tom Van Bergyk and I were in there trying to figure it out with him. What eventually happened was that Stefan made a very nice instrumental, playing at half speed! . . . Those duets Lonnie did with Eddie Lang are some of the best things ever."*
—DUCK BAKER (ANOTHER TOP GUITARIST)[49]

The Lonnie Johnson-Eddie Lang duets have been celebrated ever since as among the great guitar achievements of the century in popular music. But amazingly, in December 1931, Lonnie may have exceeded even those duets in what is the one of the most stunning virtuoso guitar performances on record. The recording in question is "Uncle Ned" (full title: "Uncle Ned, Don't Use Your Head"). The quote above is, I believe, in response to that recording. So is the following one.

In my interview with jazz guitarist Jack Wilkins, who also teaches guitar and guitar history at the Manhattan School of Music in New York, he said of his response to Lonnie Johnson's playing on "Uncle Ned": "When I first really listened to it, I said to myself, 'This can't be just one guitar!' That track just blew my mind. To this day, I play it for my students and they can't believe it—especially when I tell them it was done in 1931!"[50]

Lonnie takes this old Negro folk song and turns it into a vehicle for the most dazzling, blazing-fingered, virtuoso guitar work. The Bebop and Rock guitarists who thought they were the fastest thing on a fretboard should have gone back and listened to this recording. And even at such speed, Lonnie's playing on this tune has his usual exquisite touch and tone, nuance, and vibrato. Further, the song as a whole, and especially the stunning, intricately and creatively played bridges, with striking ascending single note lines and fast figures, accomplish an impressive thematic coherence. This version of the lyrics ranges from funky to silly and carries on with the basic tradition of the song; but the lyrics should be heard simply as an impressionistic story background to the guitar work. Other guitarists today ought to listen to this recording for inspiration; but any guitarist who heard it in 1931 or 1932 and who was in a position to play with Lonnie would more likely have responded with terminal intimidation!

That's illustrated by a comment of Johnny Shines, a Country blues guitarist who recorded a fair amount and traveled with Robert Johnson; the comment was almost certainly in reference to Lonnie's playing on "Uncle Ned." Blues guitar writer Jas Obrecht posed the question:

**Q:** One of the players you and Robert [Johnson] both admired was Lonnie Johnson. Was he one of the top guitarists in those days?

**A:** Him? Was he one of the top ones? He was *the* top. I remember one record of his was strictly jazz, and boy, he was so goddamned fast—whoo![51]

Lonnie continued actively recording through 1930, 1931, up to August 12, 1932. Nearly all the sides were blues in the manner of the tunes I've discussed in this chapter and the previous one.

One criticism that can be fairly leveled at Lonnie regarding his ongoing musical creativity was that he used a particular tune, with slight variations, for a good number of songs he recorded. A primary original example of that was "New Black Snake Blues" with Victoria Spivey in October 1928. He used that essential tune for a good number of other songs for years thereafter—as he admitted; even a Lonnie Johnson strained to come up with creative new musical themes through hundreds of songs.

Recorded on September 11, 1930, "No More Troubles Now" is a fine tune, with a bluesy yet lilting and memorable melody. Lonnie does some of his best singing of the period. It's also an interesting recording in light of the timing and the lyrics. The lyrics may have been designed to uplift people as the Depression deepened through 1930; or it could have been that Lonnie was still doing well after his triumphs in 1927 through 1929, the Midnight Steppers tours with Bessie Smith into early 1930, and the prominence gained from all that. In any case, in rich tones he sings: "I found a sweet woman, brought a new sense to me. You know I'm happy now, happy as I can be. . . ." Second verse: "Give me my good whiskey, women, wine and song. I'm going to have my fun, 'til I'm dead and gone. 'Cause I'm happy now, and I can't go wrong. 'Cause I got plenty money, I'm gonna carry these good works on." Lonnie's guitar work accompanying his singing on this side was enjoyable, with his usual creative embellishments of and accents on the main musical lines, ending with a striking, rhythmic passage with very rich tone and harmonic dimensions reminiscent of the duets with Lang; he finished with an ascending flourish. In any case, it was interesting timing for such an optimistic song. During this time Lonnie resided at 345 8th Avenue, according to notations on the back of session cards at Columbia Records, as Lawrence Cohn related to me.

Another session as accompanist is interesting to note for a special reason. Martha Raye was an Irish-American singer and comedienne who sang in the early 1930s with a couple of prominent bands; later she appeared in Hollywood films, sometimes with music, involving top stars from Bing Crosby to Bob Hope. Lonnie accompanied her for her first two recordings for Victor in 1932 (while she was only a teenager), but they went unissued. According to John Hammond and other sources, Martha was Lonnie's girlfriend around then—which cross-race relationship (and age difference) would have been quite scandalous at the time, even for New York.[52]

## Influence and Level of Artistry

In this chapter and the previous one, as I've worked through Lonnie's recordings and other developments in his epic 1926–1931 period, I have also noted examples of Lonnie's influence on other musicians regarding guitar playing, music more generally, and lyrics. As the end of the most important period of Lonnie Johnson's musical and cultural achievement is written, it's appropriate to do a summary of his accomplishments and offer some assessments.

Blues and popular music writer Elijah Wald assessed Lonnie this way (this includes the full context of a line used earlier):

Lonnie Johnson was the first male superstar of the blues era, and among musicians he was widely considered to be the finest guitar player in blues or jazz. For a young, hip musician, he was an obvious role model, both for his success and for the breadth of his innovative virtuosity. . . .

Lonnie Johnson's fastest, most complex guitar solos would have been far beyond Robert [Johnson's] technical abilities. . . .[53]

A few more notes on Lonnie's musical artistry and influence as of the late 1920s and early 1930s fill out the picture of the extraordinary impact of his recordings and other work on twentieth century music. James Sallis, author of *The Guitar Players*, guitarist and guitar teacher, offered a nice summation on Lonnie's influence:

By 1930 Lonnie's influence was sweeping, and it continued to deepen. [Blueswoman] Memphis Minnie's single-string lead guitar often sounded remarkably like his; some of Blind Blake's instrumental choruses were similar in conception to Johnson's own; and Blind Willie McTell put out several numbers such as "Death Cell Blues" and "Bell Street Blues" which both in vocal inflection and accompaniment style could almost have *been* Lonnie's.

. . . Lonnie's influence continued, not only in the cities, but also . . . in the South, where the next generation of bluesmen avidly studied his distinctive guitar style, restrained vocals, and the subtle interplay of the two.

That guitar style clearly paved the way for the first electric guitarists, Eddie Durham and Charlie Christian, and closely prefigured the postwar evolution of blues guitar.

In that latter electric guitar connection, bluesman Lowell Fulson cited Lonnie's influence, as did T-Bone Walker, who was highly influential, in turn.[54]

The Sallis point about the influence of the "interplay" of Lonnie's vocals and guitar playing was also noted by a significant blues figure. Reflecting on Lonnie's recordings, especially from the late '20s, popular bluesman Brownie McGhee said: "I had never thought that kind of music could be made with voice and guitar . . . His musical works should be the first book of the blues bible."[55]

Sallis also suggested Lonnie "paved the way for the first electric guitarists [in jazz], Eddie Durham and Charlie Christian." Jazz guitarist Jack Wilkins made this observation to me on Lonnie and the evolution of jazz guitar:

> Listening to the music of Lonnie Johnson is like listening to the history of jazz guitar. Despite his reputation of being a world-renowned blues player and singer, Lonnie Johnson was a precursor to the genius of Charlie Christian. His few solo [instrumental] recordings are proof that he could play guitar like no one before him. With the recordings he made with the also legendary Eddie Lang (aka, "Blind Willie Dunn") he was the first to play fully developed "jazz lines." One must believe that Charlie Christian heard these sounds and utilized some of it for his own playing.[56]

Charlie Christian was a brilliant, innovative guitarist of the later 1930s through 1941; in fact, most knowledgeable people would say Christian was the greatest virtuoso guitarist in American popular music after Lonnie's prime years. He played and recorded with Benny Goodman's band, was a pioneer of the electric guitar in jazz, and contributed to the beginnings of Be Bop in jazz; but sadly, he died at age 26.

As noted earlier, Bill Wyman of the Rolling Stones said, "You can trace Lonnie's playing style in a direct line through T-Bone Walker and B. B. King to Eric Clapton."[57] T-Bone Walker played with Charlie Christian in their teens in Oklahoma City in the early '30s, and if Charlie was not already aware of Lonnie's guitar virtuosity on those recordings, it's certain T-Bone would have made him aware.[58]

Indeed, the respected jazz record producer and writer Chris Albertson concluded: "But the sphere of Lonnie's influence reached beyond individual musicians to the music itself; his introduction to jazz of single-line countermelodies deeply influenced the work of such younger men as Charlie Christian and Django Reinhardt, and set the course for much of today's music."[59] Django Reinhardt was a European gypsy from Belgium and France and a unique character who was a brilliant jazz guitarist. Without question, the three greatest guitarists in the world in popular music during the first half of the century were Lonnie J, Django Reinhardt, and Charlie Christian.[60]

Speaking of Charlie Christian, Lonnie said, "I knew him in New York City when I was playing with Fats Waller at Connie's Inn." Lonnie didn't specify the year he played the Harlem club with Fats, the great jazz pianist and songwriter, but this was probably in February 1940 when Christian was in New York for recording sessions on February 7 and when Lonnie was between gigs in Chicago. It couldn't have been Connie's Inn, however, because that club closed in 1933; it must have been the similar Small's Paradise.

What a tantalizing possibility was presented by the fact that Lonnie and Charlie Christian crossed paths in New York. It's a shame nobody got those two together in a recording studio to make some dazzling guitar duets, 1940-style. Charlie would have challenged Lonnie to the highest degree, and might have re-charged Lonnie's creative guitar juices at that point. Lonnie said of Charlie, "Now that's the kid that, if he'd have lived, would have been the world's greatest guitar player."[61]

In the final review and assessment of Lonnie's influence on guitar-playing in jazz, blues and beyond in chapter 9, I add some further specifics regarding Django Reinhardt, Charlie Christian, and other leading figures in popular guitar.

Backtracking a bit in time, listen to Gunther Schuller's analysis and assessment of Lonnie's contributions to those landmark sides he made with Louis Armstrong and the Hot Five in December 1927 (a sentence quoted earlier is placed in full context):

> [Those] sides had the great guitarist Lonnie Johnson. . . . And what a difference he makes! Armstrong now . . . has a strong ally. Johnson's swinging, rhythmic backing and his remarkable two-bar exchanges with Armstrong are certainly one of the highlights of classic jazz. Johnson's influence also affects [Johnny] Dodds [on clarinet] and [Kid] Ory [on trombone], who contribute their best playing to date with Armstrong, and even Lil Armstrong [on piano] is improved.
>
> . . . With "Hotter Than That" and "I'm Not Rough" we have nearly reached the apex of Armstrong's development as an esthetic and technical innovator. Here for the first time we also encounter a highly developed sense of form and textural variety. . . .

"Hotter Than That" is a remarkable performance, in which the addition of Lonnie Johnson plays a vital part. The ensembles and solos swing in a manner that makes it quite clear why the term "hot jazz" was coined. Apart from that, the formal scheme is interesting in that it presents a greater degree of variety in the over-all structure, as well as within its thirty-two bar subdivisions.[62]

Thus, Lonnie's contribution to those historic Armstrong-Hot Five recordings went beyond his scintillating guitar work by itself.

Perhaps the best simple summary of Lonnie Johnson's recordings and abilities during this first period of his career was offered by the blues guitarist and singer John Hammond, Jr., who came into his own in the 1960s. This isn't deep analysis, but it is a nice, concise note from an excellent professional musician on the level of musical artistry Lonnie had attained: "His early recordings are staggering—the sides where he accompanies Texas Alexander in the later '20s [for example]. He played any style. He played with Duke Ellington, Louis Armstrong. He was just phenomenal."[63]

The Great Depression was in its depths by 1932. Lonnie's recording stopped, and it did not resume until 1937. The record industry was hit hard, and the number of records plummeted. But some blues and jazz musicians did continue to record. Why not Lonnie, given his popularity and the great respect in which he was held as a musician? I offer an explanation in chapter 6.

# 6

# Workin' Man; Chicago Blues

## PHILADELPHIA, NEW YORK CITY, AND CLEVELAND; NO MORE RECORDS NOW

### Resuming the Personal Story

Almost certainly Lonnie moved to the East Coast from Texas in fall 1929. The 1930 U.S. Census lists a "Lony Johnson" (I've seen that misspelling of his name elsewhere) residing in Philadelphia. He's listed as born in New Orleans, both of his parents as born in New Orleans (a significant find itself, if the census worker got that right), and his occupation is listed as "performer" in "Vaudeville-Stage"; this is surely our man. The age listing is wrong—39—but not far off; Lonnie would have been 36 at the time.

Actually, this location makes sense, since Lonnie was first introduced to Philadelphia at the beginning of his work in the TOBA vaudeville theater circuit back around 1922. It would appear that he found the city to his liking and/or hooked up with some special people, since he came back in fall 1929 and took up residence there (as he did again in the 1950s). My best guess is that he actually went to Philadelphia before he went to New York; in Lonnie's one statement about this in interviews, he simply said, "I left Beaumont, Texas, and come East."[1] He probably also decided to use the familiar Philly as his home base in fall 1929 through the first two or three months of 1930 because he was mostly touring with Bessie Smith's show during that specific period.

Two other significant items are found in the census report. One column is for "Marital Condition." For Lonnie a "D" is registered, which means divorced. Assuming no egregious mistake, this semi-formally indicates the various sources stating that Lonnie's marriage lasted until 1932 are wrong, as also suggested by various evidence discussed earlier. A second interesting finding is in the last column. It asks whether the citizen is a veteran of military service. This is answered, "yes" and "WW" is entered in the companion column that asked what war or other experience the person served in, indicating service in World War I, in this case. Again, assuming no egregious mistake, this bolsters (though it does not *prove*) the claim that Lonnie did indeed serve in World War I entertaining troops. As lamented in chapter 2, it's a shame that records from Lonnie's apparent time of service were destroyed in a fire at the U.S. archives and staff were unable to find Lonnie's service record by other documents, as they sometimes can. (Thanks to census experts for blues musicians, Bob Eagle and Eric LeBlanc, for help here.)

## New York

After that period in Philadelphia, Lonnie moved up to New York City. In New York, in addition to his recordings in fall 1929, 1930, 1931, and 1932, he found work in clubs and shows. Again, Lonnie's work with Bessie Smith's "Midnight Steppers" show tour continued into and probably through February 1930. Another example of his non-studio work: Starting on November 21, 1931, he played in a show called *That Gets It* at the Alhambra Theater (126th Street and 7th Ave., "Afternoons: 10 and 15 cents, Nights: 15 and 25 cents"; keep those prices in mind the next time you go to a New York City show today!) The other cast members are obscure today. And it appears his radio show was on in 1931 and/or 1932.[2]

## Cleveland

Lonnie said, "I left from New York and went straight to Cleveland." By 1932, the Depression was at its low point and "times was tough," to use the phrase heard from blues singers and others. Record sales had dropped dramatically; "as 1931 dawned, race records [as recordings aimed at the African-American market were called] were selling about a tenth as well as they had four years previously."[3] Things got even worse through 1931 and 1932, and work for musicians, even one at the level of Lonnie Johnson, was not easy to find. Lonnie recorded his final six sides on August 12, 1932, for OKeh Records, and his contract ran out.

In New York Lonnie hooked up with pianist and bandleader Putney Dandridge. Dandridge had worked as accompanist for the famous Bill "Bojangles" Robinson in 1930, among other musical experience. They decided to head for Chicago. It appears they left in April or May 1933 (as evidence discussed in the following indicates). They were both short on cash and Cleveland was as far as they could get, however.

They were fortunate to find a continuing gig fairly quickly at a nightclub in Cleveland, the name of which Lonnie recalled as "The Heat Wave," which was located in the Majestic Hotel. The Majestic "was *the* African-American hotel in Cleveland during the long period when Negroes were not permitted to stay in the major downtown hotels. Touring Black entertainers, including many jazz artists, stayed at the Majestic when they came to Cleveland." Correspondingly, "It was almost automatic that the Majestic present live jazz in its nightclub." The club was actually called the Furnace Room when it originally opened in 1931. The name was apparently used until summer 1933, perhaps into September, when it was changed to the "Heat Wave."[4] Evidently, Lonnie and Putney started at the Furnace Room/Heat Wave in later May or early June 1933. From Lonnie's language, it sounds like it was just the two of them hitting the road from New York, and thus, they must have recruited the other band members in Cleveland for the Heat Wave gig.[5]

Lonnie indicated that soon after they were set up in the Heat Wave, he and Putney did an audition for "Miss Ruth" (thirty years later he couldn't remember her last name), an official of a Cleveland radio station that Lonnie remembered as WHEN, but was almost certainly WTAM. They got a contract to do a regular radio show for fifteen minutes, twice a week. Lonnie also thought they were the only two Blacks hired by Miss Ruth in all the years she was at the radio station, but that was not correct. The jazz pianist Art Tatum was "heard nightly through WTAM, the National Broadcasting Company station," starting in February 1934.[6] From his comments, it appears that it was just the two of them doing the radio show, Putney presumably playing the piano. Lonnie remembered them making $400 a week, which was great money for Black guys in the depths of the Depression.

Lonnie's account of how long he and Putney were in Cleveland is at odds with some other sources, which state that Dandridge had a band and then did some solo work in the city from 1932 into 1934; but the information in those sources is not certain or specific. Lonnie offered an interesting alternative explanation for how their work ended; it is specific and has the ring of truth to it. He said he and Putney worked there for four months. (For once, Lonnie does not seem to be exaggerating the time period, though "worked there four months" should be read to mean *about* four months; in this case, it was probably a little shy of four months.) And: "We had everything sewed up, but Putney broke it up . . . He seemed to have female trouble—as usual, it was a lady. She kept writin' to him, she was so lonesome . . . So he rode back to Wildwood, New Jersey—and when he got there, he didn't find her, she'd run off with somebody else!" Lonnie added, "He didn't come back, because he had broken the contract" with the radio station, as well as ending the gig at the Heat Wave.[7]

So, Lonnie was out of a job, or rather, two jobs. He stuck around Cleveland for a while thereafter, at least through the end of 1933, playing where he could in town. One place he played was a legendary small club that was Cleveland's answer to Katy Red's in East St. Louis (with the exception of one notable factor); two sessions he played there were truly remarkable ones.

**Two Meetings of Titans at Val's in the Alley** In the early 1930s, Cleveland had a unique and extraordinary late-night music club with the quaint name, "Val's in the Alley," which was operated by Milo Valentine, an ethnic Greek. It was a place "which became a sort of magnet for all the musicians in town," and many top musicians from elsewhere would come to Val's to listen and to jam with other musicians when they were in Cleveland for a gig. Val's was different from Katy Red's in a notable way, however: It was "one of the few places where black and white could mix and play together."[8] (As I understand it, Katy Red's was, de facto, pretty much exclusively Black.)

One of those top musician visitors was Duke Ellington, who described Val's location this way: The place was "really in the alley, off an alley that was off another alley."[9] Duke might have had one alley too many there, but you get the idea. Val's was just off the fairly major east-west road, Cedar Avenue, on the east side of Cleveland; people would go north on a narrow drive off Cedar near 86th Street for 50 or 60 yards, and then would find themselves in the Vienna Court section of another cross-cutting alley. There were a few sizable two-story houses back there, behind commercial property on Cedar, one of which, on the left as you came into the second alley and Vienna Court, was Val's. The combined living room and dining room (one long space) on the main floor of the house was used as the club. (I visited the spot in October 2005, but sadly, most, though not all, of the old buildings had been razed in one of those clear-cutting frenzies of "urban renewal" in the 1960s and later, so the spot was little like it was in the early '30s.)

A musician who had played there said that, during Prohibition, Valentine "operated it as a bootlegging joint. We called it 'Val's in the Alley' because it was back off the street where the police wouldn't see it." It had good food, a pot-bellied coal stove, a rough-hewn bar, sawdust on the floor, and to the left of the bar was an old upright piano, with a den-light over it. The place could only hold about 50 or 60 people.[10] By 1934—after the end of Prohibition—Milo Valentine evidently felt Val's no longer needed to be a hidden place, since I found an advertisement for the club in the January 6, 1934, edition of Cleveland's Black newspaper, the *Call and Post*. The ad said: "In the East End, it is VAL's—Ye Rhythm Club—In the Alley by the Greasy Spoon." Those who remembered the place referred to the "greasy spoon" café in the alley on the way to Val's, but evidently it actually went by that name.

Besides being a favored meeting place for jazz musicians, Val's was a special place for a specific reason: It was the adopted musical home of that unparalleled piano genius, Art Tatum (originally from Toledo, Ohio). For readers less aware of Tatum, listen to jazz writer Dan Morgenstern: "No practitioner of the music called jazz had . . . such perfect technical command . . . as did Art Tatum. But it wasn't just his astonishing facility that inspired awe in his colleagues. It was his phenomenal harmonic sense, his equally uncanny rhythmic gift, and his boundless imagination." A famous jazz history anecdote says, when Tatum entered a club where Fats Waller was playing, Waller stopped playing and said: ""Ladies and Gentlemen, I play piano, but *God* is in the house tonight!"[11]

Tatum loved Val's in the Alley, and he also loved that old upright piano, which had some special tone and action in the keys, so he played there as much as he could over the years. As Duke Ellington said, "Famous as he became . . . he would always return to Val's in the Alley to play that piano."[12]

All that is illustrated by a marvelous tale from and of Count Basie, in his earlier professional years. As Count Basie wrote in his autobiography, augmented by Cleveland jazz historian Joe Mosbrook:

> I still remember what happened to little old smart-ass Basie.
>
> We stopped off [at Val's.] . . . I made the mistake of sitting down at that piano, and that's when I got my personal introduction to a keyboard monster by the name of Art Tatum. . . . The piano was just sitting there. It wasn't bothering anybody. I just don't know what made me do what I went out and did . . . ; I started playing and messing around . . . Somebody went and found Art.
>
> That was his *hangout*. He was just off somewhere waiting for . . . someone dumb enough to do something like that, somebody like Basie in there showing off because there were a couple of good-looking girls in the place or something like that.[13]

[Mosbrook finished the story:] Tatum sat down at the piano, like a gladiator protecting his turf, and musically vanquished the intruder. When Tatum started playing, Basie said he felt like a rank amateur. He suddenly realized this little bar in Cleveland was . . . [Tatum's] personal kingdom—not to be violated by some young Count.[14]

Now, for this book, here is the keynote of the story: Lonnie's good friend of the 1960s, Bernie Strassberg, told me, "Lonnie said he played in a place called Val's in the Alley in Cleveland in 1932. He said he played duets with Fats Waller and Art Tatum. And I said, 'Lonnie, how the hell did you keep up with Tatum?!' He said, 'It wasn't easy!'"[15] Tatum's exact whereabouts in 1932 and 1933 are not fully documented, but as James Lester reported, "we have pretty definite sightings of him at Val's in the Alley in 1933."[16] As noted above, Tatum was also in Cleveland broadcasting from WTAM as of February 1934. Their piano-guitar duet at Val's was probably in fall 1933. The timing for the duet with Fats Waller is also right: From July or August 1932 through 1933, Fats was doing a regular radio show from the powerful radio station WWL of Cincinnati, heard through much of the United States.[17] Given the fame of Val's with jazz musicians, it's not surprising that Fats made it up to Cleveland in 1933 while Lonnie was there, presumably combined with a more regular club or concert appearance.

Those 50–60 people in the club for each of those two jam sessions had an incredible musical experience. (Live recordings of the dazzling duets by those ultimate virtuosos of the piano and of the guitar in that cool club in Cleveland would have been true treasures!)

Lonnie's language in the Paul Oliver interview indicates that the first job he and Dandridge got was at the Heat Wave; as noted, that lasted only about four months. Since the following club engagement evidently began in later September 1933, it's likely that the Heat Wave job went from late May to early or mid-September.

After Putney Dandridge went back East looking for his woman and the Heat Wave gig ended, Lonnie formed a trio with singer Baby Hines (first wife of jazz piano legend Earl Hines) and Jennie Dillard and played the Club Gourmet. Memories from the jazz and blues pianist Mary Lou Williams in her earlier years (still in Pittsburgh) tell us about Baby Hines: She "never received the recognition she merits. Those days, when she began a number like 'You're an Old Smoothie' the customers showered her with tips. . . . Her torch songs brought real tears to their eyes."[18] Someone named the trio the "Mississippi Flats" (perhaps something of a pun on "blue notes," as Chris Smith suggested to me). The major Black newspaper, the *Pittsburgh Courier*, said at the end of September 1933, "this trio is all the talk in Cleveland." The *Courier* also quoted one Kuzzen George of the Club Gourmet talking about "Lonnie Johnson, the boy with the guitar and nine hundred and ninety-nine fingers." Given what has been discussed about his playing in the previous two chapters, that poetic license is understandable. The trio continued at the Club Gourmet at least through October.

Tantalizingly, a September 30 *Pittsburgh Courier* article said: "The [trio] had an audition with Warner Brothers, which will no doubt result in gratifying rewards later this year." Warner Brothers did not have a record label then, so this must have been for films. (After discovering that information, an enticing question occurred to me: Is there a segment from this audition on a film reel somewhere in the Warner Brothers' film vaults?!)

Duke Ellington had been in his first major movie, *Check and Double Check*, in 1930, and Louis Armstrong had appeared in a movie "short" in 1932 titled *Rhapsody in Black and Blue*.[19] As far as I know, however, nothing came of the Warner Brothers audition.

Lonnie reportedly also played in the Patent Leather Club, probably after the Club Gourmet gig ran out, starting in November.[20]

## Hiatus from Recording/No More Records Now—Why?

As noted, Lonnie's contract with OKeh Records ended in August 1932. He did not resume recording until November 1937. Why? It was the Depression, and there was a drastic reduction in record sales; but Big Bill Broonzy and Tampa Red recorded a series of sides throughout that period. I can't say definitively why this hiatus occurred, but, beyond the severe drop in record sales, there is another probable cause.

Peter Guralnick set the scene thusly:

> In Chicago, Lester Melrose, a White music store owner who became a music publisher, virtually controlled the blues industry. Between 1934 and his retirement in 1951, he estimated that he recorded ninety percent of everything that Columbia and RCA put out in their separate, highly successful race series. . . . Melrose, in fact, put his stamp on virtually every blues recording coming out of Chicago for more than a decade. . . .[21]

A couple of sources say Lonnie had some sort of conflict with Lester Melrose. There are two prime probabilities regarding the nature of that conflict. The first was clearly stated by another source: "Johnson was well aware of his talent and refused to sign the kind of cut-throat contracts that were being offered to blues players, leaving him without a recording contract. . . ."[22] A second possibility, which might have been a factor in addition to the contract issue, was an insistence by Melrose that Lonnie alter his approach or change the types of songs he was doing, which Lonnie refused to do. Blues writer Stephen Calt has written: Lonnie's recording was "largely foreclosed by a dispute with Lester Melrose. . . . According to Hotbox Johnson, a disciple who moved from Louisville to St. Louis in order to learn how to play like Lonnie, Melrose refused to record [Lonnie] unless he changed his too-familiar guitar style. Johnson, with a display of integrity . . . rare for a professional blues singer, refused to do so."[23] Other sources offer functionally related observations on the impact of Melrose that add insight on this question. Mike Rowe, in *Chicago Breakdown*, reports that under Melrose control, for those later 1930s and early 1940s recordings, "the instrumentation was generally the same. . . . Melrose had effected the greatest rationalization [i.e., homogenization] in blues recording."[24]

## Workin' Man

This time period is the other one in which Lonnie's whereabouts and actions are most difficult to sort out. In the two interviews in which he did talk about this general period, Lonnie gave chronologically muddled reviews of the developments in his life, as well as sometimes getting years wrong; that included a tendency for Lonnie to finish one episode or particular stretch of his life, followed by him saying, "Then . . . ", when he actually jumped *back* in time. It's no wonder a number of blues and jazz writers have been confused about what happened and when. One has to do a kind of triangulation in sorting out what he says, supported by whatever information can be garnered from other sources. Again, what follows is my best reconstruction based on all the available information.

Lonnie's luck in getting music work ran out in Cleveland in early 1934; as Lonnie put it in the 1960 Paul Oliver interview, "I was back on my own again." He followed that by saying, "So, I tried to make it in Chicago, but I had to quit the music business."[25] This indicates he first headed for Chicago, which was the original destination of Lonnie and Putney when they set out from New York, so that makes sense. This also lends implicit support to the idea of the conflict with Lester Melrose.

It may, at first glance, seem odd that Lonnie did not explicitly talk about the problem with Melrose; but, despite all the vicissitudes of his life, he rarely talked about someone who "done him wrong" in the past, to use the old blues phrase, so the lack of a mention of Melrose is not so surprising.

In his 1967 interview with Moe Asch, Lonnie said: "After the record contract gave out, I went back to the steel mill . . . in East St. Louis . . . and I started working again." Thus, it appears he went to Chicago, but in that deep Depression year, and given the problem with Melrose, he couldn't get things going in the music realm in the Windy City, so he went back to his old area and got a job at the steel mill where he had worked before. He gave us a description of the specific work he did: "I started as a sand-cutter and ended up as a molder. I was molding those big [railroad] box car wheels you see on the track." As usual, Lonnie considerably overstated the length of time he was at the steel plant (he said five years). Based on the other blue-collar jobs he noted thereafter, and keeping in mind that he was in Chicago recording again by November 1937, he was probably at the steel plant for about a year and a half.

While back in the St. Louis area, it is also likely that he kept his hand in music by playing some in the local clubs, no doubt some of the time with his brother Steady Roll. Then he took a job at a factory making railroad track ties in Galesburg, Illinois, roughly 180 miles north of St. Louis. He said he only worked there for six months "because the work was too heavy." It was more than too heavy, it was dangerous: The railroad ties were soaked in creosote and "would come out of [the creosote vats] boiling hot, and we had leather coats on and you put the ties on your shoulders" to load in box cars. The ties "weighed 150–200 pounds and only two men had to carry them, one on each end . . . , and we loaded 1,600–1,700 of those ties into the box cars. I got tired of that!" My guess is that he worked there less than six months.

Beyond wearing him out, I'm struck by the idea of this virtuoso of the guitar, with those fingers allowing Lonnie to make such masterful, intricate music, having to handle the boiling hot, 175-pound railroad ties and loading them in box cars; the same goes for his hands being used in the steel mill. Keep in mind, this was a time before there was any Occupational Safety and Health Administration or other serious oversight of working conditions, not to mention the fact that it was the Depression and people were desperate for jobs, which company executives could exploit. And this was a Black man at a time when the welfare of those citizens was widely ignored. Thank God he somehow escaped injury in such dangerous industrial conditions.

He then went to Peoria, about sixty miles east of Galesburg, where he found a nightclub gig. He said he played that club for "about three years" before it shut down, and at that point he found a job at a "steel foundry a few blocks from the club, and got a job doing the same kind of work I was doing in St. Louis." In a different interview he said he "played blues at night" in the clubs around Peoria. Regarding his work in the steel foundry, he said, "I worked there seven years." Once again, his memory exercised a time frame expander; clearly he was not there seven years or anything remotely close to it. (If one added up all the years Lonnie said he had played with particular performance partners, worked in various jobs, and lived in certain areas, he would have been closer to 100 years old when he died, instead of the 76 he actually was!) Of course, it probably *seemed* like seven years. Following the steel foundry work, he added one more blue-collar job to his resume in that workin' man realm. His characterization of the job is startling for this giant of twentieth-century music and is a comment on the tough times: "Then I got an easy job working at the golf course, taking care of the lawns. That was a *good* job; I worked there a long time." (He often said, "I worked there a long time.") What a reflection on the state of things that this seminal figure in the music of the century felt he had a "good job" tending the lawns of a golf course.[26] In terms of the chronology, all I can say is that those jobs evidently took place in that sequence from early 1934 into fall 1937.

One other thing should be mentioned here, with another Lonnie mystery involved. He filled out his application for Social Security in April 1937, and he listed his residence and employment (Maxwell House Hotel) in *Nashville*. There is some odd, inaccurate information given (like "date of birth: 8th Feb, 1909"). But it appears that Lonnie was working in some job in the Maxwell House Hotel in spring 1937. I've seen nothing else on this.

By late fall 1937 Lonnie was back in Chicago. The second recording he made in his comeback reflects his experience in those years and the general societal realm from which he came. And in it he spoke for many people who had suffered through the Depression—and many who weren't doing great before the Depression started *or* by fall '37. The song was titled, "Hard Times Ain't Gone No Where," and the opening lines were: "People is raving about hard times; tell me what it's all about. Hard times don't worry me; I was broke when it started out."

## Chicago Blues

Starting in the late 1920s and increasing in the 1930s, Black musicians, especially blues musicians, headed for Chicago; more and more it became Blues Central from the later 1930s through the 1960s. Jazz also continued to have a vital presence in Chicago in the late 1930s and early 1940s. (Kansas City was another center of jazz in the '30s, and New York was the increasingly preeminent center for jazz).

In fact, Chicago had been a prime destination for Black folks in general, who were escaping the brutal racist environment in the South in the 1920s and 1930s, as well as escaping problems in agriculture due to the infestation of the boll weevil and drought in the early '30s. As noted earlier, this was part of the Great Migration of African-Americans out of the South. Chicago was the terminus of the Illinois Central Railroad, which ran straight up from New Orleans through Mississippi. The city was also home to the de facto national Black newspaper, the *Chicago Defender*, which was widely read in the South. In fact, the newspaper's chief editor, Robert Abbott, used the *Defender* to urge Southern Black folks to escape to Chicago. Between 1910 and 1930, the population of African-Americans in Chicago increased dramatically, from 44,103 to 233,903; by 1940 it was about 280,000.[27]

As of the late 1930s into the early 1940s, there was a kind of critical mass of leading blues musicians in Chicago, which included the three biggest blues recording stars from 1926 through 1942: superb guitarist and singer Tampa Red (Hudson Whittaker), singer-guitarist Big Bill Broonzy, and Lonnie Johnson. Also based in Chicago by that time were the extraordinary singer and guitarist Memphis Minnie (born Lizzie

Douglas), the major early harmonica player, John Lee "Sonny Boy" Williamson, fine pianist and singer Memphis Slim (Peter Chatman), and others.

There was, in fact, a real *community* of blues musicians in Chicago by the late 1930s and early 1940s. Tampa Red's house became a central gathering place for the musicians—kind of a combination rehearsal hall and visitors' lodging place. The bass player, studio force, and leading blues songwriter Willie Dixon described it well. He starts with a further note on Lester Melrose: "I used to go down to Tampa Red's house on 35th and State Street. That's where Lester Melrose hung out, and Lester Melrose was the go-between man between the blues artists and the recording company. . . . Tampa Red's house was a madhouse with old-time musicians. Melrose would be drinking all the time and Tampa Red's wife would be cooking chicken and we'd be having a ball."[28]

From the later '30s on, what amounted to the crystallization of the "urban blues" took place primarily in Chicago, in its two forms. One form came from the movement of Mississippi Country blues musicians to Chicago, who then started using electric guitars and full bands. The second form was the smoother, urban, and modern blues first developed by Lonnie Johnson and a little later boosted by Leroy Carr and Scrapper Blackwell—and still later by T-Bone Walker. (Something of an off-shoot of that smoother blues was embodied in Ivory Joe Hunter and Charles Brown and was piano-based.) Those two streams of urban blues became the main thrust of the music thereafter (with a partial exception during the Folk and Blues Revivals in the 1960s). They also laid the foundations for the subsequent development of Rhythm & Blues, which then led to Rock & Roll. The Beatles and the Rolling Stones were much taken with and influenced by the Chicago blues of the '50s and early '60s, and the Stones got their name from a Muddy Waters song.

At the forefront of the continuing development of the smother urban blues were Tampa Red, Big Bill Broonzy, and Lonnie Johnson. (Leroy Carr basically drank himself to death by early 1935.) A prime influence on Tampa Red and, apparently on Big Bill, was Lonnie Johnson.[29]

The number of top bluesmen and -women in the city naturally also attracted younger musicians wanting to "make it." By the late '30s, Chicago had many good clubs offering blues music, so there were lots of opportunities to play. As Mike Rowe pointed out, "They would get their start by sitting in with the good-natured Big Bill [Broonzy], Lonnie Johnson, or Sonny Boy [Williamson], and some other bar-owner would hear or hear of them and book them into his club."[30]

The refinement of artists' *singing* was a significant part of the continued development of "urban blues" and "modern blues," along with the increasing use of electric guitars, rather than the traditional acoustics. ("Modern blues" is roughly the same thing as "urban blues," with the former basically being a further refinement of what was first called the urban blues, or what Lonnie called "city blues.") The thrust of the development was that the singing was not only smoother and often used better tone, but the language was less crude; that was in accord with the general motivation of many Blacks in the cities to present themselves as more modern and urban and less as poorly educated rural Americans. It was no less deeply soulful and moving music, however; the ultimate demonstration of that has been the music of B. B. King.

One can hear the transition from the old "*Country* blues" to urban/modern blues in certain bluesmen. John Lee "Sonny Boy" Williamson, born in Jackson, Tennessee, came to Chicago in 1934; he was increasingly popular in the city and beyond. "Perhaps more than any other blues harmonica player [Sonny Boy] was responsible for the transition of the harp from a simple down-home instrument used mainly for novelty twists and light jug band riffs to one that became an essential part of the early Chicago [urban] blues sound."[31] Big Bill Broonzy, originally from Mississippi, manifested the change in his own development as a musician. On his earlier recordings in the late 1920s through 1934, we hear not-so-refined singing and less than superb vocal tone, very much in the earlier Country blues manner. But increasingly thereafter, he sang more smoothly, with more nuance, and with better tone. In my judgment, he was influenced by Lonnie Johnson in his singing as well as in his guitar playing. Broonzy seemed to testify to this influence in his comment from his visit to St. Louis in the early '20s when he saw and heard Lonnie performing. Again, Broonzy commented on how good Lonnie was on multiple instruments and in his singing; the influence would also have come from Lonnie's great stature in guitar and vocal blues and from the fact that Lonnie was the originator of the smoother urban blues with guitar and vocals, which Broonzy proceeded to work his way into.

Beyond his celebrated guitar work, even on the singing side Lonnie Johnson led the way in the refinement of urban blues. Striking testimony to that came in 1940, when the major African-American poet and deep appreciator of the blues, Langston Hughes, said that Lonnie Johnson was "perhaps the finest living male singer of the blues." (Hughes also included the main lyrics from Lonnie's popular song, "Jelly Roll Baker," in *The Book of Negro Humor*.)[32]

## Lonnie's Chicago Club Work in the Late '30s and Early '40s

After having established himself in Chicago, the first club Lonnie played in was the Three Deuces on State Street in the "near North Side." I found an interesting description of the club in a report of May 10, 1939, from the unique New Deal Federal Writers' Project begun in the Great Depression to give work to writers:

> The 3 Deuces is a famous night spot, especially for lovers of jazz music. In the past, during the prohibition era, it was one of the few spots where musicians would come after working hours to get into jam sessions. In those days men like Bix Beiderbecke, Eddie Condon, Bud Freeman, Frank Teschmaker [*sic*], sometimes Benny Goodman, Dave Tough [leading White jazzmen from Chicago], would come down and sit together and play this music they "felt." . . .
>
> Upstairs is a bar where they have Negro performers, now including Lonnie Johnson on guitar, Lil Armstrong on piano, and Baby Dodds on drums. Downstairs is the Off Beat Room where there are usually two orchestras [bands] and where George Barnes is a featured guitarist.[33]

It's so interesting that George Barnes (a White guy) was a source for that report and was playing in the downstairs Off Beat room, because Barnes was profoundly influenced by Lonnie. Indeed, he "benefited from personal coaching by Lonnie Johnson."[34] At the time of the report Barnes was all of eighteen years old, but had been playing professionally for over a year already. One can just see young George, on breaks from his duties downstairs, going up to watch and hear Lonnie's guitar work, which was probably the origin of George's tutorials from Lonnie. George Barnes went on to become a very significant guitarist in jazz and pop music, playing on many recordings as a prime studio guitarist (including on some significant blues records) or as featured performer. Later, Country Music guitar master Chet Atkins said, "Barnes was one of my idols."[35]

Reflecting his New Orleans origins and his jazz background, at first Lonnie worked there with the pioneering, top New Orleans jazz drummer "Baby" Dodds. Just guitar and drums, with Lonnie singing, is a pretty unusual combination. Larry Gara added interesting perspective on this in his introduction to the Baby Dodds autobiography: "Baby believed that versatility is an absolute essential to a jazz musician. A good drummer must be able to play with any size or kind of outfit. . . . For one job Baby played with only Lonnie Johnson's guitar as melody instrument." Of course, Lonnie could do so much else on his guitar beyond and in addition to the melody, as we've seen. But, as the report said, by spring 1939 Lil Hardin Armstrong, Louis Armstrong's ex-wife, was playing piano with him; still later, a bass player replaced Baby Dodds.[36]

For a little while in late 1937, a fine young singer named Myra Taylor (20 years old in that year) sang with Lonnie and Baby Dodds. Then she left; but after about a year's absence, she came back and performed with Lonnie until the end of the job when the club burned down. In a 2004 interview with me, Myra had some interesting memories of her experience with Lonnie at the club. Myra, a full-of-life 87-year-old when I interviewed her, characterized herself as a "swing singer." That was appropriate given Lonnie's background and since the late '30s were the height of the "Swing Era." Myra sang standards like "My Last Affair," "You Go to My Head," etc. Lonnie would also sing, often doing his own compositions, and he would frequently take requests from the audience. I asked, "And Lonnie would know those tunes?" She answered, "Yeah, he played *everything.*" When asked how the audience responded to Lonnie, she said, "They loved him; they *loved* him!" She also echoed what others observed over the years, "He dressed very, very nice," and went on to say, "I can't say enough for him"; she also said that he was "very respectful" of her and treated her very well (as did Baby Dodds, Lil, and the bass player). Unfortunately for this book, when I asked Myra what Lonnie was like outside of the club, she said she was very young, came from a proper background and didn't drink, and after the performance she went straight from the club to her hotel room, so she really didn't get much of a sense of Lonnie beyond the Three Deuces.

Myra had a fun anecdote about their instruments: At one point Lil Armstrong had the grand piano there painted all white. The next evening Lonnie came in and his guitar had been painted white to match Lil's piano.

Myra added a note on how the Decca record company treated Lonnie, which was common treatment of Black musicians: "I was kind of disgusted with Lonnie Johnson because his record label was making big bucks off his recordings, but were only paying him $25 a side—and he acted happy to get that. It upset me no end the way they treated him!"

Lonnie played the Three Deuces until January 1, 1940, when the club burned down in the early hours of New Year's Day. Myra heard that owner Sam Beard and his partner set the place on fire themselves, or had someone do it for them, so they could collect the insurance money. She noted that jazzman Wingy Manone's band was in the Offbeat Room, along with the jazz violinist Stuff Smith, and Myra had all her performance gowns in the club; all the instruments and her gowns went up in smoke.[37] (That sort of thing happened other times in such clubs, but usually the owner(s) would discretely tell the musicians at the end of the previous evening's show that it would be a good idea if they took their instruments home that evening.)

A side note from Lonnie's time at the Three Deuces: Another blues writer sent me a copy of a program for a symposium presented by "The Record Makers" of Chicago; the symposium was titled, "My Job in Relation to the Social Trends of Today." The three speakers were author Harvey O'Connor, artist Morris Topchevsky, and Lonnie Johnson, "Swing guitarist, featured now at the '3 Deuces'—named by Hugo Pinasi as the top guitarist." The program is dated December 4, but the year is not specified; it must have been 1939. This is an indirect exemplification of the fact that Lonnie presented himself well in public.

As mentioned earlier, it appears from a comment of Lonnie's in an interview, and from other evidence, that after the Three Deuces burned down, Lonnie went back to New York to play at Small's Paradise with Fats Waller for part or all of February.

Starting in March 1940, "appearing nightly" at Square's Boulevard Lounge (104 East 51st Street, "the brightest spot in Bronzeville," i.e., Southside Chicago) were "Wilbur Hobbs and Lonnie Johnson's Swing Trio." Again, that trio name was in keeping with the "Swing Era" and Lonnie's jazz background and ability. Besides Lonnie, plus Hobbs on piano, the Trio included Andrew Harris on bass and Dan Dixon on second guitar. At times Lonnie's trio was joined at the Boulevard Lounge by a female vocalist.[38] In 1941 a series of photos was taken of Lonnie (playing a Martin acoustic guitar) and his trio performing at the Lounge. Interestingly, they were shot by Russell Lee under the auspices of the Farm Security Administration; they are now in the Library of Congress.

Lonnie and Bassman (from trio) at Square's Boulevard Lounge, Chicago, 1941. PHOTO BY RUSSELL LEE, UNDER THE AUSPICES OF THE FARM SECURITY ADMINISTRATION; IN THE LIBRARY OF CONGRESS.

On November 30, 1940, Lonnie performed in a big benefit show for needy Black musicians in Chicago. Fats Waller headed the show, and it included jazz greats Earl Hines, Roy Eldridge, Jimmie Noone, blues singer "Chippie" Hill, and others. In fall 1940 and 1941, Lonnie's trio also played at annual *Chicago Defender* banquets.

An insightful, well-written account of Lonnie performing by himself at Square's Lounge was included in a publication called *Jazz Review* produced back in the 1940s. The account was from British jazz writer Lyn Foersterling; I don't have the date, but it was probably from summer 1941. It was simply titled, "A Note on Lonnie Johnson," and came from the writer's visit to Chicago. It is striking testimony about Lonnie's achievement of greatness in *singing* by the early 1940s:

> Over our heads, a rough semi-circle of red tube spelled "Square's." The sign flickered slightly [; we walked in]. . . . We were instructed to move back through the room occupied by the bar, turn right into a narrow corridor, and turn right again. The passage opened into a long, large room, indirectly lit with a yellow-green light that spilled over in the tinted bowls placed along the walls. A fresco of three dancing nudes seemed almost to move as you looked at it. Standing near the centre of the room, resting against a polished spinet piano, stood a Negro, playing guitar and singing a blues I had never heard before. There was not the slightest doubt that the man was a folk singer of genius. . . . [They didn't, at first, realize it was Lonnie Johnson.]
>
> Then Lonnie sang, not a blues, but "Jelly Jelly," the Billy Eckstine song . . . When Lonnie sang it, it was jazz, done with unbelievable delicacy and finesse. I think Lonnie has never recorded his greatest work, or, if he has, it has been lost in the recording process. His single string guitar technique is without equal, and he puts Django to shame. As he sings, he looks out over his fretting left hand, head turned slightly to one side, working effortlessly. [He's] wearing a tan tropical weave suit and a white sportshirt, the collar spread wide and unbuttoned. . . .
>
> His singing is sincere, profoundly moving and powerful without effort; there is no suggestion that he is earning a living with his singing and playing. From the first vision of him, his lips spread in a half pout, his feet spread apart, to the later impression of his flashing diamond

ring, sparkling as he trembles the fret-board of his guitar to add a more noticeable vibrato, there is not the slightest doubt of Johnson's tremendous depth of feeling.

[Later Lonnie sat with Foersterling and his friend, and they asked him a question about his association with a musical figure of the 1920s:] He paused and stared past the piano, into the dark corners of the room and beyond. "Oh," he said in his folk voice, over the still overtones of his guitar, "Oh, old dead days." I could only guess what Lonnie saw there past the corner of the room, staring into past time, old times, visions of past things conjured up for an unkind moment by the two of us. . . .[39]

I wrote to Pete Seeger about any contacts with or influence from Lonnie. Pete wrote back and said: "I learned some beautiful blues runs in the key of D from a recording of his." He also said he saw Lonnie in "a bar on South Side Chicago, about 1941; Studs Terkel took me there." Thus, Seeger also saw Lonnie at Square's Boulevard Lounge. The job lasted through 1942.[40]

## Recordings: 1937–1942

Meanwhile, Lonnie returned to the recording studio on November 8, 1937, in Chicago, after a five-and-a-quarter-year absence. These recordings and those in the next session in March 1938 were done for Decca Records. Eight recordings were made in that first session. The first side in this comeback actually spoke to the harsher realms of the battle between the sexes; it was titled, "Man Killing Broad." Another side was about the big Mississippi flood, titled "Flood Water Blues," which drew on "Broken Levee Blues" and "Backwater Blues," and even "St. Louis Cyclone Blues." For this song and the other five done in the session, the quality of Lonnie's guitar work continued from the 1929–1932 period; the playing is strong, distinct, melodically and harmonically creative, and very rhythmic.

Two of the other five recordings from that November 8 session are worth specific note. "Swing Out Rhythm" is a very jazzy, inventive solo guitar instrumental, with a very full, rhapsodic sound; it is roughly comparable to "Playing with the Strings" in that it has the feel of experimental playing and is loose regarding standard music form. But here, his creativity didn't quite measure up to "Playing with the Strings," let alone "Away Down in the Alley Blues"; there is not as consistent and coherent a structure to the piece and the flow of the music is a bit choppy in places. Still, the song is interesting.

The other side, "Got the Blues for the West End," fondly referred to Lonnie's New Orleans origins. West End was a resort area on the shore of Lake Pontchartrain at the northern end of the city. The song title also referenced the Louis Armstrong-Hot Five masterpiece, "West End Blues." But this solo guitar instrumental was no imitation of the Armstrong tune. It's a very interesting, unique new piece. He plays single-string lines of great invention with the best of that remarkable Lonnie J touch and rich tone, and with exceptionally expressive use of vibrato and bent notes. And he creatively mixes those single-string lines with three- to six-string chording, sometimes percussively strummed primarily using the treble strings, sometimes using more strings and strummed for a deep and articulated full harmonic sound. All of this also has a good dose of thematic coherence (more so than "Swing Out Rhythm"). This tune has a unique structure and musical texture and doesn't really sound like anything else; it's an excellent addition to Lonnie's recorded output.

On March 31, 1938, Lonnie recorded eight more songs for Decca, this time in a New York City studio. For these recordings he had accompaniment from his old St. Louis friend, Roosevelt Sykes. Sykes was "one of the most important of the pre-World War II blues piano stylists. With a technique that emphasized intricate chord patterns and bass figures, along with a crisp urban blues sensibility that would occasionally slip into the jazz realm, Sykes was a first-rate solo artist and a much-in-demand accompanist."[41] You can see why Roosevelt was an ideal musical partner for Lonnie. This was demonstrated especially well in three of the first four songs recorded. The addition of Roosevelt Sykes also seemed to provide a boost in energy and spirit for Lonnie.

On the first recorded side, with its classic blues theme, "Friendless and Blue," Lonnie's guitar playing was in top form, with very sharp, creative playing, including those striking Lonnie harmonic and tonal touches. The tune included some of his better lyrics. An example was this verse about wandering in the world: "Rocks was my pillow, cold ground was my bed. (Repeat) The blue sky was my blanket, and the moonlight was my spread." The second side employs that other notable blues theme, the devil: "Devil's Got the Blues." Musically, this is a companion piece to "Friendless and Blue."

The fourth and fifth recordings from this session are genuine gems. "Mr. Johnson Swing" takes off from his first hit record of 1925 and, with help from Sykes and unknown bass and drums, turns it into a vigorous up-tempo, rhythmically driving swing blues number. Lonnie's playing is up to his high standards, especially on two instrumental breaks, with inventive guitar lines highlighted. At the beginning of the first instrumental solo, Lonnie says, "*Sing* for me, git-tar!," and his fingers sail off on some energetically picked hill and dale lines with a jazzy feel. Then he says, "Take it Mr. Piano man!," and Roosevelt Sykes plays a break with a distinctive rising set of notes, then drivingly moves on with rolling bluesy-jazz lines which remind me a bit of Earl Hines. These guys were steaming up the studio. Also, Lonnie pays tribute to Duke Ellington with new variations on the original lyrics from "Mr. Johnson's Blues": "I want all you people, to listen *while my guitar sings*. (Repeat) *If you ain't got that rhythm, it don't mean a thing.*" Lonnie's outstanding playing in that up-tempo manner continued on his remake of the "B" side of his original hit record, now called "New Falling Rain Blues," playing guitar this time. This tune, like the previous one, is so bursting with life that it is contagious. (If the feet of the person next to you aren't moving when listening to this recording, check their pulse.) Also, Lonnie's singing is superb on this tune, with great verve and a syncopated feel, very expressive tone and phrasing, and employing terrific dynamics.

In fact, his vocal work on all of the tunes recorded at this time, culminating with the singing on "Mr. Johnson Swing" and "New Falling Rain Blues," demonstrated that he was committed to continuing the improvement of his vocal work, and it was paying off. These recordings were probably at the front of Langston Hughes's mind when, in 1940, he called Lonnie "perhaps the finest living male singer of the blues."

The final recording I must note here is another remake: "Blue Ghost Blues," which was first recorded in November 1927. In the new version, Lonnie takes the coherent short story of the original side and turns this new recording into a kind of musical *movie* short by augmenting the music and singing, by lyrics with striking imagery, and by adding sound effects. He starts with a fine guitar intro, with bent strings giving a combination bluesy/haunting feel, and then sings: "Um, umm, something *cold* is creeping around. (Repeat) Blue Ghost has got me, I feel myself sinking down," with music perfectly attuned to those lyrics. A black cat is added; and he tells us, "I've been in this haunted house. . . ." The third verse is especially effective—and adds a little personal pathos: "I feel cold arms around me, and ice lips upon my cheek. (Repeat) My lover is dead, how plainly I can hear her speak," which is followed by a whispered female voice hauntingly saying, *"Lonnie, Lonnie!"* The final verse is equally good and leads to a dramatic ascending vocal flourish as the song finishes: "My windows is rattlin', my door knob is turnin' 'round [rattling sound effects added]. (Repeat) Blue Ghost has got me, I know my time won't be long." Hollywood couldn't have done it better. This is track #19 on *The* Ultimate *Best of Lonnie Johnson* CD.

In recording sessions on April 1 and October 18, 1938, Lonnie provided accompaniment for St. Louis bluesman Peetie Wheatstraw (William Bunch), who liked to call himself "The Devil's Son-in-Law" and/or the "High Sheriff of Hell." The first set of recordings does not contain particularly significant work by Lonnie,[42] so I'll be brief.

In sides like "304 Blues," "Good Little Thing," and "What More Can a Man Do" in the April 1 session, Lonnie's guitar playing works well with Peetie's piano playing and vocals. Wheatstraw's recordings were popular at the time, but for most people's ears today (at least those of non-specialists), his singing sounds mumbled at times and a bit crude, though it could conjure up some deep blues feeling.

The second session was of historic significance, however. From the first recording on October 18, 1938, "Truckin' Thru Traffic" (that's how it was spelled), we hear some guitar history: Lonnie is using an *electric* guitar for this session. That's twelve and a half months before the session of his own in which various writers have said he played electric guitar for the first time: November 2, 1939.

That October 18, 1938, session makes him a pioneer in electric guitar. The most noted early recording of significance in which an electric guitar was used was that of jazz multi-instrumentalist Eddie Durham with Count Basie's Kansas City Six. It took place on September 27, 1938—just three weeks before Lonnie's recordings with Peetie Wheatstraw. This Lonnie recording date is also significant because Charlie Christian did not make his first record with Benny Goodman's band as a much-celebrated pioneer in use of an electric guitar until Oct 2, 1939, virtually a year later. It should be further noted that blues writers tend to say the leading pioneer in use of the electric guitar in the blues realm was T-Bone Walker. But T-Bone didn't record with an electric until 1942—although his electric guitar playing subsequently had huge influence throughout blues and Rock music. There were a few isolated recordings with some individually rigged-up version of an electric guitar made even earlier than fall 1938.[43]

Lonnie's use of the electric guitar on "Truckin' Thru Traffic" is effective, employing the special tone and sustain characteristics of the electric, rather than just playing it like an acoustic guitar. This also suggests that Lonnie had been playing around with an electric for a while before that October '38 session. On another recording, Peetie says, "Now play it a little while, Lonnie," to start a Lonnie solo on "A Man Ain't Nothin' But a Fool," and he does a similar thing on "Hot Springs Blues (Skin and Bones)," but Lonnie's electric guitar playing isn't quite as innovative on those recordings as on "Truckin'. . . ." ("Hot Springs Blues . . ." has humorous lyrics about women and the Hot Springs, Arkansas, spa.)

Sources, including the authoritative reference *Blues and Gospel Records, 1890–1943*, list a September 1939 Wheatstraw recording session as "probably" including Lonnie Johnson on guitar. After careful listening, however, I am convinced this is *not* Lonnie.[44]

Because of the significance of the electric guitar in popular music and later in this narrative, it is appropriate to talk about the beginnings of its use. Especially for noisy urban clubs, and as blues increasingly turned to bands rather than musicians working solo or in duos, there was a need for an instrument that could generate more volume. There were two basic options for making an electric guitar that could generate more volume. The more obvious approach was to simply attach an electric "pickup" to the body of an existing acoustic guitar; the second option was to create a new type of guitar with a solid body (since the hollow body wasn't necessary for amplification, if electricity was to be used). Probably the first to do the latter was a Swiss immigrant living in the Los Angeles area, Adolph Rickenbacker. Rickenbacker had established a tool and die manufacturing company, and after meeting George Beauchamp, who was involved in the National steel resonator guitar company, he made parts for those guitars. The steel bodies and resonator cones in them were a first attempt to increase volume; various early bluesmen also liked the unique tone, especially played in slide guitar style. Beauchamp, in conjunction with Rickenbacker and two others, built a prototype of the first solid body electric guitar in 1931, which they dubbed the "Frying Pan" because that was basically the shape of the thing (it was not a pretty sight). In 1932, Rickenbacker made the first of his "Electro Spanish" guitars, which were simply pickups placed inside standard archtop acoustic bodies with "f" holes.[45] (Rickenbacker guitars gained fame in the mid-1960s when John Lennon and George Harrison of the Beatles used them.) Some others tinkered with electric guitars in some form in the early 1930s. In 1936 Gibson introduced the ES-100; the ES-150, "Electric Spanish" guitar (with a "hollow" arch-top acoustic body) was generally available in 1937.[46] That is the guitar Charlie Christian famously used in his first recordings with Benny Goodman.

One other note on the early development of electric guitars: Les Paul was a superb guitarist who was also an inventor by inclination. In 1939 Paul began experimenting on a solid body electric. What he produced had as funny a name as the first Rickenbacker. Paul dubbed it "The Log" because it was just a pine 4x4 with crude electronics and a neck attached. He played it in public as is, but he got such a sarcastic reaction that he later simply sawed in two a standard acoustic body with "f" holes and attached the two sides to the log. In 1941 he took his new guitar invention to Gibson Guitars. They laughed him out of the place, calling him "the kid with the broomstick with pickups on it."

But in 1947 a custom guitar maker named Bigsby made a solid body electric guitar for the Country music guitarist Merle Travis. Then, in 1950, Leo Fender and colleagues in southern California came out with the "Esquire," soon renamed the "Broadcaster," which became increasingly popular and gained its permanent name, "Telecaster." Gibson then realized they needed to get in the game and they went back to Les Paul to consult with them as Gibson developed a quality solid body electric guitar. In 1952 the Gibson "Les Paul" model came out. Ever since, the "Les Paul" has been one of the preeminent electric guitars in existence.[47]

Les Paul explained why he was moved to develop this guitar: "My reason for wanting a solid body [electric] guitar has always been that the strings would have more sustaining power, all the notes would sustain evenly and unwanted resonances would be eliminated if there was no acoustical body to contend with."[48] Put simply, a solid body electric guitar offered new musical possibilities, and further development over the next decades added an increasing series of electric tools for musical use; the result was quite a different musical instrument than the traditional acoustic guitar.

On November 2, 1939, Lonnie was in the studio for his own session using one of the new electric guitars. This session and three further ones were made for RCA's Bluebird record label, which was launched in 1933 as a less expensive line of 78 RPM records—35 cents instead of the 75 cents of their regular line.

In that session, Lonnie made eight recordings with that early electric guitar. He also had women on his mind. That was not an unusual condition for Lonnie, but in these cases he was clearly reflecting on the vagaries of man-woman relationships, as most of the titles demonstrate: "Why Women Go Wrong," "She's Only a Woman," "She's My Mary" (probably about his ex-wife), and "Trust Your Husband." "Jersey Belle Blues" is about being lonely for lost love; "The Loveless Love" is a variation on the old classic "Careless Love"; and "Nothing But a Rat" is about a man friend betraying him with his wife. It makes one wonder what was going on in Lonnie's love life in late 1939! Frankly, these recordings display pretty standard Lonnie Johnson blues music, lyrics and guitar playing; and unlike his first use of the electric on the Peetie Wheatstraw tune "Truckin' Thru Traffic," Lonnie doesn't make much use of the special nature of the electric guitar on these sides. His guitar work does combine well with the typically excellent piano playing of Roosevelt Sykes, though.

Lonnie made four more recordings as featured performer for Bluebird in May 1940. Only "Get Your Self Together" was notable; but it was excellent, starting with evocative lyrics: "I got rocks in my bed, and I can't sleep there no more. (Repeat) Ol' rocking chair's got me, and the blues is knockin' on my door." After an effective guitar intro, the music superbly fits the words. In the first verse, for example, his voice ascends and rises to a crescendo on "the blues" and then descends in marvelously syncopated and bluesy style through the rest of the line. After this recording, Lonnie used variations on the song for other performances.

On June 5, 1940, Lonnie made a pair of additional recordings for Decca, this time playing with a jazz band led by the great New Orleans clarinet player Johnny Dodds (who died shortly thereafter). The band included his brother Baby Dodds on drums, Natty Dominique on cornet, John Lindsay (who played with Jelly Roll Morton) on bass, Preston Jackson on trombone, and Richard M. Jones on piano (composer of one of the best-ever blues songs, "Trouble in Mind"). All were originally from New Orleans. The two sides, "Red Onion Blues" and "Gravier Street Blues," amounted to sparkling revivals of original New Orleans jazz in pure ensemble-style playing. The first had a march feel to it, and Lonnie simply played rhythm guitar; the second included a short, rollicking solo by Lonnie on guitar, with strong accents. These two recordings contributed to the revival of "Dixieland" or traditional jazz that occurred in the 1940s.

The other most notable Lonnie J recordings of the early '40s were some privately made "live" recordings on acetate records (before tape was available) of Lonnie and his Trio at Square's Boulevard Lounge on January 6, 1941. The first is his original "Falling Rain," and it's interesting because we hear a rare return by Lonnie to piano playing in a public gig. His very nice, rolling, jaunty, blues piano playing takes up where he left off in those 1926 recordings with his brother. On higher notes, his singing voice sounds a little raw on this one (too much smoke in the club at that point?), but his singing technique in general matched those 1940 recordings. He also demonstrates on this tune and on the following one how he just got better and better at syncopation in his singing, which gave a jazzy enhancement to the feel of the song.

"Rocks in My Bed," the second recorded song, is a variation on "Get Yourself Together." It starts with a heavy beat by the bass, and then Lonnie takes off on guitar, backed by rhythm guitarist Dan Dixon and the bass player. The trio's strikingly rhythmic performance in the first section of this recording sounds like a precursor to 1950s Rock & Roll recordings, especially with the room acoustics sounding like the atmospherics of those mid-'50s Rock & Roll 45s. Later, Lonnie adds more intricate Lonnie-style guitar lines. He is playing acoustic guitar for these recordings, yet he and his partners really *rock*, especially in the early part of the song. The final recorded tune was Lonnie's take-off on Gershwin's famous "I Got Rhythm," here appropriately titled "More Rhythm." This is also driving, energetic music that is fun to hear—basically a Rhythm & Blues version of the Gershwin tune. It is a treasure to have these windows on Lonnie's club performances in the period.

On February 7, 1941, Lonnie was back in the recording studio, this time with Lil Armstrong accompanying him on piano and Andrew Harris on bass from the Three Deuces gig. They first recorded a new version of Lonnie's song "Crowing Rooster Blues," for which he added two new verses on the story of men spending their hard-earned money on the pimps and prostitutes, and he hits the moral of that story pretty hard. This is the best version of this tune Lonnie recorded, and his singing is especially good, infusing the lyrics with meaning, with excellent dynamics and his best rhythmic sense. The vocal *tone* is rich and resonant in the middle and lower registers, but thins out and is less aesthetically pleasing in the higher register, as is the case with many singers. This is track 20 on *The* Ultimate *Best of Lonnie Johnson* CD.

On "That's Love," with Lil Armstrong's supportive but not flashy piano accompaniment, we see the first step in what would become Lonnie's increasing inclination to sing pop ballads. The final song they recorded in that session was another emotive ballad, "In Love Again." In

CD liner notes, blues researcher-writer Chris Smith offered this worthy comment on Lonnie's ballad singing tendencies and abilities: "'In Love Again' is one of the ballads that Lonnie was so good at, to the despair of those who want to put blues singers into musical straitjackets." Blues and jazz writer Sam Charters offered another perspective on Lonnie's desire to sing ballads: "It is obvious that in the ballads he found a counterbalance to the cynicism of the blues."[49]

Lonnie's "Chicago Blues" (which I borrowed for the second part of the chapter title) is quite negative about people in Chicago, at least those he had connected with: "My first night in Chicago, my friends they treated me fine. But overnight, they changed like daylight savings time. And everything I really wanted, I had to lay my money down on the line." Must have been a bad spot with his people in Chi-town. The melody on this tune is rather repetitive, and is sung in a repetitive way. Finally, "I Did All I Could" had creative variations on the melody that is essentially that of the famous Mississippi Sheiks' song, "I'm Sitting on Top of the World."[50]

Lonnie made one more set of recordings for RCA Victor's Bluebird label before the war and a recording ban stopped recording for a good while. In that February 13, 1942, session he was joined by the outstanding blues pianist Blind John Davis. Throughout the session, Blind John's vigorous, richly textured, bluesy, rolling and rhythmic piano work made a big contribution to the recordings; and his piano and Lonnie's guitar playing coordinated beautifully. Various of these recordings, like the 1941 live recordings at Square's Boulevard Lounge, demonstrate how Lonnie was already updating his music to the Rhythm & Blues era that was just under way.

Just two months after the Pearl Harbor attack, with World War II raging in Europe and now in the Pacific, war matters were on people's minds. Lonnie responded with three recordings in this session. Two of those recordings were "From 20 to 44" (the age range of men who could be drafted), which included well-toned singing by Lonnie; the other was "The Last Call," with a superb piano solo by Blind John.

"Rambler's Blues" was a direct take-off from his 1927 "Roaming Rambler Blues" and it is the real standout from this session. Thus, this was the second of two versions of the song that B. B. King said was the one record he would take to that proverbial desert island. There was good reason for that: Lonnie's singing on this tune is excellent, with real power and dynamics, superbly employed syncopation, deepened nuance, and rich tone quality, all dramatically expressing the meaning of the lyrics. On "Rambler's Blues," the piano playing of Blind John and Lonnie's guitar work are in especially effective coordination.

His singing on all of these recordings shows the continuing development of his vocal technique and style. From "Mr. Johnson Swing," "New Falling Rain Blues," and "Blue Ghost Blues" in his March 1938 session to "Get Your Self Together" in May 1940 to "Crowing Rooster Blues" in February 1941, Lonnie demonstrated how he had increasingly become one of the best singers in the blues and Rhythm & Blues realms. "Rambler's Blues," along with the club work in Square's Boulevard Lounge described earlier, showed the beginning of Lonnie's achievement of *greatness* as a singer—in addition to his long-proven greatness on guitar.

The other recordings from the February 1942 session are not especially noteworthy. They include "The Devil's Woman," which is a remake of "You'll Be Making Whoopee in Hell Tonight," with a few changes in lyrics; it's charged with more energy, and is more in an Rhythm & Blues mode than the earlier recording.

## Playing for the Public in Chicago, 1943–1947

After the engagement for Lonnie's trio at Square's Boulevard Lounge ended at the end of 1942, he started playing at Joe's Hickory House on South Park Avenue in the South Side in late January 1943. By March the club had been renamed and the entertainment was billed as "Joe's Deluxe Club presents Valda Gray with Lonnie Johnson, King of the Blues, and Marl Young and His Orchestra." Lonnie continued working there through the rest of 1943, though in October Marl Young's band was replaced by another.

In an interview I did with Marl Young—a sharp 87 at the time of the interview—he distinctly remembered the owner of the place, Joe Hughes, saying to him: "We're gonna make this place *jump*; I'm gonna bring in Lonnie Johnson." Marl said Lonnie was the featured musical artist there. But the place also had a show with a difference: female impersonators performed. Marl Young's five-piece band backed up Lonnie, who mostly sang, but sometimes would play his guitar; they did the blues. Marl told me, "The response [to Lonnie] from the audience was great, and the crowds were fantastic, he really drew them in."[51]

On June 29 and 30 and July 1–4, 1944, Lonnie made special appearances on a bill for the "Grand Opening of the Greater Grand Terrace Café," with singer Billie Holiday receiving top billing. This continued with Billie through much of July; Lonnie got second billing as "Famous Blues Singer and His Guitar." Square's, now called "Square's Steak House," featured "Lonnie Johnson's Gang," which was Lonnie and Ernest Smith's Trio.

Significantly, in August in the Rhumboogie club, just a few blocks from Square's, the other greatest blues guitarist was performing, namely, T-Bone Walker. T-Bone increasingly demonstrated his guitar virtuosity and verve as the 1940s rolled along.

Speaking of the remarkable T-Bone Walker, in an interview, reflecting on those years and Lonnie's appearances in Chicago, he gave a vivid word picture of Lonnie's sartorial splendor, as well as paying tribute to his singing: "Lonnie Johnson. . . . Wonderful blues singer. . . . Sharpest cat in the world, wore a silk shirt blowing in the wind in the winter, nice head of hair, and a twenty-dollar gold piece made into a stick pin."[52]

Square's Steak House was clearly glad to have Lonnie Johnson back performing there. From November 1944 to May 1945 the establishment put a series of ads designed to look like news articles in the entertainment section of the *Chicago Defender* about Lonnie's work there, with headings like, "Lonnie Johnson Gets in Groove at Square's Now" (which said, "Lonnie is a big favorite on the Southside and he is proving a fine tonic for the place right now"). As best I can tell, he continued at Square's through 1946. On September 6, Lonnie played in a concert at Orchestral Hall featuring the "rediscovered" original New Orleans jazz trumpet standout, Bunk Johnson.

Speaking of such jazz folks, in the mid-1940s Lonnie also played in what was a combination of concerts and jam sessions with the Chicago Hot Club (jazz aficionados and musicians). There is a good photo of him at the front at a summer 1946 session with blues pianist Little Brother Montgomery, jazz trumpeter Lee Collins, bassist John Lindsay, and others. He occasionally played in monthly concerts with the "New Orleans Wanderers," as well, which included most of the same people, and sometimes included bassist Bill Johnson, in his mid-70s, who had played with the Original Creole Band, one of the founding groups of jazz. Lonnie played in these sessions as late as October 19, 1947.[53]

Author Bruce Cook offered insightful observations of Lonnie at one of those mid-1940s Chicago Hot Club performances. His father had introduced him to jazz as a young fellow, and then he got interested in the blues:

> I remember my impression in listening to him was that it would be hard to imagine anybody playing better. There is a quality that the real virtuoso communicates, an added dimension to his playing, that makes it immediately and recognizably distinct from that of one who is merely proficient. Lonnie Johnson had it . . . , playing deep rolls and treble runs that he extended with amazing subtlety, torturing out the last nuance of melody from those simple blues chords.
>
> . . . I remember his voice as hushed and rather insinuating in tone; he was a singer with a style that managed to say more than words alone might allow. . . . He was the very picture of the urban bluesman, and that was the image he projected as he sang—knowing, worldwise, a man who had no illusions left but who still had pride in himself, a kind of played-out masculinity that you might associate with Bogart. All that was Lonnie Johnson.[54]

The final major job of his Chicago years was at the Flame Club on Indiana Avenue. From early 1947 through May '47 he was joined by his old friend Roosevelt Sykes on piano and by "Big" Crawford on bass. (The latter is notable as the bass player on six of the earliest Muddy Waters recordings.) Then a September 13, 1947, ad in the *Chicago Defender* for Club Georgia announced its "first anniversary party," and the featured attraction is a "'Battle of the Blues' between (John Lee) Sonny Boy Williamson and Lonnie Johnson," who are listed as going at it "every Friday, Saturday and Sunday."

That calls up a moving tale Lonnie told in an interview:

I went into the Flame Club . . . [and] I was workin' with Roosevelt Sykes . . . And Sonny Boy Williamson was workin' right around the corner. So we would alternate on our intermission time and [I'd] go 'round to the Plantation Club and . . . play with him, and on his intermission time he'd come 'round to the club where I was workin' at . . .

So, he just come 'round, and then he went back, went 'round the corner. He said, "I'll see you after a while, when you get off. Come on 'round to the club." I say, "OK." And about five minutes later a feller come 'round and say he's dead. . . .[55]

We know Sonny Boy Williamson was murdered on June 1, 1948, so this indicates Lonnie was back in the Flame Club with Roosevelt Sykes in late spring 1948. Lonnie played a couple of other clubs in late 1947 and early 1948 like Gatewood's Tavern, informally called "the Gate."

## Meanwhile, on the Home Front

Here's another of those personal realm mysteries that abound in Lonnie's life: On his Membership Record Card for the Chicago Musicians' Union, I found the line, "Beneficiary: Mrs. Kay Johnson. Relationship: Wife." The card is dated December 19, 1944. Evidently sometime before that date Lonnie took a wife. From indirect but strong evidence related in the next chapter, this appears to have been a formal marriage. However, in no interview did Lonnie ever say anything about her and I have no background on her.

Maybe this is the place to relate what Lonnie told his friend Roberta Barrett (nee Richards) years later: He said he didn't much like being married.[56]

## Recordings, 1944–1947

From the fourteenth of February 1942 until December 14, 1944, Lonnie made no recordings. For the World War II effort, the government began to restrict use of shellac, essential material for records in those days. Then in July 1942, the President of the American Federation of Musicians, James Petrillo, announced a ban on recording (applying to all instrumentalists, but not to vocalists) because they were concerned about the flourishing jukeboxes and the royalties musicians were not getting from that outlet, as well as the effect on live playing.[57]

On December 14, 1944, Lonnie made his final four sides for the Bluebird label, but there were no standouts here. Lonnie then signed with DISC records and on a July 1946 session he made twelve recordings. Blind John Davis again provided fine piano accompaniment. Several sides further demonstrate Lonnie's increasing inclination to perform emotional ballads, including "My Last Love," "I'm in Love With You," "Why I Love You," and "In Love Again." "Blues for Everybody" and "Blues in My Soul," were instrumentals, with Lonnie and Blind John serving up good, creative playing. Finally, Lonnie cut six tunes for another independent record company, Aladdin. But none were noteworthy. At this point in Lonnie's recording there was a sameness about them, and his singing was only fair; it seemed uninspired, with not much in the way of dynamics and so on. To my ears, Lonnie lost a bit of his groove and got into a musical rut in his final year of recording in Chicago.

# 7

# Rhythm & Blues

## Rhythm & Blues—And the First Rock & Roll Record?

The Blues Collection reissue label put out two CDs of Lonnie's recordings from 1937 to 1952. They were titled, *Lonnie Johnson: The Rhythm & Blues Years*. This was appropriate because Lonnie moved with the times, amped up many recordings, intensified the rhythm in his music in the 1940s, and contributed to the Rhythm & Blues era—though his most famous recording in this period was a ballad. (The term "Rhythm & Blues" was actually initiated in *Billboard* magazine in 1949 to move beyond the old "race records" label, but the musical genre that the new term denoted and better characterized was underway by the early 1940s.)

As Mark Humphrey pointed out: "Johnson updated fluidly without compromising his musical personality, and this, even more than his virtuosity and influence as a guitarist, may be the quality that makes him one of the truly heroic figures of the blues."[1]

Indeed he did, and certain of his recordings are especially striking demonstrations of that, as he took himself into the Rhythm & Blues era. We got a nice peek at the beginnings of Lonnie's energized Rhythm & Blues development in the second of those live private recordings made at Square's Boulevard Lounge in Chicago in January 1941, "Rocks in My Bed"; this was a significant part of what he was doing in his club work in the 1940s, one of the reasons he "made the place *jump*," as the Chicago club owner said. "Mr. Johnson Swing" and "New Falling Rain Blues" from March 1938 demonstrate how elements of swing jazz led to

Rhythm & Blues music, especially in the hands of someone like Lonnie with his rhythmic blues and jazz background.

Then in February 1947 Lonnie was lead electric guitarist on "Home Last Night," with "Dirty Red" Nelson singing. The title almost sounds like a lullaby. It was anything but. This recording has a driving Rhythm & Blues feel, rockin' rhythm and style on the guitar by Lonnie, and what, seven to ten years later, became the essence of the early electric guitar and overall sound of the recordings that established the new musical genre of Rock & Roll.

If you compare the guitar work and overall sound in those prime founding documents of Rock & Roll—Chuck Berry's "Johnny B. Goode," "Memphis," and "Back in the USA," and Buddy Holly's "That'll Be the Day" and "It's so Easy"—the stylistic connection and evolution of electric guitar playing from Lonnie Johnson's performance on "Home Last Night" and other '40s Rhythm & Blues numbers to such prime early Rock & Roll recordings is striking.

Those connections are not surprising. Buddy Holly's favorite guitarist was Lonnie Johnson. As Jerry Allison, the drummer from Holly's band, the Crickets, has reported: "We used to sit around and listen to blues pickers like Lonnie Johnson. Like, there was a song called 'Jelly Roll' [presumably meaning 'Jelly Roll Baker' from 1947], and the style of guitar that Buddy played on 'That'll Be the Day'—that was the sort of guitar that that old blues picker played." "That'll Be the Day" was Holly's first big hit. In his autobiography, Chuck Berry said he "became a fan of Lonnie Johnson" from listening to his records played on the Black East St. Louis radio station.[2]

In fact, Lonnie's electric guitar playing on that early 1947 record sounds suspiciously to my ears like the first Rock & Roll record. Many informed observers see the prime candidates for the first Rock & Roll recording as "Good Rockin' Tonight," on two separate 1948 releases by Roy Brown and Wynonie Harris, Fats Domino's 1949 tune, "The Fat Man," or "Rocket '88" of 1951 sung by Jackie Brenston and backed by Ike Turner and his Kings of Rhythm. But since "Home Last Night" was recorded in February 1947, it could be seen as the first Rock & Roll record. There is no scientific formula for deciding what is a Rock & Roll record verses a Rhythm & Blues recording, however; it's a judgment call. And it was a process of evolution and development.

Robert Palmer suggested that assigning such exclusivist musical categories is more a convenience for nonmusicians. Indeed, for some of the first generation of rockers, asserting that what was newly called Rock & Roll was a separate category of music was suspect. Dave Bartholomew, who provided the backing for the early Fats Domino hits, said: "We had rhythm and blues for many, many a year, and here come in a couple of White people and they call it rock and roll, and it was rhythm and blues all the time!" Still, a new genre of music gradually evolved that we validly came to call Rock & Roll. It's interesting to consider the origins of the music that became so huge in the second half of the twentieth century and to look at the stage in which Rhythm & Blues was evolving into Rock & Roll music. The evidence I've just presented shows that Lonnie Johnson was, if anything, ahead of the wave in that transition, and was a significant influence on the musical minds of key founding fathers of Rock & Roll.[3]

## "Tomorrow Night" and King Records

On December 10, 1947, Lonnie made his first four recordings for King Records of Cincinnati. The fourth tune recorded that day was "Tomorrow Night"—which was *not* written by Lonnie and had been previously recorded.[4] But he liked the song—as noted at the end of chapter 6 he was increasingly drawn to emotional ballads—and he drew on his ever-developing vocal skill and recorded a marvelous version. It became the biggest hit of his career, reaching number one on the Rhythm & Blues chart and number 19 on the pop chart in 1948, the year of its release. And it kept reverberating in the musical world. Lonnie's vocal work isn't great in the first line of the recording, with a thin and nasal tone; but it got much better thereafter. And he used his other vocal skills to sing the song passionately, with excellent dynamics, and to convincingly and movingly convey the meaning of the lyrics. More generally, he created a musical atmosphere in the recording with how he delivered the song that made it resonate in people's hearts and souls.

Indeed, "Tomorrow Night" was one of those songs that captured the spirit of the time and became a key part of the "soundtrack" of people's lives in those immediate postwar years when folks in America were longing for some good feelings after the terror and turmoil of World War II. It also had quite an impact on other major musicians.

B. B. King loved the record. In his autobiography he spoke with deep insight about Lonnie's broader approach to music-making and commented on the quality of his singing on ballads and similar music and how "Tomorrow Night" reflected all that:

> Lonnie was more sophisticated. His voice was lighter and sweeter, more romantic, I'd say. He had a dreamy quality to his singing and a lyrical way with the guitar. . . . Lonnie sang a wide variety of songs. I liked that. I guess he found the strict blues form too tight. He wanted to expand. When he sang "Tomorrow Night," probably his most famous ballad, I understood that he was going to a place beyond the blues that, at the same time, never left the blues.[5]

(B. B. referred to Lonnie's voice as "lighter and sweeter, more romantic"; but from the 1940s through 1967 Lonnie demonstrated on a number of other recordings that he could also sing with power, grit and soul. The sixth track on *The* Ultimate *Best of Lonnie Johnson* CD, "Don't Ever Love," is perhaps the most dramatic demonstration of that ability.)

The great blues guitarist Buddy Guy fondly remembered hearing "Tomorrow Night" on the radio down in Louisiana when he was in his teens. Even Robert Lockwood, Jr., loved the song. Lockwood was an outstanding blues musician and was a much more sophisticated guitarist than many other blues musicians, sometimes merging into jazz. By his later years he was at times rather cynical, even bitter, feeling he had never gotten the attention he deserved. So, it surprised me a bit when Lockwood told me in a fall 2005 interview: " 'Tomorrow Night,' I never will forget it. I don't have it on record now; I wish I could find it." (I sent him a copy.)[6]

## Lonnie and Elvis

Then there was Elvis. Let me first remind you of what Peter Guralnick reported in the first volume of his biography of Elvis Presley: "Charlie's Record Shop in Memphis . . . was where Elvis first played for girlfriend Dixie the original of one of the songs *he sang all the time*, Lonnie Johnson's 'Tomorrow Night'"[7] (emphasis added).

Elvis recorded "Tomorrow Night" in late 1954 in the very beginning of his recording career at the subsequently famous Sun Studio in Memphis. What makes Lonnie Johnson's vocal performance on this song particularly notable in the history of popular music is that Elvis copied Lonnie's performance, from rushed phrasings in certain places to vocal tone, dynamics, and general style. This can be heard on *The Ultimate Best of Lonnie Johnson* CD, with Lonnie's original and the Elvis version back-to-back (tracks 22 and 23). Especially important to note is a specific vocal technique Lonnie used that Elvis copied: a soulful cascading down several notes as "night" in "tomorrow night" is sung in the chorus. It's more than a vocal glissando on a descending line, with the distinct steps involved, yet there is a smooth flow of line; that and the special, ultra-rich and emotive vocal tone gives the technique deeper musical and expressive character. This particular vocal technique became a signature element of the Elvis singing style. You can first hear this specific element at one minute and twelve seconds into Lonnie's original of "Tomorrow Night" and at one minute eight seconds into the Elvis track on the CD. (Elvis's cover of the song was not released at the time; but the influence on his singing is very evident.)

**. . . And Bob Dylan** "Tomorrow Night" evidently continued to reverberate for a long time: A fellow named Bob Dylan recorded his own version of the song, borrowing some of Lonnie's phrasing, on his late 1992 CD, *Good As I Been to You.*

The success of "Tomorrow Night" and a couple of other hits re-energized Lonnie, and they led to some significant concert and club bookings. Most notable was his dual headlining appearance in June 1948 with jazz tenor saxophone great Lester Young at the ultimate temple of Black music, Harlem's Apollo Theater. Lonnie's billing in an Apollo ad in the *New York Age* amusingly said, "The Newest Recording Star"— over twenty-two years after his first hit record was released! Underneath Lonnie's name it more appropriately said, "Tomorrow Night," which further demonstrates the impact of that recording. Starting in late July,

Lonnie played at another major club, the Baby Grand Café in New York (specifically, in Brooklyn); the corresponding ad, again, simply had "Tomorrow Night" listed under his name, this time with the further note: "(Latest Hit Record)." On August 11, Lonnie appeared in another of those big benefit concerts, in this case, at the large Lewisohn Stadium. This one had a remarkable list of performers, including Ella Fitzgerald, Duke Ellington, Louis Armstrong, Sarah Vaughn, Billie Holiday, Bill "Bojangles" Robinson, Count Basie, and others. What a show that must have been![8]

In later 1948 through 1950, Lonnie played with major New Orleans jazz veteran Kid Ory and band at Carnegie Hall as part of the "Dixieland Jazz" revival trend, and he played clubs in Detroit and Chicago.[9]

In the second half of 1948, Lonnie, with his wife Kay Johnson, moved to Cincinnati. With royalties coming in from "Tomorrow Night" and with a home loan from East Clifton Savings & Loan, they bought a nice three-level house with a turret on the right at 828 Rockdale Avenue.

Lonnie's house in Cincinnati, 1940s. PHOTO BY DEAN ALGER, 2007

## King Records

King Records was formally started in August 1944 with Syd Nathan as leading force, although they had actually released their first two records in late 1943. An interesting side note on Lonnie's signing with King: On his artist information sheet, besides writing that he was born in 1900, as he had begun to regularly claim, Lonnie said, his "favorite pastime is watching ballet." (That's the only place I've come across that bit of information, but given the depth of his musical and artistic appreciation, why not?)[10]

From the late 1940s on, Lonnie was increasingly concerned about people—including the younger ladies he preferred—thinking him *old*. So, he routinely claimed he was born in 1900—or avoided the subject. But there was a second reason for claiming 1900 as his birth year, in my interpretation of Lonnie psychology; and, as in historic musical matters, he again parallels Louis Armstrong. Louis always said he was born on July 4, 1900, while later research revealed he was actually born in August 1901. Both Louis and Lonnie wanted to be registered as born in 1900 because they wanted to be perceived as children of the twentieth century—and as central figures in the development of the leading music of the century, which they were. This interpretation is implicitly confirmed in something Lonnie said to Max Jones in 1963: "I was born in 1900, so I'm as old as the century."[11]

King was one of those independent record companies that sprang up in the postwar years and produced recordings and boosted music and musical trends that the big older companies like RCA Victor and Columbia were slow to grasp. King was interesting in that it actually started by recording what was then called "Hillbilly" music, which were released on the King label; in 1946 King put out *Hillbilly Boogie* by the Delmore Brothers, for example. Soon thereafter Syd Nathan was recording Black blues, Rhythm & Blues, and jazz musicians and released them on the Queen label. But in August 1947 they retired the Queen label, and all the Hillbilly/Country and Black music was released on the King label.

That melding of the two different musical—and sociological— realms on one label was symbolic. Steven Tracy found a 1949 *Cincinnati*

*Post* story that reported on how King "had a commitment to smashing Jim Crow":

> "Cincinnati is a border town," said the skeptics, "you can't get Negroes and White people to work together. It's too close to the South." [But Ben Siegel] told Syd Nathan . . . that he'd be King's personnel manager only if they'd let him run his department as he saw fit. They backed his policies.
>
> King hires 400 employees, and the non-discrimination policies have needed no "backing." Here's the way things stand today: The musical director, assistant office manager, foreman of the mill room, set up man on the production line, assistant promotion director, legal secretary, a dozen stenographers, and 20 percent of the factory workers are Negroes.
>
> There is a Chinese bookkeeping machine operator and a Japanese comptometer operator.
>
> All groups have joined in on summer picnics, Christmas parties, and baseball games. . . . "We pay for ability," says Mr. Siegel, "and ability has no color, no race, and no religion."[12]

Thus, it was quite appropriate that Lonnie became a King recording artist. It was appropriate in another way, in light of Lonnie's move into Rhythm & Blues music and his several precursor-to-early-Rock & Roll recordings: The Wynonie Harris recording of "Good Rockin' Tonight" was recorded by King in December 1947 and released in '48, and Roy Brown's version of "Good Rockin' Tonight" was also released in '48, on the new King subsidiary label, De Luxe. A string of important R & B artists recorded for King, from Hank Ballard and the Midnighters to sax king Earl Bostic; those R & B artists culminated in James Brown and the development of soul music. (Brown's recordings were released on another King label, Federal.)

Further, as a much later Cincinnati newspaper article on the King Records story pointed out: "A decade before Sam Phillips' Sun Records revolutionized pop music by signing Elvis Presley to sing white country tunes and black blues, King was mixing and matching the music of black and white artists."[13]

That "mixing and matching" of Hillbilly/Country music and the music of Black artists directly involved Lonnie Johnson. In a late 1949 session, Lonnie made recordings of two songs by one of the leading Country music acts of the time, the Delmore Brothers: "Troubles Ain't Nothing But the Blues" and "Blues Stay Away from Me." Those song titles are still another illustration of what a profound impact the blues had on Country music. The "B" line of the standard 12-bar blues form of "Troubles Ain't Nothing But the Blues" includes a wonderful manifestation of the cross-breeding of blues and Country: "Worries, so doggone hard to lose." "Doggone" is a real Country music colloquialism used as the accent word in that line in the Delmores' blues song; we could call this "*Country* Blues" in a different sense. Lonnie sang both of those tunes quite well, in a blues style, and added very good electric guitar solos in the middle of each.

In other ways King furthered the "music and Civil Rights" phenomenon introduced in chapter 1. As it was articulated by Ralph Bass, who ran the Federal Records label for King and later was a key player at Chess Records:

> We brought Blacks and Whites together with music. I remember in Atlanta, Georgia, when "The Twist" came out, Hank Ballard was the featured act at this big club and . . . they were lined up, Blacks and Whites together all down Auburn Avenue, to try to get into this club. The police came, man, and they said, "We'll have a riot. Let 'em alone; let 'em go." So, here [we had] Whites and Blacks together. We gave them a common denominator, a common love. We appealed to the one emotion that the law couldn't do a damn thing about, their common love of music.[14]

Lonnie's other recordings for King released in 1948–1952 included several remakes of earlier songs: "Friendless Blues" (recorded December 1947, from "Friendless and Blue"), "Falling Rain Blues" (December '47), "Working Man's Blues" (a December '47 version of "Crowing Rooster Blues"), and "Jelly Roll Baker" (December '47). In my judgment, this rendition of "Jelly Roll Baker" is his best recording of this classic Lonnie J tune. It's track 21 on *The* Ultimate *Best of Lonnie Johnson* CD. Illustrating how other blues musicians valued the song, the great blues pianist and singer who was a prime figure in the Muddy Waters band, Otis Spann, made a superb recording of the tune as featured performer in studio sessions in Europe in 1963.

A more up-tempo, Rhythm & Blues approach is used in this newer recording of "Jelly Roll Baker," with effective employment of the electric guitar. Lonnie sings at a high level, with fine resonance, phrasing, dynamics, and some very effective syncopated lines. A couple of times he also uses a hint of stop time effects to add drama and some musical tension to the recording.

The other sides are well done, with use of the electric guitar and more of a Rhythm & Blues approach giving a different feel to the new versions of the songs. "Friendless Blues" has special interest because Lonnie was backed by a band led by jazz trumpet player Oran "Hot Lips" Page; it also included jazz tenor sax player Hal Singer, who later provided a jazzy solo and fine backing on saxophone for Lonnie's masterful 1960 recording, "Don't Ever Love." Hot Lips doesn't play a special solo on this record, but the band adds enriched texture to the tune.

Then there was "Backwater Blues," recorded in August 1948. In this new performance of the Bessie Smith classic Lonnie used the unique characteristics of the electric guitar, especially the greater capacity for sustain and the special electric guitar tone. Along with extraordinarily creative employment of bent notes, he used those electric guitar capacities to produce a stunning aural impressionist painting of the rising floodwaters and their impact on people, all the while maintaining a remarkable level of overall thematic coherence in the guitar music. And, when he sings "the wind began to blow," he uses the electric guitar for an effective artistic impression of the wind blowing and for musical punctuation; other similar effects are added.

I commented earlier that many have missed the artistic value of this "Backwater Blues" because they have too narrow a notion of great guitar playing as being only about fast finger-work and razzle-dazzle. Musical art is much more than that, which Lonnie demonstrated with this recording. He tops it off with truly masterful *singing*. From the first notes, Lonnie employs rich, resonant vocal tone, among his best ever, great dynamics and nuance, and with his vocal lines and inflections he compellingly conveys the meaning of the lyrics and the *feeling* of people experiencing this natural disaster. In short, with this recording, Lonnie Johnson further demonstrated he'd reached the level of greatness as a singer. With the addition of his sublime, stunningly artistic guitar work, this is no less than a masterpiece of twentieth century musical art, in my judgment. This is track 4 on *The Ultimate Best of Lonnie Johnson* CD.

King Records ad, run in *Billboard*, Dec. 1948.

Indeed, in "Backwater Blues," Lonnie's creation of that "aural impressionist painting of the rising flood waters and their impact on people," with effective expressive use of the electric guitar, is an excellent illustration of what I wrote about in the "Interlude" section in chapter 2 regarding music and modern art.

Let me briefly review some other highlights of Lonnie's King recordings. A couple of the other King records were also big hits: "Pleasing You" and "So Tired." (On the latter, a King ad said it was the "top tune in England the last ten weeks," though without record charts there until 1952, what King based that claim on is unclear.) In general, these recordings had a strong Rhythm & Blues feel. In almost all cases, Lonnie's singing was very good, with power, dynamics and verve.

"Pleasing You," from August 1948, and "Just Another Day," from the last King session in June '52, were pure emotive ballads—sometimes with lyrics, especially in the latter, edging into the sappy. But Lonnie sang them sensitively, with generally good delivery, though sometimes with less than his best vocal tone. "Nobody's Lovin' Me" (September 1950) was written by King's Artists and Repertoire man, Henry Glover, and is like a bluesy version of an old Tin Pan Alley song—very polished, with written-to-please lyrics and a nice, catchy melody. Lonnie sang it well, and performed it with strong Rhythm & Blues rhythm; but it is not a really significant recording.

"Playing Around," on the other hand, was a pure instrumental. This one is a bit of a gem, with Lonnie playing hot electric guitar licks and lines, and with Paul Renfro playing soulful tenor sax inspired by Lester Young ("Prez"); in fact, the intro and ending, especially, sound much like Prez on his premier recording with the Basie band, "Lester Leaps In." Herman Smith adds some jazzy piano backing and a fine solo.

The rest of the King recordings are strong Rhythm & Blues work. In one tune, Lonnie did a direct take-off from a big R & B hit by Louis Jordan, the combination novelty-funky-silly tune, "Ain't Nobody Here But Us Chickens," recorded in August 1946. In September 1950, Lonnie made "Nothin' Clickin' Chicken," which included a rockin' Lonnie electric guitar solo in this intensely R & B number, and also included a very good piano solo. Other recordings in the King sessions were: "It Was All in Vain," "Me and My Crazy Self," "You Can't Buy Love," "You Only Want Me When You're Lonely," and "Just Another Day." One downside to Lonnie's playing on these recordings is that, on four or five of the sides, he plays a guitar intro that is just a slight variation on the intro to "Tomorrow Night." There was a lack of creativity in the guitar playing on these recordings.

While in Cincinnati, Lonnie performed across the Ohio River in Newport, Kentucky. Newport, for a long time, was a wide-open town, and the clubs would keep going all night; it could also be a pretty wild place, at times. His principal gig was at the 333 Club, appearing as guest artist with the Frank Payne Trio, which continued through much of 1949. Frank Payne said, "He was very popular with the fans there, the patrons."[15] Lonnie also made several recordings for King with Payne's trio in April and May 1949.

Lonnie returned to Cleveland to play at Jack's Musical Bar starting in later October 1951. His performances there were well received; succeeding weekly ads for Jack's in the *Cleveland Call and Post* said, "Held over!

2nd Smash Hit [week]!"; "Held Over! 3rd Smash Hit!"; . . . "Held Over! 5th Big Week." His engagement ended in January.[16]

## England, Leaving Cincy and Gone to Philly, Rama Records

**A Performance Tour in England, 1952** In 1952, with more interest in the blues in Great Britain, Lonnie got the opportunity to do a concert tour in England (England only, it didn't extend into the rest of Great Britain). He was enthused about this tour, but his reception was not as good as he hoped. Lonnie's increasing embrace of ballad singing was a good part of the problem. It wasn't that he sang the ballads poorly, rather, it was a matter of expectations.

The Dean of British blues researcher-writers, Paul Oliver, wrote to me about his observations regarding Lonnie's performances, and about the English blues fans who knew of Lonnie and were drawn to his shows in that '52 concert tour:

> There were great expectations of Lonnie's visit; but there was much dis-
> appointment during and after it. He had misjudged the audience. This
> was probably based on his experience of U.S. White audiences and folk
> clubs. Here, he played and sang too sweetly, with items like "I Left My
> Heart in San Francisco" losing, not gaining, him an audience.

Jazz writer Steve Voce, however, had a little different take on Lonnie's performances:

> Lonnie made his second visit over here in 1952 [after the apparent
> 1917–1919 trip] and delighted his audiences with a high percentage
> of previously unheard material. Some of the diehards were hugely dis-
> tressed by the proportion of ballads which Lonnie included in his pro-
> grammes. He has a fetching manner with these songs and, although
> some of them are banal, I find them largely attractive, and since Lonnie
> has such a determined fondness for them, they must be accepted as a
> vital part of his work.[17]

I should note that it was not Lonnie who served as a principal spur to the growing British interest in the blues in the early 1950s. Instead, it was a performance tour the previous year by Big Bill Broonzy that provided the principal spark, along with a 1950–1951 tour by Josh White.

While British expectations and Lonnie's current musical inclinations made for an English concert tour that was not as successful as he would have liked, one development was both very satisfying and was still another manifestation of the pervasive influence of Lonnie Johnson.

Tony Donegan, originally from Glasgow, was one of the British fellows who got very interested in American blues, jazz and folk music. He boosted his knowledge of that music by listening (in these immediate post-World War II years) to American Armed Forces Radio and by going to the library of the American Embassy in London and listening to "everything they had" in those areas of music. He built his skills as a musician and formed the Tony Donegan Jazz Band. In June 1952 his band got the chance to play in a show at the Royal Festival Hall supporting American pianist Ralph Sutton and "one of Donegan's idols, Lonnie Johnson." After they played, Donegan got Lonnie to autograph his banjo, "something he was very proud of." The official emcee for the show was evidently under-informed about these musicians, because he introduced Lonnie as "Tony Johnson" and Donegan as "Lonnie Donegan." His band members had lots of fun thereafter calling him "Lonnie Donegan," and, with his great appreciation for Lonnie Johnson's musical artistry, he made his stage name Lonnie Donegan thereafter. (The lead acoustic guitar-playing, especially in the intro, on the recording "Dead or Alive" from 1956 by Donegan and his band shows striking evidence of Lonnie Johnson's musical influence; but I'm told by British music writer Chris Smith that it is almost certainly Denny Wright of that band who is doing the Lonnie-like guitar-playing. But then, that's still more evidence of Lonnie's wide influence.)[18] Recordings were made of nine or ten of the songs performed at the concert, though they were not issued; there are also reports that backstage recordings were made of Lonnie J playing with "Lonnie" D.

Lonnie Donegan went on to be the leading figure in the "skiffle band" movement of the second half of the 1950s in Britain, which was focused on playing folk and blues music. In the late '50s through the beginning of the '60s, skiffle bands served as the launch pad for the musicians who went on to make up the Beatles, the Rolling Stones, etc., and in turn, made Rock music history. George Harrison, for example, was at first a bit intimidated by the American Rock & Roll music. Then "he discovered reigning skiffle superstar Lonnie Donegan. George was electrified by . . . Donegan's music and the emotions it brought out in him."[19] And Harrison was aware of Donegan's interest in Lonnie.

## Leaving Cincinnati, Gone to Philly, Recording for Rama

Lonnie made his final records in the '50s for King on June 3, 1952, just before he left for the English tour. By 1953, things were deteriorating for Lonnie Johnson. Once again he had money problems, despite the big hits of just four and five years earlier. In addition to his fortunes in the musical world declining again, he was probably irresponsible with the big royalty checks he had gotten from "Tomorrow Night," and others. (He said his first royalty check for "Tomorrow Night" was $41,000; according to the U.S. Bureau of Labor Statistics, that would be $394,750 in 2013.[20]) He was not making his monthly mortgage payments, his troubles mounted, and on September 15, 1953, East Clifton Savings & Loan began a foreclosure action against the Johnsons' house; a division of King Records was also involved. Later, an officer of a King subsidiary got a legal order to stop distribution of any profits from sale of the house going to the Johnsons, but only Kay was named as defendant, and Kay was listed as "whereabouts unknown." It appears Lonnie hastily left Cincinnati under a debt cloud regarding his house, and Kay did the same, and they apparently went their separate ways.[21]

**Back to Philadelphia** Lonnie's retreat led him back to friendly territory in Philadelphia. At first, he still had some public presence and momentum from his big hits for King Records. For example, he had a return engagement at the Baby Grand Café in New York in August 1953. At times he also did some local club playing. As late as 1956, he made a few more recordings for the small, short-lived label, Rama. Little is known about these sessions, and the original master recordings are not available.

There is not even certainty as to where these recordings were made. Lonnie was backed by Frank Payne on piano, with whom he'd worked in Cincinnati/Newport, Kentucky, and unknown persons performed on bass and drums. He recorded eight titles. Perhaps the first that should be mentioned is "Will You Remember," which was a follow-up or "answer" to "Tomorrow Night." This song uses the "Tomorrow Night" lyrics as the base, and then does variations on a number of the lines to make it a follow-up. It uses the same electric guitar intro that was used on its forerunner. Lonnie sings the song in similar manner as the original, and generally as well. On the surface, another standout here is unusual: Lonnie sings a very fine and passionate version of the classic ballad, "Vaya Con Dios." The guitar used here is not his usual electric one of this period; it sounds rather like he found one of those old Mexican 12-string guitars to use for some interesting and unusual guitar music, but I can't swear to that.

The eight Rama recordings were actually made in two sessions. The musicians backing Lonnie for the first four songs illustrate just how obscure these sessions are: Otherwise authoritative discographies such as that by Mike Leadbitter list "Don't Make Me Cry Baby," "My Woman Is Gone," and "Stick With It Baby" as having only Frank Payne on piano and unknown bass and drums musicians backing Lonnie. But listening to the recordings makes clear there is actually a full Rhythm & Blues band backing him, including horns. These records, instrumentally and vocally, carry on directly from Lonnie's work at King, producing very good, driving Rhythm & Blues recordings. ("My Woman Is Gone" borrows the gist of its opening line of lyrics from T-Bone Walker's signature 1946 song, "(They Call It) Stormy Monday": "Ev'rybody cries the blues Tuesday, but Monday's just as bad.") Two of the songs recorded in the second session, "This Love of Mine" and "I Found a Dream," were pure emotive ballads, which Lonnie sang quite well. On these tunes he used an acoustic guitar, and on "I Found a Dream," a favorite ballad of his own composition, Lonnie makes especially effective use of the acoustic for accompanying himself, and plays a guitar solo that's perfectly suited to the music.

Mostly, after the initial year or so in Philadelphia, Lonnie was back again being a "workin' man," however. Indeed: "The old guitar sat while Lonnie did home construction work as a carpenter's helper."[22] Evidently, he also did some club playing, given the following.

**Meanwhile, on the Home Front** After Lonnie settled into life in Philadelphia, and while playing at a local club, he met Susie Small and they got involved. Susie was much younger than Lonnie and was the daughter of Tommy Small, a DJ ("Dr. Jive") on WWRL radio in New York. Tommy was also the brother of Ed Small, founder of Small's Paradise, one of the Harlem clubs that were a significant part of the history of jazz and other Black music; Tommy later took over as owner of Small's Paradise.

## Race, Records and Young People—And a Culture in Transition

This chapter and previous ones included discussion of ways the music, musicians and the whole process of musical performance played an increasingly significant role in progress on civil rights. In two segments in this chapter we saw how the King Records organization played such a role, and how some of the records they produced and concert performances of their artists began to chip away at racist restrictions in the South.

Indeed, the developments in Black music and culture and Whites' increasing response to them, especially on the part of young people, continued to make waves in and intensified their transformation of American society. The mid- to late-1950s saw Rock & Roll burst on the scene, evolving from Rhythm & Blues; it increasingly took by storm the music scene and young people's attention and enthusiasm. As many have noted, it drew especially on the powerful music developed by Blacks, from Louis Armstrong to Lonnie Johnson to Louis Jordan, as well as Country music sources. In the mid- to late-'50s, the founding fathers of Rock & Roll were electrifying young people.

But it wasn't just about music. As with the earlier meaning of jazz and blues, Elvis Presley, Chuck Berry, Carl Perkins, and others meant something more: Elvis Presley "personified Rock & Roll's youthful promise of liberation, its inarticulate defiance of the decade's bland conformism." Speaking of Carl Perkins, and implicitly referring to Chuck Berry, Little Richard, etc., Bob Dylan articulated what these musicians meant to him and many others when they heard and saw them in the late 1950s: "He really stood for freedom. That whole sound stood for all the degrees of freedom. It would just jump right off that turntable. . . . Everything—the vocabulary of the lyrics and the sound of the instruments."[23]

Now, that quote above spoke of "inarticulate defiance of the . . . bland conformism." Well, with Dylan in the lead, singer-songwriters in the 1960s produced articulate, powerful music that questioned the status quo and stimulated and expanded people's musical, cultural, and political thinking.

Further, the tale of Chuck Berry's observation to Carl Perkins about how their music was having an impact on breaking down racial barriers, related in chapter 1, was profoundly true. Making it all the more interesting was the fact that the epicenter of this brazen new music was the Southern city of Memphis, Tennessee, and the upstart Sun Studio. This new music in general featured White artists from the South like Carl Perkins, Jerry Lee Lewis, Elvis Presley, and Buddy Holly, as well as Black artists from the South like Fats Domino from New Orleans and Little Richard from Georgia. Additionally, there was Chuck Berry from St. Louis, whose initial recordings were released by Chess Records of Chicago.

A striking illustration of the impact of all that came in May 1962. At the all-White University of Alabama, a survey of students was conducted by the Cotillion Club, which asked what performers they would like to have on campus. The survey sheet listed performers in several categories—*but no Black names were included.* The questionnaire did have two final questions that indicated the Club had some sense of what was happening: "Would you favor Negro entertainers on this campus?" and, "Would you favor a complete Rock and Roll show?" In the male vocalist category, Ray Charles was favored by an "overwhelming majority"—with a write-in vote, since he was not named on the questionnaire. Many responded yes even to the generically phrased question about favoring "Negro entertainers on campus."[24]

That response by University of Alabama students in 1962 was not an isolated case, and these developments that were disturbing old Southern sensibilities started years earlier. The following story also takes us back to the section of chapter 1 on "Radio and the Transcending of Racial Barriers."

Radio station WLAC out of Nashville was one of those powerful "clear channel" stations that could be heard throughout much of the U.S. WLAC had a disc jockey named Gene Nobles who, in 1946, "was the first guy anywhere to play Black music on a power [clear channel] station." And: "As early as 1952, he was voted the most popular DJ by the students at the University of Mississippi"—which was as all-White as the University of Alabama. The other popular and pioneering WLAC DJ, "Hoss" Allen, continues the story—and adds some vital music history:

> In most Southern college towns [in the '50s], you couldn't *get* a lot of radio stations. It was often a choice between listening to country music on WSM [Nashville], or to our blues, and they'd rather listen to blues than country. We found this to be true at the University of Alabama, LSU, Georgia, Florida, all the colleges, we had them locked up. And out in the country also. White guys growing up in Tennessee, Louisiana, Mississippi, Arkansas, Texas, Alabama, if they were musically inclined, they *played* country music, but they *listened* to WLAC, as well as to the Grand Ole Opry on WSM, and it influenced them. They started trying to hold those guitar chords like blues guys, play in minor keys and stuff, but it didn't come out like Muddy Waters or Howling Wolf, it came out Rockabilly, and from rockabilly came White Rock & Roll.[25]

That helped set the scene for the extraordinary developments in the 1960s. And as Martin Luther King, Jr., said to a conference of Black radio DJs in the later '60s:

> In a real sense, you have paved the way for social and political change by creating a powerful cultural bridge between Black and White. School integration is much easier now that they share a common music, a common language, and enjoy the same dances. You introduced youth to that music and created a language of soul and promoted the dances which now sweep across race, class and nation.[26]

In a written message to the 1964 Berlin Jazz Festival, Dr. King carried the point further:

Jazz speaks for life. The Blues tell the story of life's difficulties, and . . . they take the hardest realities of life and put them into music, only to come out with some new hope or sense of triumph. This is triumphant music. . . .

It is no wonder that so much of the search for identity among American Negroes was championed by Jazz musicians. Long before the modern essayists and scholars wrote of "racial identity" . . . , musicians were returning to their roots to affirm that which was stirring in their souls.

Much of the power of our Freedom Movement in the United States has come from this music. It has strengthened us with its sweet rhythms when courage began to fail. It has calmed us with its rich harmonies when spirits were down. And now Jazz is exported to the world. For in the particular struggle of the Negro in America there is something akin to the universal struggle of modern man. Everybody has the Blues. Everybody longs for meaning.[27]

# 8

# Blues Revival in the '60s: Comeback Again

## Rediscovered

Lonnie Johnson's situation in the later 1950s was well described in liner notes to his first comeback album in 1960: "Lonnie's slip into obscurity was so complete this time that many persons thought he was dead." Alternatively, one writer claimed he had seen Lonnie down and out in Chicago in 1958. Indeed, Lonnie commented, "I've been dead four or five times. But I always came back. . . . I always knew that someday, somehow, somebody would find me."[1]

In late 1959 Lonnie was working as a janitor in the Ben Franklin Hotel in Philadelphia. Chris Albertson (who had come to the U.S. from Denmark not too long before) "rediscovered" him, which led to what amounted to his third comeback. Albertson subsequently became a respected jazz record producer and author of the definitive biography of Bessie Smith. At the time, however, he was a DJ at jazz radio station WHAT in Philadelphia.. (In an interview, Chris said, "The woman who owned the station was rather strange. The FM station was all White [music] and the AM station was all Black. And she had a white dog named FM and a black dog named AM."[2]) In my interview with Albertson, I asked him how the rediscovery happened:

> I was on the air seven days a week . . . , and I played everything from [saxophone jazzman John] Coltrane to Ma Rainey.

One day on air in 1959 I said, "I wonder whatever happened to Lonnie Johnson?" . . . Then I got a call from Elmer Snowden, who said, "Well, I just saw Lonnie in a supermarket; he's in Philly." [A jazz guitarist and banjo-player who also played saxophone, Snowden's first notable experience in music came when he led a band in the early 1920s, joined a little later by a young pianist named Duke Ellington; the band then became "The Washingtonians."]

And then I got a call from someone who said, "I work at the Benjamin Franklin Hotel and there's someone here, a janitor, named Lonnie Johnson. I don't know if that's the one you're looking for—he's never mentioned any music—but I can tell you he's very careful with his hands, he always uses gloves."

So I went down to the hotel . . . And when he came in, I easily recognized him. We talked, I got his phone number, and I then said I wanted someone to hear him. He had a guitar, a beat-up old guitar. I called John Hammond [of Columbia Records], whom I'd never met, and I called Orrin Keepnews of Riverside Records, whom I'd never met, and said I was going to have Lonnie Johnson over to my apartment to play on Saturday. Much to my surprise, they both said they'd be there.

So I had both Lonnie and Elmer over (they'd never played together before). I had an old British tape recorder, and I taped them as they played. Hammond was his usual self, saying, "Oh, it's marvelous, marvelous!" (That was his favorite saying.) John and Orrin talked to Elmer and Lonnie, they all had a wonderful time, and they left—and nothing happened. So, a little later I took the tape to Bob Weinstock at Prestige Records. He listened to the tape, and then he said, "Let's do an album." So, we did."[3]

(Amusingly, Lawrence Cohn, former Columbia/Epic Records Vice President, told me that John Hammond, who was famous for his discovery of great musicians, from Bessie Smith to Count Basie to Dylan and Springsteen, tended to discount Lonnie's importance, mostly because Hammond couldn't claim credit for discovering him. Larry took special delight in needling Hammond whenever he came across something else attesting to Lonnie's greatness. This is "inside baseball," Columbia Records-style, but fun anyway.)

A little later I will discuss the album they made and other things; but first I need to set the scene with some developments in the early 1960s that were of major importance for music and for broader societal matters.

## Blues and Folk Music Revivals

Starting in the later 1950s with a few intrepid White blues lovers and 78 record collectors, several of whom were also writers, interest in the older blues musicians developed and then increased into the early 1960s. A "Blues Revival" was underway; and the rediscovery of such major early Country blues musicians as the extraordinary Son House, Big Joe Williams, Skip James, and others in the early '60s boosted that revival.

There was a parallel, overlapping development in the realm of folk music. The Folk Revival had its origins in the later 1940s and early '50s, with the playing of Woody Guthrie, Pete Seeger, The Almanac Singers and The Weavers, Josh White, Leadbelly and others, and included some crossover into the blues. The seminal LP record set, the *Anthology of American Folk Music*, released by Folkways in 1952, was a major contributor to these early developments. The 1958 release and big success of the Kingston Trio's reworked old North Carolina murder ballad, "Tom Dooley," however, really started the folk boom, which gained steam in the early '60s.

In light of this book's thesis on music and the image of African-Americans and progress towards Civil Rights, it's important to point out that the Folk Revival was not just about college kids growing beards and long hair and strumming acoustic guitars. A vital element of the Folk Revival, drawing on the heritage of Woody Guthrie and Pete Seeger and their musical partnerships and brotherhood with Black musicians like Leadbelly, Brownie McGhee, and Sonny Terry, was an active concern about America's societal problems and striving to realize the nation's proclaimed ideals. In the 1950s and 1960s the great folk and blues singer and guitarist Josh White was a significant part of that, who expressed himself in music and talk in powerful, effective manner. He—and his son, Josh White, Jr.—were deeply influenced by Lonnie. Indeed, Josh White, Jr., sent me this thought in an e-mail: "Enough cannot be said about Lonnie. I don't remember where we met and all I remember about him was that he was just a wonderful, friendly man who remembered fondly my mom and dad. We shared a stage together after my old man died and that's where I got to know the man, just a little. He was a hell of a guitar player."

These concerns were manifest in various forms, from protest songs to the involvement of Peter, Paul and Mary, Bob Dylan and Harry Belafonte in Civil Rights marches. Something of a culminating event for this involvement came at the end of the 1963 Newport Folk Festival in late July when Pete Seeger, Bob Dylan, Joan Baez, and Peter, Paul and Mary linked arms with the (Black) Student Nonviolent Coordinating Committee's Freedom Singers and sang "We Shall Overcome" and Bob Dylan's "Blowin' in the Wind."[4] One month later the historic March on Washington occurred, with Martin Luther King, Jr., presenting his now-famous "I Have A Dream" speech. Bob Dylan, Joan Baez, Peter, Paul and Mary, Josh White, Odetta, and Mahalia Jackson gave musical offerings to that event—and registered for history the folk music community's contribution to the Civil Rights movement.

Blues writer Elijah Wald made an excellent point about the development of the Blues Revival, with special focus on that much-discussed Delta blues figure, Robert Johnson. In his book *Escaping the Delta*, Wald analyzes how the current notion that people have of Robert Johnson and his significance was boosted in a major way by developments in the 1960s, especially the embrace of his music by Eric Clapton, the Rolling Stones, Led Zeppelin, and others. Robert Johnson was fairly influential and significant in the history of the blues, from the time of his recordings in 1936–1937 until the 1960s. But since the '60s, frankly, too much has been made of his role in blues history. Even many blues specialists are getting tired of endlessly hearing about Robert Johnson. Other singers and instrumentalists were more influential before the '60s, from Lonnie Johnson to Muddy Waters (Muddy was influenced by Robert, but was influenced more by Son House),[5] and their importance continues. I'm not denigrating Robert Johnson's striking music; it is simply to note that the Robert Johnson mania has been overdone. In truth, Lonnie Johnson was far more important—and a greater musician—than Robert. As Lawrence Cohn wrote me: "Lonnie Johnson's importance in Twentieth Century music is monumental—far transcending other Johnsons, including Robert"[6]—this from the man who produced the Grammy Award-winning boxed set, *Robert Johnson: The Complete Recordings.*

In the early to mid-'60s the mostly White record collectors and writers got fascinated with the old Country blues musicians, as did some White British and American Rock and blues musicians. Robert Johnson's personal story in particular provided wonderful material for myth-making (especially since he died young and in a mysterious way). The Blues and Folk Revivals and the feelings behind them were in accord with what I discussed in the "Interlude" in chapter 2 regarding people's search for more authentic experience and modes of expression in the modern, disjointed world of the twentieth century; and the '60s were prime time for such searching. Thus, as Wald wrote: "That is why Leroy Carr and Lonnie Johnson have disappeared from the pantheon, along with almost every other major [blues] star of the 1920s and 1930s. They were geniuses, perhaps, but also smooth, intelligent professionals. And as we now know [that is, as the notion developed in the "Blues Revival" of the '60s], that is not *blues.* Blues is . . . raw, dirty, violent, wild. . . ."—and from rural Mississippi Delta country and like areas.[7]

The striking irony here is that Eric Clapton was the White Rock musician most intensely interested in (some say obsessed with) and pushing the myth of Country Blues musician Robert Johnson. But in truth, Clapton's sophisticated guitar style come more from Lonnie Johnson than Robert Johnson (principally via Lonnie's profound influence on T-Bone Walker and B. B. King). Correspondingly, it's a sad injustice that Clapton has never given Lonnie the credit he deserves. I hope that will happen with this book out in the public domain. Clapton's silence stands in stark contrast to the strong statements B. B. King has made regarding Lonnie's influence and his general importance in the development of twentieth century music; and, as is noted later, T-Bone said Lonnie was his number one influence. (Clapton *has* attested to the influence of B. B. King and to his joy in recording a CD with B. B., *Riding with the King*.)

## Third Comeback

So, to return to the studio, Lonnie got the chance to start recording again. But as Chris Albertson wrote at the time, "records are not made one day and issued the next, so the day after that first album was recorded, Lonnie was back working at the hotel. After the record was released things began to happen, however." On July 8 and 9, 1960, Lonnie played an engagement at the Center, a coffee house in Philadelphia. Meanwhile, Albertson was striving to get him more substantial performance work, and the first significant job he got for Lonnie is hugely amusing, given his orientation to the ladies. Chris Albertson takes the story from here:

> Lonnie was making just $65 a week at the hotel . . . I called the William Morris office. I was naïve at the time, so I just called them up. Well, as it happened, I got a guy there named Gold who was a big Lonnie Johnson fan. He said, "He's still playing?!" He was so excited and said he'd get back to me. He called back and said, "How's four weeks in Chicago at the Playboy Club?" I said it sounds great. I think it was $350 a week.

Lonnie was at the Playboy Club from July 12 to August 8. "He was such a success that he was asked for a return engagement" at the Club. Lonnie must have thought he'd died and gone to heaven![8]

Speaking of heaven, as well as the Folk Revival, Albertson related to me what happened after Lonnie started performing at good gigs and recording again:

> And then, of course, the folk music fad was on, with Joan Baez, etc., and there was renewed interest in people like Lonnie. He benefited from that. And all of a sudden, there were all these young people who really got into Lonnie; all these young people were going out and getting his records, reading about him. He was in seventh heaven.

*1960*

- 2 -

We don't know too much about the political views of Professor Corey, but we are sure that they are as hilarious as his views on "Sex: Its Origin and Application," which were featured on Pages 79-83 of the June issue of PLAYBOY. He has advised us that he is "against U-2 and for ME-2." His campaign battle cry, which it might be handy to memorize, is "Throw the Rascal In!--Nominate Corey." Corey has also informed us that if he does win the nomination (either or both) he is going to demand "equal time," not from radio and television stations, but from his landlady. (He lives in a boarding house where they only have one bathtub.)

After Professor Corey leaves The Playboy Club on July 11 to wrap things up at the Democratic convention in Los Angeles, Rose (Chi-Chi) Murphy and her Trio, featuring Slam Stewart on bass, will open with the great guitarist and blues shouter, Lonnie Johnson, as an extra on the bill. They'll all be on hand from July 12 to August 8 in the upstairs room.

We want to apologize for the rubber-stamped message which appeared on your last statement. Unless you were already "past due," the rubber-stamped message did not apply to you, of course. Some mischievous Bunny (after all, we do hire them for their looks) made the mistake of stamping all the statements instead of just those few that were about to become past due, and a tremendous amount of confusion ensued. That rubber stamp was meant only for those members who had an unpaid balance as of the time that the new statements were being sent out.

Don't forget that your Club will be featured in a big six-page cover story in the August issue of PLAYBOY. If you're not already a PLAYBOY subscriber, you can enter a subscription by just jotting the words, "Enter my subscription" on the top portion of the statement that you return with your payment. Add an additional $6 to your payment for a one-year subscription, or $14 for a three-year subscription. You'll start receiving the magazine with the August "Playboy Club" issue. (Incidentally, PLAYBOY goes up to 60¢ on the newsstand in September, so this is an excellent time to subscribe.)

We hope that you are enjoying your Club, and that you'll let us know if you have any suggestions. We appreciate and give serious consideration to all comments received from members.

Sincerely,

THE PLAYBOY CLUB

*Hugh M Hefner*

Hugh M. Hefner
PRESIDENT

HMH/ad

Second page of letter to Playboy Club members, signed by Hugh Heffner, with note of Lonnie's appearance, 1960. COURTESY OF JOHN STEINER COLLECTION, CHICAGO JAZZ ARCHIVE, UNIVERSITY OF CHICAGO LIBRARY.

## 1960–1961: Albums, Gigs, Concert with Duke, and a Special New Friend

In spring 1960 Lonnie made three successive LP record albums for the Bluesville label of Prestige Records that were supervised by Chris Albertson. On March 8, for the first album, simply titled *Blues by Lonnie*

*Johnson*, they laid down twelve tunes at the Rudy Van Gelder recording studio in Englewood Cliffs, New Jersey, just across the Hudson River from New York. A number of the greatest jazz records were recorded at Van Gelder's studio, which many considered to be unique. According to sax player Hal Singer, the group for this session was informally called "the Lonnie Johnson All Stars."[9]

The LP included a masterpiece, "Don't Ever Love"; Albertson and Bluesville Artists and Repertoire guy, Esmond Edwards, must have quickly realized how good that recording was because it was placed first on the album (it was the eleventh song recorded). Most striking on "Don't Ever Love" is Lonnie's vocal artistry. The man who was an ultimate virtuoso guitarist in popular music sings with such power, nuance, dynamics, expressiveness, timing, and meaningful phrasing on this recording that he shows, even more compellingly, how he had achieved the level of greatness in his *singing*, as well. This song is another very good Lonnie Johnson composition; it starts with an excellent line of lyrics, words that resonate profoundly: "Did you ever love a woman, with your *whole* heart and mind?," with the extended vocal note on "*whole*" given intense emphasis. The music and Lonnie's singing are perfectly and powerfully attuned to the words. Thereafter, the lyrics explore the impact of betrayal and the lies people can tell in such relationship situations. This is the *blues*, but played in a jazz setting.

One of Lonnie's greatest strengths was his extraordinary versatility. On "Don't Ever Love," Lonnie's vocal work was anything but "lighter and sweeter" with a "dreamy quality," as B. B. King spoke of at one point; rather, this song is sung with remarkable punch and power, and has penetrating emotional impact (though in a few places the pure vocal tone is less than perfect). For this song Lonnie drew on decades of continued development of his singing technique; and that stunningly expressive singing came from a lifetime of living, from a lifetime of the ups and downs of relationships with the opposite sex, and from the deepest human feelings in general.

This track—number 6 on *The Ultimate Best of Lonnie Johnson CD*—displays work on the electric guitar that was effective for this song and well coordinated with lines, musical layers and tone colors of the rest of the band, using the tone and other characteristics of the electric guitar to appropriate effect. But there were no genuine Lonnie J gui-tar pyrotechnics here. Lonnie was more focused on his singing. He is joined here by two first-rate veteran jazz musicians: Hal Singer on tenor sax and Claude Hopkins playing perfect piano accompaniment. There are also good men on bass and drums. It is a tribute to Chris Albertson that he conceived of this session and brought these superb musicians together with Lonnie for these recordings.

This is a jazz group session, and the track shows how well Lonnie worked with a top jazz ensemble; these guys click musically like they had played together as a unit for years. It's also interesting that Lonnie didn't feel the need to hog the spotlight; he gave space for a beautiful, soulful, soaring sax solo by Hal Singer, and Singer actually opens the recording with a sax line. A fun, spirited part: As Lonnie finishes the verse and just as the sax solo is about to start, someone urges Singer on, saying, "*Rock it, rock it, ROCK it!*," and Singer soars on that sax. (That someone might have been Lonnie himself, since on the eleventh song on the album we hear an urgent, spoken "*Rock it, baby!*," which sounds more clearly like Lonnie.) Then the band, with Lonnie in the lead, kicks it into even higher gear. The spirit of the players on this recording is a joy to behold. The track is also one of those ultimate demonstrations of how the blues is a prime foundation of jazz, and how the blues can add such emotional depth and rich yet gritty texture to jazz music, especially when performed by top musicians.

Working with that excellent jazz group also seemed to energize and stimulate Lonnie. In fact, it was typical for Lonnie to be energized when working with a group in recordings, as has been mentioned earlier. His energy and intensity, passion, and soulfulness on all of the songs on this album are striking—and belie his sixty-six years of age and the long, difficult road he had traveled.

Lonnie continues his excellent singing throughout the album. All of the songs were composed by him. On tracks two through five his sing-ing is especially expressive and powerful. The second track, "No Love for Sale," also includes piano backing, which included a solo by Claude Hopkins, with fine harmonic touches and rich, rolling figures, drawing on his many years of jazz lead and accompaniment work. Again, on that tune and most of the others, Lonnie offers good, characteristic Lonnie J

guitar work, but nothing extraordinary, being more focused on his singing. On the third and fifth tracks, "There's No Love" and "She Devil,"
Hal Singer stands out again, providing excellent backing on the sax and
fine solo work. On the fourth song, "I Don't Hurt Anymore," Lonnie
adds some greater guitar pyrotechnics, starting with a more interesting
and compelling intro and a characteristic, intense, and swinging solo in
the middle, as he does on "One-Sided Love Affair."

On the seventh song on the *Blues with Lonnie Johnson* album, "Big
Leg Woman" (the title draws on a funky old blues theme), Lonnie and
the band take it up a notch and the group really *cooks* on this number, with Singer again offering an intense solo on his sax. Speaking of
cooking with the band, the tenth tune is a jazzy instrumental, but with
the soul and feel of a Rhythm & Blues number: "Blues 'Round My
Door." (That title phrase borrows the line from his song, "Sun to Sun
Blues," from way back in early 1926.) Lonnie starts it off with an interestingly different, intensely rhythmic guitar intro, with Singer's sax then
taking it for another inventive solo. Then Hopkins adds a characteristic piano interlude, followed by Lonnie increasing the intensity further with a driving guitar solo. Marvelous, musically moving stuff this
is. Oddly, Prestige reversed the song title positions for tracks 8 and 9:
"She's Drunk Again" (from a theme he used years before) is actually the
eighth track, and "There Must Be a Way" is actually number 9. Those
tunes and the final two on the album are good blues songs played in
a jazzy Rhythm & Blues manner. The album was well received at the
time; the respected jazz writer Ralph J. Gleason gave it four stars in his
review for *Down Beat*.

In April 1960, Chris Albertson brought Lonnie back to the studio, this time with Elmer Snowden. An LP album was released from
that session; and then in the CD era, Prestige (now owned by Fantasy
Records) in its "Original Blues Classics" series, put out a second CD
with ten previously unreleased songs from the session. The approach
to the recording session was interesting and laudable, which Albertson
explained in the liner notes: "The repertoire had not been planned
ahead, both had been told to play whatever came to their mind; it
is not often that a record company allows its artists such freedom,
but this system inevitably produces the best results." The results were

good; but *I* think the *unreleased* set is actually better than the originally released album.

In my interview with him, Albertson told me about the environment (in two senses) for the recording session: "It was a very rainy, blustery day outside, and it lent something to the atmosphere. We went into the studio and you could hear a pin drop, it was very quiet *inside*. And a little later, as Lonnie and Elmer got to the point where they were starting to dig each other and the music each was producing and were listening to each other, with that blustery day outside in the general background, it was very nice."

The original album, *Lonnie Johnson with Elmer Snowden: Blues and Ballads*, manifested Lonnie's increasing interest in emotive ballad singing. The Prestige Artists and Repertoire man, Esmond Edwards, and Chris Albertson had intended for it to be a blues album, but Lonnie sang a favorite ballad, "Memories of You," and then was invited to do a couple more. "Memories of You" and Lonnie's own composition, "I Found a Dream," two of his favorite ballads, are emotive, romantic, slow tempo ballads about the glories of love. That's well illustrated in the opening lines of the second tune: "I found a dream  . . . ; I found a dream when I found you." Lonnie sings them sensitively, with much emotion and nuance. He also added extended guitar solos to each song that were not typical Lonnie lead work; rather, they were lilting, gentle, subtly expressive lines that were very appropriate to the song subjects and nature of the music. I must confess, however, that I'm in partial agreement with various critics: I do not find his singing on these two tunes, or on the third ballad, "I'll Get By Somehow," to be among his better vocal work. The vocal tone is not his best for significant parts of the songs—a bit thin and breathy, and not in an artistically effective way—and the very slow tempos seem to put a damper on maintaining his best vocal styling; the songs' momentum seems to drag and, at times, become a bit uncertain; it's subtle, not dramatic, but that's what I hear. (His vocal tone and general delivery are much better on his first recording of "I Found a Dream" from the obscure Rama label in 1956.) I find the song "I'll Get By Somehow" itself to be lacking focus and structure; it really seems to meander and plod along. As I've shown earlier in the book, I am not one who automatically dismisses Lonnie's ballad singing, and I appreciate his desire not to be confined to one genre of music. But I just don't think these particular performances are his better work—though, after a not-so-excellent start, Lonnie's singing on "Memories of You" develops well and he sings it with sensitivity and passion. But: A *different* view of his ballad singing is noted later in this chapter.

For four other tracks on the original album, Lonnie recycles two of his own earlier songs, plus "St. Louis Blues" and Bessie Smith's "Backwater Blues." "Haunted House" is a redo of "Blue Ghost Blues," which he had recorded twice before. This one is well done, but the '38 version is his best. Lonnie's new recording of his "Jelly Roll Baker" is more extended than the earlier versions since the three-minute confines of the old 78 records are no longer a problem. Lonnie sings with verve and potency, adding some vocally playful bits here and there. He plays and sings "Backwater Blues" very well, but it's tough to top a master-piece like his 1948 version. For example, the thematic coherence in his guitar music here is not as great and consistent as on the '48 recording. This version of "St. Louis Blues" is, frankly, a little odd. Lonnie plays it in a bouncy, jaunty, up-tempo manner, and he changes the lyrics quite a bit in a seemingly off-hand manner, often not for the better. He was probably tired of singing the song the same way he had two hundred times before. The performance isn't bad in absolute terms; it's probably more the jarring of expectations regarding this classic tune.

Perhaps the most aesthetically pleasing songs on the album were the three instrumentals. That isn't surprising, given the long experience of these two musicians in jazz. "Blues for Chris," named for the man who brought Lonnie back and Elmer Snowden and Lonnie into the studio, is a slow tempo piece led by Snowden, with a mellow feel and with a gen-tle constant sense of moving along. The combined guitars, with deep bass backing, produce an excellent rhythmic sense, with rich musical texture and accents. This one is a treat for the ears. The old jazz classic "Savoy Blues " (one of the tunes Lonnie played with Louis Armstrong in 1927), with its memorable main musical theme, and "Elmer's Blues," offer more fine instrumental work in the same vein.

The CD of unreleased songs from the April '60 session, appro-priately titled *Lonnie Johnson with Elmer Snowden: Blues, Ballads and Jumpin' Jazz*, includes what I think are the two best tracks for the entire session; they are so good, it's a puzzle why they weren't part of the original album. "Blue and All Alone" (second track) is a slow blues. In this case, the slow tempo is used by Lonnie to draw out all the meaning of the lyrics as he produces increasingly powerful, evocative, and soulful singing, with great timing and phrasing. His singing includes very effective use of "melisma," which, in English, is drawing out a single syllable of the lyrics over several notes, in this case, often ascending and/or descending for dramatic and extra musical effect. In a series of places he soars impressively up to high notes, strikingly adding to the power and artistry of the music and to the meaning of the words. Added to all that is effective use of his electric guitar; the tone and use of sustain for expressive purposes that he draws from it and the lines he plays perfectly fit and complement the other elements of the recording. He ends the tune with an equally appropriate guitar solo. This is an outstanding musical performance, with his singing literally *rising* to the level of greatness as the song goes along.

Then Esmond Edwards asks Lonnie to do something from his old hometown. He responds with "New Orleans Blues," which is even better than "Blue and All Alone." This is Lonnie's own song in tribute to and remembrance of his hometown, which includes his lament that it had been a long time since he'd been in the place that spawned him and his music. It's on *The Ultimate Best of Lonnie Johnson* CD. His lyrics:

> I've been away so long, I've been gone so many years
> Yes, I've been away so long, from my old hometown
> That my heart begins cryin', ev'ry time that ev'nin' sun goes down.
> …
>
> Dear old New Orleans, they call it the land of dreams
> Yes, dear old New Orleans, it's known as the land of dreams
> It's my old hometown, it's dear old New Orleans.
>
> I've traveled so many miles, still got a long way to go
> I've traveled so many miles, still got a long way to go
> Yes, if I can't hitchhike my way, I'll start walking down that long ol'
> lonesome road.

In my hometown you lay down sleepin', ev'ry day you wake up
  with a smile on your face
Yes, at night you lay down dreamin', wake up with a smile upon
  your face
That's why I want to go home to New Orleans, that's the only place.

Lonnie takes the song at a slow tempo, smoothly flowing along like it was the Mississippi River gliding down to the Crescent City. He starts with a characteristic intro on his electric guitar, but with extra rich guitar tone and style and especially sublime touch and feel. His playing in the intro and later in the song illustrates how Lonnie could use the particular tone and sustain characteristics of the electric guitar to enrich and add further character to the lingered-over and very expressive bent notes he employs so effectively. He sings the lyrics with an extraordinary depth of feeling, with excellent timing and phrasing, with knowing, strategic use of syncopation, and with verve, yet in a smooth, lyrical manner. His dynamics are stunning; he employs striking power, often as he swoops up to a high note, adding emphasis to the meaning of the lyric, but also sings at quieter levels to enhance the mood and massage the meaning in a different way. The vocal tone he produces is superb, some of his very best pure vocal quality. Thus, on this recording he again rises to the level of greatness in singing, including more of that soaring up to vocal heights with rare vocal ability and with power and beauty. This is one of his four greatest vocal performances, along with the '48 "Backwater Blues," the March 1960 "Don't Ever Love," and his unique December 1960 recording of "Summertime," which I review shortly. (All are on *The Ultimate Best of Lonnie Johnson* CD.) Lonnie took all that original, rich New Orleans musical background and, with its inspiration, produced a superb, moving recording in celebration of the Original Music City.

*Blues, Ballads and Jumpin' Jazz* also includes six instrumental tracks, including one usually done with the vocal featured. These include "Lester Leaps In," their version of the famous Lester Young-Count Basie gem, the old classic, "On the Sunny Side of the Street," which various jazz players have taken off from, and the Duke Ellington gem, "C-Jam Blues." Two other old classics are also included, "Birth of the Blues," and "Careless Love" (which is usually sung); all of these tracks have memorable, catchy and delightful keynote intros and/or main melodic themes. Each of these instrumentals was a selection by Elmer (who didn't sing), sometimes prodded by Lonnie, so Elmer generally took the guitar lead on them. He showed that he was a fine professional guitarist, still in good form—though not at Lonnie's level of virtuosity. The two work well together, with Elmer's acoustic guitar making for a nice contrast and complement to Lonnie's electric. These veteran jazzmen also display an excellent rhythmic sense. Amusingly, at the beginning of track 6 Elmer asks Lonnie if he remembers "Careless Love." Lonnie had first recorded the song in November 1928 and sang it well; he did so again in August 1948 and had sung it numerous times in clubs and concerts; he remembered it, indeed.

Finally on that CD let me give special attention to Lonnie's version of one of the best and most loved popular songs in American history, "Stormy Weather." Actually, there are two takes. After the first take, in the background you can faintly hear Edwards tell Lonnie there is just room on the master recording tape for a second take of the song. Lonnie, as a seasoned recording musician, doesn't miss a beat and says, "I didn't do it right last time; let's do it *good* this time." That's amusing for two reasons. First, many a blues or other popular singer would *love* to have recorded a vocal performance as excellent as Lonnie's was on that first take. The second reason is that, in my judgment, his performance on the first is actually the better one. For that reason, I'll focus my note on the first take. Lonnie sings this tune, with its memorable melodic theme line and perfectly matching lyrics, in superb style, with outstanding timing, phrasing, and dynamics, and he beautifully conveys the meaning of the lyrics. (My one minor criticism is that in a few places his vocal tone is merely pretty good—not so rich.) His electric guitar is also put to excellent use. Most notably, later in the song, he says, "*talk* to me guit-tar" and sails off into a superb solo that is stylistically perfect for the song; and overall he plays with excellent tone and touch. This whole CD is a treat.

The last 1960 album, *Losing Game*, was recorded in late December 1960 and includes another masterpiece: Lonnie's unique, virtually re-composed version of "Summertime." On this recording he offered extraordinarily powerful, expressive, and artistic singing, infusing the lyrics with meaning and drama; his early years on the vaudeville stage were evident in his presentation here. From the tone and style of the first notes he perfectly captures the essence and the musical feel of this Gershwin classic, especially the A minor tonality, and thereafter he carries it on even more richly. That includes extraordinary stretched and bent vocal notes that dramatically enhance the meaning of the particular lyrics and the basic feel of the song. And in some places he produces a subtle, sublimely nuanced cascading down several notes, with an aesthetic fading from a strong top note to a more hushed sound, all perfectly directed and controlled, yet feeling very natural.

In his return to an acoustic guitar, he produces stunningly creative, artistic work for this version of "Summertime." His opening of percussive strums and acoustic guitar tone immediately establishes the atmosphere of a hot summer day in the South—again, in the musical context of that A minor tonality. And his guitar work thereafter continues and deepens that feel. Further, he adds creative little figures on the guitar that serve musically as accents, but also impressionistically convey other elements of the summer experience. (In a place or two one is stimulated to imagine a programmatic element such as bees buzzing around.)

All of that vocal and guitar work is perfectly woven together and presented with an exceptional thematic coherence (even by the standards of a song that lends itself to such coherence). This is greatness in vocal work; and with the remarkably inventive re-composition of the song *and* his unique artistry on the acoustic guitar, this recording is a genuine masterpiece. To come up with a creative, artistically superb and *new* arrangement of this classic that had been recorded hundreds of times over the previous 25 years is itself an impressive achievement. This is track 5 on *The Ultimate Best of Lonnie Johnson* CD.

As I mentioned earlier in the book, some astute observers, from writer James Sallis to bluesman Brownie McGhee, recognized that Lonnie Johnson was a pioneer in development of the superb *combination* of voice and guitar. His work on this 1960 version of "Summertime" is an ultimate illustration of how that combination and interaction of voice and guitar can produce great music; each took off from or augmented the other and added dimensions to the vocal and instrumental expression.

"Evil Woman," on the *Losing Game* album, had a bit of a surprise: Lonnie returned to playing the piano. His rolling harmonic keyboard work is played like only a month or two had passed since he played piano, in similar style, on those 1926 records. Another song worth special note is the second track, "My Little Kitten Susie," Lonnie's love song to his young partner Susie Small: "I've got a *cool* little kitten, her name is Susie Mae. . . ."

The first track on the album is "New Orleans Blues." Now, why would he record that again for Prestige/Bluesville when he just did so earlier in the year? Well, besides playing *acoustic* guitar this time, Lonnie turns it into a different song; it's different stylistically, and has substantial changes in the lyrics:

> Well, I'm goin' back to New Orleans, Philadelphia ain't the place
> for me (Repeat)
> 'Cause these chicks don't want no *one* good man, they want ev'ry
> man they see.
>
> Well, I'm goin' back home, if I have to hitchhike all the way
> (Repeat)
> That's where I can make love in the moonlight, lay in the shade all
> through the day.
>
> Creole babies got big bright eyes, coal black curly hair (Repeat)
> And they know how to love a man, *that's* why I'm goin' back there.

This was an interesting variation on the original, well played and sung. (It is a bit jarring, however, in light of the very next song: his love song to Susie! But then, this is a *blues* album.) Speaking of blues songs, he offers two others that one could call very good, regular Lonnie J blues tunes, "Moaning Blues" and "Losing Game," both played and sung very well, with typical Lonnie Johnson lyrics, music, and guitar work. The tenth track is an instrumental that basically harks back to his halcyon days in '27 and '28 creating those extraordinary solo guitar instrumentals. Using his acoustic guitar, Lonnie offers up an excellent "Slow and Easy" blues, as per the title, with a beautiful, lilting yet soulful main musical theme, and, later on, with interesting and lovely harmonic touches and excellent dynamics. Additionally, it being Lonnie, he adds a widely sung ballad, "What a Difference a Day Makes." In my judgment, he sings this song more effectively than the ballads on the first 1960 album, though there are a few falters in tone and phrasing.

Two other tracks are real standouts. Track seven, "Lines in My Face," is played and sung exceedingly well, with deep feeling, and he conveys the meaning of the lyrics with great effectiveness. The lyrics are among his best—they are pure blues poetry, with some wisdom from a long life; again he showed he was one of the premier lyric writers in blues history:

> Heartaches have caused, the deep lines in my face (Repeat)
> When you've been disappointed in love, your heart has no resting place.
>
> Each line in my face tells a story, the tears tell the reason why.
> Deep lines in my face tell a story, the tears tell the reason why.
> When you've been hurt in love, it shows on your face until the day you die.

His singing masterfully brings out the meaning of those lyrics. This song is a gem, musically, vocally, and lyrically.

The second to the last song on this album is the other real standout and it leads to an interesting additional comparison: "Four Walls and Me." This is a superb song, lyrically and musically, that is a bluesy meditation about languishing in a room, surrounded by those four walls, reflecting on and lamenting a lost love. Again, this was recorded in December 1960. In 1961 Country music star of the time Faron Young recorded a new song by the emerging Country music songwriter and not-yet-famous Willie Nelson, titled, "Hello Walls." This was a very good song with marvelous lyrics that were about languishing in a room, surrounded by those four walls and lamenting a lost love. It became a hit later in 1961. From the rather vague narrative in Joe Nick Patoski's biography, apparently Willie wrote the song in later 1960, so he evidently came up with the song idea independently of Lonnie's recording—and the music and lyrics are quite different. The conjunction of those superb songs on the same theme at about the same time is quite interesting, though. I guess it's a case of "great musical minds think alike." It's also worth noting, as Bill C. Malone reports, that Willie "absorbed music from a wide variety of cultural and ethnic sources," and his radio listening led him to jazz (among other music). Further, Willie employed "blues inflections and off-the-beat phrasing" borrowed from such sources.[10]

**A Downside to Lonnie's Conduct** I have noted some very positive aspects of Lonnie as a person, and more are noted in chapter 9 But he did have his faults. Chris Albertson understood Lonnie's musical importance and did significant things for Lonnie to recharge his career. But Chris also had experiences with Lonnie's not-so-admirable side. Lonnie's principal fault was being irresponsible about money—a good deal of it spent on lady friends. The Cincinnati house problem was noted in the previous chapter. A specific example from the time period discussed here: When Chris rediscovered Lonnie, he had a beat-up old guitar, as noted. Despite having only a modest income himself at the time, Chris bought a nice new Gibson guitar for Lonnie, so this master guitarist could have an instrument worthy of his talents. But even after Lonnie made several recordings in 1960 and got some good-paying club appearances, all he ever gave Chris for the guitar was a first payment of $25. Lonnie's rather irresponsible tendencies regarding money manifested themselves in other ways, but I see no reason to linger over other cases.[11]

I think that part of Lonnie's mental make-up on this is that he was at the top of the music world in the later 1920s and had feedback to the effect that he was a great musical artist; so, he probably had the feeling that he deserved to have ample money. The fact that he, like many other Black musicians, had been ripped-off by the record companies (like Decca) surely added to his state of mind regarding money. He wrote a couple of poignant letters to his friend Bernie Strassberg about how hurt he was that his manager in the '60s, Peter Rachtman, "let me down after I put all my trust in him" regarding getting work and being paid appropriately for that work. Being short-changed by a record company was not just something that happened in the earlier decades, however. In late '61 or early '62, he showed Bernie his royalty statement from Prestige/Bluesville and complained bitterly about not receiving his due. As Bernie put it to me in an interview, "Pennies, *pennies* he was getting—because somehow he didn't have the rights."[12] (Veteran record producer Richard Shurman pointed out to me that there were probably other elements in this situation that Bernie—and Lonnie—didn't fully understand. Still, record companies taking advantage of musicians was an issue that continued into the 1960s and beyond.) In any case, I see little purpose in any further armchair psychoanalysis regarding this pattern of Lonnie's behavior. This downside has been duly noted; let's move on with those things he did that are of importance for musical and cultural history.

**A Special Friend** Bernard Strassberg is a long-time New Yorker of Jewish ethnicity who was a knowledgeable jazz and blues lover and a record collector. He met Lonnie, understood his musical significance, was moved by him as a person, and became Lonnie's friend. In fact, Bernie and his family adopted Lonnie as part of the family, and Lonnie did the same from his side. Bernie also told me that "in accord with the old Southern Black tradition, he always called my wife 'Miss Ann;' it was never 'Ann,' as well as he got to know her." In an interview I conducted with Bernie in 2004 and in subsequent phone and in-person conversations, he provided a good deal of information and insight, as well as many documents, for this book. Let Bernie tell the story of how he first met Lonnie, with a notable cameo appearance by another musical legend—a legend to be, in his case:

> The first time I saw Lonnie was at Gerde's Folk City in Greenwich Village [New York], in 1961. Lonnie was on a bill with Victoria Spivey. A little into the performance, a young man came up and took out his harmonica and backed up Victoria Spivey. That young fellow was Bob Dylan.

As can be seen from the announcement flyer, Lonnie's appearance at Gerde's was September 12–24 (1961); Dylan's own engagement, with the Greenbriar Boys, followed, from September 26 to October 8. Dylan's first appearance on a commercial recording was playing harmonica backing for Victoria Spivey, whose album was released in 1962.

Flyer for Lonnie Johnson and Victoria Spivey then Bob Dylan appearances at Gerdes Folk City, Greenwich Village, New York, 1961.

Bernie then continued the story of his initial experience with Lonnie, and added a little inside look at the person and performer:

He was staying in a fleabag hotel. I said, "You can't stay here, man!" Lonnie said, "Oh, I have no money" [a regular refrain from Lonnie]. So I said, well, you can come stay with me. And so, for almost ten years, when he was in New York, I'd pick him up at the bus station and he'd stay with my family.

And by the way, like an old pro, he'd have these two suitcases. I'd say, "What the hell you got in there, man?!" Lonnie replied, "A change of clothes." He sang at this dinky Greenwich Village club, and he'd change suits *every* set—different tie, different shirt. The only thing he wore with all the outfits was this little diamond-studded guitar stickpin [which looked more like a violin—see photo in chapter 9]. He'd also take one shot of Gordon's Gin before he went on stage to loosen up a bit. He certainly wasn't a boozer; I never saw him drink any significant amount of booze.

Bernie offered two other closer looks at Lonnie. First, there was a bit of physical evidence of the guitar player. Everyone who starts to play guitar, especially steel-string guitar, has painful fingertips at first from pressing down on those steel strings until they can build up some calluses. In Lonnie's case, after playing guitar countless hours for decades, "his finger tips were like pieces of stone." Rather more significant is the fact that Bernie remembered Lonnie in the Strassberg home "playing along with records we were playing; and when he got particularly into it, his eyes would be closed and his head thrown back, his fingers dancing over those strings." A special example was a time they had put on the early Louis Armstrong-Hot Five masterpiece, "West End Blues," and Lonnie played some fine lines along with the record. "I had this on reel-to-reel tape, but it is now lost." (What a shame!) That is also interesting as a precursor, since Lonnie later made an excellent, unique recording of "West End Blues" with a Canadian jazz band in late 1965.

I should add here that in 1965, Bernie Strassberg made some recordings of Lonnie singing and playing guitar in the living room of his home in Forest Hills, Queens, New York City, that were recorded on his home reel-to-reel Wollensak tape recorder. As an ultimate labor of love, Bernie got a CD made of the recordings, which was released in 2000 on the Blues Magnet label. Unsurprisingly, the CD suffers bit in sound quality, compared with what we are used to today or with major studio recordings of the time; but these are unique, very personal home recordings of the legendary Lonnie J, so most folks will understand. And especially in the home setting of this family who had cared so much for him, it is unsurprising that Lonnie's sentimental side came out in his performance of some ballads/popular songs like "This Love of Mine," "September Song" and "My Mother's Eyes." To my ears, he sings "September Song" well, with nuance, fine phrasing, and lots of

Lonnie Johnson with Bernie Strassberg in the Strassberg Brooklyn home, about 1965. PHOTO COURTESY OF BERNIE STRASSBERG.

well-channeled feeling. He offers a seven-minute version of "St. Louis Blues" that is much better than the *different* version he recorded for *Losing Game.* Performing in the living room, he appropriately finished up and faded out with the Hoagy Carmichael classic, "Rockin' Chair."

**Playing at Other Clubs and Recordings—1961** In '61, besides playing at Gerdes Folk City, Lonnie performed at another Greenwich Village club called the Night Owl. For one of those gigs at the Night Owl veteran Country bluesman Sleepy John Estes was also on the bill. Bernie Strassberg added another highlight from his club appearances during this time: "And one memorable night at Gerdes Folk City, Muddy Waters had just given his concert at Carnegie Hall, and after the concert he brought his whole band into Gerdes to join Lonnie—and on the bill with Lonnie that night was [blues pianist] Little Brother Montgomery. What a night that was!"

Lonnie also appeared in Detroit at Café Gallerie in the first two weeks of November 1961. A *Detroit Free Press* newspaper article titled, "Guitarist Lonnie Johnson—Saw Birth of Blues," adds interesting perspective—starting with a personal description: "Slender, of medium build, soft-spoken with courtly manners, Johnson's looks belie the years he has seen—several more than sixty of them"—67, to be exact. (Lonnie was 5' 10" tall.) That was an old story with Lonnie. For example, in an article in the British *Jazz Quarterly* from 1945, writer Mark Thomas had seen Lonnie performing in Chicago in '45 and said: "When I first went to see Lonnie Johnson I expected to find a much older man, for at fifty-six, Lonnie looks little more than thirty-seven." (Thomas thought Lonnie was born in 1889, so in this case, he over-estimated Lonnie's age, which was actually 51—but he still looked 14 years younger.) The *Detroit Free Press* article went on to discuss Lonnie's partner on the bill at Café Gallerie, folk singer Len Chandler. The article noted Len's rich voice and ability to play "several string instruments," along with holding a master's degree from Columbia University. And: "'I'm a continual student of folk music,' Chandler said, and then with admiration in his eyes he added, 'but it always seems I'm listening to Lonnie's records'."[13]

Bernie also remembered that Lonnie appeared on the *Today* show; his vague recollection was that this was somewhere in 1964–1966. But since by '64 he was fading in public attention and from mid-1965 on he was mostly in Toronto, it was more likely to have been a bit earlier, when his comeback was in full swing and when the Folk and Blues Revivals were at their height, like 1962 or 1963, or perhaps just after he returned from the '63 American Folk Blues Festival tour of Europe.

In July 1961 Chris Albertson and Prestige/Bluesville brought Lonnie and Victoria Spivey together for a reunion, which produced the album, *Idle Hours*, with Cliff Jackson playing piano in support. That was the title of one of their late '20s duet recordings. Lonnie is again playing acoustic guitar. This wasn't exactly a reunion album, however, since Victoria sang on only three of the twelve tracks. For two of those songs, "Long Time Blues" and a redo of their late '20s recording "Idle

Hours," Lonnie and Victoria reprised their duets from long ago. Both are delightful, with the two mostly trading verses; the first song was, in effect, a celebration of their reunion. The second song took the duet/duel approach to the vagaries of man-woman relationships. Victoria is in fine voice for those two tunes and for her solo singing on "I Got the Blues So Bad." On the latter, Victoria plays piano herself, offering interesting and rather rhapsodic playing. All the other tracks were regular 1960s Lonnie Johnson blues songs and guitar playing. Again, it is nice to hear the deep tone of his acoustic guitar playing, though he generally doesn't do anything special—and often uses his standard '50s and '60s guitar intro.

Chris Albertson related to me a humorous story from that recording session, which is part of the reality of Lonnie Johnson's nature, self-perception, and orientation towards women: At the recording session, "Victoria was very interested in Lonnie; she was flirting with him. But Lonnie would have none of it; she was too old for him. At one point Lonnie came to me and said, 'Victoria wants me to come to [her house] for a chicken dinner, but I don't think that's what she wants me there for. You gotta help me, Chris!' "

**"The Duke and the Janitor"** Chris Albertson also told me the story of a reunion concert with Duke Ellington in November 1961. Lonnie's performance and its reception in the concert also lead to consideration of a question blues and jazz writers have posed regarding Lonnie's *lack* of fame.

CA:  "I had read that Duke was giving a concert at Town Hall in New York. So I called Duke's manager. He didn't know about Lonnie; but when he mentioned Lonnie to Duke, Duke was very excited. I said it would be nice to have a reunion. Duke said, 'Of course, let's do it.' Then, after the word got out, the *Daily News* had that headline. [The *Daily News* may have had a similar headline, but a story in the November 22, 1961 *New York Herald Tribune* had the heading, "THE DUKE AND THE JANITOR TO HOLD A JAZZ REUNION."] Lonnie, a proud man, was so unhappy about that headline."

[The Duke-Lonnie J reunion concert had promise, but:] "It didn't produce anything that even approximated what he had done with Duke in the '20s—"Hot and Bothered," "The Mooche," etc.—'cause Lonnie had gotten into playing clichés. There was a certain opening he almost always played at that point. It was as if he had just sort of settled in and his creativity wasn't quite there as before; he didn't seem inspired . . . I thought once he got together with Duke, some of the old spark would come in and he would dazzle us or something. But he didn't. It also didn't fit with Duke's 1960s band; whereas back then it was a perfect combination.

DA: "Did the headline spoil it for him?"

CA: "It might have; I know he was very upset about it, and I understand why. I don't know if he had that actively in mind while in the concert, but it did kind of set the tone; I mean, here was the lowly janitor meeting the Duke. They were not on stage as equals. But also, Lonnie hadn't played with a band like that in many years, and I think he may have been a little uncomfortable."

DA: "That surprises me, given his genius and his versatility."

CA: "He just wasn't with the program. He played a solo, in the right key and all that, but it was nothing out of the ordinary. And I think a lot of people were in awe of the fact that this was Lonnie Johnson, but then were somewhat let down by what he played because it wasn't the Lonnie Johnson you heard on the old records . . . I also think the electric guitar got in the way a bit."

Apparently, that rather negative assessment of Lonnie's performance with Duke and band was not universally shared. John S. Wilson, music writer for the *New York Times*, wrote a review of the Ellington concert for the next day's paper, which included this final paragraph (though it only addresses Lonnie's singing):

> Lonnie Johnson, the veteran blues singer and guitarist, joined the band after intermission and not only gave a useful demonstration of how to sing a potent and unpretentious blues, but also developed what started out as a rather glib treatment of "September Song" into a performance of such moving strength that even the usually implacable Mr. Johnny Hodges gave visible evidence of joy as he blew in the background.[14]

(Alto saxophone player Johnny Hodges, one of the greatest soloists in the long history of the famous Ellington band, was much noted for his impassive face, even while producing sublimely moving blues from his horn.)

The Albertson tale is one illustration of why Lonnie Johnson did not, in the end, develop the fame one would have expected.

## Great Music and Influence, So Why Didn't He Become as Famous as Louis Armstrong or Bessie Smith?

A question various blues and jazz writers and aficionados have posed is, given the greatness of Lonnie Johnson's music and his wide and profound influence, why didn't he become as famous as the few other blues and jazz greats at his level of musical artistry?

First, as mentioned previously, there is some truth in the Albertson statement that Lonnie had settled into use of some guitar licks repeatedly. But then, it would take someone superhuman to be truly different and creative for every recording and public performance when that musician had recorded hundreds of songs and had played in thousands of clubs and concerts of every conceivable sort for 45 years—and given the ups and downs of Lonnie's life in particular. But it is incorrect to state that he *routinely* settled into standard riffs and patterns and did not make great music in his later years, as I pointed out earlier and as is compellingly demonstrated on the *Ultimate Best of Lonnie Johnson* CD. We still have to solve the puzzle just posed, however. The main answers to the question are as follows, as I see it.

**Pop songs, Bad Timing and Led Astray by a Big Hit** That phrase sums up the central answer. Ironically, the huge ballad hit Lonnie had in the Rhythm &Blues era, "Tomorrow Night," along with Lonnie's strong desire—like that of Duke Ellington—to avoid being stuck in one narrow, confining musical category, seems to have been the key. Because Lonnie had such a huge hit singing a ballad later in his career (with a big royalty payoff) this encouraged him to try more of the ballad stuff and pop standards. Additionally, as discussed previously, Lonnie was a model of class and dignity, and he wanted to transcend the race problem and appeal to Whites as well as minorities. Pop standards could appeal to that wide, trans-racial audience, he thought. Further, Black man Nat King Cole moved from pure jazz musician to pop singer, developed an extraordinarily wide appeal throughout American society and beyond during the 1950s and into the 1960s. The same was the case with Sam Cooke in the late 1950s and early 1960s. Those examples were not lost on Lonnie. The fact that his friend Louis Armstrong had a giant, society-wide hit with the show tune "Hello Dolly" in spring 1964 probably further encouraged this inclination at that time. Also, Lonnie was a very passionate, emotional, and romantic man, and he loved to sing emotive ballads and standards. So, Lonnie sang more ballads and pop standards. But despite the brilliant vocal work in various blues and jazz songs, and his fine singing in the ballad "Tomorrow Night," *some* of his pop song vocal work was not so great. Some of the recorded pop songs didn't come across as genuinely or compellingly as the blues and jazz material, and even some of the phrasing and vocalizing of words did not work well—in my assessment. (But again, see just below for an alternative view on this.)

Roberta Barrett, from his last years in Toronto, gave me a description of Lonnie's performing style that yields another clue to why he didn't develop and maintain the level of fame his artistry merited. She describes her first time seeing him in a club: "Two things I noticed immediately: First, his guitar stylings were absolutely fabulous. Second, he barely moved." The latter is probably a product of the dignity with which he conducted himself and his wish to not come across like the stereotype of a Black entertainer: all flash, jiving suggestive movements, and so on. One can see the dignity and the lack of movement in his appearance in the DVDs of the American Folk Blues Festival tour of Europe, especially Volume 1. That probably limited his appeal to the mass audience—and wasn't splashy enough to generate much media attention—even though in smaller club settings he could connect very well with audiences and inspire enthusiasm for him as we have seen.

Then there was the timing factor. As illustrated by the case of the Town Hall concert with the Duke, there were some key points and prominent public events where Lonnie missed significant opportunities to show his greatness, bolster his standing, and register his important place in music history. This was especially the case in the early- to mid-1960s when the Folk and Blues Revivals were going strong and the reputations of these older musicians were being revived.

Chris Albertson related another prime example to me. With the Folk Revival and young people's enthusiastic involvement in it, there was renewed interest in people like Lonnie. "Then there was a big folk music concert at Town Hall [New York; this may have been the concert on March 11, 1960, with Jean Ritchie, Cynthia Gooding and others, which was advertised as "The Folk Concert of the Year!."[15]] They wanted Lonnie; he was to represent the blues. And they asked him, 'Are you sure you can do the blues now?' But Lonnie did not want to be put in that compartment of the blues; he wanted to show he could do much more than the blues. So at the concert I said, 'Well, this time Lonnie, do the blues; you're representing a concept for the concert.' He said, 'That's fine.' But he came out, and I was sitting in the concert, and he said, 'I want to dedicate this song to my friend Chris Albertson, for everything he has done... It's his favorite song, 'This Heart of Mine'. [Albertson laughed at the memory of that pop song being cast as his favorite.] He did it well, but it was out of place." And Lonnie lost another chance to reinforce his place of greatness in music history with a new generation.

**. . . But, Another Perspective on Lonnie's Ballad Singing** In chapter 6 I offered this quote from the blues researcher-writer Chris Smith: "'In Love Again' [is] one of the ballads that Lonnie was so good at, to the despair of those who want to put blues singers into musical strait-jackets." Indeed; and while *sometimes* his singing on ballad and pop standards wasn't as compelling and artistically effective as on many of his blues numbers, in a number of cases he did sing such ballads beautifully. Bernie Strassberg, who is a knowledgeable appreciator of blues and jazz, gave me this impassioned statement on the issue:

> You know, he was vilified for singing ballads like "My Mother's Eyes," because he was such a sentimental guy. A lot of critics couldn't see past that to realize what he *did* with that material. That's what pisses me off. . . . I mean, I hear Lonnie's version of "Memories of You" and it still sends chills down my spine. I've had a lot of musicians to my place, and when I've pulled out that album with Lonnie singing "Memories

of You," the musicians all would close their eyes, then develop big grins, and then they'd say, "How come I never hear of him?!"

The record on which that song appears is the album from the Prestige/ Bluesville session with Elmer Snowden (the LP album released at the time). Again, I'm not quite as taken with that specific recording of "Memories of You" as is the estimable Bernie Strassberg, but as the recording spins along, one can hear how Lonnie's singing was more and more beautifully expressive and moving as he worked his way through the tune. And thinking of my impression alongside Bernie's, I'm reminded of the comment by British jazz writer Lyn Foersterling from his observation of Lonnie's performance in Square's Boulevard Lounge in Chicago in the early '40s: "Then Lonnie sang, not a blues, but 'Jelly Jelly,' the Billy Eckstine song . . . When Lonnie sang it, it was jazz, done with unbelievable delicacy and finesse. I think Lonnie has never recorded his greatest work, or, if he has, it has been lost in the recording process." I have no doubt that Bernie and others heard marvelous, moving renditions of that and similar songs by Lonnie in club dates and concerts.[16]

Another angle on this, which illustrates the Strassberg comment about Lonnie being "such a sentimental guy," is offered by Albertson in his original liner notes for the LP album in which "Memories of You" appears. This part narrates developments in the recording session:

> Side one opens with "Haunted House," a very moving blues which literally drove Lonnie Johnson to tears as he sang it in the studio. It was actually recorded towards the end of the session and, after he had concluded it, he went, almost without stopping, into "Memories of You." This was originally planned as a blues album, but Lonnie has always liked to sing ballads . . . and we liked this one so much that Prestige Artists & Repertoire man Esmond Edwards asked Lonnie to sing a couple more. The result was "I'll Get Along Somehow" and his own "I Found a Dream." By the time he had sung those he was so choked up from crying that we had to end the session.[17]

I mentioned that Lonnie emphatically did not want to be seen as an "*old* Country Blues singer." By the 1960s, he was very sensitive to being seen as old in general. This is colorfully illustrated by an anecdote from

Charles Keil's *Urban Blues*. I asked Keil about the source of this quote and he told me, "this was the first thing out of Lonnie's mouth when I started interviewing him!" The quote: "Are you another one of those guys who wants to put crutches under my ass?"

## Club Work, More Recordings, Developments on the Home Front

After his late 1961 appearance in Detroit, Lonnie had an engagement in San Francisco in early 1962 at the club, "Sugar Hill, Home of the Blues." The club's proprietor was Barbara Dane, a White woman who was a terrific folk and blues singer herself, especially prominent in the late '50s into the early '70s. (Check out her superb, soulful album from 1965, *Barbara Dane and the Chambers Brothers*, especially track 2, "You've Got to Reap What You Sow," for an excellent example.) Despite the title of the club, Lonnie was into singing emotive ballads and other pop songs and, apparently, that's what he mostly sang at Sugar Hill—to "mixed feelings from the audience, since they expected the blues but got pop songs." As Barbara told me in an interview, it was clear from things Lonnie said and did that "he would have done anything to break into the pop world." But there is an irony in Barbara's comments on his ballads and pop song inclinations at the club, which is manifest in a song from the album I review next.

Lonnie also played a number of times at Gerdes Folk City from December 1961 into spring 1966, appearing with folk singers like Jean Ritchie, Bonnie Dobson, and Barbara Muller.

In April 1962, Prestige/Bluesville brought him in for one more album: *Lonnie Johnson: Another Night to Cry*. The fifth song on this album, with the excellent blues title, "Fine Booze and Heavy Dues," is actually a very bluesy tribute to the Sugar Hill blues club: "I've got the blues for San Francisco, it's San Francisco where I long to be. There's a club they call 'Sugar Hill,' and that's where I long to be." This makes me think Lonnie probably sang a mixture of ballads and pop tunes *along with* the blues, but Barbara's memory tended to focus on the pop songs because she and her audience were expecting pure blues. In any case, this one's a good tribute to the club and is played and sung very well. It's also interesting to note that there were no ballads on this album, only blues; that was, no doubt, what Bluesville wanted.

Another tune seems to have a specially directed message: "Goodbye Kitten." On the December 1960 album *Losing Game* Lonnie recorded a love song to his partner, "My Little Kitten Susie." But this one's about problems between them. (A hazard of involvement with a musician is that problems may get written into a song, recorded, and left in the public realm.)

Despite problems with his Susie, Lonnie recorded a song for his new daughter in June '64, "Brenda," which was one of four recorded in a brief return to King Records. There is a nice instrumental on the album, "Blues After Hours," which has characteristically good Lonnie guitar lines and harmonic touches, though it isn't at the level of the inventive virtuosity of his late '20s and early '30s recordings—a comparison he must have gotten sick of hearing. The other songs are pretty much his regular 1960s blues songs, with nothing really noteworthy.

**Personal Life**   From Lonnie's letters to Bernie Strassberg, it appears that by about March 1962 Lonnie and Susie were no longer living together on West Oxford Street, at least not continuously. Lonnie's address was now 3212 West Dauphin Street, Philadelphia (by Fall 1961 he'd started to refer to that as his business address). This other place may explain another mystery: In an interview, Lonnie referred to his ninety-year-old mother living with him in the early–mid '60s. But Susie and Brenda told me Angieline never lived at Oxford Street. So, maybe Lonnie had this separate residence with his mother there, which he also used as his business address for mail, and then mostly lived there. This basic status was impressionistically confirmed in his song, "Teardrops in My Eyes," when he sings, "Goodbye little Susie . . ."

## American Folk Blues Festival Tour, Recordings in Europe

In fall 1963 Lonnie performed on the important American Folk Blues Festival (AFBF) tour of Britain and Europe. They first did a 29-day tour of nine different nations on the Continent, and then toured Great Britain.

The American Folk Blues Festival tours were organized and conducted by two German jazz and blues lovers and promoters, Horst Lippmann and Fritz Rau, and were sponsored by the German Jazz Federation; they had help from the great Chicago bluesman Willie

Dixon. The first tour was in 1962. As European producer-promoter Philippe Rault said:

> Through the American Folk Blues Festival, it was really the first time any serious presentation of blues was made and brought to European audiences. This was a really pivotal period, 1962–1964—people were so starved for those shows because it was the real thing finally happening. . . .

Those shows had a big, double-dimension impact. In the earlier phases of the Rolling Stones, the Beatles, Eric Clapton, and other British musicians, they had been struck by American blues records they'd managed to obtain; but hearing the real thing live was a moving experience and provided a powerful impetus to deepen their playing of the music. A number of writers since then have pointed out the second dimension of the impact: Many White American young people actually got their introduction to the blues of African-American culture and found their avenue to the great blues musicians through those *British* musicians, who became hugely popular by the mid-1960s. (When the Beatles first came to America in 1964 and took questions from the press, they said they especially wanted to see Muddy Waters. A news guy, who was just as clueless about this powerful music in his own land as most White American youth, said, "Where's Muddy Waters?," thinking it was some obscure location.)

Lonnie was part of the second annual American Folk Blues Festival tour in 1963, which included Dixon, harmonica master Sonny Boy Williamson II (Aleck "Rice" Miller), great blues pianists Otis Spann and Memphis Slim, Country bluesman Big Joe Williams, young blues guitarist Matt "Guitar" Murphy, and Lonnie and Victoria Spivey. Lonnie's reception was considerably better than that of his 1952 tour of Britain. A writer for the British *Jazz Journal* reported at the time on Lonnie's appearance at Britain's Fairfield Hall, Croyden: "The second half opened with Lonnie Johnson. A smooth, and at times almost sentimental performer, he has great charm and is a magnificent guitarist. He was obviously moved by his reception, and the audience took him right to their hearts." British blues writer Paul Oliver (who was and is a blues purist) had a somewhat different perspective on Lonnie's performances in a couple of the concerts in England: "He sang with spirit and played better—far better—than he did on his [1952] trip. 'Falling

Rain Blues' sounded good, but there is a latent sentimentality in most of his work, and he followed this up with an embarrassing 'I Left My Heart in San Francisco'. . . . [But] the audience applauded wildly, I have to record. . . . But on Sunday he suddenly swung into a rocking, superbly sung and played "See See Rider," leaving one confounded and delighted."[18] Val Wilmer took the terrific, artistic photo of Lonnie playing at Fairfield Hall, shown here.

Fortunately, film was shot of some appearances on these AFBF tours, including two song performances of Lonnie at separate concerts and one of Lonnie introducing and then accompanying Victoria Spivey. Sadly, film of Lonnie is extremely rare, so it is a treat to be able to actually *see* and hear him, even if it's only at that late point in his career.

On the DVD, *Volume 1, The American Folk Blues Festival—1962–1966*, Lonnie is seen performing his title song from the 1962 album, *Another Night to Cry*. His singing is very evocative and rhythmic, with good tone. It is also of historical interest to see him playing his guitar, in this case, his '60s electric guitar. (The guitar was an inexpensive

Lonnie Johnson performing in Fairfield Hall, Croydon, England, October 18, 1963, during the American Folk Blues Festival tour. PHOTO BY AND COURTESY OF VAL WILMER.

Kay, with a body roughly like a Gibson Les Paul. In his interview with Val Wilmer, Lonnie said: "They make a light instrument . . . and the execution on the finger-board is so fast. You just touch it and you have no trouble playing it. I love it!"[19]) There is an all-too-brief close-up (as is too often the case, the cameraman or film director did not understand music well enough to pan in on a feature guitar solo).

When I first saw this film, I was immediately struck by how much Eric Clapton's playing style owes to Lonnie. I have three concert videos featuring Clapton, which I've looked at closely and repeatedly. Another thing very apparent in this film is the restrained dignity with which Lonnie carried himself. An additional segment of visual interest: It's enjoyable to see Muddy Waters put his arm around Lonnie and be playful with him in the "all-cast" closing, with most of the musicians taking a turn doing a variation of "Bye Bye Blues" or their own song adapted to the sequence of performances; it's a visual/behavioral demonstration of Muddy's affection and respect for Lonnie.

The performance seen in volume one was in a concert auditorium (Fairfield Hall, Croydon, south of London, I believe). The second Lonnie song performance on film, on volume four of the DVD series, was in a very different setting. It's more informal, with people sitting all around the floor (in Free Trade Hall in Manchester, I believe). Lonnie switched to acoustic guitar, and played it superbly, giving us a chance to see his flat-picking style, touch, and vibrato in action on the original type of instrument he played. It is especially nice to observe that playing on an extended solo—though, unfortunately there was, again, only a brief close-up on his playing. He sang even better on this number. Lonnie's dignified introduction of Victoria Spivey and accompaniment for her are seen on volume two of the DVD series. (Victoria's performance was perhaps the *least* effective on the DVD's, with too many vaudevillian eye-rolls and singing that fell well short of her vocal work on the 1961 reunion album with Lonnie, *Idle Hours*.) These DVD's are an historic treat, with film of Sonny Boy Williamson II, Muddy Waters, Sonny Terry and Brownie McGhee, T-Bone Walker, Howlin' Wolf, and so on.

Len Kunstadt, co-editor of *Record Research* magazine and writer, related an interesting incident from that tour that illustrates Lonnie's concern for his voice (at 69 years of age) and the respect others had for him. To set the scene, I should note that Willie Dixon, the Chicago bluesman and helper on the tour, was about 6' 4" tall, weighed at least 280 pounds, and had been a heavyweight boxer in his younger days; Big Joe Williams was just shy of six feet tall, but must have weighed 250. The story:

> Willie Dixon saved the show from a major altercation over a window being open on the bus. Lonnie Johnson had such a pure voice he didn't want to get a cold, and Big Joe Williams, who had high blood pressure, was always hot and wanted a window open. An altercation started and Sonny Boy Williamson, who was in the front of the bus doing a radio announcement, got into the middle of it and told Big Joe to shut the window.
>
> Big Joe Williams reached into his pocket like there was something there [like a knife] and I remember Willie Dixon grabbing Big Joe around the waist and getting him in the back of the bus.[20]

Sonny Boy Williamson II, the great harmonica player, was pretty sizable himself. But to me, what best explains his actions can be literally seen and heard on the Volume One DVD of the AFBF. Sonny Boy does the introduction of Lonnie before he comes out on stage. Now, you must understand that Rice Miller, aka Sonny Boy Williamson II (*not* the original John Lee "Sonny Boy" Williamson with whom Lonnie played in Chicago in the '40s), was widely seen in the blues and recording community as a very irascible, ornery dude who was always ready to draw out his knife and threaten somebody. (Also, in some photos he rather looks like an image of the devil; a number of people crossing his path in the early '60s would have said that image was appropriate.)

So for the introduction, Sonny Boy comes out, uses his hands to quiet the strong applause for him, and says (here I smooth out the language just a little to make it more coherent because Sonny Boy was not very literate): "It give me great pleasure and make me feel so good to introduce a *very nice* musician; one of the best bluesmen from way back in the '20s; a boy that can put rhythm with blues and blues with rhythm. He can do such a wonderful solo with the blues, and with soul; and when I say 'soul' I mean *soul.* I bring him to the stage now, the *one and only Lonnie Johnson!*" Sonny Boy used a tone of voice in those last words that conveyed deep admiration; his profound feeling for the musician and the man Lonnie Johnson was very evident.

While on the AFBF tour on the continent, Lonnie made recordings of his own and with pianist Otis Spann for the Storyville label in Copenhagen, Denmark. The recordings with Spann as the featured musician included an absolutely masterful version of one of the greatest blues songs ever written, "Trouble in Mind." Spann played his usual ravishing, yet deep blues piano. And, though he was known for his great piano work in the Muddy Waters band, on this recording he showed he could offer some outstanding, very soulful blues singing. Lonnie provided exquisite accompaniment on his electric guitar, adding accents and guitar phrases in support of Otis's piano work and singing. In the bridge he added a line that climbed the scale with superbly placed, rich electronic guitar notes and then descended in a way that enhanced the harmonic dimensions of the music and sublimely complemented the piano lines Otis was playing. (Otis mentioned Lonnie's name twice just before and at the beginning of the bridge, and then he pauses the piano a bit and one can sense that he looked over at Lonnie, in effect saying "take it" for a couple of bars.) This is the seventh track on the *Ultimate Best of Lonnie Johnson* CD, and it's a not-to-be-missed gem.

Otis Spann, who was arguably the greatest of all blues pianists, continued his outstanding playing on the recordings featuring Lonnie. Johnson seemed inspired and energized from his reception in Europe and while playing with Otis; one can hear the increased energy and enthusiasm in his singing. His album opens with a revisit of his old hit, "Tomorrow Night." This was not only a very good version of the song, but I think Lonnie sang it even better than on his hit '48 recording. Spann's playing (again) adds ravishing, yet deeply bluesy piano backing and embellishments. The second track is a six-minute "Clementine Blues" (bearing *no* relation to the old American folk song, "Oh My Darling, Clementine"). It's a genuine blues song, which Lonnie sings superbly. Spann adds even better piano work, with his trademark rich tone and stunning dynamics greatly enhancing the tune; Lonnie's guitar playing and the piano playing of Otis work especially well together here. A very jaunty, rollicking, rhythmic version of the old, old tune, "See See

Rider" came next, played and sung like Lonnie did in the AFBF concert described above, with a terrific Spann solo break mid-way through.
Lonnie added variations of his own on the lyrics, in many cases improv-
ing on the coherence and interest of the story told in the lyrics.

The rest of the tunes are characteristic Lonnie J blues tunes,
done well, plus two ballads, also done well. Further, Lonnie offered
the popular/jazz song, "Jelly Jelly." Here he sings the song brilliantly,
reminding me of the eloquent description of Lonnie's singing of that
song at Square's Lounge in Chicago in the '40s, quoted in chapter 6.
(Some of his softer singing techniques on this recording, while maintaining quality and expressive capacity, would have improved his ballad
singing on his 1960 comeback album.) Finally, "Swingin' with Lonnie"
is an instrumental, starting with a blazing guitar intro. Otis and Lonnie
really cook on this jazzy Rhythm & Blues-style number.

After returning from his good reception during the American Folk
Blues Festival tour of Europe, Lonnie recorded six tracks for the Spivey
label that Victoria Spivey had established, with Len Kunstad, to produce blues records. To my ears, the most interesting of these recordings
is the appropriately titled, "Mr. Johnson's Guitar Talks," an instrumental. It's a fine piece with characteristic 1960s Lonnie licks and general
approach, played with style and verve. But it doesn't reach the level of
inventive music or the remarkable thematic coherence that Lonnie's late
'20s and other masterpieces achieved.

Lonnie's career then declined again, though, as mentioned earlier, he
did continue to play some gigs in coffeehouses, in New York, especially.

At the end of my interview with him, Bernie Strassberg reflected on
the series of ups and downs of Lonnie's professional life. In a keynote
of those reflections he added an interesting point on Lonnie Johnson's
perspective on his own career and musical achievements: "But he really
didn't complain that much about being overlooked. He knew what he
had done; he knew what he was worth." Chris Albertson told me the
same thing.

But Lonnie wasn't done *yet*. And he made still another comeback,
which developed in what, at first glance, was a rather unlikely place:
Toronto, Canada.

# 9

# The Legacy of Lonnie J: The Guitar in Twentieth-Century Music

## The Metro Stompers and the Old Man

In June 1965, Jim McHarg, the leader of a fine Dixieland jazz band in Toronto, had a good idea. He was aware of Lonnie Johnson's past accomplishments in blues and jazz, as well as his origins in New Orleans, and he thought he'd bring Lonnie in to play with them; so, McHarg made arrangements for him to come up for a gig. On June 21 he and John McHugh, owner of the well-known Penny Farthing coffeehouse in the Yorkville area of Toronto where they would play, went to the bus station "to meet a 65-year old guitar-playing blues singer. I had sold John on the idea of booking this old timer for a two-week engagement." But McHarg wondered, "How would this . . . old man, a star from another era, compete with blaring Rock 'n' Roll, the good-looking young folk singers," and so on in that hip area of Toronto in the mid-1960s?

Well, Lonnie Johnson, who was actually 71 years old, not 65, came in and dazzled the audience and led that traditional jazz band to heights they had probably never before reached in making music; it was the young Canadian musicians who had to strive to keep up with that "old man" in vigor and musical creation—as can be heard on the fine album they made later, *Lonnie Johnson: Stompin' at the Penny*, with *Jim McHarg's Metro Stompers*, as the Columbia release was titled. (The

Design and mock-up of the album cover for the original Canadian LP of *Stompin' at the Penny* with *Jim McHarg's Metro Stompers featuring Lonnie Johnson* (fall 1965). COURTESY OF BERNIE STRASSBERG.

LP was recorded in Toronto and was originally released by Columbia's Canadian subsidiary essentially as a Toronto regional record, titled: *Jim McHarg's Metro Stompers featuring Lonnie Johnson*. Lawrence Cohn recognized the significance of this album and arranged for its release in the main Columbia Roots & Blues series. Cohn and Columbia were sued by McHarg for changing the original title, which was settled out of court; but the album would have been long forgotten without the presence of Lonnie Johnson.)

As McHarg reported, that first night:

The audience was electrified, his superb interpretation of ballads and blues enthralled them. Wave after wave of sustained applause greeted every number. His first set lasted an hour and ten minutes; we had expected the usual 20 minutes . . . Within 24 hours the word was out and the Penny Farthing was being crammed to the door. The age group [included] 50-somethings, but also college kids, courting couples, Mums and Dads, and even Rock 'n' Roll musicians from across the street [from another club].

In an article written shortly afterward, McHarg said, "The truth of the matter is that when he started to sing he just pulled us along in his musical slipstream." But let me also say that, on the recordings, the Metro Stompers played very well indeed, with some especially fine work by cornet player Charles Gall ("Scotland's greatest gift to jazz since Chivas Regal") that backed and added complements to Lonnie's singing and guitar.[1]

The area press grasped what was happening: A writer for the *Toronto Daily Star* newspaper wrote, "I heard a genius at work, a man who loves to sing, has given his life to it, and bares his heart and soul in song. He takes us from the scramble of our modern scurrying world and makes us take a hard look at ourselves." Sid Adilman of the *Toronto Telegram* offered a different laudatory perspective: "Lonnie Johnson, at sixty-five years of age [*sic*], outplays, outsings, outdraws the bulk of hippy modernists." Lonnie's two-week gig turned into a six-week extended engagement a little later.[2]

McHarg added a note that showed something about the kind of person Lonnie was: "He remembered every waitress and dishwasher by name and did the rounds of the staff to greet them every evening before playing his first set."

McHarg added a second note on Lonnie's nature, in this case another illustration of how he would encourage young musicians: "We went all the way out to a home in Don Mills on his only day off to sing to a group of 15-year old boys who had formed a jug band, then he enthused to me about their playing all the way back to the hotel."[3] That little story has an interesting additional element: The teenage jug band Lonnie and Jim went to play for and see used the wonderful extended name, "The Tubby Fats Original All-Star Downtown Syncopated Big Rock Jug Band." (That would have been tough to put on a business card!) A key force in the band was a young man named Ken Whiteley. Subsequently, Whiteley became a very prominent folk and blues musician in Canada and beyond—and still is.

In a telephone interview with me, Ken said he first saw and heard Lonnie at The Penny Farthing during that June '65 booking. Ken was all of fourteen years old. He still remembers that night quite vividly: "It was a hot night—a good eighty degrees or more. Lonnie comes in *immaculately dressed*, with wide leg pants, perfectly pressed, and a stylish shirt, and he had his Kay electric guitar, which he always used in this period." This is the guitar that can be seen in the Val Wilmer photo taken during the '63 AFBF tour, displayed on the frontispiece. Ken said he found Lonnie's playing and his presence "thrilling"; he was greatly inspired by Lonnie Johnson. Later he had the chance to meet Lonnie at a private party to which Ken had brought a 12-string guitar. Lonnie proceeded to play the guitar and, in effect, Ken got some lessons. Whiteley's summary statement on Lonnie: "Lonnie Johnson was elegant and generous, and he was a versatile and awesome musician." And, like many others, in answer to my question about how audiences responded to Lonnie, Ken said, "People *loved* him."[4]

In an article for *Coda* magazine, McHarg (originally from Scotland) put his interest in Lonnie in fascinating perspective regarding McHarg's personal history, music history, and the remarkable power, spread, and impact of earlier jazz music:

> My interest in this guitar-playing blues singer was born twenty years ago in Glasgow, Scotland. At that time I was a member of a small group of individuals who had banded together to form a club. The unusual aspect of this club was that the membership included doctors, lawyers, plasterers, butchers, and other representation from the professional and artisan fields. To bring such a diverse group together in what was still very much a class-conscious society was unheard of.
>
> The subject matter that interested us all and lowered the class barrier was our common love of jazz music. Each member took it in turn to bring along part of his record collection and give a recital . . . One evening a noted Glasgow doctor was in the chair. He had chosen as his subject the famous Louis Armstrong recordings of 1927. Introducing one of the discs, he said, "I would like you all to pay particular attention to the guitar player. It is popular opinion among collectors that, in spite of the genius of Armstrong's trumpet, this version of 'Savoy Blues' owes its greatness to this comparatively unknown guitarist who

completely dominates the rhythm section and sparks Armstrong to one of his finest solos. This, in my opinion, is the greatest jazz guitar work ever [recorded]." The guitar player on that very famous recording was Lonnie Johnson.[5]

(Again, that "Savoy Blues" side is track 10 on the companion CD.)

Lonnie found people welcoming and club work available, so he stayed in Toronto, other than some trips back to Philadelphia, and to New York for club gigs and a recording session. His five years in that Canadian city were to be the final act in the extraordinary saga of the legendary Lonnie J.

He found a particular someone who became a very special factor in what turned out to be the last years of his life. Her name was Roberta Richards (now Barrett). She was a music booking agent (starting at age 16!) in Toronto. But she didn't initially cross paths with Lonnie through music gigs. Roberta told me this story, and she was a tremendous source of information and insight on these years. We all owe her a debt of gratitude for her friendship with and caring for this giant of twentieth century music. As Roberta (in her early twenties at the time) related the story:

> I had a good friend who was a writer for *Jazz Journal* named Verum Clapp. He and I would exchange records. I'd listened to Lonnie Johnson records, among others . . . , and I heard from Mr. Clapp that Lonnie was influential and that he really liked his style.
>
> One day after visiting Verum and exchanging records, I and my son were walking through the park across the street from my house, and as we were walking, I saw a man ahead of me, wearing an overcoat, fall. I ran over to him and asked if he was OK. He looked up at me—I can still see his face, he had this child-like look on his face, with large, twinkling eyes—and he asked me, "Can you sew?" I said, "I can do a lot of things, but sewing isn't my forte." Then he showed me a big tear in his trousers and said, "You gotta help me; I'm on my way to see about a job and I've got to have my pants repaired." He said he didn't have another pair of good pants, and the smile left his face. I felt bad for him, said I lived across the street, and said I'd give the sewing a shot. (Wouldn't happen today, but I did it then!)

I bandaged his knee and sewed the pants (not terribly well). Then he said, "Thanks, baby," and he left. But we forgot to exchange names, since he was in a panic to get to the job interview and I was in a panic faced with doing that sewing. The next day I hear a knock on the door, and there he was, big smile on his face, elated, with two huge containers of ice cream, and said, "I just wanted to thank you, 'cause I got my job." We had the ice cream. Then he asked if I'd have dinner with him. He said he "played a little guitar and sang some"—those were his exact words. He said he'd like to have me see what he did, that he wanted me to see him play, just as a thank you. I said OK.

So, that Friday night he came by to pick me up. He came with his guitar (all of his guitars he called "Baby") and a small amp. The gig was at The Villa in the west end of Toronto. When I walked in, I met the owner, Doug Cole, who I knew—I'd booked musicians with him before. Behind Doug I saw a playbill that said, "Appearing: the great Lonnie Johnson." And I said, "*That's* who he is!"

And that was my personal introduction to Lonnie Johnson.

Roberta became Lonnie's booking agent and friend. (Lonnie Johnson saying "I play a little guitar" was like Rembrandt saying "I mess around a little with paint brushes and canvas.")[6]

From evidence in Roberta's memory and a newspaper article I obtained, Lonnie had actually played at a Toronto coffeehouse called the New Gate of Cleve in the Yorkville section (around the corner from The Penny Farthing) in late May '65. He then went back to Philadelphia, before getting the call to appear at The Penny Farthing. The newspaper article had a photo with the caption, "Lonnie Johnson, 65, an authentic living legend in jazz."[7]

From later in 1965 through early 1969, after that appearance at The Penny Farthing, Lonnie played at The Villa and other places around Toronto like Castle George in George's Spaghetti House (often just called "George's Club"), the Kibitzeria (also owned by George), the Golden Nugget, Steele's Tavern, and the Riverboat Club—in which Neil Young and Joni Mitchell began their careers and people like Gordon Lightfoot and Kris Kristofferson performed. Lonnie appeared at the Riverboat with bluesmen Brownie McGhee and Sonny Terry. Lonnie

Lonnie Johnson and Louis Armstrong reunion in a Toronto concert hall dressing room, 1965.
PHOTO BY JIM MCHARG.

occasionally came to the Monday evening "Hoots" of the Toronto Folk Guild, which were held at the Riverboat Club. He also appeared a few times elsewhere in Canada, including Ottawa. (Mark Miller has tracked down and offered some more details on Lonnie's appearances in Canada.)[8] He didn't work constantly—by this time he was getting a pension from his years in the Chicago Musicians' Union, as well as some continuing song and record royalty money—but he got enough gigs to generally stay in Toronto.

For a while, Lonnie also had his own club, "Home of the Blues," established with financial help from an appreciator of his music, which was located at Huron Street and Harbor in Toronto. But it lasted less than a year; Lonnie was not the type to effectively manage a club business.

Jim McHarg related another event of interest. During this time, Louis Armstrong came to Toronto to give a concert at the O'Keefe Center and

McHarg arranged to get Louis and Lonnie together; Lonnie told him he hadn't seen Louis "for close on twenty years." They met in Armstrong's dressing room. As McHarg related it:" 'Ole Satchmo' was a figure I had been exposed to before [in public concerts]. The man talking to Lonnie was a different person entirely. Absent was the big grin, the flashing teeth and the popping eyeballs. In their place was registered the genuine pleasure of seeing an old friend."[9] McHarg took the photo of these two reunited old masters from New Orleans.

## *Stompin' at the Penny* —The Album

Drawing on their successful collaboration at The Penny Farthing, in November 1965 Lonnie and McHarg's band recorded the album, *Lonnie Johnson—Stompin' at the Penny, with Jim McHarg's Metro Stompers.*

Lonnie performs on only six of the thirteen tracks on the album. I'll focus on those tunes. The album opens with a sparkling, up-tempo version of the old jazz tune, "China Boy." The band, with Lonnie on electric guitar, plays the song in jaunty, classic New Orleans ensemble style, with propulsive momentum. He plays guitar in a vigorous, rippling, then romping manner and melds perfectly with the band. By the middle of the tune these guys are really cookin'.

Speaking of New Orleans music, the sixth track is a Stompers-Lonnie J version of the old Louis Armstrong-Hot Five masterwork, "West End Blues." Cornet player Charles Gall opens with his version of the famous (and daunting) Satchmo descending line, and manages to do his own (somewhat more modest) version quite well. Lonnie follows with ringing electric guitar work producing inventive variations on the main theme. He periodically punctuates those lines with sharply but richly played notes, and later adds some percussive strumming that adds to the texture. Meanwhile, Gall continues to contribute excellent counterpoint and complementing lines on cornet. All this is done while maintaining an energetic rhythmic pulse, with verve. Thus, the group turns in a very fine rendition of this classic, employing their own arrangement.

The ninth track on the album is a Lonnie Johnson instrumental, "Go Go Swing," which is essentially a successor to such late '30s Lonnie Swing-to-Rhythm & Blues tunes as "Mr. Johnson's Swing." In accord with Lonnie's strong ballad tendencies, they also do "My Mother's Eyes." The band's very nice Dixieland-style backing gives extra verve to this old emotive ballad and seems to boost Lonnie's energy in his singing—and keeps Lonnie from getting overly schmaltzy. The Stompers also add excellent accents and harmonic and tonal complements that add interest to the tune. This is my favorite of Lonnie's recordings of this song.

The real standouts on this album are two Lonnie J blues numbers, however. "Mr. Blues Walks"—on *The Ultimate Best of Lonnie Johnson* CD—is one of his very best, with Lonnie again showing he could rise to the level of greatness in his singing. He presents the words with power, nuance, verve, and excellent phrasing, and conveys the meaning of the lyrics in compelling, dramatic manner. The lyrics were still another demonstration of Lonnie's outstanding skills in that department, with his music, again, perfectly and powerfully suited to them:

> When the town is fast asleep, Mr. Blues be getting 'round (Repeat)
> Ev'ry time he knocks on somebody's door, he leaves 'em with a
>     mournful sound.
>
> Oh, woman screams out my man is gone, Lord, what am I gonna
>     do?! (Repeat)
> I never knew how much I loved him, until he said we were through.

Lonnie's brilliantly sung presentation of the lyrical story is accompanied by his strong electric guitar work, though nothing especially inventive and virtuosic, and by fine support from the Stompers. The latter includes particularly well-timed and well-cast backing, accents, and fill-ins between Lonnie's phrases by the cornet player; he played with punch, verve, style, perfect timing, and terrific cornet tone. This song is great music that is also very accessible to a wide range of people; and it's an excellent demonstration of how the blues is a prime foundation of jazz, which two musical forms Lonnie bridged so well. The ending is a superb demonstration of how superbly Lonnie could *swing* with the guitar and a "trad" jazz band.

His singing is equally great on the other core blues number, which is another outstanding Lonnie J song, "Bring It on Home to [Me] Mama," again with good electric guitar work and excellent support from the

Metro Stompers. It's impressive that, after forty years of songwriting, he could produce two more terrific tunes.

McHarg and the Stompers offered some excellently played Dixieland-style instrumentals without Lonnie, as well. Those tunes included "Dippermouth Blues," McHarg's own "Stompin' at the Penny," and "Canal Street Blues." Further, they do a good, soulfully played version of the blues classic, "Trouble in Mind," which includes a beautiful cornet-clarinet duet. Finally, they offer another gorgeous cornet-clarinet duet on a real oldie, "The Old Rugged Cross."

## Lonnie Johnson, the Person—From Interviews with Roberta Barrett

Roberta Barrett is a White woman of Jewish extraction. In my interviews with her she gave a good sense of what Lonnie Johnson the person was like, part of which comes in tales poignant and humorous:

**DA:** "Will you describe how he presented himself as a person? Earlier you said, 'The presence of this man was incredible.' Will you talk about how he presented himself and how people responded to him?"

**RB:** "Dean, he was the classiest guy I ever met. He always wore a suit; he always wore a tie and nice shirt; he always wore a diamond stickpin— that was kind of a statusy thing [the guitar stickpin—see photo opposite]. And he was always immaculate . . . And he carried himself with much *dignity* . . . He had a presence

Close-up of Lonnie Johnson with guitar and showing guitar diamond stick-pin, 1960. PHOTO BY AND COURTESY OF CHRIS ALBERTSON.

about him that was, I can't even describe it. It was amazing. . . . The only other man in my life, as a long-time musical booking agent, who got that kind of reaction was Louis Armstrong . . ."

RB (cont.): "And he had a child-like face . . . His eyes were huge, and they had this twinkle, almost like a very mischievous child."

[Lonnie also had some grace and perspective in dealing with other people, even when they could be trying:] "During Lonnie's first set at a Toronto club, a gentleman went up to the stage and asked him to play 'Red Sails in the Sunset' for he and his wife's anniversary. Lonnie said fine and sang it. But this guy and his wife talked all the way through the song. Then, during the break between sets, that guy came over to Lonnie and said he and his wife had missed the song and would Lonnie do it again for them? He said OK and went back up, again dedicated it to the couple and sang it again. When he finished and was packing up, a waiter, who was also a budding musician, came up to Lonnie and asked him: 'Mr. Johnson, I have to ask you this: That fellow requested a tune and you played it, but the guy talked all the way through it—in fact, he talked through the entire first set. Why would you ever play it again for him?!' Lonnie said, 'I do that all the time because I never want to be as rude as some of the customers.'"

Speaking of caring about his audience, Roberta also related this tale: "When Lonnie found out someone in his audience had an anniversary or a birthday, he would sometimes impulsively have the waiter take a bottle of champagne or wine to them 'on the house.' But that bottle would actually go on Lonnie's own tab; and when it came time for Lonnie's pay after the gig, there would be little—or he'd even *owe* the club! This happened several times." (That's unlike various other blues and jazz guys who would drink up their pay *themselves*.)

He also had a remarkable perspective on race, given all he had been through in life. And, while he generally thought Canadians showed little prejudice (Roberta warned him that it was there, just not as great as in the U.S.), he could also respond to racism sharply—but sometimes with a good dose of pointed humor. Roberta Barrett told me this illustrative tale:

One time, with my two little kids, I took a walk with Lonnie through Yorkville Village. We were passing a church and two older women looked at us in disdain. Now I must admit, it might have looked to some like an odd picture. Here was an older Black man pushing a baby carriage, two very blond children, and me, a young, White, red-headed girl. Anyway, as we were passing, these two ladies were making some crude remarks out loud. Lonnie overheard them. He then pushed the carriage closer to them and said, "I see you're interested in my baby; would you like a closer look?" Then he pulled the blanket away from my one year old daughter, showing this blond, blue-eyed child. And he laughed; I've never seen him laugh so hard. Then he turned to me and said, and this is a direct quote: "You know, them women need church, and a lot of it, to clean up their minds."

Lonnie made clear he didn't hate those with racist attitudes; he only felt sorry for them and what it did to their minds and spirits.

## Recordings for Folkways

In 1967 Lonnie was brought to Moses Asch's Folkways Records to make what turned out to be his final recordings. (Neither the CD nor leading discographies specify the exact date; in fact, the original tapes were filed away and then rediscovered and prepared for record release by Sam Charters in 1982. Moe Asch's independent record company operated in a more informal manner than the big commercial companies like RCA and Columbia[10]). The remastered CD of the album (from Smithsonian/Folkways), *Lonnie Johnson: The Complete Folkways Recordings*, includes all 23 recordings he made in that '67 session. Fortunately for music history, while there, Moe Asch conducted an interview with Lonnie, which has been drawn on for this book. The CD includes a four-and-a-half-minute segment of that interview, so people can hear Lonnie discussing his music and life in his own voice.

Starting with the first two songs he recorded, Lonnie, now age 73, showed he still had excellent vocal and guitar artistry to offer. On the first two tunes, "Raise the Window High" and "Tears Don't Fall No More," Lonnie's singing is excellent in pure quality and expressiveness, displaying nuance, soulfulness, and power. Those two songs, though no composing credits are explicitly given in the CD liner notes, are clearly Lonnie's own new compositions. The lyrics for both are very good (though perhaps not quite at the level of his most masterful lyrics) and the music works excellently for both. For example, the following are the opening two verses of "Tears Don't Fall No More." In his singing, he does a masterful job of evocatively extending the note for and enunciation of the word "cried" in the "B" line of the first verse and the same for "please" and "blues" in both lines of the second verse (which I denote by adding vowels in the right places):

Darling the day you left home, everything was all right

Darling the day you left home, I thought everything was going
all right

When I found that empty pillow, I walked the floor and
*CRIIIIED* . . . all night

Baby, baby *pleeease* . . . , *PLEASE* hurry home to me (repeat)

'Cause I've got rocks in my bed, and these *BLUUUES* . . . is
killin' me.

"Long Road to Travel" is a redo of his December 1960 version of "New Orleans Blues," but in faster, more jaunty manner. It's well done, but his magnificent April 1960 version can't be beat. "Old Rocking Chair" is Lonnie's second recording of this Hoagy Carmichael classic; he takes it at a faster clip than usual, which results in some rushed phrasings, and also results in some less-than-great vocal tone in his higher range; the same goes for "How Deep Is the Ocean."

"Lazy Mood" is a well-constructed instrumental, with interesting and rich harmonic touches, that creates a nice overall feel. "Mister Trouble" is a redo of his 1965 song with the Metro Stompers, "Mr. Blues Walks"; it is played at a faster tempo which doesn't allow him to draw out and dramatize the excellent lyrics, some of which are changed. There are also several standard 1960s style Lonnie blues numbers on the album, with his regular '60s style electric guitar work. "Summertime" is also redone, but it's hard to top the masterpiece he produced in December 1960. This one is taken too fast, with some rushed phrasings;

but the guitar solo has interesting variations on the musical theme. The early blues standard "C. C. Rider," employing some of his own lyrics, is well done, in a jaunty manner and again at a rather fast pace. (Did he have extra coffee before and during this session?!) Lonnie also did several emotional ballads; the most notable are still another recording of "Careless Love" and "My Mother's Eyes."

The last song recorded in this final Lonnie Johnson record session was its own perfect ending for his remarkable, historic recording career. After he recorded the series of tunes and after he asked Lonnie to talk about his past in the interview, Asch said, "Play one more blues song. . . ." Coming around full circle, he then played and sang the "B" side of his very first hit recorded some 42 years earlier in November 1925, "Falling Rain Blues." Unlike the original, he plays it on guitar; and unlike the three-minute restriction of the old 78 records, he does an extended version of the song, taking four and three-quarters minutes to offer an excellent rendition.

## A Meeting of Giants—The Once and Future Kings of Guitar

Surprisingly, given how much influence Lonnie had on B. B. King, as of late 1968 they had never met in person. In late 1968 or early 1969 (nobody involved remembers the exact date), B. B. King was appearing in Toronto. He called concert promoter Richard Flohil and said, "I've never met Lonnie Johnson. I hear he lives in Toronto; do you know where he is?" Flohil called Lonnie's friend Howard Mathews, owner of a soul-food restaurant, the Underground Railroad, to ask him where Lonnie was. (Earlier Mathews had managed the Kibitzeria, where Lonnie had performed.) Howard said, "He's sitting in my living room." Flohil picked up B. B. and took him to the house of Howard Matthews and wife Salome Bey (a fine singer) in Toronto. Brownie McGhee and Sonny Terry were also present. Sadly for history, Flohil thought he would be intruding, so he didn't stay in the kitchen where B. B. and Lonnie had their primary conversation. When I interviewed B. B. he said of the meeting: "Lonnie seemed to be very happy to meet me. He'd heard of me, and he heard things I'd said about him, and he thanked me for all of that." In our 2005 interview, "B" couldn't remember much in the way of the specifics of the conversation, just that they were delighted to meet one another and had a nice, warm talk. Interestingly, after relating to me how much he respected Lonnie and what a model Lonnie was for him and others, B told me that when he met Lonnie he thought to himself, "I just wish I could have that kind of influence on some of the young people. But he had it on me—ever since I was quite young." Of course, B. B. King went on to have a tremendous influence on musicians and young people of all sorts; he certainly made that wish come true.[11]

## Lonnie Johnson and the Guitar in Twentieth-Century Music

Over the course of this book I have presented many testimonials, analyses and examples demonstrating Lonnie Johnson's tremendous, pervasive impact on guitar playing in twentieth-century popular music. This section offers a summary of those impacts; and it discusses how artistry on the guitar in popular music developed over the century. It begins with two special cases of his influence, along with a bit of historic testimony regarding Lonnie's later use of the electric guitar, which has been criticized by some writers.

## Crucial Connections for Music History:
## Lonnie and B. B. King; Lonnie and Buddy Guy

In my interview with B. B. King he said:

> "Out of the many guitarists, there's five that stays with me. This is my MP3 [points to his MP3 player on the table in the back of his tour bus]. There Lonnie is right now; I have several of his songs right there. Lonnie was number one in my book. Number two was Blind Lemon Jefferson, three was Charlie Christian, four was Django [Reinhardt], and five was T-Bone Walker. Those five people was my idols. But when you mention guitar, the first thing I think of is Lonnie Johnson."

It's interesting how he used the present tense in talking about Lonnie's music on his MP3 player; Lonnie and his music are a continuing presence for King. That was exemplified by B. B.'s recording of "Tomorrow

Night" and "My Love Is Down" (from 1944) for his 2008 CD, *One Kind Favor*. Then he switched to the past tense, thinking of blues history.

In the interview I asked him: "In *Blues All Around Me* [his autobiography] you said Lonnie was a prime early influence, and you noted that he 'had a lyrical way with the guitar.' Would you tell me how he influenced you? For example, was that 'lyrical way with a guitar' a significant influence?" King responded: "His technique was just different from anyone else, to me . . . If you listen to some of the instrumental things he did, you can hear blues that nobody else was playing, putting that kind of stuff in them." He specifically cited the guitar duets Lonnie and Eddie Lang did in 1928–1929. With Lonnie's masterful solo guitar instrumentals like "Away Down in the Alley Blues" and "Playing with the Strings," in addition to the 10 duets with Lang, the "kind of stuff he put in" those "instrumental things he did" included exquisite touch, tone and vibrato and a lyrical style that, indeed, "nobody else was playing"; and that included virtuoso guitar lines of great melodic invention. As noted in chapter 4, listening to the unequalled tone and lyrical playing of Lonnie on recordings from the later 1920s on, and then listening to B. B. King's playing, especially that famous vibrato, touch, and tone, Lonnie Johnson's profound influence on the guitar artistry of Mr. King is clear. That influence subsequently extended from there to the legions of blues, Rock and even jazz guitarists influenced by B. B. King.

When I asked about other Lonnie Johnson songs he was influenced by, B. B. cited "The Devil's Woman" (the 1942 remake of "She's Making Whoopee in Hell Tonight"), "Broken Levee Blues" and "Lonesome Road" from 1942. And as related in chapter 4, B. B.'s favorite tune was either "Roamin' Rambler Blues" (1927) or the 1942 version, "Rambler's Blues," released when he was seventeen and beginning serious pursuit of music. Listening at his Aunt 'Mima's house in his teens included 1920s recordings, as well as those of the late '30s and early '40s.

More broadly, as stated in *The B. B. King Treasures*:

> It was Johnson's ability to cross musical boundaries without losing track of his identity as a blues musician that B. B. emulated throughout his life. . . . As his popularity grew, he would introduce people around the world to the blues by doing exactly what Lonnie Johnson had done:

He would take the blues beyond nearly everyone's expectations, without ever leaving the blues behind.[12]

**Lonnie Johnson, B. B. King and the Electric Guitar** B. B. then added to his statement on Lonnie's influence, noting to me how Lonnie updated his playing, as time went on and as technology and musical exploration took the guitar into the electric domain: "And then it was so nice when Lonnie started to play the *electric* guitar. Oh God, when he started playing the electric guitar—he'd already been doing it to me, but he did it *even more* then!"[13]

That is especially interesting and historic testimony, since a number of critics and writers have suggested that later in his career, when he had switched to the electric guitar, Lonnie had declined as an instrumental artist—that the electric guitar "got in the way" of Lonnie's better playing, as an astute observer put it about one prominent event—and that Lonnie sank into lesser work and playing standard riffs over and over. There is some validity to the latter complaint for a number of Lonnie's later recordings. But B. B. King's comment suggests reconsideration of that complaint as a general conclusion.

Indeed, *The* Ultimate *Best of Lonnie Johnson* CD provides compelling musical evidence that, for a number of recordings at least, Lonnie played superbly with the electric and used its unique characteristics to add dimensions to his artistry. That companion CD is arranged so that the first seven tracks are all masterpieces, spanning his recording career, as well as being music that is accessible to a broader audience. It is not an accident that on four of those first seven tracks, Lonnie plays an electric guitar. Chronologically, the first of those is his masterful 1948 recording of "Backwater Blues," in which he uses the unique characteristics of the electric guitar, especially including the special tone and greater capacity for sustain, to create a recording of stunning artistic merit, maintaining superb overall thematic coherence in the guitar music *and* making his playing perfectly fit the lyrics. His 1960 recording of "New Orleans Blues" again shows how effectively he could use an electric guitar to enhance his musical art; the touch and use of extended bent notes are striking in their expressive effect.

**Buddy Guy on Lonnie J** Buddy Guy is one of the greatest guitarists in blues history; Eric Clapton once called him "the greatest guitarist alive." He was a protégé of Muddy Waters in Chicago starting in the late 1950s, after coming up from Louisiana. In my interview with him, I asked Buddy, "When I listen, for example, to your 1963 recording, 'Worried Mind,' I hear such smoothly flowing guitar lines. The style is distinctly Buddy Guy, but do I hear a little Lonnie Johnson influence there?"

Buddy responded: "Yes you do! Anything I got, it started from Lonnie—and from Lightnin' Hopkins, Arthur Crudup and a few others." And he remembered avidly listening to Lonnie Johnson records on the radio in his earlier years back in Louisiana.

Then he related this delightful story:

> I said, hey man, if I make it to school, I want to be taught this. First time in high school in Baton Rouge, I went to a guy there and said, "I want to take lessons." And the teacher, he said, "OK, I can teach you, but you gotta get Book 1." I said, "No, I already got Book 1, and it was Lonnie Johnson and the early Muddy Waters records." He said, "I can't teach you that!" I said, "Well, you can't teach me then."

**Lowell Fulson and Albert King on Lonnie** Lowell Fulson was a major blues guitarist and singer from the later '40s through the '80s. He liked Blind Lemon Jefferson. "But the guy whose guitar playin' I like better, which I didn't hear till I got older when I really got to playin', was Lonnie Johnson." Blues great Albert King (who was a big influence on Stevie Ray Vaughan, among others) cited Lonnie Johnson (and T-Bone Walker) as principal among the musicians he liked and was influenced by.[14]

## Beyond B. B. and Buddy: Lonnie Johnson and the Development of Artistry on the Guitar in the Twentieth Century

This discussion continues with a review of key figures in the development of artistry on the guitar in the decades after Lonnie laid down most of the foundations of guitar lead and solo work in the second half of the 1920s through 1931. Of course, a section of a chapter is not the place for a comprehensive review, so this discussion must be selective and concise, and it focuses especially on guitarists whom Lonnie influenced, directly or indirectly. This review is important, however, for the broader musical perspective in the book. But it's also intended to add a few notes on key elements of the development of artistry on the guitar beyond but building on Lonnie Johnson's influence. This book has demonstrated that Lonnie was the prime founding father of virtuoso guitar work for all of popular music, and he laid down many of the principal elements and techniques of such guitar playing. Later, others took it further and added elements of their own; it's valuable to briefly trace that whole development here. As I've said, this book is about much more than simply a biography of an old musician. The bibliography I've included lists additional readings on this subject for those who want to explore further.

The first guitarist of major significance after Lonnie Johnson and Eddie Lang was actually from Europe: Django Reinhardt.

**Django Reinhardt** (1910–1953)  This Manouche gypsy of Belgium and France was a unique genius of the guitar. At first he was an accompanist and played gypsy and French café-type music. But especially starting with records played for him by his friend Emile Savitry in summer 1931, he began intensely listening to jazz.

In his 2004 biography, Michael Dregni reports that Django listened to Duke Ellington's band, Joe Venuti's Blue Four with Eddie Lang on guitar and Venuti on violin, etc. But Django was most moved by Louis Armstrong's powerful, soulful playing, especially in the "Hot Five" and "Hot Seven" records. Dregni then draws on Savitry's memories (from an interview), and notes that Django and Savitry specifically listened to the Armstrong-Hot Five record, "Savoy Blues." Regarding that recording, Savitry reported Django saying, "the guitarist who accompanied Armstrong is out of tune!" The problem with that report is that *two* guitarists played on that recording and neither Dregni nor (apparently) Savitry relate Django's assertion of which one is out of tune. The first one to be heard on that side is Johnny St. Cyr, playing rhythm guitar. And listening to the recording, he does sound a bit out of tune. Of course, the second guitarist on the recording, playing an impressive solo and adding a new voice to the Hot Five, was Lonnie Johnson—who *was* in tune and whose playing has been so highly praised by everyone from Gunther Schuller to that Scottish physician in the 1950s, whose comments were related early in this chapter. Unfortunately, either Savitry didn't report the rest of Django's thoughts on that record or Dregni didn't relate them (though Savitry was no music expert). What a shame. But this is evidence that Django directly heard Lonnie Johnson's guitar work, at the beginning of Django's development of his jazz playing. As noted, he also heard Eddie Lang (who was important in his own right, but was also influenced by Lonnie). Django's trademark was scintillating lead and solo guitar work, with remarkable, creative lines. Since Eddie Lang was nowhere near Lonnie as a creative melodic improviser, as discussed in chapter 5, Django had to have been more influenced by Lonnie. Now, remember what the music writer Tony Russell said about that Hot Five recording, "Savoy Blues," on which Lonnie played alongside Johnny St. Cyr: "To hear these three sides is to hear the turning of a page. St. Cyr was a well-respected musician, and not an old man . . . , but in approach, technique and even temperament he belonged to another era. . . ." Thus, Lonnie was laying down the foundations for the future of jazz guitar as a lead and solo instrument. Indeed, his virtuoso, lyrical improvised lead lines, countermelodies, and accents were striking for Django to hear, and he had to have been influenced by Lonnie Johnson's playing. After hearing "Savoy Blues," he must have sought out the other two Hot Five recordings with Louis and Lonnie, as well—especially "Hotter Than That," which, as Schuller said, was "a highlight of classic jazz."[15]

Django's playing was a brilliant development in jazz guitar, and he is recognized as one of the few truly great jazz players produced in Europe (though there have been many very good ones). Along with his prime partner, violinist Stephane Grappelli, and the rest of the "Quintet of the Hot Club of France" (two other rhythm guitarists including Django's brother and a bass player), their recordings from 1934–1939 received a lot of attention in Europe and America. Django's speed, flair, and creativity gave a further boost to the guitar's status as a lead and solo instrument. (The featured pair of Django and Stephane Grappelli, *as a duo,* had their original inspiration from the 1920s recordings of Eddie Lang and his Philadelphia partner, Joe Venuti.)

More specifically, Django seems influenced by Lonnie Johnson in the following ways. In his expert analysis of key features of Django's playing, Dan Lambert points out that "with his sense of melodic invention and ear for musical drama, Django could transform the most familiar song into a musical adventure." As I've documented, starting about nine years before Django's first significant recordings, Lonnie was the original guitarist with an unparalleled ability for creative melodic invention, and he certainly had an "ear for musical drama," in solo guitar instrumentals, in guitar duets, with voice and guitar, and as part of small band music; just listen to "Away Down in the Alley Blues," "Midnight Call Blues" with Lang, "Hotter Than That" and "Savoy Blues" with Armstrong and the Hot Five, etc. And, in the most extraordinary manner, he could also "transform the most familiar song into a musical adventure," a prime example being Lonnie's transformation of the old Negro folk song "Uncle Ned" into a dazzling display of creative guitar virtuosity in 1931. That's especially interesting because the song Lambert focuses on to explore Django's playing was none other than his own version of that same song, called "You Rascal You" in this case. That was the title used when Armstrong had recorded the song, which was surely the immediate inspiration for Django's version. Lambert also notes that Django liked to "mix chords and single notes"—which, again, Lonnie was doing with unparalleled virtuosity in various recordings in the 1920s. But let me be clear: I'm not saying Lonnie was Django's primary influence, simply that, given what was just noted, he must have had some significant influence on Django. Django was explicit in stating that the recordings of Louis Armstrong were his greatest inspiration. It's also important to note what Django did *not* achieve at Lonnie's level: the exquisite *touch, tone, and vibrato.*[16]

**Charlie Christian** (1916–1942) Charlie Christian provided the next big boost for the guitar as a virtuoso lead instrument in jazz, and beyond. There is no explicit evidence of a direct influence by Lonnie on Charlie Christian. But there is strong circumstantial evidence, along with the assessment of some top jazz writers. At two points in the early 1930s, young Aaron Walker (later dubbed "T-Bone") and younger

Charlie Christian got together while both were in Oklahoma City, Christian's home, and played guitar together on street corners and elsewhere, exploring guitar technique and trading ideas. (Charlie grew up in a very musical family.) It is inconceivable that T-Bone would have failed to pass on to Charlie awareness of the very urban/urbane leading guitar virtuosity and musicianship of Lonnie Johnson and recommend recordings to listen to (see below). Further, both T-Bone and Charlie "took guitar lessons on a regular basis from . . . [African-American] Chuck Hamilton" of Oklahoma City. As a professional on guitar and a guitar teacher, there is no question that Hamilton would have been very aware of the best and most important guitarist in jazz and blues in the late '20s and early '30s, Lonnie Johnson. And he would have learned what he could from Lonnie's records and probably from seeing him live, especially while Lonnie was in the Dallas area, just 200 miles to the south; Hamilton surely would have passed on what he learned to very promising students like Charlie Christian and Aaron Walker. There is testimony that Charlie was influenced by Django Reinhardt, as well.[17]

Also, as Chris Albertson observed: "Lonnie's . . . introduction of single-line countermelodies deeply influenced the work of such younger men as Charlie Christian and Django Reinhardt, and set the course for much of today's music."[18]

In August 1939, after record producer and talent scout John Hammond urged Benny Goodman to try out Charlie, he became a dazzling addition to Goodman's small group music. Charlie had a tremendous feel for the music and a deep commitment to jazz playing, and he came along in the first years of the electric guitar.

In fact, a few years after electric guitars became available, Christian quickly developed a distinct idea of what the electric guitar could do. "He heard it as a distinct voice, not just a loud guitar playing guitar-type music, but a new instrument, playing single-line solos, like a saxophone . . ." with a clear, ringing sound. Most importantly, he was "the first to play [the electric guitar] with complete authority." And thus, while Lonnie and a couple of others actually recorded with an electric before Christian, it was Charlie who first compellingly showed how distinct, artistic, and powerful an instrument the electric guitar could be, which had a profound effect on popular music thereafter. Besides many jazz guitarists, B. B. King cites Christian as an important influence on his growing sense of what could be done with an electric guitar. Charlie also had a great rhythmic sense and used a creative flexibility of beat; that, along with his inventive melodic lines, "lines that flowed from him with such grace, like the flight of birds, free and unforced, emerging without any apparent effort," gave his playing an excitement and aesthetic that provided a big further boost to the guitar as featured solo instrument.[19] Tragically, due to tuberculosis and not taking care of himself, he died in 1942 at age 25.

But, as with Django, Christian did not achieve the level of touch, tone, and vibrato that Lonnie Johnson did.

**T-Bone Walker** (1910–1975) In his "biographical encyclopedia of the blues," Robert Santelli offered the generally accepted assessment of this artist, who was born in Texas in 1910 and grew up in Dallas: "Aaron T-Bone Walker was a creator of modern blues and a pioneer in the development of the electric guitar sound that shaped virtually all of popular music in the post-World War II period. [And,] Walker was the quintessential blues guitarist. He influenced virtually every major post-World War II [electric blues] guitarist, including B. B. King, Jimi Hendrix . . . Buddy Guy . . . Eric Clapton." When asked by blues writers Jim and Amy O'Neal, "Who did you listen to when you were trying to learn guitar? Who were your main influences?" T-Bone replied: "Lonnie Johnson and Leroy Carr and his guitar player, Scrapper Blackwell." He also said he saw and heard Lonnie in Dallas several times in his early years in the area. As discussed earlier, Lonnie was based in Dallas from mid-1927 through the summer of 1928. At that time Aaron Walker was seventeen to eighteen years old and in the first years of his serious guitar playing—prime time for being influenced by the brilliant and urbane guitarist and singer, Lonnie Johnson. Remember what the jazz musician Buddy Tate said of the time in his youth near Dallas when he had the chance to play a professional gig with Lonnie in that precise period: "Lonnie Johnson was a big man, you know, he had hits one after another . . . To play with Lonnie Johnson! You *know* we were all excited."[20] That is just how T-Bone had to have felt. And that feeling was surely enhanced because T-Bone aspired to be a sophisticated *urban* guitarist and singer of blues and, to some extent, jazz music. Lonnie was the perfect model for him.

After Lonnie, T-Bone was the next leading figure in blues guitar to employ more sophisticated, jazz-like playing. Mark Humphrey has summarized T-Bone's playing well: He used "crisply articulated notes interspersed with sexy slurs in the manner of a jazz trumpeter. His storming vamps with chords, often echoed by a horn section, were a six-string imitation of blaring brass and reeds . . . [And he employed] impeccable phrasing, subtle syncopation, and thoughtful depth [in] his lean guitar monologues."[21]

I should also note **Charlie Byrd** (1925–1999), especially since he's mentioned in the tale of Lonnie's accident and recuperation that follows shortly. A very interesting and unique guitarist, Byrd basically had one foot in the jazz world and the other in the classical world. Charlie took a master class from Segovia, for example. And even when playing in jazz bands, he often used a classical guitar. I have to assume that Byrd's interest in Lonnie and his recognition of Lonnie Johnson's importance came especially from his appreciation of Lonnie's almost classical guitar-like playing on solo instrumentals like "Away Down in the Alley Blues" and from the Johnson-Lang duets, as well as from his recordings with the Louis Armstrong and Duke Ellington bands.

His trio of the late '50s and early '60s, "which featured Charlie Byrd's original finger-style jazz guitar, made an enormous impact on the jazz world." And then in 1961 the U.S. State Department sponsored a South American tour with Byrd's trio. "During this tour the idea occurred to Byrd to mix jazz improvisation and harmony with the samba" and other popular Brazilian music. In 1962 he linked up with popular jazz saxophone player Stan Getz and made a best-selling record of that music.[22]

Speaking of jazz guitarists, as well as other ethnic music, British photographer-writer Val Wilmer told me that Lauderic Caton of Trinidad, who later was a pioneer of electric jazz guitar in Britain, "arrived at his tone listening to Lonnie Johnson on his landlord's Victrola." He was especially influenced by Lonnie's playing on the 12-string guitar used in the duets with Lang.[23]

(Beyond Django Reinhardt and Charlie Christian, jazz writers have too often ignored the guitar in jazz. For example, there are but a very few pages on Django and Charlie Christian, very brief and inaccurate mention of Eddie Lang and Lonnie Johnson, and almost nothing else in James Lincoln Collier's *The Making of Jazz*. Another example: Despite an entry featuring a jazz performer of relatively modest significance as Don Pullen, no section in *Visions of Jazz* by Gary Giddins featured a guitarist—though his 2009 general history with Scott DeVeaux offered some attention to guitarists. A blessed exception to this poor treatment of guitarists by jazz writers in general histories is the multiple editions of Joachim Berendt's *Jazz Book*.)

## Country and Rock Guitarists

I've taken note of the major impact of the blues on Country music. But even jazz had an impact on that music, most prominently with the very influential and popular band of the 1930s and 1940s, Bob Wills and His Texas Playboys, who were the great force in what came to be called "Western Swing." A leading guitarist in that particular school of music, as well as in the major stream in Country Music called "honky-tonk," was Floyd Tillman: "His single-string solos modeled after Lonnie Johnson's, Tillman, while with the [Blue Ridge] Playboys, helped popularize the use of the electric guitar in country music." Tillman, in turn, was a significant influence on Rockabilly founding father of Rock & Roll, **Carl Perkins**; but, as the Perkins biography/autobiography says, it's very likely that Carl also directly heard Lonnie's impressive single-string runs and other guitar work on the radio in his youth and was influenced by Johnson's guitar playing.[24]

In chapter 7, I discussed how Lonnie was a significant influence on **Buddy Holly** and **Chuck Berry**. Their guitar work as founding fathers of Rock & Roll brought the electric guitar to the forefront of popular music and started the establishment of the electric guitar as the prime icon of Rock.

**Chet Atkins** (1924–2001) became arguably the greatest and most influential virtuoso guitarist in the history of Country music—though Atkins often transcended the Country music genre. He was strongly influenced by Lonnie. Chet said: "Another Black musician I listened to and admired was Lonnie Johnson, one of the great guitar improvisers of his time."[25] A very versatile player, Atkins drew on the blues, jazz and Ragtime, traditional Country music, and even an occasional touch of Classical music, and he played everything from sophisticated jazzy instrumentals to tastefully embellished pop tunes. In effect following in the footsteps (or finger-steps) of Lonnie and Eddie Lang, Chet also made fine guitar duet albums, perhaps the best of which was with Doc Watson (the superb Country and Folk acoustic guitarist), *Chet Atkins and Doc Watson: Reflections.*

**Eric Clapton** is so universally known and widely written about that little needs to be said here. Let me just highlight two things. As he has talked about, he was profoundly influenced by American blues guitarists and other bluesmen, starting in the early 1960s. And in the '60s he increasingly realized that he could take the old Country blues and "modernize them," as he said. Well, as shown in this book, Lonnie Johnson had started doing that thirty-five years earlier. But Clapton began his intense musical development during the Blues Revival of the early '60s, when the rediscovery of the old Country blues musicians was getting lots of attention, and he paid special attention to the Country blues artists, especially Robert Johnson.

Interestingly regarding another source of his musical beginnings, Clapton has said: "Ever since I first heard the guitar introduction to Buddy Holly's 'That'll Be the Day,' listening to, and eventually making music has been a very serious business to me." In chapter 7 I reported that Holly's band "used to sit around and listen to blues pickers like Lonnie Johnson. Like, there was a [Lonnie J] song called 'Jelly Roll' ['Jelly Roll Baker'], and the style of guitar that Buddy played on 'That'll Be the Day'—that was the sort of guitar that that old blues picker played."[26]

As Clapton grew with the '60s burgeoning of Rock music, he was a central figure who brought into Rock the deep blues feel, making musical lines that soared with that feel. Clapton also offered a level of sophistication in his virtuoso guitar work that was virtually unprecedented in Rock music. And though he has never explicitly recognized Lonnie's influence, he drew on the foundations Lonnie laid to offer tonal purity, great melodic invention, and superb touch and vibrato, and his style was really developed from Lonnie's original, via T-Bone Walker and B. B. King. Actually, Clapton saluted that influence in an indirect but striking way: In a superb Martin Scorsese-directed film titled *Nothin' But the Blues* (not easy to find, for some reason) of concerts related to his *Back to the Cradle* album, Eric said:

> There were a couple of people that had something that I didn't hear anywhere else taken to its furthest development, which is the finger vibrato. . . . T-Bone would play a lot of phrasing, but he wouldn't really end up on a note and make it [here Clapton hits a nice-toned note with rich, resonating vibrato]—give it that vibrato thing. That's what it was. It's almost like a *voice*, like a human voice. . . . And the great players, and B. B. is one of them, have the kind of vibrato that you would *die* for."[27]

In fact, it was Lonnie Johnson who first took the finger vibrato "to its furthest development." And as this book has shown, the great vibrato that B. B. King developed was directly inspired by Lonnie Johnson's extraordinarily expressive vibrato. It should also be noted that, while with John Mayall's "Bluesbreakers" band, Clapton lived with Mayall and "studied [his] extensive collection of blues records." Put that together with Mayall's statement that, "I was initially inspired by guys like Josh White, Leadbelly and Lonnie Johnson," and there is more reason for concluding Clapton was influenced by Lonnie."[28]

Clapton was also much better than most of the noted Rock guitarists in being able to maintain a full thematic coherence in his guitar work, again, first developed by Lonnie.

A prime early inspiration for **George Harrison** was Lonnie Donegan—strongly influenced by Lonnie J; and in a *Guitar Player* interview, George noted Lonnie J's influence on Donegan.[29]

There has also been much public note and writing about Jimi Hendrix. Most important to note is that Hendrix took the great *expressive* capacity of the guitar that Lonnie first developed, drew on what Charlie Christian, T-Bone Walker, and B. B. King established with the special capabilities of the electric guitar, and "turned [the electric guitar's] sound into an elemental force," as Robert Palmer put it. Hendrix took all the electric capacities that had been developed for the guitar and related amps by the '60s and used them to further an ultra-modern, wailing expressionism. But I must add here what is a bit of Rock heresy (normally a Rock oxymoron): For my aesthetic sense, Hendrix, with his extraordinary mastery of technique on the guitar (from endless hours of practice), tended to get too lost in the electric guitar effects wailing and sailing off in all directions, so that the actual quality of the music he produced suffered at times. In the momentary experience of a concert setting (or even a recording), that can be exciting, but a fair amount of it was more experimental effect than successful production of enduring, great *music*. In his last months Jimi himself said essentially that, implicitly referring to his lack of "thematic coherence," which I discuss below in review of Lonnie's artistry: In a discussion, someone said of another guitarist, "He's all over the guitar. Sometimes it sounds like it's not too orderly." Hendrix commented: "Sounds like someone we know" and laughed at himself.[30] And as Charles Shaar Murray wrote, in his last months, "Hendrix was bored to death with power-trio hard rock."[31]

Guitarist Michael Bloomfield and others reported that Jimi listened to and studied the main forms of Black music, from the early blues guys to Muddy Waters and B. B. King to Rhythm & Blues players and even jazz; "he loved the real old Black music forms, and they poured out in his playing."[32] Hendrix was very influenced by B. B. King; as he said to a stage partner in an early year of his playing, late 1962: "I was trying to get that B. B. King sound." He learned from T-Bone Walker records, as well.[33] It's also revealing that late in his short life Hendrix said, "The background of our music is a spiritual blues thing. Now I want to bring [my playing] down to earth. I want to get back to the blues, because that's what I am."[34] So, Jimi was perhaps directly, and certainly was indirectly influenced by Lonnie Johnson. A suggestive element is his use of Lonnie-like striking vibrato, especially derived from King, but maybe directly from Lonnie, as well. For example, see Jimi's vibrato on a blues on acoustic guitar and on an electric version of "Purple Haze" on the video, *Experience Jimi Hendrix*.[35] I don't know of Hendrix explicitly mentioning Lonnie's music; Lenny Carlson suggests Jimi "cited Johnson's influence," but doesn't offer the source for that statement.[36]

As mentioned, a central aspect of that influence was in the *expressive* use of the guitar. Let me offer some interesting perspective on that. Speaking of the finest acoustic guitars, classical guitarist Julian Bream said, "the guitar . . . is an instrument of the senses. . . . ; it can convey beautifully a delicate thread of poetry." Then he made a striking two-part observation: "It is the constant reminder of such a thread in this, the noisiest and most violent century in history, that I believe to be Segovia's greatest achievement."[37] A profound thought. *But*, the following also shows how the *electric* guitar, in the hands of a virtuoso who understood *that* instrument, could use it to musically "comment" on that noisy, violent century in very effective manner: A particular Hendrix guitar performance shows that *and* brings me back to the theme of music, modern art, and society. First, some artistic perspective: In 1936 during the Spanish Civil War, Picasso was personally horrified but artistically inspired by the appalling bombing of the village of Guernica in Northern Spain by Franco's "Nationalist"/fascist army. He painted a powerful, wrenching, moving masterpiece of modern art, simply titled *Guernica*. In mid-August 1969 a who's who of Rock and Folk music performed at the now-legendary Woodstock music festival. At Woodstock Jimi Hendrix played what, in form, was the national anthem, but used his electric guitar to produce what we might call a musical expressionist "painting" that stunningly evoked and depicted the sound and fury of bombing in the Vietnam War and powerfully commented on the destruction and madness of the actions. Thus, with his electric guitar, Hendrix "painted" the "Guernica" of and for America at that stage in its public and cultural history; it was a masterpiece of modern musical art. That form of expression was appropriate since in the 1960s Rock and Folk music were the leading modes of artistic and social expression in the culture. And so, Hendrix took the expressive use of the guitar that was primarily and originally established by Lonnie Johnson and carried it to extraordinary artistic heights—and to powerful musical commentary on socio-political matters.

**Carlos Santana** (born 1947): It should also be mentioned that Santana was still another Rock guitar great, with one of the most sublimely, soulfully, powerfully and expressively distinctive guitar styles ever. He was profoundly influenced by B. B. King—and hence, at least indirectly influenced by Lonnie.[38]

**Duane Allman (and Jimmy Page)—and the Symbolism of the Allman Brothers Band** Another key passage from Robert Palmer in his Rock & Roll history spelled out the key elements of Duane Allman's artistry on guitar—one of the greatest "guitar heroes" of Rock history. Palmer pointed out the "tonal elegance, long-lined lyricism, and coherent thematic development" of Duane's playing. Starting in chapter 4 I noted how Lonnie Johnson originally developed those key elements of artistry on the guitar. Further, in his biography of Duane Allman, Randy Poe points out that B. B. King was one of Duane's biggest influences, if not *the* greatest influence; in illustration, Duane recorded "B. B. King Medley" in 1968. *This* book has spelled out Lonnie's profound influence on B. B. King. It's also worth noting that on their greatest album, the *Allman Brothers Band at Fillmore East*, they play T-Bone Walker's "Stormy Monday." In his autobiography, Gregg Allman also stressed B. B.'s influence on Duane.[39]

Rock Guitar God **Jimmy Page** summed up the huge influence of B. B. King:

> He has proved of fundamental importance to the development of modern popular music. He has influenced nearly every . . . successful blues player and rock artist, too, from Chuck Berry, Buddy Guy and Jimi Hendrix to Prince and Eric Clapton. . . . Myself, Jeff Beck, Billy Gibbons, and Keith Richards have all had B. B. King as a vital common denominator and source of inspiration. . . .[40]

Regarding the broader societal theme of this book about the impact of music on progress towards Civil Rights, I should also underline the role of the Allman Brothers Band; additionally, this demonstrates that it was not just leading Black musicians who contributed to that progress, as has been demonstrated with other examples in this book. Duane Allman had a strong sense of social justice; and most importantly, "this interracial act, formed in the South of the late 1960s, was making a bold statement by referring to itself as a band of brothers."[41]

The characteristics of the guitar discussed in chapter 4, Lonnie's influ-ence that spread like waves in a pond, the nature of blues, Country, Rock, and jazz, and the impact of the "guitar heroes" in each musical genre, combined to make the guitar a dominant instrument. A man-ifestation of this came in two prime waves of guitar sales. The first wave came in the mid-late-1950s, in the wake of Chuck Berry, Carl Perkins, Buddy Holly, etc. "The real peak of activity, though, began around 1963, when total sales figures for all guitars almost doubled from the previous year, from just over 300,000 to over 600,000. By 1965, total guitar sales had jumped to 1.5 million; the Fender com-pany alone was producing 1,500 guitars a week, most of them electric models."[42] That surge came in the direct aftermath of the big wave of interest in folk music and, given the sales of the Fender electric gui-tars, it especially came from the early years of the Beatles, the Rolling Stones, Eric Clapton, etc. By the later '60s, the guitar had become a prime cultural icon.

## "I Will Never Die in a Hospital, and I Will Perform Again!"
## Accident

One day in March 1969 Lonnie was standing outside Wester's Restaurant on Avenue Road in Toronto when two cars collided; one was thrust up on the sidewalk and hit Lonnie, he fell forward, and then the second car hit him. There was a horrific irony here: Chris Albertson told me that Lonnie was terribly afraid of an auto accident, and in the 1960–1961 period when Chris was doing so much for Lonnie, as Chris would drive him around, he would insist that Chris drive very slowly.[43]

It was Roberta that Toronto General Hospital called after Lonnie was taken there by ambulance. They said her "father" had been in a serious auto accident and was asking for her. Roberta went to the hos-pital, asked for her father Lonnie Johnson, and found the doctor who had called (he'd found her number in Lonnie's wallet "in case of emer-gency"). "He was shocked and said, 'But you're White!' I said, 'I am, yes.'" (See the photo of Roberta, Lonnie in a wheelchair, and Roberta's daughter Marla on his lap.)

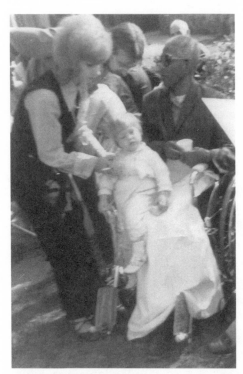

Lonnie Johnson in wheelchair with red-haired Roberta Richards (now Barrett) and child on Lonnie's lap. PHOTO COURTESY OF ROBERTA BARRETT.

The physician took her to the emergency room. Roberta told me: "He was nearly unrecognizable, he was swollen to such proportions, and he was semi-conscious. But then Lonnie mumbled, 'You made it!' . . . The doctor said the prognosis wasn't good; Lonnie had many internal injuries, plus fractures." In fact, the doctor said he rather doubted Lonnie would survive. He then wanted to know Lonnie's age. "My answer: 'Who knows?!'" (It was later that she learned his birth year.) "So, I stayed at the hospital for the whole night. And suddenly, in the early morning, he awoke and mumbled to me, 'What are you doing here?! Who's minding the babies?'"

The physician also told Roberta that, if he survived, Lonnie was in for a very long process of recovery. And indeed, after being transferred to the long-term hospital, Riverdale, he was in that facility for months. After four or five months in the hospital, they said he could be released, but couldn't be alone, so Roberta took him to her house; she had help from visiting nurses. There were also periodic doctor visits. "One of the later visits with the doctors, they became alarmed and had him readmitted to the hospital. Three or four days later he had the first of three strokes. The strokes left him partially paralyzed on his left side. After that he became despondent; he wanted to play guitar, but couldn't." But they gave him very good therapy in the hospital; and "he really won the nurses over!" He gradually got better. A little later he was able to go out for the occasional weekend visit to Roberta's place.

Another little tale, again related by Roberta, illustrates how others were thinking of Lonnie while he was in his extended stay in the hospital. Lonnie had wanted a guitar in his room, but Roberta thought that was a bad idea because a couple of items of Lonnie's jewelry had been stolen. So, "Jim McHarg led an effort and they got some balsa wood and made a kind of model guitar out of it and brought it to him. And people would sign it. It was painted white" [which probably reminded him of the guitar he had painted white when he was playing with Lil Armstrong in Chicago's Three Deuces club].

Gradually his spirits returned; and with that indomitable spirit of his, at about that time he said to Roberta, "I will never die in a hospital, and I will perform again!"

While Lonnie was in the hospital, Louis Armstrong, Bill Cosby, his pianist partner in 1940s recordings, Roosevelt Sykes, and other notables visited him. Among those who visited Lonnie while he was recovering at Roberta's house were jazz guitarist Charlie Byrd, jazz violinist Joe Venuti (again, Eddie Lang's violin-guitar duet partner and friend from Philadelphia), another pianist partner on recordings in the 1940s, Blind John Davis, and bluesman Booker T. "Bukka" White (a relative of B. B. King's). Later, when Lonnie was able to walk a little, Roberta took him to visit Duke Ellington at the Royal York Hotel when he was in town for a concert.

Brownie McGhee also visited Lonnie. In a fond remembrance that he wrote for *Living Blues* magazine just after Lonnie's death, Brownie took note of his first meeting with Lonnie in a Chicago club in about 1946: "At our first meeting I had the chance to play with Lonnie on the same stage. It took lots of courage, but I did it. I'll never forget that day."[44] Brownie was a terrific bluesman with a fine voice and a winning way with audiences. He was a good guitarist, but wasn't at Lonnie's level of virtuosity (like nearly everyone else); he was reflecting on playing with the ultimate guitar magician. That major musical figures like Brownie McGhee, Buddy Guy, and others said of their chance to be on stage with Lonnie, "I'll never forget that day," is quite a testament to Lonnie's historic importance.

Lady Iris Mountbatten, of the British Mountbatten family, loved jazz and blues and she had heard Lonnie in the Toronto clubs and was a fan. She heard of the accident, went to see Lonnie in the hospital, and then asked Roberta about the money situation to pay the hospital bills. When Roberta said the American Federation of Musicians was sending some money, but not a lot, Lady Iris then suggested a benefit concert. So they formed a committee for this, with Lady Iris, Roberta, promoter Richard Flohil, and a couple of others. On May 4, 1969, the concert was held in Ryerson Auditorium at Ryerson College in Toronto; the famous Canadian folk singers Ian & Sylvia, bluesman John Lee Hooker, fine jazz pianist Sir Charles Thompson, and a few others performed. Canadian folksinger Gordon Lightfoot couldn't make the concert due to conflicting schedules, but he contributed $500 to the cause (which was equivalent to over $3,000 in 2013).

## Final Concert—and Passing the Torch of Guitar Greatness

Toronto concert promoter Richard Flohil and Dick Waterman (manager of rediscovered blues great Son House, and masterful blues photographer) put together a concert at the famous Massey Hall in Toronto. The concert was called the "Blue Monday" event. It was held on February 23, 1970. It was to feature Son House, young, up-and-coming blues guitarist Buddy Guy, and famous singer Bobby "Blue" Bland, plus a local band, Whiskey Howl; but Son House couldn't make it. It was also in tribute to Lonnie Johnson. They hoped Lonnie could appear, but nobody was at all sure he could make it. Roberta asked the doctors if she could take him to a concert—not perform in one, just "take him to a concert"; the doctors said absolutely not, he had to remain calm and quiet.

Lonnie had been able to get out of the wheelchair and was walking some by early 1970, "but he was still very shaky and weak," said Roberta. Lonnie was adamant about appearing in the concert, however; he realized he couldn't play guitar, due to partial paralysis from the strokes, but Buddy Guy could do that duty. Roberta takes the story from here:

> It's not nice to say I lied to the doctors, so let's just say I *omitted* some stuff. I just made it sound like I was taking him home for a weekend,

but I asked if I could extend it one more day. They said no. I intended to simply not bring him back until a day later, but he wasn't feeling well on Sunday and I took him back to the hospital. Then on Monday morning he said, "I'm going to that concert!" I was frightened, but I said to the doctors that he really hadn't had a full weekend out, so just let me take him out for this evening.

So, we get the suit and shoes ready, get the diamond stick pin in his tie . . . We took him to Massey Hall. He was walking with a cane and he was very shaky . . . We get to the stage wing and he tells me, "All right, this is how it's gonna go: I'm going out there and I'm not using any wheelchair, I'm not using any walkin' stick, I'm going on my own, and *you're* not taking me!" I stood there, and he took about three steps and then said, "You know, I think I'm comin' back for my walkin' stick. I think it won't look too bad—even looks kinda distinguished, so I'll use it." (He spoke this like he was doing me a big favor using the cane.)

And so, people in the audience saw Buddy Guy sitting on a chair on the right with his Fender Stratocaster guitar, a microphone on a stand in the middle, a stool on the left just high enough so Lonnie wouldn't have to bend his legs much to sit down, Jim McHarg stood on the left side with his stand-up acoustic bass, and Bobby Bland's band stood in a semi-circle in the shadows behind Buddy and the drum set.

Lonnie appears out of the stage wing, painfully shuffling along, leaning heavily on his cane, slowly making his way towards center stage. Meanwhile, in the front row, Roberta, Roberta's friend Helen Townley, Richard Flohil, Lady Iris and a couple of others who knew the full story, sat there, each holding his or her breath, hoping, praying that Lonnie would not collapse right there. But he kept on going and finally made it to that stool, sat down, kept the cane in his right hand, took the mic in his left hand, looked to his left at Buddy, spoke the name of the song he was going to sing and nodded, and they were off.

Richard Flohil and Roberta remembered him singing three songs: "Tomorrow Night," "Careless Love," and either "St. Louis Blues" or "Jelly Roll Baker" (memories differ on the third song). But when I interviewed Buddy, he couldn't remember just what songs they did—for a special reason.

Buddy, in fact, hadn't been aware that he would be on stage with Lonnie until just before the concert started. In his memoir, Buddy said they briefly met just before the concert and Buddy said to Lonnie: "Man, there wasn't a time when I wasn't in love with your guitar and your voice."[45] Here is Buddy's description of the occasion, as related to me in our interview:

> When they told me he was there, that he would come out on stage with me, I forgot every damn thing I knew . . . I can remember him coming out there, and I said to myself, "I will never forget this day, I will never forget what happened." I was so excited, and the songs we did didn't matter; what mattered to me was that I got a chance to be on stage with *history*. And I said to myself, "You back in class, Buddy; you just sit down and listen and pay attention to what's goin' on so you can *learn* something."

"Passing the Torch of Guitar Greatness." Historic photo of Lonnie Johnson performing at his final concert with Buddy Guy, with guitar, looking admiringly at Lonnie, February 1970. PHOTO BY AND COURTESY OF ROBERTA BARRETT (NEE RICHARDS); NOT PREVIOUSLY PUBLISHED AND EXCLUSIVE TO THIS BOOK.

Richard Flohil and Buddy Guy told me his singing got stronger as he went on, and that he sang well. Flohil also said, "Buddy played many of those great Lonnie Johnson guitar licks." Roberta Barrett said that Buddy's guitar playing was inspired by Lonnie—"Buddy was fabulous that night."

It was a fitting and moving symbolic moment: Buddy Guy was the new generation and was taking the torch of guitar greatness from the man who was a principal inspiration. Buddy's look up at Lonnie in that previously unpublished photo (taken by Roberta) speaks volumes.

Lonnie Johnson walking off the stage at the end of his performance in his "final concert."
PHOTO BY AND COURTESY OF ROBERTA BARRETT (NEE RICHARDS); NOT PREVIOUSLY PUBLISHED AND EXCLUSIVE TO THIS BOOK.

Buddy, along with B. B. King and others, carried the legacy of Lonnie Johnson's monumental impact on blues guitar playing—and music in general—through the last third of the twentieth century and into the twenty-first.

At the end of his three songs, Lonnie won a standing ovation; it was wonderfully symbolic that many in the audience were young people. As he slowly made his way off stage, leaning on that "walkin' stick," he turned his head to look at the audience and beamed; he left the stage with tears streaming down his face.

In his memoir, *When I Left Home*, Buddy Guy added to his thoughts on Lonnie:

> Other entertainers at the end of their careers got to enjoy comfort and fame. . . . Yet here was . . . a bluesman who wasn't just good but was goddamn great, an artist whose spirit inspired dozens of other great artists, a musician who deserved the respect of presidents and kings. Yet, when Lonnie Johnson died a few months after I got to play with him, you had to look in the back of the paper to see any little mention of him. Most papers didn't mention him at all.[46]

## No More Troubles Now—The Legacy of Lonnie J

Lonnie Johnson died in his apartment on June 16, 1970, at the age of 76. There was another sort of extended effect of the accident and hospitalization, an impact that, effectively, was another missed opportunity for Lonnie to register and affirm in public recognition his proper place as a top figure in blues history—and beyond. After that Massey Hall concert, there was some hope that he might continue to recover and resume performing. Indeed, he was scheduled to appear at the big Ann Arbor Blues Festival in Michigan later that summer, where, in the setting of that premier festival, he might have received the accolades he was due—that were, in fact, long overdue. But he passed away, and another opportunity for broader recognition passed him by.[47]

A memorial ceremony was held in Our Lady of Lourdes Catholic Church in Toronto, which was packed with mourners. (Despite his Baptist origins, he liked the church and had worshipped there often,

Roberta Barrett told me.) His friend, the outstanding Toronto singer Salome Bey, sang Lonnie favorites, "Tomorrow Night" and "My Mother's Eyes" for the ceremony. There was actually a private ceremony at Mount Hope Cemetery in Toronto, with the casket. This led to reports that Lonnie Johnson was buried in Toronto. But this is not correct. His body was taken to Philadelphia and he is buried in White Chapel Memorial Park in Feasterville, Pennsylvania, just outside Philadelphia.

**Interesting Citation in Classic American Book** There is an intriguing citation of Lonnie in that American literary and documentary classic from the Depression years, *Let Us Now Praise Famous Men*, written by James Agee, with photos by Walker Evans. The opening section, "Persons and Places," that lists the people they closely observed, includes this: "Unpaid agitators: William Blake, Ring Lardner, Jesus Christ, Sigmund Freud, Lonnie Johnson" (and two others). I did not discover the specific reason for that reference. But later Agee wrote of "race records" as one of the important elements of history that inspired him. And perhaps the summary assessment on the dust jacket of the newer, fine edition of the book[48] is a clue: It's a portrait of three tenant farm families in the South, "and a larger meditation on human dignity and the American soul." The dignity with which Lonnie Johnson carried himself and the role he, Louis Armstrong, Duke Ellington, and some others played in our society, including the profound, soulful music they produced, may be what is referred to here, with Lonnie being more of a humble "man of the people" than Duke. And as Ralph Ellison said, people like Duke Ellington and Lonnie Johnson gave such "a sense of *possibility*." Indeed, Agee began the book's section on "Education" by saying: "In every child who is born, under no matter what circumstances, and no matter of what parents, the potentiality of the human race is born again. . . ."[49]

**Installed in the Gennett Records "Walk of Fame"** Gennett Records was one of the pioneering independent record companies that produced important jazz, blues, and Country music recordings in the 1920s; it was actually a subsidiary of the Starr Piano Company of Richmond, Indiana. Lonnie did a number of recordings with them, primarily as an accompanist.

In September 2010, Lonnie was installed in the Gennett Records Walk of Fame, which is along the road where the original factory is located (brick shell still standing, with old Gennett Records logo still visible) and not-so-sophisticated recording studio (gone, but they've outlined on the ground where it was). I spoke at the installation ceremony. Here is the fine "medallion" placed on the Walk:

Gennett Records "Walk of Fame" Medallion of Lonnie. Plaque reads: "Johnson was among the great blues performers of the 1920s. Best known for his guitar playing, he also played violin, piano, and celeste on anonymous recordings for Gennett in 1927." The lower part tells who donated the medallion and their relation to the Gennett family.

## The Legacy of Lonnie J

Lonnie Johnson has been most recognized for his brilliant, pioneering guitar work. That is central to his legacy and importance in music history. Lonnie also developed a distinctive, unique guitar style. As bluesman John Lee Hooker admiringly expressed it: "He was a genius. . . . Nobody sounded like him. You could tell it was Lonnie every time he picked up the guitar."[50] B. B. King said the same thing, as reported earlier. As has been noted through this book, Lonnie's extraordinary virtuosity and unique style included unparalleled touch, tone, and vibrato, all enhancing his pioneering expressive guitar playing. And as jazz guitarist and teacher of the history of guitar at the Manhattan School of Music, Jack Wilkins, told me: "Listening to the music of Lonnie Johnson is like listening to the history of jazz guitar. Despite his reputation of being a world-renowned blues player and singer, Lonnie Johnson was a precursor to the genius of Charlie Christian. His few solo [instrumental] recordings are proof that he could play guitar like no one before him. With the recordings he made with the also legendary Eddie Lang (aka, Blind Willie Dunn) he was the first to play fully developed jazz lines."

A related element of his masterful guitar work was well articulated by jazzman Wynton Marsalis: "The highest level of instrumental technique is *nuance*."[51] (In that statement, Marsalis was referring to Louis Armstrong. That's one of a series of musically important parallels between Louis and Lonnie, as detailed below.) Lonnie was a pioneer in that way as well, strikingly shown in such works as his solo instrumental "Away Down in the Alley Blues" and his duets with Lang on "Blue Guitars" and "Midnight Call Blues" (in the later '20s) through his unique version of "Summertime" on acoustic guitar in 1960, employing his rich, sensitive touch and tone, timing and dynamics.

Two other dimensions of his music have *not* received the credit they deserve:

**Underappreciated for Caliber of Singing** I've discussed how his singing was good in the later 1920s and continued to improve thereafter. As documented through this and the three previous chapters and in the recordings, Lonnie kept getting better and by the 1940s his singing rose to the level of greatness, at least on a number of recordings and in clubs. For prime examples, see tracks 1, 4, 5 and 24 on the companion CD.

**In a Rarified Class of Greatness** That leads me to a very significant point. Lonnie Johnson was one of only a handful of musicians who attained greatness both as an instrumental musician *and* as a singer.

Who else genuinely belongs in that ultimate elite category of musicians? Well, two clear choices are, first, Louis Armstrong, and second, B. B. King. As was discussed at the beginning of chapter 5, B. B. has been one of the supreme guitar players in popular music. Jazz guitarist Jim Hall expressed it perfectly: "I would rather hear B. B. King play *about four notes* than hear most other guys play all night. He just really *reaches* me."[52] (Just listen to the opening notes of the B. B. album *Live and Well*.) Hall was pithily but eloquently referring to that great touch and tone and that profound *expressive* capacity, all in the service of deep blues feeling, that B. B.'s playing displayed. Jim Hall was a White guy who grew up in Buffalo and Cleveland, and his comment is also a manifestation of the nature and power of the blues to express more profound human experience and feelings that spread widely in the context of the changing and alienating modern society and the development of American music and culture that was discussed in the "Interlude" section in chapter 2.

This book has documented how that great touch, tone, vibrato, and expressive guitar playing in general that B. B. King's work displayed so magnificently was originally developed in all its essentials by Lonnie Johnson, starting in the 1920s. As guitar virtuoso and teacher Stefan Grossman has written, "The roots of modern electric blues and rock guitar can be found in the playing of Lonnie Johnson." Blues singer Victoria Spivey expressed it well: "Everywhere I turn I hear Lonnie in T-Bone Walker, B. B. and Albert King, Muddy Waters, and the younger fellows like Buddy Guy. And, of course, all the White kids are playing Lonnie, most of them thinking they're being influenced by B. B. What I like about B. B. and T-Bone is that they give Lonnie the credit. . . ."[53] It's also notable that, while B. B. recognized Robert Johnson's significance, B.B. said, "but I didn't idolize him like I did Lonnie Johnson."[54]

Further, drawing on Lonnie Johnson's early vocal influence, B. B. King became the greatest *singer* in the history of the blues, in my judgment, and one of the greatest in all of popular music. Bessie Smith and Son House, two other prime candidates for the distinction of greatest blues singer, had power, intensity, and emotion. But B. B. developed greater versatility and a more full range of expressive techniques in his singing, while losing nothing in the power and emotion dimensions, and he also had a remarkable richness of vocal tone. For excellent examples, especially his unparalleled use of dynamics for drama and to infuse the lyrics with meaning, listen to the second and third tracks, "Sweet Little Angel" and "It's My Own Fault," on his historic *Live at the Regal* CD. (It's interesting that in 1952 he recorded a pure ballad a la Lonnie J, "You Know I Love You.")

I leave it to notable specialists, as well as to regular folks who love the music, to ponder and produce a listing of who else belongs in this special Double Distinction, Ultimate Musical Hall of Fame: those who attained greatness as singers *and* instrumentalists. Let the discussion and debate begin.

**Lonnie and the Advent of the Microphone** Writers have often said that Bing Crosby was the original singer to make full, effective use of the microphone, allowing more subtlety and nuance in vocal recording than the old vaudeville tradition and than was possible under the original acoustic recording technology, where singers had to basically shout into the recording horn. Bing's first hit was actually in 1928 while still singing with his trio, The Rhythm Boys, performing with the Paul Whiteman Orchestra; and he didn't really come into his own and develop his mastery of solo use of the microphone until 1929.

Lonnie Johnson's 1926 recordings were made under that old, crude acoustic recording technology, and he had to shout into the horn; it distorted his vocal quality. But after OKeh was acquired by Columbia later in 1926 and could record with microphones, Lonnie quickly adapted in his recordings in 1927. Listening to his August 1927 recording, "Roamin' Rambler Blues" (track 11 on *The Ultimate Best of Lonnie Johnson* CD) one can hear a fine use of the microphone and significant nuance in his singing (in rather stark contrast to his 1926 recordings, starting with "Mr.

Johnson's Blues," track 8 on the CD). Thus, Lonnie was also a pioneer in use of the mic for vocal recordings—actually in advance of Crosby.

Also regarding Lonnie's singing, another interesting and notable fact is that a number of recordings with his best vocal work were produced quite late in age, when he was in his late sixties and older. Indeed, he demonstrated genuine *greatness* in his singing on "Don't Ever Love" (March 1960), "Blue and All Alone" and "New Orleans Blues" (April 1960), and "Summertime" (December 1960) when he was 66 years old, and on "Mr. Blues Walks" (1965) when he was 71. And he served up singing that was at least at the near-great level on "Tears Don't Fall No More" (1967) when he was 73.

**Inadequately Recognized for Excellence in Lyrics**  The second dimension of Lonnie Johnson's music that has not received adequate credit is the lyrics for his songs. He was actually one of the better writers of song lyrics in blues or jazz history, as has been demonstrated with many examples through this book. He produced lines that reverberated through the history of the blues, like the poetic line "Blues, falling like showers of rain." He wrote songs that told a coherent story of people in compelling manner with music perfectly suited to the lyrics, like the whole story in "St. Louis Cyclone Blues," along with the tale of his "dear old New Orleans" hometown in "New Orleans Blues." And into the 1960s he could write pure blues poetry like his late 1960 song "Lines in My Face." And that song, again, had music that perfectly suited the lyrics and beautifully and powerfully conveyed their meaning. It's not only that he produced songs with excellent, compelling and coherent lyrics; it's the large number of songs with very good and mostly *original* lyrics that is the point, unlike many blues song writers who just borrowed various phrases and lines that were generally floating around.

**Exceptional Thematic Coherence in Guitar Work**  Another element of the greatness of Lonnie Johnson's music was the exceptional *thematic coherence* of his artistry on the guitar. Starting with the "A" side of his first hit record, "Mr. Johnson's Blues," developing further in guitar instrumentals like "Away Down in the Alley Blues" and "Blues in G" from 1928, through "Uncle Ned" of December 1931 to "Backwater

Blues" of 1948 to "Summertime" of December 1960 and many songs in between, Lonnie demonstrated a remarkable ability to maintain a coherence to the themes played on his guitar, and often built an over-all "architecture" that gave superb structural logic to his musical art. An aspect that makes the best compositions of Mozart and Beethoven among the greatest artistic achievements in human history is the overall architecture and structural logic of the entire composition, along with excellent thematic coherence in the various movements and sections within that overall structure.

To my ears and aesthetic sense, a number of other musicians seen as top guitarists in Rock, blues and jazz play lots of notes on their solos, in the right key and often with some fine signature licks, some with impressive speed, but they basically meander up and down the fret-board without an overall coherence, a musical logic and architecture for the whole set of notes making up the complete song and sections of it—"aimless solos," as jazz writer and trumpeter John Chilton aptly expressed it. Like few popular guitarists have ever done, Lonnie was able to build that architecture for the whole song and coherently continue his musical themes through inventive variations, emphases, and accents in sections of the songs, as the examples just noted demonstrate espe-cially well. I do not hear Lonnie's level of thematic coherence in the playing of either Django or Charlie Christian.

**Louis Armstrong and Lonnie Johnson: Two Titans Who, in Parallel, Changed Much of Popular Music** In a fascinatingly insightful com-ment in his chapter on "The Negro Spirituals" in his landmark 1925 book on African-American culture, *The New Negro*, Alain Locke wrote: "Up to the present, the resources of Negro music have been tentatively exploited in only one direction at a time—melodically here, rhythmi-cally there, harmonically in a third direction. A genius that would orga-nize its distinctive elements in a formal way would be a musical giant of his age."[55] Louis Armstrong and Duke Ellington did just that for jazz music and beyond in the years following that comment, and they did indeed become musical giants—not only "of their age," but for the ensu-ing century. Lonnie Johnson did the same for guitar-playing in blues, jazz, and beyond, and is today a relatively unsung giant of music history.

Many scholars and writers on popular music suggest that Louis Armstrong had the greatest impact of any musician in the century. As I've discussed, Lonnie Johnson was a second titan who changed much of popular music. A major finding of this book is that, in multiple ways, Lonnie's historic development of artistry on the guitar—and voice-with-guitar—strikingly paralleled that of Louis Armstrong on the horn and in his singing. Again, the height of that work occurred during precisely the same period as Louis Armstrong's landmark records using trumpet and voice, from the first Hot Five recordings in November 1925, eight days after Lonnie's first recordings as featured performer, with record releases and first impacts in 1926, and continuing through 1931.

In his noted study *Early Jazz*, Gunther Schuller explicitly hailed and implicitly alluded to that stature of Lonnie: "Four of the [Armstrong-Hot Five] sides had the great guitarist Lonnie Johnson. And what a difference he makes! Armstrong now . . . has a strong ally."[56] That is, Louis now had a musician with him who could play at his level and be a seminal co-creator.

The pinnacle of Armstrong's historic Hot Five recordings came with "West End Blues," recorded in June 1928. Lonnie added a significant dimension to the three historic Armstrong-Hot Five recordings in late 1927 and spurred Louis and the rest of the band to greater heights. Then Lonnie matched Louis's tremendous, creative trumpet work with equally historic and impressive virtuoso guitar playing on "Playing with the Strings," "Away Down in the Alley Blues," etc., in February 1928, in the first of the great guitar duets with Eddie Lang recorded in November 1928, and then in the rest of those historic duets in 1929. And he continued the groundbreaking work up through his stunning "Uncle Ned" recording in December 1931. In those records and other work Lonnie Johnson was the prime creator of powerful, innovative, virtuoso lead and solo work on guitar in jazz and blues, and he was the leading figure who laid down the main foundations of guitar artistry for all of popular music thereafter. And, with help from Eddie Lang and later from Django Reinhardt, Charlie Christian, T-Bone Walker, Chuck Berry, B. B. King, and then Eric Clapton, Lonnie thereby established the dominance of the instrument in the second half of the century.

B. B. King put it simply and powerfully: "Lonnie Johnson was the most influential guitarist of the 20th Century."[57]

There are several specific ways Louis and Lonnie had parallel impacts on popular music of huge and fundamental importance, and were similar in how they purveyed their music. First, as Terry Teachout discusses in his excellent 2009 book on Louis Armstrong,[58] Satchmo was the supreme original developer of great *tone* on the trumpet and of extraordinarily *expressive* playing of the horn itself, not using mutes and other "trick" add-ons.

Lonnie Johnson did the same for the guitar—without use of a "slide" and before later electronic effects. An introduction to a section titled "The 50 Greatest Guitar Tones of All Time" in a book of collected articles from *Guitar Player* magazine expressed it well: "Tone. It's one of the most magical and beautiful aspects of the guitar . . . We know great tone when we hear it, but achieving it is still a tall order . . . Tone is what makes all music come alive and hit you in the face, gut and heart. Without it, music is just a collection of dots on a page."[59] It was Lonnie Johnson, more than anyone else, who demonstrated the pure musical and general expressive possibilities of superb and creative tone achieved on the guitar, which was one of the key factors leading to the guitar's dominance.

As Teachout put it in comparison with a trumpet challenger to Armstrong, Jabbo Smith: "What Smith lacked, however, was Armstrong's ability to use the upper register of the trumpet to *expressive* effect, soaring above the staff in a manner reminiscent of the 78 [opera records] of Caruso and John McCormack that he had heard in New Orleans."[60] The same was the case with Lonnie; his touch and tone on the guitar and his expressive capacities on the instrument were well beyond anyone else in the later 1920s and early 1930s (and almost everyone else since)—and like Louis, some of that came from absorbing the great opera music from his New Orleans days, along with drawing on the expressively lyrical playing that was characteristic of both the French and "Spanish tinge" traditions in the Crescent City around 1900.

A prime example of those characteristics of Lonnie's playing is his masterpiece guitar instrumental, "Away Down in the Alley Blues," from February 1928. The first 37 seconds of that recording are an especially good illustration of Lonnie's accomplishments with those artistic characteristics and, again, of how he parallels Louis Armstrong. The illustrative culmination of the playing comes at 31 seconds when, in the course of perfect thematic coherence, for a transition from one beautifully constructed phrase to the next, he bends the string, with exquisite touch and tone, to slide up to the next note and then down and on into the next phrase, *while also maintaining a perfect sense of rhythm and timing* during that extended bent note of great expressive feel. It sounds simple on casual listening, but it is simply sublime musical art, developed *in motion* (i.e., improvised). A quote about Armstrong from jazz pianist Teddy Wilson expresses Lonnie's extraordinary artistry as well, so strikingly in evidence in "Away Down in the Alley Blues": "Armstrong had all the factors in balance, all the factors equally developed. Such a balance was the essential thing about Beethoven, I think, and Armstrong, like Beethoven, had this high development of balance: lyricism, delicacy, emotional outburst, rhythm, complete mastery of his horn."[61] Indeed; and just substitute "guitar" for "horn" and the observation applies to Lonnie J. James B. Dalton has done considerable authoritative review of Lonnie's recordings. After a detailed analysis of Lonnie's superb 1927 instrumental, "Woke Up This Morning with the Blues in My Fingers," Dalton reached a similar conclusion: "Many of Lonnie Johnson's solo guitar pieces have the same nearly-classical balance and structure."[62]

Teddy Wilson said something else about Louis that also applies as profoundly to Lonnie: "He was such a master of melodic improvisation, and he never hit a note that didn't have a great deal of meaning. Every note was pure music."[63] As I documented in chapters 5 and 6, Lonnie was the supreme creative melodic improviser on guitar in both jazz and blues over the first third of the century, during which time the foundations of those musical genres were being laid.

The development and mastery of all those artistic capacities by Louis and Lonnie, in conjunction with their extraordinary creativity and imagination, led to something still further. Again, Terry Teachout expresses the point well, in this case regarding one of Satchmo's recordings, "Sweethearts on Parade," from 1930. The song itself Teachout rightly calls a "footling ditty," meaning a low-grade pop tune of little inherent artistic merit. But this bit of musical cottage cheese,

"Armstrong, in one of his most stupendous feats of alchemy, turned into a three-minute trumpet concerto of the utmost splendor."[64] Lonnie was able to do the same thing. The best example was, again, his December 1931 recording of "Uncle Ned," which was a funky old Negro folk song. But as I said in chapter 5: "Lonnie took this old Negro folk song and turned it into a vehicle for the most dazzling, blazing-fingered, virtuoso guitar work" (he also sang the song quite well). And that stunningly virtuoso guitar-playing included "exquisite touch, tone, nuance, and fine thematic coherence"—all while playing at a speed nobody could match in the early 1930s—and few since.

That pioneering development of thematic coherence is still another thing Lonnie shared with Louis. In his study of seven Armstrong Hot Five and Hot Seven recordings, Brian Harker noted: "Before Armstrong, cornet players tended to play paraphrases of a song's melody or . . . short [solo] breaks. . . . Armstrong was among the first to play lengthy solos on the abstract material characteristic of breaks. More important, he managed to connect the various phrases of his solos, creating a sense of ongoing coherence." Harker also noted that the structural conception involved would later be characterized by musicians as "telling a story," with those thematically coherent lines, almost giving the feel of a narrative. He finds that coherence starting to fill out in "Potato Head Blues" of May 1927. Lonnie was demonstrating that unprecedented thematic coherence on the guitar beginning at least with "Steppin' On the Blues" recorded in April 1927, and fully realizing that story-telling coherence in his guitar instrumental, "Woke Up This Morning with the Blues in My Fingers" of May 1927. A crucial Harker conclusion adds this historic point: "The phrases relate to one another motivically, binding the entire solo together in a coherent statement. In this way, 'Potato Head Blues' offers a new approach to jazz based on structurally integrated variations of a chord progression rather than [merely] embellishments of a fixed melody."[65] This is exactly what Lonnie Johnson did, culminating in that masterwork, "Away Down in the Alley Blues" of February 1928.

Terry Teachout, Gary Giddins, and other jazz writers have pointed out that Louis Armstrong loved a good melody, and employing a good melody, understandable by regular folks, was part of how he connected so well with such a wide range of people of all races and types—while bringing superb jazz-playing to them (despite the carping of some elitist jazz snobs about Satchmo's later years). Again, Lonnie did the same. As guitar music expert Lenny Carlson said in his analysis of one of Lonnie's recordings: "This is an example of his flair for creating interesting and beautiful melodies. Lonnie Johnson's popularity with the listening public and his pervasive influence over other guitarists were based on such melodies, which he composed and improvised with remarkable ease and consistency."[66]

Ted Gioia summarized Armstrong's profound impact on music: Other jazz players of the era "lacked the technical resources and . . . the creative depth to make the solo the compelling centerpiece of jazz music." None of those others "could match Armstrong's vast range of rhythmic devices, his variegated ways of phrasing, or just the sheer inner momentum and outer logic of his melody lines."[67] As discussed earlier, these attributes also apply to Lonnie J, from his superb rhythmic accompaniment of, then response counterpoint to Armstrong on, "Hotter Than That" and the other Hot Five sides to his categorically similar but creatively unique counterpoint to the Ellington players in "The Mooche" and "Hot and Bothered" to his remarkable, unparalleled, variegated phrasing and logic of melody lines in "Away Down in the Alley Blues" to the same plus that "sheer inner momentum" of his solo work on "Playing with the Strings" and "Uncle Ned" and his duet work with Lang on "Handful of Riffs" and "Hot Fingers."

In summary, in six years from late 1925 through late 1931, Louis Armstrong and Lonnie Johnson, those two old friends from the musically seminal city of New Orleans, engaged in a burst of extraordinary aesthetic creativity that changed popular music and produced artistic outpourings of historic musical importance.

In addition, Lonnie's *singing in combination with his guitar work* originally established and was a key force in the further development of one of the two main strains of "urban blues" that led to Rhythm & Blues and then to Rock & Roll. And the continual development of his singing by itself significantly affected some hugely influential figures in popular music in the second half of the century, most notably B. B. King and Elvis Presley.

To Louis Armstrong's widely acknowledged central role in affecting the course of popular music of the century must be added Lonnie Johnson as the another of the greatest forces in the development of that music.

These two masters also paralleled one another on race and American society. As Michael Cogswell reported, the personal tapes Louis made included stories of discrimination, where one would expect outrage; "but his attitude is one of pity for the discriminators, and the accounts are delivered in a 'Can you believe this one?!' mode. . . ."[68] As noted earlier, Lonnie's basic response was feeling sorry for what such mentality did to the racist's mind and spirit—though like Louis, when provoked, he could issue sharp satirical comment on the stupidity involved.

**Lonnie Johnson, Jazz and Blues Music, and Modern Art** One of the historic Lonnie Johnson-Eddie Lang guitar duets was titled, "Blue Guitars." It's appropriate that a famous "Blue Period" painting by Picasso is informally known as the "Blue Guitar" work, implicitly referenced in the Johnson-Lang title. From Lonnie's masterpiece guitar instrumentals like "Away Down in the Alley Blues" and "Blues in G" and his duets with Eddie Lang like "Midnight Call Blues" and "Blue Guitars" to his featured guitar work on the Louis Armstrong-Hot Five recordings and on the early Ellington masterwork, "The Mooche," to Lonnie's 1948 aural impressionist painting of "Backwater Blues" to his masterful recomposition of "Summertime" in late 1960, it seems to me that he was a signal contributor to music and modern art. And as noted in chapter 1: "British composer Constant Lambert wrote: 'I know of nothing in Ravel so dexterous in treatment as the varied solos in the middle of the ebullient "Hot and Bothered"'." A featured counterpoint to those "solos in the middle" of "Hot and Bothered" was the guitar-playing of Lonnie Johnson.

Again Lonnie paralleled Louis Armstrong. As a *New York Times* review of Teachout's biography of Louis Armstrong, said: "Louis Armstrong . . . was to music what Picasso was to painting, what Joyce was to fiction: an innovator who changed the face of his art form, a fecund and endlessly inventive pioneer . . . [who] helped remake 20th century culture."[69] Once again, those words apply to Lonnie Johnson, as well.

**Johnson-Lang and the Glories of Great Guitar Duets** The guitar duets recorded by Lonnie Johnson and Eddie Lang in 1928 and 1929 were historic achievements in guitar playing. The exquisite interweaving of their guitars produced supremely creative, sublimely melodic and harmonic works of music at the highest level of art. They also inspired later guitar duets in jazz, starting with two that Lang recorded with Carl Kress in 1932, and continuing with examples like the first electric guitar duets with Kress and George Barnes in the early 1960s, which also included the first improvised choruses since the Johnson-Lang duets (again, Barnes drew on the tutoring Lonnie gave him in Chicago in the late '30s). Beyond jazz, a number of albums have offered special duet guitar treats in popular music, such as *Chester and Lester*, with Chet Atkins and Les Paul, or, even better, *Chet Atkins and Doc Watson: Reflections*. And in classical guitar the Julian Bream-John Williams duet albums of the 1970s are extraordinary contributions to musical art.

**The Symbolic Importance of the Johnson-Lang Duets—and their Successors** A continuing broader societal theme running through this book has been about the impact of major musical figures on progress in Civil Rights. Beyond their historic importance in the development of artistry on the guitar, the duets Lonnie Johnson and Eddie Lang recorded in 1928 and 1929 were something special in that regard, producing the first full partner interracial recordings. Lonnie Johnson, Black man from New Orleans, and Eddie Lang (Salvatore Massaro), White man of Italian ethnic stock from Philadelphia, had great respect for each other's musicianship and appreciated each other personally. Indeed, as Lonnie said: "Eddie was a fine man. . . . He didn't tell me what to do; he would ask me. Then, if everything was OK, we'd sit down and get to jiving. I've never seen a cat like him since. And he could play guitar better than anyone I know."[70] (Again, Eddie died too young to get his later reflections.)

To offer an important double entendre, Lonnie Johnson and Eddie Lang, in those duets and in their respect for each other, created a perfect symbol for what racial *harmony* could be like in and for America's future.

Also, while Lonnie Johnson was not a march-in-the-streets Civil Rights activist, it is interesting that one of his very best and most powerful songs, "Broken Levee Blues," was an artful musical protest about the neo-slavery of forced-labor levee work by Black folks along the Mississippi River in the late 1920s.

That development of major musicians contributing to progress on Civil Rights was carried forth over the ensuing decades by Lonnie Johnson, Duke Ellington, Louis Armstrong, Jack Teagarden, Bing Crosby, Jimmie Rodgers, Woody Guthrie, and others. Sinatra said it well in celebrating Duke Ellington's 75th birthday: "Maybe the political scientists will never find the cure for intolerance. Until they do, I challenge anyone to come up with a more effective prescription than Duke Ellington's music, and Duke Ellington's performance as a human being."[71]

That development was carried through the rest of the century and into the twenty-first century by B. B. King, Harry Belafonte, Pete Seeger, Dizzie Gillespie, Josh White, Tony Bennett, Bob Dylan, Joan Baez, Eric Clapton, Buddy Guy, Taj Mahal, Carlos Santana, Willie Nelson, Stephen Stills, Bonnie Raitt, Stevie Wonder, Bruce Springsteen, U2, Cheryl Crow, Ben Harper, and other great musicians, Black and White—and Brown and other colors too.

# Appendix I

## THE LEGENDARY LONNIE J

Song in tribute to Lonnie Johnson by Dean Alger

To$^E$ music he was born
Greatest $^A$guitar in those days
In $^{B7}$both blues & jazz
The $^E$legendary Lonnie J

He came from New Orleans
Went up St. Louis way
Then on to Chicago
The legendary Lonnie J

With Satch and the Duke
Hot guitar he played
With Bessie and others too
The legendary Lonnie J

Bridge

Django to Charlie Christian
Robert Johnson to BB King
Learned great jazz & blues
When Lonnie would play & sing

Yes and then Rock & Roll
Rocked on night and day
And they all drew on
The legendary Lonnie J

He influenced them so
One and all just the same
Indeed he did, and
Lonnie Johnson was his name.

# Appendix II

## BLUES, JAZZ AND THEIR SIGNIFICANCE: MUSICIANS AND CIVIL RIGHTS

As was introduced in chapter 1, the powerful, evocative nature and sociological significance of blues and jazz were profound factors in the evolution of the self-image of African-Americans and had, through major Black musicians and some White ones, an increasing impact on their standing in the broader society and progress on Civil Rights. This appendix more fully presents my own vision on the subject, and it casts the net more broadly than the material in chapter 1, looking beyond the primary focus on Lonnie Johnson to wider developments in music and Civil Rights.

The winding road to fully realizing democratic citizenship for all Americans was manifest in such significant detours as the 1896 Supreme Court decision in the *Plessy v. Ferguson* case. The Court ruled that "separate but equal" facilities were constitutional; but the ruling effectively affirmed African-Americans as unequal and further legitimized segregation. Jazz writer Charles Edward Smith connected blues music with the decision: "Blues had emerged from the welter of Negro folk music most forcefully by the 1890s, providing another Minority Opinion than that of Justice Harlan in *Plessy v. Ferguson* . . . For it was the cry of a people, as well as a song or a way of singing it."[1]

In the introduction to his powerful book *Blues People* (1963) Leroi Jones (later, Amiri Baraka) offered this keynote to his discussion of the evolution of Black folks/"Blues People": "The one peculiar referent to the drastic change in the Negro from slavery to 'citizenship' is his music. . . . I cite the beginning of blues as one beginning of American Negroes" in their development from slavery to *citizens*.[2]

In his fascinating memoir *Treat It Gentle* (1960—his original title was, "Where Did It Come From?"), Sidney Bechet gave us a look into the heart of that precise point, with elemental eloquence and folk wisdom:

> The slaves felt a trouble on them . . . The only thing they had that couldn't be taken from them was their music. Their song, it was coming right up from the fields, settling itself in their feet and working right up, right up into their stomachs, into their spirit, into their fear, into their longing . . . It was like it had no end, nowhere even to wait for an end, nowhere to hope for a change in things. But it had a beginning, and that much they understood . . . it was a feeling in them, a memory that came from a long way back. It was like they were trying to work the music back to its beginning and then start it over again, start it over and build it to a place where it could stop somehow,

to a place where the music could put an end to itself and become another music, a new beginning that could begin *them* over again. There were chants and drums and voices—you could hear all that in it—and there was love and work and worry and waiting; there was being tired, and the sun, and the overseers following behind them so they didn't dare stop and look back. It was all in the music . . .

All the music I play is from what was finding itself in my grandfather's time . . . Because all the strains that went to make up the spirituals, they were still unformed, still waiting for the heart of ragtime to grab them up, mix in with them, bring them out of where only a few people could feel the music and need it, bring it out to where it could say what it had to say . . .

Mostly there was this big change: a different feeling had got started.

Go down Moses
Way down to Egypt land;
Tell old Pharaoh,
Let my people go . . .

It was years they'd been singing that. And suddenly there was a different way of singing it. You could feel a new way of happiness in the lines. All that waiting, all that time when that song was far-off music, waiting music, suffering music; and all at once it was there, it had arrived. It was joy music now. It was Free Day . . . *Emancipation.* And New Orleans just bust wide open."[3]

Most African cultures were primarily oral, rather than written; and song and telling the stories of their people were key elements of those cultures. After being taken from their native lands to America, Black folks used the oral tradition, especially through song, as a primary means of expressing their feelings and telling their story. The only thing they had that couldn't be taken away from them was their music, indeed—and their soul and spirit. And that spirit, once they adopted Christianity and adapted it to their needs and styles, produced the deep soulfulness and soaring feelings of the "Negro Spirituals"—which often included veiled expressions about their bondage and desire for escape to freedom. Thereafter, the collective work in cotton fields and on the levees gave rise to work songs and field hollers, which later led, along with inspiration from the Spirituals, to that profound music of the people called the Blues. As Bechet said, "and become another music, a new beginning that could begin *them* over again."

The nature of the blues and jazz, especially as performed by major musicians, began to have a significant impact on Blacks' self-image *and* standing in the broader society in the later 1920s. After such top Black musicians as Louis Armstrong, Duke Ellington, and Lonnie Johnson, plus White ones like Bix Beiderbecke and Jack Teagarden, initiated things through the power of the music and from their mutual appreciation, these developments had wider and wider impact throughout American society. As leading African-American bass player Milt Hinton said, "Musicians had been integrating way before society decided to do that."[4] (Prof. Houston Baker, Jr., has written powerfully and insightfully about the Black experience, music, and modernism in the 1920s and thereafter in his fine book, *Modernism and the Harlem Renaissance*.[5]

Further, the top musicians were themselves important models of accomplishment and success. As Giles Oakley said of people like Bessie Smith and Ma Rainey as they appeared on stage in major theaters for Black folks in the 1920s and early 1930s: "At such moments the blues stars became virtually heroines, symbols of success and glamour, dressed in resplendent outfits . . . In a society which denied Black people the dignity of human equality, denied them the means to even strive for it, the trappings of riches and success were symbols of great potency."[6]

Here let me point out that the developments in the 1920s and those I relate more fully in the following are of interest and significance because they are also one of the most *inspiring* trends in the history of American society. The artistry and courage of great Black musicians *and* of a number of White ones, plus the outrage at racial prejudice and determination to work to overcome it that animated various White music promoters, night club owners, writers and others, is a profound story of people putting themselves on the line to make America finally live up to its proclaimed ideals; and ultimately, it is a triumph of the human spirit.

A good example of the role of non-musicians in this was John Hammond (from the Vanderbilt family), discoverer and producer extraordinaire of musicians. As he said in his autobiography, "To bring recognition to the Negro's supremacy in jazz was the most effective and constructive form of social protest I could think of."[7] His "Spirituals to Swing" concerts in Carnegie Hall in 1938 and 1939 were historic examples of this.

Following the attention and praise Armstrong and Ellington, especially, received by the early 1930s, further striking events and developments from the '30s into the '50s boosted racial progress. For example, in summer 1937 Louis Armstrong "vaulted over yet another [racial] barrier by becoming the first Black to host his own network-radio variety show" when he substituted for singer Rudy Vallee's long-running NBC Blue Network show with Satchmo's own commercially sponsored show called 'Harlem'." And: "Vallee was one of many Armstrong fans in show business; Louis's artistry had long since transcended categories."[8]

Other events contributed to this progress, like John Hammond's December 1938 "From Spirituals to Swing" concert and the much-celebrated Marian Anderson concert before 75,000 people in front of the Lincoln Memorial in Washington in April 1939. This outdoor concert was set up after she had been denied Constitution Hall by the Daughters of the American Revolution, who controlled the Hall. That prompted First Lady Eleanor Roosevelt to resign her membership in the DAR.[9] And there was the powerful protest song about lynching, sung so evocatively by Billie Holiday on a 1939 recording, "Strange Fruit." Two years later Sidney Bechet recorded a stunningly powerful instrumental version. See the end of this Appendix for my special review of this recording—which is a microcosm of the broader theme of this book.

As the years wore on in the century, others in blues, jazz, and folk music with supreme talent, personality and exceptional humanity steadily made inroads on racial stereotypes and barriers from their prominent public platforms. Beyond those noted in chapter 1, significant examples were jazzmen Dizzy Gillespie, with his musical brilliance and incandescent personality (and as one of the hippest people alive), and Oscar Peterson, with his stunning virtuosity on the piano and great dignity; handsome, broadly popular folk musicians Josh White and Harry Belafonte (plus movie appearances); hugely popular jazz pianist, then pop singer Nat "King" Cole, and gospel, then pop singer Sam Cooke (speaking of handsome guys).

Additionally, in the mid-1930s though the 1940s, tremendously popular White Big Band leaders like Benny Goodman, Artie Shaw, and the Dorsey brothers worked with Black musicians and had some Black musicians as featured performers in their bands, and they took public stands against incidents of racial prejudice. George Gershwin made jazz and blues central to his most noted compositions like "Rhapsody in Blue" and *Porgy and Bess* and respected the musicians who created and brilliantly played the music he drew on.

In the 1940s and 1950s producer Norman Granz brought top jazz musicians to concert halls all over America in his Jazz at the Philharmonic programs. He demanded that his Black musicians stay in excellent hotels and that seating at the JATP concerts be integrated. As bass player Ray Brown said: "Black musicians couldn't stay in decent hotels until Norman came along. People forget about what he did." Granz said, "I insisted that my musicians were to be treated with the same respect as Leonard Bernstein or [classical violin great] Heifetz because they were just as good—both as men and as musicians." Barney Josephson's Café Society nightclub in New York, from the late '30s through the '40s, was a place "where blacks and whites worked together behind the footlights and sat together" in the audience.[10]

In 1949, Louis Armstrong appeared on the cover of *Time* magazine, which was of far greater cultural and societal importance at that time. Soon after, that huge star of music, movies, and radio, Bing Crosby, invited Armstrong to appear on his network radio show. He introduced Louis saying: "I got a big charge out of seeing a bright satchel-mouthed face beaming at the world from the cover of *Time* magazine—the face of one of my best friends . . . Tonight I'm just poppin' with pride to give a friendly five to the most sensational horn of them all, Louis 'Satchmo' Armstrong."[11] This was six years *before* the Montgomery Bus Boycott, launching the active phase of the Civil Rights movement.

And in that crucial stage of American society and race relations, the mid-1950s, it's also interesting to note that Louis Armstrong, on his 1955 album *Satch Plays Fats* and in concerts with White audiences, performed the powerful, moving Fats Waller-Andy Razaf show song, "(What Did I Do to Be So) Black and Blue," which Satchmo had originally turned into an anthem of racial injustice back in the late 1920s. In a 1956 live recording, you can hear the mostly White audience responding with recognition, applause, and cheers for Satchmo's version of "Black and Blue"—and a storm of applause at the end.

A wonderful illustration of the impact of all this even in the South, featuring Duke Ellington and his great orchestra, came in a reminiscence of African-American singer Earl Coleman from his youth:

> He told of a magical afternoon in Mississippi . . . where he heard the sound of Duke Ellington's brass men warming up, the light hitting those silver or golden horns through which they eased so much heat and sophisticated feeling. Then he spoke of looking through the windows at the Ellingtonians, inside the private Pullman cars that sat on those Mississippi train tracks like luxury hotel rooms on wheels. . . .
>
> Earl attended the dance where Ellington's band was performing. Negroes took to the floor on every tune, and whites sat behind ropes, enjoying Ellington's music and the floor show of romance and rhythm so superbly provided by the local people who became, in Dizzy Gillespie's words, "the mirrors of the music." Earl remembered that during intermission the smooth-looking Ellington sat at a table with the whites who ran the town, but that he sat not as the target of a joke or as some version of inferiority. He charmed and laughed and told tales as a man of talent and aristocratic bearing whose humanity took a back seat to no one's.[12]

In 1956, Satchmo appeared playing himself, with his band the All Stars, in the film, *High Society*, which starred Bing Crosby, Grace Kelly, and Frank Sinatra; it was the fourth-highest grossing film of the year. The admiration Bing Crosby had for Louis Armstrong is evident in their interactions in the film. (Some people think Satchmo stole the show with his performance. The elegant Grace Kelly was still another Armstrong fan.) In 1957, the famous and hugely respected figure in broadcast journalism, Edward R. Murrow, made a feature documentary film of Louis and His All Stars called *Satchmo the Great*, which was an expansion of the profile of Armstrong done on Murrow's popular CBS TV show, *See It Now*. The film showed Armstrong as "a good will ambassador and a man loved and respected throughout the world"—he played before 100,000 people at one concert in Africa. The film ends in the U.S. with Armstrong performing "St. Louis Blues" with the New York Philharmonic Orchestra led by Leonard Bernstein; a photo was taken of Bernstein with his arm around Armstrong's shoulders and a look of pure delight and admiration on his face. Still further, humorously alluding to the international stature and appeal of Louis Armstrong around this time, an editorial cartoon in 1958 in the prominent magazine, *The New Yorker*, had distinguished men around a Washington conference table saying: "This is a diplomatic mission of the utmost delicacy. The question is, who's the best man for it, [Secretary of State] John Foster Dulles or Satchmo?"[13] As noted in chapter 1, Murrow and Bernstein were seen by *Life* magazine as among the most important Americans of the century. So was Louis Armstrong.

(Let me add that, further demonstrating Armstrong's prominence, and in accordance with the "music and modern art" discussion in the "Interlude" section in chapter 2: "Arthur Dove, the first American abstract artist, painted a canvas [in 1938] called 'Swing Music (Louis Armstrong)' . . . [which was] a visual evocation of an Armstrong solo."[14])

Two other observations add perspective on the impact of these musicians, especially regarding Louis Armstrong, Duke Ellington, and Lonnie Johnson. Modern jazz trumpeter Lester Bowie once said: "The true revolutionary is one that's not apparent. The revolutionary that's waving a gun out in the streets is never effective; the police just arrest him. But the police don't ever know about the guy that smiles and drops a little poison in their coffee. Louis . . . was that sort of revolutionary."[15] The poison in the coffee was not the best metaphor for how he affected things, but the gist of it is quite right; ultimately, Louis Armstrong's impact on race and society was profound. Second, Harvey Cohen noted the similar importance of Duke Ellington's "nonverbal communication" in all this. And: "For him, the most effective protest in the American scene was to live and create in a way that undermined racial barriers and stereotypes. His career shows how much the racial changes in the United States owed to infiltrators like Ellington, who softened the enemy so that protests could develop effectively."[16] As shown throughout this text, the dignity and great artistic creativity with which Lonnie Johnson operated was like that of Duke; and the numerous major guitarists and singers he influenced added to his impact.

Remember, as well, that a very significant element was how *participatory* were blues and earlier jazz performances among Black folks. As jazz researcher Lynn Abbott wrote: "Contemporaneous black press reports suggest that early African-American theater settings fairly *thrived* on interaction between performers and audience . . ." in the 1920s and 1930s in large theaters of that sort in major cities like St. Louis, Washington, D.C., Chicago, New York, Atlanta, and Philadelphia. (It continues today in places like the Apollo Theater in Harlem.) This communal and participatory element of the music and Black folks' involvement was a factor in the increasing solidarity and impetus to take collective action to enhance their Civil Rights.

But it wasn't just Black audiences who were being brought into that more active involvement—and into a connection with these Black musical artists and their displays of commonality. I reviewed for a jazz website the "Basin Street Blues" track from the marvelous album of Louis Armstrong and his All Stars recorded live in 1956 before what evidently was a mostly White audience. Let me quote the key passages:

> This live recording opens with Louis Armstrong's spoken introduction of the song title. The immediate roar of approval from the audience is a good illustration of how, by the mid-1950s, so many reveled in Louis and his All Stars, and how the band had brought this music to a wide public and made something of a cultural icon of "Basin Street Blues" . . . As Barney Bigard, the great clarinetist who formerly played with the All Stars and Ellington, said, "That band was the main group that brought jazz to the people, all over the America and all over the world. . . ."

> . . . With Louis Armstrong as the master of ceremonies and maestro of the
> trumpet, they brought this art to the audience in a most engaging way. "Engaging"
> is meant literally, as Armstrong's personal magic, love of the music, and unique con-
> nection with his audience brought them into active involvement with the experience
> of making this music. . . . One can hear this in the audience response; beyond
> the rousing applause at Satchmo's announcement of the tune title and the storm of
> applause at the end, the audience is part of the action when Armstrong, after sing-
> ing ". . . in New Orleans, the land of dreams," goes into a scat vocal with flair
> (no doubt accompanied by some delicious mugging) with the audience's delighted
> response completing the performance.[17]

As briefly noted in chapter 1, the most crucial impact of all those great musicians and their extraordinary humanity was on each succeeding generation of *young
people* from the 1920s on, who increasingly embraced Black music and style as cool
and as significant for their lives and social feelings.

The historical point at which young people of the majority race began to affect
things, and a view of how this music and the spirit behind it were starting to spread
widely as early as the late '20s, is well articulated by Gary Giddins in his biography of Bing Crosby in his earlier years. It also relates to the discussion in chapter 2
regarding developments in modern society and music. Here Giddins speaks of Bing
and his singing partner Al Rinker, in their early twenties, at the beginning of Bing's
singing career—after having been strongly influenced by jazz and blues:

> They were . . . two clean-cut White boys bringing a variation on Black music to
> the vaudeville stage [late in the vaudeville era] with panache and charm. They rep-
> resented something borderline radical: a trace of danger, a current from a generation
> that threatened to bust out of old and settled traditions. At no time between the Civil
> War and Prohibition had the nation's young people clamored for a music of their
> own or rebelled against the songs of their parents. . . . They charmed everyone, yet
> were harbingers of a break with conventions. . . .[18]

That was "the Jazz Age." Further, in the early 1930s college students were
among Louis Armstrong's biggest fans. Those college students then became adults
and many took the appreciation of that great African-American artist and others
into the broader society and thereby contributed to lessening the racist orientations
in America.

Young people's exposure to the music and style and to Black folks as fellow
Americans kept broadening and made them less and less inclined to buy into the
racist system.

Here let me draw on my expertise in my *other* professional realm. Confession:
I was actually trained as a political scientist, with a Ph.D. in that discipline; that
includes work on public opinion and political socialization. A leading book on the
field (to which I contributed suggestions for a new edition) spelled out a key type of

opinion change: "A *generational* effect exists when a specific age cohort [like 16–25 year olds] is uniquely socialized by a set of historical events" and developments. The increasingly pervasive developments and high profile events involving music and related style that are discussed here and elsewhere in the book provided just such impacts on majority/White young people's attitudes towards race. This increasingly resulted in change from the previous generations. As reported in two studies of young people's development in modern societies, especially America, the increasing pattern over the twentieth century was this: "Contemporary youth spend much of their lives outside the formal economic and political spheres, but in a milieu that reflects the larger structure and is designed explicitly for them. It is marked by clothes . . . music, entertainment, and the like, and is recognized as belonging to youth but excluding adults." And: "Young people's behavior within this autonomous sphere is enormously consequential." The changes in young people's attitudes on race have been registered more and more strikingly in opinion surveys and other studies for decades. A 2007 study summarized the general pattern of opinion on an issue particularly fraught with racial tension: "Each new generation has entered adulthood with more positive attitudes toward interracial marriage. . . ."[19] That attitude change and others related to racial tolerance was not solely caused by the musical factor, but all the developments discussed here were very significant contributors, as the previous material and the following paragraphs detail.

In chapter 9 I note Lonnie's indirect influence (via B. B. King) on Duane Allman and the Allman Brothers Band; and I point out the sociological significance of the mixed race Southern Allmans calling themselves "a band of brothers" in the late 1960s. An interesting personal story of how the racial attitudes of young White *southerners* were increasingly influenced by all this is told by Mark Kemp in his book, *Dixie Lullaby: A Story of Music, Race, and New Beginnings in a New South*. Kemp and his friends were profoundly influenced by the Allman Brothers: "They talked like us, they looked like us, they sang about issues and landscapes that we could feel and see. . . . For me and many kids like me, the Allman Brothers and the southern rock movement that they spawned in the early 1970s . . . changed our lives and gave us a sense of community and purpose. . . ." And, "it was the beginning of a healing process" amongst southerners. The Allman Brothers sometimes made the racial connection explicit: Gregg Allman said, "'God Rest His Soul' was a song I wrote in tribute to Martin Luther King right after his assassination. . . . I thought [he] was a beautiful man, and he was trying to bring us together and end the strife in the country."[20]

An additional element of the music and the societal circumstances involved in it among African-Americans was very significant (and drew on traditional African performances); and it rather directly prepared the way for collective action on Civil Rights. Blues players and their audiences participated in a kind of collective cultural ritual that was often cathartic for those folks Leroi Jones/Amiri Baraka called "Blues People." The blues performances, in that cultural situation, also "dramatized the cultural vitality and rebelliousness of the participants, evoking race and class sol-idarity." The blues and various of its leading performers provided a further historical impact as prominent purveyors of the call for urban migration: Many rural blues artists plus *non*-rural blues and jazz artists "were in the forefront of this exodus [from the cotton belt in the first half of the twentieth century]; they were the oracles of their generation, contrasting the promise of freedom with the reality of their harsh living conditions, using their imagination and insight to reformulate the common complaints and aspirations of African Americans."[21]

## Other Perspectives and Questions

*But,* Black Middle Class Aspirations and Doubts About Blues and Jazz   Despite the previous discussion, I must note that the aspirations of many Blacks for middle class respectability and their effort to overcome White stereotypes about Black folks led them to express doubts about jazz, especially until the mid-1930s, and about blues through the 1950s. These Blacks, occupying "respectable" positions in the African-American community, suggested the music and the musicians did not reflect well on the middle class, mainstream American orientations they were promoting for Blacks folks. Dave Payton, influential columnist of the *Chicago Defender*, was a prominent African-American figure who, in the '20s and '30s, expressed negative observations of blues and of the jazz musicians who didn't conform to his notion of enhancing the race. As Arnold Shaw also pointed out regarding Blacks and the "country blues" as late as the '50s: "The Black people . . . I knew never lived in the country. They looked down on country music. Among themselves, the Blacks called country blues 'field nigger' music. They wanted to be citified."

That's why Lonnie Johnson appealed so widely to African-Americans and always insisted, "I don't play country blues, I play *city* blues." And that's part of what B. B. King meant when he said: "Singers like Blind Lemon Jefferson formed the backbone of the music. [Then] I got to see how those blues were modified and modernized by artists like Lonnie Johnson"—who performed in an urbane manner and presented himself with dignity, style and sophistication.[22]

As jazz got a more and more positive reception from notables in the general society and was increasingly recognized as a significant art form starting in the 1940s, however, the attitude of "respectable" Blacks softened, though it took much longer for them to recognize the value and importance of blues. Then, starting in the later 1940s, more challenging notions came forth:

(Sort of) Contrary Conceptions   More stark questions have been raised by some, though not all of these questions and claims are relevant to this particular discus-sion. An example: Miles Davis once said (in characteristically arrogant, popping-off manner), "Whites can't play jazz." A few other Black jazz guys have said something similar. Well, this is hard to take seriously since White jazz pianist and arranger Bill Evans was central to the Davis-led "jazz masterpiece" album, *Kind of Blue*, and at other times Davis defended the use of White jazz players in his other bands. Louis Armstrong praised the playing of pioneering White jazzmen like Jack Teagarden and Bix Beiderbecke, sax great Lester Young credited early White sax player Frankie Trumbauer as a prime inspiration, and so on. Benny Goodman's swinging clarinet solo, following Teddy Wilson's intro, on the great Billie Holiday recording, "He Ain't Got Rhythm" (1937), shows it's foolish to say Whites can't play jazz—and the melding of Goodman's clarinet with Wilson's piano, Buck Clayton's trumpet and that Basie "All American Rhythm section" are a sublime combination of artistic sensibilities. Black jazzman Milt Hinton (in a fine book of his photographs) wrote: "Whenever there was good jazz being played . . . [White baritone sax player] Gerry Mulligan was there. He's been a mainstay of jazz for forty years."[23]

There was much comment on the exclusion of Whites from performing in jazz programs at Lincoln Center by director Wynton Marsalis; it was even called "racist" by jazz writer Whitney Baillett in a much-discussed *New Yorker* article.[24] Works by jazz writer Gene Lees and others deal with the issue and related claims.[25] That particular flap is not really relevant to this discussion, but some of the heated debate on it moved into the broader issue of jazz as Black music, etc. The first part of a Baillett comment echoes the claims of some Black jazz performers in that regard, then suggests broader perspective: "Blacks invented jazz, but nobody owns it."

Actually, that first part is not accurate. Creoles of New Orleans (part French, part Hispanic, Black, or other) were a significant part of the creation of jazz. They played in bands that led to the creation of jazz and boosted the earliest years of jazz like the Onward Brass Band and the Reliance Brass Band; and Creoles like George Bacquet, Paul Barbarin, and Lorenzo Tio Sr. (born in Mexico) and Lorenzo Tio, Jr. taught future jazz greats like Sidney Bechet (best characterized as a Creole of color), as well as playing in founding jazz bands. Statements by some Black musicians (and a few writers) flatly claiming that African-Americans "created" jazz ignore those facts. Further, two of the four most important bands in the original establishment of jazz used "Creole" in their names: Joe Oliver's Creole Jazz Band and The Creole Band (or Original Creole Band) of Freddie Keppard and Bill Johnson; use of those names was a reference to the Creole role in the creation of jazz (although leader Oliver was pure African-American). Another of those original jazz bands, The Red Hot Peppers, was led by Creole Jelly Roll Morton and included Creole Kid Ory and Creole of color, Johnny St. Cyr. St. Cyr and Ory also played on the Armstrong Hot Five recordings; and St. Cyr and Creole of color Honore Dutry played in Oliver's band. And so on. (Buddy Bolden's band was the first of the principal original jazz bands. The misnamed Original Dixieland Jazz Band was all White; but their significance in jazz history is much debated, other than making the first jazz recordings.)

Further, saying Blacks "created" jazz is vague. After those founding father bands for jazz, Whites played significant roles in first making jazz a major genre of music and a great art form during the 1920s and early 1930s. White Texan Jack Teagarden was the real father of the powerful, virtuoso trombone role in jazz bands, starting in the later 1920s. The Trumbauer and Beiderbecke examples were noted above. One of the most seminal and greatest jazz clarinetists was Creole Barney Bigard, who began with the Albert Nicholas Band in1923 in New Orleans and made important recordings with Ellington, Armstrong, etc.; his ethnic heritage was part French, part Spanish. (It's also interesting that Ray Charles said an early musical hero was White jazz clarinet master Artie Shaw: "I didn't even know he was White and didn't care. [He] . . . had the clarinet technique I loved. That perfect tone... [and] he swung-his ass off. . . ."[26])

Jazz writer Richard Sudhalter summarized the beginnings and establishment of jazz: "But a growing body of . . . research into the origins and early development of jazz has [found] that the music may not be so much a black American experience as an *American* experience, with various racial and ethnic groups playing indispensible and interlocking roles"—including many White musicians, not just a relative few. Sudhalter exhaustively documented the latter in his study, *Lost Chords: White Musicians and Their Contributions to Jazz, 1915–1945.*[27]

Various African-American musicians have also complained that often, Black musicians have not reaped their just rewards as prime creators in and performers of the musical art form of jazz. Most jazz writers agree. But, as they and various Black musicians rightly point out, the principal problem has been with White-owned record companies and media, along with more or less racially based responses from *some* of the general public. Black poet, music critic and composer Ron Welburn said it well (amending a radical essay from his younger years): "It became clear to me that the racial issues involving jazz rest more on the onus and shoulders of promotion, production, journalism, and advertising than on the musicians . . . [T]he convenient paradigms for lashing out at white musicians I increasingly deemed as self-serving. . . . "[28]

It's ironic that Black *blues* guys have rarely said those things, despite that fact that the blues is the soulful foundation of the claim by African-Americans that this whole music is *their* cultural possession, and the blues *was* primarily the creation of Black folks. Blues greats like Muddy Waters, B. B. King, and Buddy Guy have expressed appreciation for the blues artistry of White musicians like Eric Clapton and Stevie Ray Vaughan, and have thanked the Rolling Stones, Clapton, and others for helping bring their music out to a wider American audience. The title of a Muddy Waters album says a lot about all this: *Fathers and Sons* (with a great album cover that's a delightful take-off on the Sistine Chapel mural). It refers to young White musicians like Mike Bloomfield and Paul Butterfield who learned from the Black Chicago blues guys and played with Muddy for that live album—Bloomfield playing superb bluesy guitar—and were inspired by him. Indeed, that's a big part of the beauty of this whole development and how this profound music increasingly spread and had such impact.

Many points made by Baraka in *Blues People* are in accord with what I've written in this book, including the profound human expression in the music and its significance, the "expanded sense of communal expression so characteristic of Afro-American music," the importance of *urban* development in blues and jazz, and the way the music and musicians reflected changes in the condition of Black folks (Baraka's emphasis) and helped *drive* those changes (my emphasis).

One assertion by Baraka seems, at first glance, to take us beyond the themes in this book. He wrote of how soulful Black-based music like jazz, blues and Rhythm & Blues constituted "an attempt to reverse the social roles within society by redefining the canons of value." Further: "The complete domination of American society by . . . the economic sensibility [and big corporations' influence], discouraging completely any significant participation of the imaginative sensibility in the social, political and economic affairs of the society, . . . made the formal culture . . . anemic and fraught with incompetence and unreality."[29] He suggested that the Black modes of expression through blues, jazz and R & B *did* offer the extraordinary imaginative sensibility so lacking in American society. In those passages he was especially referring to the modern jazz musicians of the '40s and '50s, but he sees a broader societal significance. Well, that actually points to what I discussed in the "Interlude" section of chapter 2, noting how capitalist economics and the Victorian social order had dominated America, but were increasingly and variously challenged by the rise of modernism and the new music and all that went with it. The challenges to the oppressive and discriminatory order continued with the first stirrings of Civil Rights, Beat Poets, etc., in the later 1950s, then the developments summarized as "the '60s," with the height of the Civil Rights movement, and millions of Whites, Hispanics and others challenging the socio-economic and political order, and the start of the environmental movement. Music was a major accompaniment to all that in the '60s. (My own contribution to musical critique of capitalist practices in the current era is my protest song, "The Bankers' Greed Blues." The lyrics, with a nice note by Pete Seeger, are on my website[30], along with our performance video.)

**On the Other Hand** Given the racial history in America, one can understand the inclination of some Black jazz musicians to lay an exclusivist claim to jazz and blues. But in truth, most major Black musicians appreciated the mutual musical stimulation and comradely partnership of accomplished White musicians (and those of other ethnic origins). *But,* the virtually hostile, exclusivist attitude by *some* Black musicians led to problems and even reverse racist conduct.

Gene Lees, jazz writer and former editor of leading jazz magazine, *Down Beat,* noted an unfortunate example, originally revealed in a *New York Times* interview with the African-American sax player Sonny Rollins. Rollins wanted a different sound for his next album and he got the White jazz guitarist Jim Hall to play with him. "Jim had an incredible harmonic sense, he's such a sensitive player. So to me, he was the perfect guy. . . ." But, "after 'Freedom Suite' . . . some people expected me to behave in a certain way and wondered why I'd hire a White musician. I took some heat for that. [But I thought] it was a healing symbol. . . ."[31] In *Cats of Any Color: Jazz, Black and White*, Lees had strong words for such exclusivist orientations towards jazz. Lees flatly said: "Any statement that jazz is 'Black music' and only Black music is racist on the face of it"; he cited the role of Creoles, etc., noted above. He also worried that exclusionary actions were becoming institutionalized with such things as American Jazz Masters Fellowship Awards almost totally shutting out major White musicians, as well as Wynton Marsalis' conduct at Lincoln Center (now eased up).[32]

Two other books that have thoughtfully wrestled with this are *Where the Dark and Light Folks Meet: Race and the Mythology, Politics, and Business of Jazz* by Randy Sandke, White jazz trumpet player and writer, and *Jazz in Black and White* by White saxophone player Charley Gerard. Gerard regularly felt pushed aside by Black jazz guys due to his being White; in Lester Young's unique, hip lingo, Gerard "felt a draft," that is, he felt discrimination, reverse discrimination, in this case, and noted examples of what he'd experienced. Like Sandke and Lees, this is a man who revered the great Black jazz musicians, so it was doubly disappointing.

In light of the horrible story of racism in America for so long, it's a wonderful thing that African-Americans have been increasingly recognized for being prime creators and developers of these great forms of expression and musical art. But it seems to me that the exclusionary attitudes and actions of *some* actually betray the essential spirit of the music and the main thrust of the constructive impact the music has had on human relations and American society. In the end, due to the power of the music, the interaction of musicians of every demographic category, and the other developments I've reviewed, the perspective of a fellow named Duke Ellington may be the best conclusion (offered in 1945): "Jazz . . . is modern and it's American. The Negro element is still important. But jazz has become part of America. There are as many white musicians playing it as Negro . . . We are all working together. . . . We learn from each other."[33] Gene Lees summarized and editorialized well about the four great Black jazzmen (including Dizzy Gillespie) he wrote of in *You Can't Steal a Gift*: His four essays told the story of "the magnificence of the legacy they bequeathed to their country . . . and the munificence of their humanity. All are men who had every reason to embrace bitterness—and didn't."[34] The rich interactions in the community of jazz musicians took them to a higher level.

Founder of the Jazz at the Philharmonic concerts, Norman Granz, was a fierce fighter of discrimination against Black musicians. But as registered in his biography, "Granz was troubled by the attitude of some European jazz fans . . . who he thought practiced a form of reverse racism by presuming black musicians to be more authentic jazz artists than white players simply on the basis of skin color. This is just as wrong as the bias . . . that's directed the other way."[35]

Ultimately, it's about great music and the magnitude of the humanity of key figures. Dizzy Gillespie spoke out about race problems starting in the 1940s. His genius and his principled humanity made great contributions. His orientation was about real values and a decent society, as he showed when he said: "Pete Seeger is outspoken politically, [but he is so] warm. . . . He's a great man."[36]

And about the blues that is fundamental to jazz and most other popular American music, here's the perspective of W. C. Handy, composer of "St. Louis Blues" and a key early force in originally bringing the blues to the wider American society: "The blues is a thing deeper than what you'd call a mood. Like the spirituals, it began with the Negro, it involves our history, where we came from, and what we experienced." But then the blues spread out and had wider influence. "So the blues helped to fill the longing in the hearts of all kinds of people. They took it to their hearts and felt the same thing we felt . . . . The blues and jazz have become American music. . . ."[37]

Jack Teagarden, in a stage appearance with his old friend Louis Armstrong, summed up simply and well regarding those who have a profound feel for and commitment to great jazz and blues, whatever their ethnic origins: He said to Satchmo, "You're a spade and I'm an ofay, but we got the same soul. Let's blow." Seeing those two together on film in the '50s and hearing their combined music, with that line included, in the documentary *Satchmo*[38], is a beautiful thing that embodies the essence of what I've said here.

## . . . And Spreading the Music and Respect for the Musicians Nationwide

It's worth taking special note of two White singers who drew on that music, became hugely popular, and brought their influence from that music and their respect for and occasional musical partnership with significant Black musicians to most of American society—beginning in the late 1920s: Bing Crosby and Jimmie Rodgers.

Music writer Gary Giddins summarized: "As the most successful recording artist of all time [and] an abiding star of movies, radio and television . . . Bing Crosby helped transform and define the cultural life of the United States. . . . He was inspired by his idol and lifelong friend, Louis Armstrong. . . . [By the late 1920s-early 1930s,] Bing brought something new to [mainstream] American song: rhythmic excitement, virile authority, emotional candor." Crosby said: "I'm proud to acknowledge my debt to the Reverend Satchelmouth. He is the beginning and the end of music in America."[39] ("Satchelmouth" was the full, original version of Armstrong's nickname, later transmuted and shortened to "Satchmo.")

Bing's success gave him leverage in Hollywood. In 1936 he insisted that Louis Armstrong be in the film, *Pennies from Heaven*. And: "Though his part was small . . . , Louis would be top-billed as part of a quartet of stars. No Black performer had ever been billed as lead in a White picture."[40] Thereafter, Louis appeared in a series of films, and his musical genius (even when employed in odd movie settings) and charisma conveyed his exceptional humanity to mainstream audiences all over America.

Jimmie Rodgers is often called "the Father of Country Music." Following his big 1927 hit, "Blue Yodel (T for Texas)," and up to his early death in 1933, Jimmie became hugely popular; his reach extended well beyond the newly recognized Country Music realm. And, as Barry Mazor wrote in his fine book on Rodgers, Jimmie "found ways to further the spread and acceptance of the blues without an ounce of condescension to the musical material he loved. . . . No Caucasian singer before Jimmie Rodgers had so successfully digested the basic, inherent ethos of the blue.s . . . From his very first hit, this was a central attraction of his act and style for audiences and [other] performers, White and Black alike."[41] His respect for the musicians who created the blues was manifest. In further illustration of this, Louis Armstrong accompanied him on the Rodgers recording, "Blue Yodel #9," as well. (On his TV show in late 1970, Johnny Cash showed sheer delight and honor in having Louis on his show, and the two of them performed a re-creation of that Jimmie Rodgers recording with Armstrong—in the temple of Country music, Nashville's Ryman Auditorium. It's on DVD.[42])

The impact of all this kept broadening through society and helped change history; and ultimately all this helped set the scene for the election of the first Black President of the United States in 2008.

## Perfect Expression of the Broader Themes:
## Sidney Bechet's Masterful "Strange Fruit"

SIDNEY BECHET: STRANGE FRUIT

TRACK    Strange Fruit

ARTIST    Sidney Bechet (soprano sax)

CD    Really The Blues (Living Era)

**Musicians:** Sidney Bechet (soprano sax), Willie 'The Lion' Smith (piano), Everett Barksdale (guitar). Composed by Lewis Allan.

**Recorded:** New York, September 13, 1941

RATING:   100/100
(learn more)

The Billie Holiday recording of this song is justly famous. By contrast, this version is not well known outside the limited ranks of jazz writers and the most intense jazz lovers. That is a cultural tragedy because this is one of the ultimate masterpieces of musical art performed and captured on record in the 20th century. (Astonishingly, in his major biography of Bechet, John Chilton basically dismisses this recording with a one-sentence wave of his hand.)

Besides pure musical art, this is drama of the highest order. It is the tragedy Shakespeare would have created if he had lived as a black musician in the American South during the Jim Crow era (1876-1965). The title "Strange Fruit" refers to two African-American men in Marion, Indiana, hanging from a tree upon which they'd been lynched by a white mob in 1930. Haunted by a photograph of this grisly event, a Jewish high-school teacher in the Bronx named Abel Meeropol wrote the song under a pseudonym in 1936.

With its striking lyrics, Billie Holiday's recording is transfixing. But to me, Bechet's instrumental version is even more powerful. And his soprano sax, with its famous intense, throbbing vibrato, offers the perfect instrument for expressing the meaning and emotion of this ultimate cry of the heart and protestation against the stark inhumanity of lynching. The recording can be enjoyed purely for the stunning music; but the societal meaning adds an extraordinary dimension to this American cultural expression.

Bechet provides a climbing and descending opening with rich tone and great poignancy, making a kind of mini-overture to the story. He plays with less volume than usual, the first use of dynamics in this song that has rarely been equaled for enhancing meaning and art. Everett Barksdale's guitar next offers a reflective transition, in descending steps, to the main musical lines, followed by pianist Willie "the Lion" Smith introducing the main theme with simple virtuosity of touch and tone. Now Bechet plays the theme with embellishments, starting in still restrained manner, like a lament. Then he steadily increases the intensity and passion, climbing higher and higher, taking the lament to a profound cry of the heart and then to a keening protest with that throbbing Bechet vibrato in full cry, only to climb even higher and end on a dramatic high note that is simultaneously an ultimate anguished wail and an appeal to the heavens to end this insanity. It is sublime musical art, yet also carries profound social meaning.

And then, all too quickly—in 2½ minutes—it is done. Rarely has such great musical art and human expression been accomplished in so short a time.

Reviewer: Dean Alger

Alger track review of S. Bechet recording of "Strange Fruit" from *www.jazz.com*

# Appendix III

## GUIDE TO RECORDINGS BY LONNIE JOHNSON AND RELEVANT OTHERS

### Lonnie Johnson on CD

Special companion CD to this book, compiled by Dean Alger:

*The* Ultimate *Best of Lonnie Johnson* (2012, record company arrangements pending). The first 7 tracks are accessible masterpieces spanning Lonnie's career, then the rest are important recordings arranged in chronological order; all are specifically cited and reviewed in the book.

### Other principal Lonnie Johnson CDs:

*Lonnie Johnson: Steppin' on the Blues*, Columbia. Columbia-selected best of Lonnie Johnson's recordings from 1925 to 1932 on OKeh Records.

*Eddie Lang and Lonnie Johnson: Blue Guitars, Volumes I & II*, BGO Records double CD (see *www.bgo-records.com;* doesn't seem to be available on *Amazon.com*), with all 10 of the Lang-Johnson guitar duets and other recordings with Louis Armstrong, Texas Alexander, etc. A wonderful CD!

Document Records has *Lonnie Johnson: The Complete Recorded Works*, from 1925 through August 1932 in seven "volumes"/CDs, and then in three more CDs from 1937–1947, in chronological order. WARNING: be aware that these are simply direct transfers from old 78 records; they are not remastered for the digital-CD era, so the sound quality is often not so good.

*Louis Armstrong: The Hot Fives and Hot Sevens* with Lonnie Johnson on "I'm Not Rough," "Hotter Than That" and "Savoy Blues" (Dec. 1927) are available on various box sets and individual CDs.

*The OKeh Ellington* 2-CD set, tracks 17 "The Mooche," 18 "Move Over," and 19 "Hot and Bothered" on Disc One with Lonnie Johnson (1991, Columbia).

*Lonnie Johnson: He's a Jelly Roll Baker*, RCA Bluebird, with recordings from 1939 through 1944.

*Lonnie Johnson: Blues in My Soul: 1937/1946*, Blues Collection-EPM Musique (this is, in effect, "The Rhythm & Blues Years," Vol. 1).

*Lonnie Johnson: The Rhythm & Blues Years, Vol. 2: 1947–1952*, Blues Collection-EPM Musique.

*Blues By Lonnie Johnson*, Prestige-Bluesville (1960, "Original Blues Classics" series).

*Blues and Ballads: Lonnie Johnson with Elmer Snowden* and *Blues, Ballads and Jumpin' Jazz, Vol. 2*, Prestige-Bluesville (1960, "Original Blues Classics" series).

*Losing Game*, Prestige-Bluesville (late 1960, "Original Blues Classics" series).

*Idle Hours: Lonnie Johnson with Victoria Spivey*, Prestige-Bluesville (1961, "Original Blues Classics" series).

*Lonnie Johnson: Another Night to Cry*, Prestige-Bluesville (1962, "Original Blues Classics" series).

*Lonnie Johnson: Stompin' at the Penny, with Jim McHarg's Metro Stompers*, Columbia Legacy (1965, originally on the "Roots & Blues" series).

*Lonnie Johnson: The Complete Folkways Recordings* (1967, Smithsonian-Folkways).

*Lonnie Johnson, The Unsung Blues Legend: The Living Room Session* (2000, Blues Magnet Records, recorded 1965 in Bernie Strassberg's living room).

*Dealing with the Devil: 25 Essential Blues Classics*, track no. 1, "Tomorrow Night" (2004, Varese Sarabande Records-King Records). Lonnie's big hit, "Tomorrow Night," is actually difficult to find on CDs. In addition to this CD, it is also available on the following box set.

Cheap Box Set: *Lonnie Johnson: The Original Guitar Wizard*, Proper Records (of England): 4-CD set with substantial booklet: selected recordings from 1925 to 1952, but just in raw chronological order. ("Tomorrow Night" is on CD 4.)

### Lonnie Johnson on DVD

*The American Folk Blues Festival, 1962–1966, Volume One*, track 5, "Another Night to Cry" (2003, Experience Hendrix-Reelin' In The Years Productions). Reverentially introduced by Sonny Boy Williamson II, Lonnie plays his regular '60s electric guitar and performs the title song of his album of the previous year.

*The American Folk-Blues Festival: The British Tours 1963–1966*, track 3, "Too Late To Cry" (2007, Experience Hendrix-Reelin' in the Years Productions). Here Lonnie plays an acoustic guitar and performs in a more intimate setting.

*The American Folk Blues Festival 1962–1966, Volume Two*, track 6, "Black Snake Blues" (2003, Experience Hendrix-Reelin' In The Years Productions). Here Lonnie introduces and then accompanies singer Victoria Spivey.

### Superb Recent Performances of Lonnie Johnson Songs

*Rediscovering Lonnie Johnson* – Blues Anatomy with special guest, Jef Lee Johnson (and Geoff Muldaur) (Range Records, Philadelphia, 2007). Superb covers of nine Lonnie J songs, two others he recorded and a tribute to him, with full Rhythm & Blues band and great guitar work by Jef Lee Johnson.

### B. B. King on Selected CDs

*The Fabulous B. B. King* (1991, Flair/Virgin Records America). Early B. B. King recordings, 1951–1954; here one can hear the influence of Lonnie Johnson at the beginning of B. B.'s recording career.

*B. B. King; Live at the Regal* (1964/1997, MCA). Shows B. B. King at the height of his artistic and performance powers and shows why he was the greatest of all blues singers, as well as one of the greats on guitar.

*B. B. King: Live and Well* (MCA, originally released in 1970; import CD available). One side of the original LP was a recorded live in a club, the other side was a studio recording; considered one of his best albums in B. B.'s prime.

*B. B. King: Deuces Wild* (MCA, 1997). A delightful series of duets with other artists, including Van Morrison, Eric Clapton, Bonnie Raitt, the Rolling Stones, and Country musicians Willie Nelson and Marty Stuart.

*Riding with the King: B. B. King and Eric Clapton* (Reprise, 2000). Grammy-winning CD with the two ultimate guitarists influenced by Lonnie Johnson playing joyously together.

(There are various best of B. B. King albums and box sets; an ultimate career perspective 10-CD box set, with substantial liner notes by Richard Shurman, is in production as this is written.)

### Robert Johnson on CD

*Robert Johnson :The Complete Recordings: The Centennial Collection*, Columbia (2011, with all the songs he recorded, from the two earlier albums Columbia released in the 1960s).

*Robert Johnson: The Complete Recordings*, Grammy Award-winning Columbia 2-CD box set with fine booklet (1990; with all recordings Robert made, including alternate takes).

### Buddy Guy on Selected CDs

*Buddy Guy: Buddy's Blues* (1997, Chess-MCA). Buddy's early recordings, especially track 1, "Worried Mind," in which one can hear Lonnie's influence on Buddy's guitar playing (as confirmed by Buddy).

*Alone and Acoustic: Buddy Guy and Junior Wells* (Alligator Records, 1991). A marvelous, interesting album with Buddy playing acoustic guitar, with the great harmonica player Junior Wells accompanying him.

*Damn Right, I Got the Blues* (Silvertone/Jive Records). A break-out album for Buddy, including guest appearances by Eric Clapton, Jeff Beck and Mark Knopfler, with a terrific version of "Mustang Sally," among other good tunes.

### T-Bone Walker on Selected CDs

*Blues Masters: Very Best of T-Bone Walker* (Rhino Records, 2000); the best of T-Bone's earlier recordings.

(There are various "Best of" or "Essential" T-Bone Walker CDs with his later work.)

### Django Reinhardt and Charlie Christian on Selected CDs

*Django Reinhardt with the Quintet of the Hot Club of France: Are You in the Mood?* (*Jazztory, 1994*); my favorite collection of 21 of Django's best recordings.

*Django Reinhardt: Chronological Volume One* (JSP Records, 1992); Django's earliest recordings.

*Charlie Christian: The Original Guitar Hero* [*sic*] (Columbia-Legacy, 2002), with 8 of Charlie's best recordings with Benny Goodman small groups.

### Charlie Byrd on Selected CDs

*The Guitar Artistry of Charlie Byrd* (Original Jazz Classics-Riverside, 1997).

There are a number of Byrd albums. A pair of very nice, accessible ones also feature two other top jazz guitarists:

*Great Guitars: Charlie Byrd, Herb Ellis, Barney Kessel* (Concord Records, 1978/ 1990); *Great Guitars Live: Charlie Byrd, Barney Kessel, Herb Ellis* (2-CD, Concord Records, 2001).

### The Evolution of Jazz Guitar

*Pioneers of the Jazz Guitar* (Yazoo Records, 1992); includes some Lonnie Johnson-Eddie Lang guitar duets and some of their successors, like Carl Kress and Dick McDonough.

*Hittin' on All Six: A History of the Jazz Guitar* (4 CD set, with extensive, well-done booklet; Proper Records—PROPERBOX 9, 2000)

### Three Favorite Guitar Duet Albums

*Chet Atkins and Doc Watson: Reflections* (Sugar Hill Records, 1980/1999); wonderful, Country-flavored virtuoso guitar-pickin' in the mature prime of these guitars legends, and starts with a sparkling, delightful "Dill Pickle Rag."

*Chester and Lester* (RCA, 1976/2007—with extra tracks), with guitar masters Chet Atkins and Les Paul.

*Together Again: Julian Breams and John Williams* (1993 [recorded 1973, 1978], RCA Victor-Gold Seal). Masterful guitar duets by two of the greatest classical guitarists of the twentieth century.

### General Listings of Blues and Jazz Recordings:

For a comprehensive listing of blues recordings up to World War II, see Robert M. W. Dixon, John Godrich and Howard Rye, *Blues and Gospel Records, 1890– 1943*, 4th ed. (Oxford, UK: Clarendon Press, 1997). For postwar blues, see Mike Leadbitter and Neil Slaven, *Blues Recordings 1943–1970, 2nd revised edition* (London: Record Information Services, 1987).

For perhaps the best general listing of jazz recordings, see the Tom Lord Jazz Discography. Online information: *www.lorddisco.com*

# Notes

## Notes to Chapter 1

1. Interview with the author, 23 March 2005, Minneapolis.

2. James Sallis, *The Guitar Players* (1982; repr., Lincoln: University of Nebraska Press, 1994), 50–51.

3. Bill Wyman with Richard Havers, *Bill Wyman's Blues Odyssey* (London: Dorling Kindersley, 2001), 106.

4. One guitar-playing expert suggested to me that Nick Lucas could be considered the "Original Guitar Hero." I deal with this early in chapter 4.

5. Lonnie's birth date: According to Big Bill Broonzy, Lonnie said it was 1894. See *Big Bill Blues: William Broonzy's Story as Told to Yannick Bruynoghe* (1955; repr., New York: Da Capo Press, 1992), 119. Lonnie also told two other credible sources that 1894 was the year (see chapter 2 for details). For some other details on Lonnie's life, there is a four-and-a-half-minute interview with Lonnie included on the Smithsonian/Folkways CD, along with a comment after the final song. It's fascinating to hear him talk of his life in his own speaking voice (though a couple of dates are inaccurately remembered).

6. Gunther Schuller, *Early Jazz* (New York: Oxford University Press, 1968), 109.

7. Duke Ellington, *Music Is My Mistress* (Cambridge, MA: Da Capo Press), 102.

8. Martin Williams, *Jazz Heritage* (New York: Oxford University Press, 1985), 37.

9. Gerard Herzhaff, *Encyclopedia of the Blues* (Little Rock: University of Arkansas Press, 1992).

10. *Chuck Berry: The Autobiography* (New York: Harmony Books, 1987), 25; John Goldrosen and John Beecher, *Remembering Buddy: The Definitive Biography of Buddy Holly* (New York: Penguin Books, 1987), 41.

11. Bob Dylan, *Chronicles, Vol. 1* (New York: Simon & Schuster, 2004), 157–158. Also see interview with Dylan in *Rolling Stone*, issue #882 (Nov. 22, 2001).

12. Quoted in Nick Tosches, *Where Dead Voices Gather* (Boston: Back Bay Books-Little Brown, 2001), 151.

13. B. B. King with Dick Waterman, *The B. B. King Treasures: Photos, Mementos and Music from B. B. King's Collection* (New York: Bulfinch Press, 2005), 118 (epigraph for chapter 13).

14. *Blues All Around Me: The Autobiography of B. B. King*, 23. In an interview with the author King expanded on that thought (March 23, 2005, Minneapolis). Interviews with Buddy Guy (February 11, 2005, by phone) and Hubert Sumlin (April 21, 2005, by phone).

15. Interview with the author, July 16, 2004, New York City.

16. Paul Oliver, *Conversation with the Blues*, 2nd ed. (Cambridge, UK: Cambridge University Press, 1997), 107.

17. E-mail message to author, 22 June 2004.

18. Chris Morris, "Legend Lonnie Johnson Resurrected Via Intimate Set From Blues Magnet," *Billboard*, June 24, 2000.

19. Martin Williams, *Jazz Heritage* (New York: Oxford University Press, 1985), 93–95.

20. Ted Gioia, *Delta Blues* (New York: Norton, 2008), 16.

21. "Blues in the Mississippi Night," Alan Lomax recording, available on Rounder Select CD.

22. Gary Giddins, *Visions of Jazz: The First Century* (New York: Oxford University Press, 1998), 9.

23. Quoted in Alan Pomerance, *Repeal of the Blues*, 217–218.

24. Quoted in Geoffrey C. Ward and Ken Burns, *Jazz: A History of America's Music*, 10.

25. Quoted in Craig Werner, *A Change Is Gonna Come: Music, Race and the Soul of America* (New York: Plume Books/Penguin, 1999), 70.

26. Paul Garon, *Blues and the Poetic Spirit* (San Francisco: City Lights Books, 1996), 2.

27. Dizzy Gillespie with Al Fraser, *To Be or Not to Bop: Memoirs—Dizzy Gillespie* (New York: Doubleday, 1979), 424.

28. *The Republic of Plato*, translated with introduction and notes by Francis MacDonald Cornford (New York: Oxford University Press, 1945/1970), 115 (IV. 424), and 90 (III. 401).

29. Dean Alger interview with Henry Townsend, July 8, 2004, St. Louis.

30. Quoted in Alan Pomerance, *Repeal of the Blues: How Black Entertainers Influenced Civil Rights* (New York: Citadel Press-Carol Publishing Group, 1988), 217. Unfortunately, Pomerance did not specify the year Robeson said this, nor did he supply a source for the quote.

31. Alan Lomax, *The Land Where the Blues Began* (New York: Delta Books/Dell, 1993), 16–23.

32. Samuel A. Floyd, Jr., *The Power of Black Music* (New York: Oxford University Press, 1995), 98.

33. Ted Gioia, *The History of Jazz* (New York: Oxford University Press, 1997), 125.

34. Paul Oliver, *The Story of the Blues,* rev. ed. (Boston: Northeastern University Press, 1997), 109.

35. Giles Oakley, *The Devil's Music: A History of the Blues*, 2nd ed. (New York: Da Capo Press, 1983/1997), 164.

36. Bill Wyman with Richard Havers, *Bill Wyman's Blues Odyssey*, 106.

37. Ralph Ellison with Robert O'Meally, ed., *Living With Music: Ralph Ellison's Jazz Writings* (New York: The Modern Library, 2002), 48, 79–81.

38. Camille F. Forbes, *Introducing Bert Williams* (New York: Basic Civitas Books, 2008), 94.

39. On that period, see David G. Nielson, *Black Ethos: Northern Urban Negro Life and Thought, 1890–1930* (Westport, CT: Greenwood Press, 1977). Also see John Hope Franklin, *From Slavery to Freedom: A History of Negro Americans*, 3rd ed. (New York: Vintage Books, 1967).

40. Chris Smith liner notes for *Lonnie Johnson: Complete Recorded Works 1925–1932 . . .* , Volume 4, 9 March 1928 to 8 May 1929, Document Records CD.

41. Randall Sandke, *Where the Dark and the Light Folks Meet: Race and the Mythology, Politics, and Business of Jazz* (Lanham, MD: Scarecrow Press, 2010), 234.

42. A photo of his mother, Louise Monette, can be seen on page 26 in *Jazz* by Geoffrey Ward and Ken Burns (companion book to the PBS documentary).

43. John Edward Hasse, *Beyond Category: The Life and Genius of Duke Ellington* (New York: Omnibus Press, 1993/1995), 112.

44. Quoted in the context of related discussion in Dean E. Alger, *The Media and Politics*, 2nd ed. (Belmont, CA: Wadsworth Publishing, 1996), 6. (Original source: D. McQuail, *Sociology of Communications* (Penguin books, 1972).

45. Taken from radio listings in the *New York Amsterdam News*, September through November, 1929.

46. Peter Guralnick, *Last Train to Memphis: The Rise of Elvis Presley* (Boston: Little, Brown, 1994), 38, 76.

47. Chuck Berry, *Chuck Berry: The Autobiography* (New York: Harmony Books, 1987), 14, 25.

48. Marc Miller, "Louis Armstrong: A Cultural Legacy," chapter 1 in *Louis Armstrong: A Cultural Legacy* (New York: Queens Museum of Art and University of Washington Press, 1994), 17.

49. For the full story on Granz, see Tad Hershorn, *Norman Granz: The Man Who Used Jazz for Justice* (Berkeley: University of California Press, 2011). On a key particular in the Granz actions see Dizzy Gillespie with Al Fraser, *To Be or Not to Bop: Memoirs—Dizzy Gillespie* (New York: Doubleday, 1979), 407.

50. Quoted in Penny Von Eschen, *Satchmo Blows Up the World: Jazz Ambassadors Play the Cold War* (Cambridge, MA: Harvard University Press, 2004), 11–12.

51. Craig Werner, *A Change Is Gonna Come*, 265.

52. Peter Guralnick, *Sweet Soul Music: Rhythm and Blues and the Southern Dream of Freedom* (New York: Harper Perennial/HarperCollins, 1986), 2.

53. *The American Folk Blues Festival, 1962–1966, Vol. 1* (Experience Hendrix/Reelin' In the Years Productions—Hip-O Records).

54. Paul Oliver, *Conversation with the Blues*, 2nd ed., 140.

55. Jas Obrecht, ed., *Rollin' and Tumblin': The Postwar Blues Guitarists* (San Francisco: Miller Freeman Books, 2000), 300.

56. Interview with author, 8 July 2004, St. Louis.

### Notes to Chapter 2

1. Quoted in Nat Shapiro and Nat Hentoff, *Hear Me Talkin' to Ya* (1955; repr., New York: Dover Publications, 1966), 3.

2. James Lincoln Collier, *The Making of Jazz* (New York: Delta Book-Dell Publishing, 1978), 58–61. On Gottschalk: Geoffrey Hidley, ed., *The Larousse Encyclopedia of Music* (Secaucus, NJ: Chartwell Books, 1971), 437.

3. Material from Henry Kmen, *Music in New Orleans* cited in Samuel Charters, *A Trumpet Around the Corner: The Story of New Orleans Jazz* (Jackson: University Press of Mississippi, 2008), 17.

4. Barney Bigard, *With Louis and the Duke* (New York: Oxford University Press, 1986), 5.

5. Geoffrey C. Ward and Ken Burns, *Jazz—A History of America's Music* (New York: Alfred A. Knopf, 2000), 11.

6. David Fulmer, *Chasing the Devil's Tail* (New York: Harcourt, 2003); David Fulmer, *Rampart Street* (New York: Harcourt, 2005); David Fulmer, *Jass* (New York: Harcourt, 2006).

7. Marshall W. Stearns, *The Story of Jazz* (New York: Oxford University Press, 1958), 69; Samuel Charters, *Jazz: New Orleans, 1885–1963* (1963; repr., New York: Da Capo Press, 1983), 3. For revised year, see Donald Marquis, *In Search of Buddy Bolden* (New York: Da Capo 1978), 43–47; Samuel Charters, *A Trumpet Around the Corner: The Story of New Orleans Jazz*, 83–90.

8. Nat Shapiro and Nat Hentoff, *Hear Me Talkin' to Ya* , 7.

9. Howard Reich and William Gaines, *Jelly's Blues: The Life, Music, and Redemption of Jelly Roll Morton* (Cambridge, MA: Da Capo/Perseus, 2003), 18. Alan Lomax, *Mister Jelly Roll* (New York: Pantheon, 1950), 24–25.

10. Frederic Ramsey, Jr., Charles Edward Smith, eds., *Jazzmen* (London: Sidgwick and Jackson, 1939/1957), see especially pp. 12–13, 30. On this, also see Gunther Schuller, *Early Jazz* (New York: Oxford University Press, 1968), especially on page 67: "the only tributary source of jazz that seemed to remain constant was the blues . . . And one can be sure that

when Bunk Johnson says that as a kid he 'used to play nothin' but the blues' in New Orleans barrelhouses, he was playing essentially the same instrumental blues that spread like wildfire in 1920s race recordings. . . ." "Big Eye" quoted in Thomas Brothers, *Louis Armstrong's New Orleans* (New York: Norton, 2006), 66.

11. *Pops Foster: The Autobiography of a New Orleans Jazzman, as told to Tom Stoddard* (Berkeley: University of California Press, 1971), 23. "Interchapter" explanations by Ross Russell.

12. See Howard Reich and William Gaines, *Jelly's Blues* (Boston: Da Capo Press, 2003), 14.

13. Quoted in Ward and Burns, *Jazz*, 7.

14. *Pops Foster: The Autobiography*, 63.

15. George Lewis quote from Thomas Brothers, *Louis Armstrong's New Orleans* (New York: Norton, 2006), 52. For discussion of the Creoles, their status and role in the development of jazz, etc., see, e.g., Collier, *The Making of Jazz*, 59–65; and see Ward and Burns, *Jazz*, 4–18. On the general evolution of condition of African-Americans, see John Hope Franklin, *From Slavery to Freedom: A History of Negro Americans*, 3rd ed. (New York: Vintage Books, 1967— or newer edition). "Marriage of the two schools" quote: *Pops Foster: The Autobiography*, 23.

16. David A. Jansen, Gene Jones, *Black Bottom Stomp* (Routledge: New York, 2002), 184.

17. Interview with Danny Barker from 7/22/74, Hogan Jazz Archive transcript.

18. Barney Bigard, *With Louis and The Duke*, 7.

19. Stearns, *The Story of Jazz*, 51, 54. Review of recent research: Randall Sandke, *Where the Dark and the Light Folks Meet: Race and the Mythology, Politics, and Business of Jazz* (Lanham, MD: Scarecrow Press, 2010), 44–48.

20. *Pops Foster: The Autobiography*, 63. Presuming Foster meant the early players in jazz, etc., in the late 1890s through the early 1910s, this is a touch over-stated, especially since he doesn't mention Creoles; Creole guitarist Charlie Bocage (born 1894) is a prime example of the latter. But, a review of Rose and Souchon's.*New Orleans Jazz: A Family Album* (Baton Rouge: Louisiana State University Press, 1967) makes clear the basic tendency is correctly stated.

21. *Pops Foster: The Autobiography*, specific quote on p. 64.

22. *Oh, Didn't He Ramble: The Life Story of Lee Collins, as told to Mary Collins* (Urbana: University of Illinois Press, 1989); Digests of St. Cyr interview reels I, II, III, IV and VI at Hogan Jazz Archive, Tulane University.

23. Transcript of 5/30/1957 Braud interview from Duke Ellington Oral History Project, NMAH, Smithsonian Institution; transcript in Hogan Jazz Archive, Tulane University, p. 19.

24. Court Carney, *Cuttin' Up: How Early Jazz Got America's Ear* (Lawrence: University Press of Kansas, 2009), 94.

25. Michael Hoffheimer, "Stringing the Blues," *The Strad*, November 2002, pp. 1185; and see Samuel Charters, "Workin' on the Building: Roots and Influences," chapter 1 in Lawrence Cohn, ed., *Nothing But the Blues* (New York: Abbeville Press, 1993), 14–15. Jefferson quote related in Marshall Stearns, *The Story of Jazz*, 54.

26. *Pops Foster: The Autobiography*, quotations on 75 and 46.

27. William S. McFeely, *Frederick Douglass* (New York: Norton, 1991), 306; Lewis Porter, *Jazz: A Century of Change* (New York: Schirmer Books, 1997), 109.

28. Lynn Abbott and Doug Seroff, *Out of Sight: The Rise of African American Popular Music, 1889–1895* (Jackson: University Press of Mississippi, 2002).

29. Copy of application for Social Security account obtained by author; application dated April 29, 1937. In the absence of definitive birth, church or census records so far, 1894 is the author's best conclusion. It's what Lonnie told Big Bill Broonzy: *Big Bill Blues: William Broonzy's Story as Told to Yannick Bruynoghe* (1955; repr., New York: Da Capo Press, 1992),

119. Chris Albertson, who "rediscovered" Lonnie in 1960, produced recordings of him, and interacted with him substantially, reported that Lonnie, while tending to overtly claim he was born in 1900 so as to seem younger, inadvertently revealed his birth date once by saying he was a certain age in a certain year, and Albertson did the arithmetic that led to 1894 as the birth year: Interview with author, 15 July 2004, New York City. (February 8 is consistently used, so we at least know his birthday!) Lonnie also, in a moment of frustration, blurted out to Canadian music booking agent and friend, Roberta Barrett, "I hate being called old, even if I was born in 1894." Lonnie's Chicago Musicians' Union cards are in a Lonnie Johnson file, Harold Washington Library Blues Archive, Chicago. Most oddly, Lonnie's application for his Social Security account lists his birth date as Feb. 8, 1909-?!

30. For a good review of searching such records and many more, especially for African-Americans, see Tony Burroughs, *Black Roots* (New York: Fireside Book/Simon & Schuster, 2001). Lonnie on the family Bible: from author interview with Roberta Barrett 3/21/05. Flood years: information obtained from the US Army Corps Engineers, New Orleans District, "The Mississippi River and Tributories Project" website, *http:www.mun.usace.army. mil/pao/misstrib.htm.*

31. Mark Thomas, *Jazz Quarterly* 2, no.4 (1945); the same wording is used in liner notes by George Hoefer for Disc Records #710 from 1946. These were the earliest references found. Thereafter, articles seemed to just repeat some variation on that line, or they say "at Rampart and Franklin," as in Keith Briggs, "Sam You Can't Do That to Me: A retrospective on Lonnie Johnson . . . ," *Blues & Rhythm*, March 1987.

32. 1883 New Orleans Atlas, Robinson and Pidgeon, New York, published by E. Robinson, found in a Tulane Library special collection.

33. In an interview with British jazz and blues writer and photographer Val Wilmer, she quotes Lonnie as saying he had "six sisters and five brothers" who played music: *Jazz Monthly*, Dec. 1963, pp. 5–7; and Paul Oliver quotes him saying he had "five sisters and six brothers" who played. See *Conversation with the Blues*, 2nd ed. (Cambridge, UK: Cambridge University Press, 1997), 84. But then, in a recorded interview with Lonnie by Moe Asch in 1967, Lonnie says "two sisters played music" (interview on Smithsonian/Folkways CD, *Lonnie Johnson: The Complete Folkways Recordings*, SF 40067). For the first two, it seems likely that Oliver or Wilmer got the sister and brother numbers reversed. But it's hard to explain the latter ver-
. sion, in Lonnie's own voice on the recording. The "in my family you'd better play something" quote is from chapter "Lonnie Johnson: Chased By the Blues" by Chris Albertson in Pete Welding, Toby Byron, eds., *Bluesland: Portraits of Twelve Major American Blues Masters* (New York: Dutton, 1991). Mother apparently played piano: Max Jones, "The Men Who Make the Blues," *Melody Maker*, 30 August 1969; Max Jones writes that he got this information directly from Lonnie.

34. Val Wilmer, "Lonnie Johnson Talks to Valerie Wilmer," *Jazz Monthly*, Dec. 1963.

35. Interviews with Bernie Strassberg, 7/16/04, New York, and with Roberta Barrett, 3/21/05 and 4/4/05, by phone; "Lonnie Johnson Talks to Valerie Wilmer, *Jazz Monthly*, December 1963, first page of article.

36. *Pops Foster: The Autobiography*, p. 92.

37. Paul Oliver, *Conversation with the Blues*, 2nd ed., p. 84. Interview with Moe Asch on *Lonnie Johnson: The Complete Folkways Recordings,* Smithsonian/Folkways CD #SF40067 (track titled "The Entire Family Was Musicians").

38. Key publication asserting 1910–1917 dates: Sheldon Harris, *Blues Who's Who* (New Rochelle, NY: Arlington House Publishers, 1979), 279.

39. Chris Albertson chapter in Welding and Byron, eds., *Bluesland*; Al Rose, Edward Souchon, *New Orleans Jazz: A Family Album* (Baton Rouge: Louisiana State University Press, 1967), 62.

40. Charlie Bocage interview, July 18, 1960, Reel II–Digest, Hogan Jazz Archive, Tulane University.

41. Punch Miller interviews, 9/1/59, Reels I and III summaries, and and 9/25/59 Reel I summary, Hogan Jazz Archive, Tulane University. "Lived in Raceland for 2 or 3 years": Letter from Richard Allen, Hogan Jazz Archive Director, dated Feb. 12, 1971, to Bob Groom of *Blues World* magazine; copy of letter in Hogan Jazz Archive Vertical File on Lonnie Johnson.

42. Paul Oliver, *Conversation with the Blues*, 2nd ed., p. 84.

43. Punch Miller interview, 9/1/59, Reel III summary, Hogan Jazz Archive.

44. Both quotes: Paul Oliver, *Conversation with the Blues*, 2nd ed., p. 84.

45. "widespread proliferation" and "Contemporaneous black press reports" are both from Lynn Abbott and Jack Stewart, "The Iroquois Theater," *The Jazz Archivist* 9, no. 2 (Dec. 1994).

46. Sheldon Wolin, *Politics and Vision* (Boston: Little, Brown, 1960), 363–364.

47. See Alfred Appel, Jr., *Jazz Modernism: From Ellington and Armstrong to Matisse and Joyce*, chapter 1, "Jazznocracy," especially pp. 14, 48–49. In 1917–1919: Vera Stravinsky and Robert Craft, *Stravinsky* (New York: Simon & Schuster, 1978), 175. See "When Picasso Changed His Tune," and "It's the Craftsmen, Not the Singer of the Song" (Holland Cotter and Ken Johnson respectively), *New York Times*, February 11, 2011, pp. C25–C27.

48. Kathy J. Ogren, *The Jazz Revolution: Twenties America and the Meaning of Jazz* (New York: Oxford University Press, 1989), 7. Originally quoted in J. A. Rogers, "Jazz at Home," in Alain Locke, ed., *The New Negro* (1925; repr., New York: Atheneum, 1968), 221–222.

49. Walter Isaacson, *Einstein* (New York: Simon & Schuster, 2007), 280; quote from Philip Courtenay, "Einstein and Art," in Maurice Goldsmith, et al., *Einstein: The First Hundred Years* (New York: Pergamon Press, 2000), 145.

50. Warren Sussman, *Culture as History: The Transformation of American Society in the Twentieth Century* (New Yok: Pantheon Books, 1984), 106.

51. Paraphrased in Robert M. Crunden, *Body and Soul: The Making of American Modernism— Art, Music and Letters in the Jazz Age, 1919–1926* (New York: Basic Books, 2000), 97.

52. Phyllis Rose, *Jazz Cleopatra* (New York: Vintage Books, 1989), 39.

53. Ted Gioia, *Delta Blues* (New York: Norton, 2008), 16.

54. Christine Stansell, *American Moderns: Bohemian New York and the Creation of a New Century* (New York: Metropolitan Books, 2000).

55. Houston Baker, *Modernism and the Harlem Renaissance* (Chicago: University of Chicago Press, 1987).

56. Data cited and quote on p. 77 of Arnold Shaw, *The Jazz Age* (New York: Oxford University Press, 1987). Also see the 2010 book by Peter Muir, *Long Lost Blues: Popular Blues in America, 1850–1920* (Champaign: University of Illinois Press), which well documents how widely blues, or the basic blues idea, pervaded American music as early as the 1910s. RCA best of album: *Country Legends: Jimmie Rodgers*. Malone quote: Bill C. Malone, *Country Music U.S.A.*, rev. ed. (Austin: University of Texas Press, 1985), 104.

57. Harvey G. Cohen, *Duke Ellington's America* (Chicago: University of Chicago Press, 2010), 116, 127.

58. "Armstrong and Ellington: Portrait of the Artist as a Young Man" in Dan Morgenstern, *Living with Jazz* (New York: Pantheon, 2004), 21.

59. Page Smith, *The Rise of Industrial America*, Vol. 6 of his "People's History" of America (New York: McGraw-Hill, 1984), 917.

60. Court Carney, *Cuttin' Up: How Early Jazz Got America's Ear* (Lawrence: University Press of Kansas, 2009), 129.

61. From Panassie, *The Real Jazz* (1942) as quoted in Ted Gioia, *The Imperfect Art* (Palo Alto, CA: Stanford [University] Alumni Association, distributed by Oxford University Press, 1988), 29–30.

62. Robert Santelli, *The Big Book of the Blues* (New York: Penguin Books, 1993), 215.

63. "I'm a Roamin' Rambler," *Jazz Quarterly* 2, no. 4, p. 18. Oliver interview with Lonnie in Paul Oliver, *Conversations with the Blues* (Cambridge, UK: Cambridge University Press, 1997), 140.

64. Bill Haesler, liner notes for album *The Jazz Makers: The Blues of Lonnie Johnson*, Swaggie (Australia) S1255.

65. Steve Voce, "The Return of Lonnie Johnson," *Jazz Journal*, May 1963, p. 13. First article (?) saying "epidemic took all 13 of Lonnie's immediate family": Mark Thomas, "I'm a Roamin' Rambler," *Jazz Quarterly* 2, no. 4 (1945): 18.

66. CD: *Lonnie Johnson: The Complete Folkways Recordings*. The complete interview was posted on National Public Radio in relation to a story on the release of a new CD, *Rediscovering Lonnie Johnson*. Information on statement by Susie Smalls supplied by Rick Bates, and daughter Brenda statement from interview by the author, 3/4/05.

67. Paul Oliver interview with Lonnie on July 17, 1960, in Philadelphia. Much of the interview material is published in Oliver, *Conversation with the Blues*.

68. Dean Alger interview with Henry Townsend, July 8, 2004, in St. Louis.

69. Quoted in liner notes by David Bitten for Prestige/Bluesville album, *Blues by Lonnie Johnson* (his first album in his last "comeback," recorded March 1960).

70. Mark Thomas, "I'm a Roamin' Rambler," *Jazz Quarterly* 2, no. 4 (1945): 18.

## Notes to Chapter 3

1. Kevin Belford, *Devil at the Confluence: The Pre-War Blues of St. Louis Missouri* (St. Louis: Virginia Publishing, 2009), 17.

2. W. C. Handy, *Father of the Blues* (NP: Da Capo Press, 1941/1969?), 142. On the 8-bar interpretation, see Jeff Todd Titon, *Early Downhome Blues* (Urbana: University of Illinois Press, 1977), 26. "Stump" Johnson statement: Paul Oliver, *Conversation with the Blues*, 2nd ed. (Cambridge, UK: Cambridge University Press, 1997), 101.

3. Henry Brown on "Blackmouth": Paul Oliver, *Conversation with the Blues*, 2nd ed., 104.

4. Cecil Brown, *Stagolee Shot Billy* (Cambridge, MA: Harvard University Press, 2003), quote on p. 22.

5. Brown, *Stagolee Shot Billy*, 8.

6. Rudi Blesh and Harriet Janis, *They All Played Ragtime*, 4th ed. (New York: Oak Publications, 1971), 41.

7. Lynn Abbott and Doug Seroff, *Ragged But Right: Black Traveling Shows, "Coon Songs," and the Dark Pathway to Blues and Jazz* (Jackson: University Press of Mississippi, 2006), 3–4.

8. Harriet Ottenheimer, "The Blues Tradition in St. Louis," *Black Music Research Journal* 9, no. 2 (Autumn 1989): 138–141, quote on p. 138, which originally appeared in David A. Jason and Trebor Jay Tichenor, *Rags and Ragtime: A Musical History* (New York: Seabury Press, 1978), 70–71.

9. Leroy Pierson, "80 Years of the Blues," *St. Louis Post-Dispatch*, March 29, 1981, p. 11. James "Stump" Johnson on Son Long: Paul Oliver, *Conversation with the Blues*, 101.

10. Interview with Zutty and Marge Singleton by Steve and Lee Smith for the book *Jazzmen* by Ramsey and Smith, fall 1938; transcript and related notes held in the Hogan Jazz Archive, Tulane University.

11. The prime source, though not an original document, is the respected *Blues Who's Who* by Sheldon Harris (1979; repr., New York: Da Capo Press, 1981), 279. On playing the violin with Creath on the "St. Paul" riverboat: Paul Oliver, *Conversation with the Blues*, 2nd ed., 107.

12. Danny L. Read, "Lonnie Johnson: Groundbreaking Soloist When Recording Was Young," *Guitar Player*, November 1981, 62.

13. William Howland Kenney, *Jazz on the River* (Chicago: University of Chicago Press, 2005), 12–13.

14. David Chevan, "Riverboat Music from St. Louis and the Streckfus Steamboat Line," *Black Music Research Journal* 9, no. 2 (Autumn 1989): 163–167, quote on p. 163. Second quote on adaptation of New Orleans jazz is from Kenney, *Jazz on the River*, 47.

15. Paul Oliver, *Conversation with the Blues*, 140.

16. Interview with Lonnie by Moe Asch of Folkways Records in 1967, four-and-a-half minutes of which are included on the Smithsonian/Folkways CD, *Lonnie Johnson: The Complete Folkways Recordings*. This information was not on the segment included on the CD.

17. Paul Oliver, *Conversation with the Blues*, 2nd ed., 140.

18. See especially Lynn Abbott, "'For Ofays Only': An Annotated Calendar of Midnight Frolics at the Lyric Theater," *The Jazz Archivist* 17 (2003), from the Hogan Jazz Archive, Tulane University Library.

19. Interview with Henry Townsend, St. Louis, July 8, 2004. Mark Miller said he lived in the East St.Louis suburb of Lovejoy, Illinois, but the respective reference note is a bit vague on this: Mark Miller, *Way Down the Lonesome Road: Lonnie Johnson in Toronto, 1965–1970* (Toronto: Mercury Press & Teksteditions, 2011), 29 and reference note 17.

20. Interview with Lonnie by Moe Asch of Folkways Records in 1967, 4 and a half minutes of which are included on the Smithsonian/Folkways CD, *Lonnie Johnson: The Complete Folkways Recordings*; this information is towards the beginning of that segment. The Townsend information on Lonnie in East St. Louis is from Dean Alger's interview with him in St. Louis on July 8, 2004. Carpenter and cook as trades: "Lonnie Johnson Talks to Valerie Wilmer," *Jazz Monthly*, December 1963, 5–7.

21. See the photo of Mary in Sheldon Harris, *Blues Who's Who*, 297.

22. Dean Alger interview with Bob Koester at Delmark Records in Chicago on January 9, 2004.

23. 1967 Asch interview with Lonnie.

24. Verum Clapp, "I Remember Lonnie," *Jazz Journal*, January 1972, 22, 39.

25. Talk with Susie and Brenda in Richmond, Indiana, September 11, 2010, while we were at the Gennett Records Foundation Walk of Fame ceremonies.

26. Chris Albertson, *Bessie*, 2nd ed. (New Haven, CT: Yale University Press, 2003), 203–204.

27. Audio files made from original tapes of interview with Lonnie by Paul Oliver on July 17, 1960, in Phildelphia.

28. Giles Oakley, *The Devil's Music: A History of the Blues*, 2nd ed. (New York: Da Capo Press, 1983/1997), 164–167.

29. For lyrics see Oakley, *The Devil's Music*, 166; Michael Taft, *Talkin' to Myself: Blues Lyrics, 1921–1942* (New York: Routledge, 2005), 318.

30. Dean Alger interview with Townsend, 2004.

31. Paul Oliver, *Conversation with the Blues*, 110.

32. Edmund Morris, *Theodore Rex* (New York: Modern Library, 2002), 172, 261–262. Buck-and-wing at White House: *Theodore Rex*, 80. Arnold Rampersad, *Jackie Robinson: A Biography* (New York: Knopf, 1997), 10–11.

33. Quoted in Jas Obrecht, "Introduction," in Stefan Grossman, *Masters of Country Blues Guitar, Featuring Lonnie Johnson* (New York: Warner Bros. Publishing, 1993), 7.

34. "Better than me": Oliver, *Conversation with the Blues*, 107. Alger interview with Henry Townsend, 2004; Oliver, 105, 107.

35. See Mark Miller, *Way Down That Lonesome Road*, 27–28.

36. Cited in the Lonnie Johnson entry in the Louisiana Blues Hall of Fame.

37. C. A. Schicke, *Revolution in Sound: A Biography of the Recording Industry* (Boston: Little, Brown, 1974), 84–85. The acoustic method was the way recordings were made into 1925. That technology was pretty crude, made recording *groups* especially difficult, and tended to force singing and instrumental playing to be sufficiently loud and targeted to get through the horn and onto the recording disc. In 1925, the Bell Laboratories (related to the Bell Telephone system) released the new electrical recording microphone and (to simplify the story) it was bought and *exclusively* used by the big two record companies, Victor and Columbia. OKeh Record label (a division of General Phonograph) did not have access to the new electrical recording technology. So, from late 1925 until October 1926, when the OKeh label was sold to Columbia, OKeh records were acoustically recorded—and suffered from poor sound quality.

38. Mark Miller, *Way Down That Lonesome Road*, see chapter 3.

39. Henry Townsend, as told to Bill Greensmith, *A Blues Life* (Urbana: University of Illinois Press, 1999), xiii.

40. Lynn Abbott, Jack Stewart, *Jazz Archivist* 9, no. 2 (Dec. 1994): 2.

41. Ben Sidran, *Black Talk* (New York: Holt, Rinehart and Winston, 1971), xiii–xv.

42. Interview by Dean Alger, 2004.

43. Henry Townsend, *A Blues Life*, 36–37.

44. Michael Cogswell, *Louis Armstrong: The Offstage Story of Satchmo* (Portland, OR: Collectors Press, 2003), 27–28.

## Notes to Chapter 4

1. Quoted in the "Introduction" to Jas Obrecht, ed., *Blues Guitar* (San Francisco: Miller Freeman Books, 1993), vi.

2. Lorraine Glennon, ed., *Our Times: The Illustrated History of the 20th Century* (Atlanta: Turner Publishing, 1995), 197.

3. Richard Chapman, *Guitar: Music, History, Players* (London: Dorling Kindersley, 2000), 17. And see Maynard Soloman, *Beethoven* (New York: Schirmer Books, 1977), Chapter 15, especially p. 175 and its footnote.

4. Richard Chapman, *Guitar*, 17.

5. For the vogue in guitar in Europe in the first third of the nineteenth century and significant guitarists and composers, see Chapter 6, "Guitaromanie," in Frederic V. Grunfeld, *The Art and Times of the Guitar* (New York: The Macmillan Company, 1969). Liner notes for *Itzhak Perlman and John Williams: Duos—Paganini and Giuliani* (alternate title), Columbia Records. Henry VIII's guitars: Chapman, *Guitar*, 11.

6. Tony Bacon, *The Ultimate Guitar Book* (New York: Knopf, 1991), 8.

7. Quoted in Tony Palmer, *Julian Bream: A Life on the Road* (New York: Franklin Watts, 1983), 51.

8. Foreword by Stills in Jim Washburn and Richard Johnston, *Martin Guitars: An Illustrated Celebration of America's Premier Guitarmaker* (Pleasantville, NY: Reader's Digest Press, 1997).

9. Andres Segovia, *Segovia: An Autobiography of the Years 1893–1920* (New York: Macmillan, 1976), 42.

10. Quotes in both paragraphs: Robert Palmer, *Rock & Roll: An Unruly History* (New York: Harmony Books, 1995), 193–194.

11. Lawrence Gushee, "The Nineteenth-Century Origins of Jazz," *Black Music Research Journal* 14, no. 1 (Spring 1994): 11.

12. See Tony Palmer, *Julian Bream,* 49 and the discussion through that chapter.

13. Henry Townsend, as told to Bill Greensmith, *A Blues Life* (Urbana: University of Illinois Press, 1999), 18.

14. Francis Davis, *The History of the Blues* (New York: Hyperion, 1995), 62.

15. Tony Russell, *The Blues: From Robert Johnson to Robert Cray* (New York: Schirmer Books, 1997), 17–21.

16. Sylvester Weaver accompanied vaudeville blues singer Sara Martin and then recorded one blues guitar instrumental and a guitar rag instrumental in November 1923; and in mid-1924 he recorded four more sides. But he is not generally seen as a major pioneering influence; this is roughly illustrated by the fact that there is no biographical entry on Weaver in Sheldon Harris's, *Blues Who's Who*, Gerard Herzhaft's *Encyclopedia of the Blues*, or Robert Santelli's *Big Book of the Blues*—though part of the reason for that absence is the fact that little biographical information was available. One Ed Andrews also recorded two blues sides in spring 1924, but the crudely played and sung country blues tunes had no impact. Papa Charlie Jackson, who came from the minstrel and "medicine" shows, was a little more significant. In about August and September 1924, he recorded four blues songs, singing (passably well) and playing good banjo-guitar (physically like a large banjo and sounding like one, but strung and tuned like a guitar); the most notable of them were "Papa's Lawdy Lawdy Blues" and "Salty Dog Blues." He recorded another 16 sides in 1925, mostly blues. Some of his records sold well, so he was a legitimate pioneer in this realm. But again, he did not have a wide impact, though he did help start the process of getting the record labels to cast a wider net.

Nick Lucas was the first good solo guitarist to record pure instrumentals, in 1922. The two sides were, "Pickin' the Guitar" and "Teasin' the Frets." He did not play the blues or jazz; it was general popular music. He was quite good as a finger-picking guitarist; Gibson even made a special model of guitar named after him in the '20s. By the late 1920s and through the '30s Lucas had a strong career on stage and was mostly known as a singer.

Meaning of "Guitar Hero": This term/phrase in Western music and culture refers to a genuinely *virtuoso* guitarist who had very wide impact, and impact that *lasted*. Lucas had rather wide recognition as a guitarist for a few years, but he did not have wide, enduring impact on twentieth-century guitar playing; and the guitar playing on "Pickin' the Guitar" and "Teasin' the Frets" was good finger-style guitar work in a general popular music mode, but was not even close to Lonnie's work as a creative guitar virtuoso.

17. The national tours in the mid- to late-1910s of the "Original Creole Orchestra," so well documented by Lawrence Gushee, are an exception that doesn't overcome the rule. Lawrence Gushee, *Pioneers of Jazz* (New York: Oxford University Press, 2005).

18. "Lonnie Johnson Talks to Valerie Wilmer," *Jazz Monthly*, Dec. 1963.

19. Lenny Carlson, *Away Down in the Alley: The Great Blues Guitar of Lonnie Johnson* (Pacific, MO: Mel Bay Publications, 1993), 14.

20. Bill Greensmith "Introduction" in Henry Townsend, *A Blues Life*, xii.

21. Lenny Carlson, *Away Down in the Alley Blues*, 52.

22. E-mail communication from August 28, 2009.

23. E-mail communication (Aug. 16, 2009) from Chris Smith, co-author of *The Penguin Guide to Blues Recordings*, writer of many CD liner notes, etc.

24. Humphrey's "Bright Lights, Big City" chapter in Lawrence Cohn, *Nothing But the Blues* (New York: Abbeville Press, 1993), 159.

25. Pete Welding, "Ramblin' Johnny Shines," *Living Blues*, July–August 1975, p. 29.

26. Francis Davis, *The History of the Blues*, 133.

27. Peter Guralnick, *Listener's Guide to the Blues* (London: Blandford Press, 1982), chapter 9, pp. 60–61.

28. The phrase "steady rolling man" had apparently been in general use, though how widely I don't know, so maybe Robert just took that saying. But Robert had surely been exposed to Steady Roll as brother of Lonnie from listening to the records they made together in 1926. (Testimony, some of it on the previous page and later in this book, indicates Robert avidly listened to Lonnie's records from various years, as B. B. King told me *he* did at his Aunt Mima's house as a kid. This was common for young, developing blues musicians; those records were treasured in many houses.) Robert may have heard Steady Roll in person in his ramble through St. Louis in 1934 or 1935. At that time, Henry Townsend was an established recording blues musician, and he not only had huge respect for Lonnie Johnson, but also thought Steady Roll was essentially at Lonnie's level as a musician. It was common practice in blues and jazz for one musician to recommend to a second one that he listen to an accomplished other musician; it was especially the case for an established performer to recommend that an up-and-coming younger musician, like Robert Johnson at that time, go hear a particular superb musical artist. Thus, it is a reasonable inference to think that, when Henry played with Robert Johnson during his visit to St. Louis, Henry would have recommended that Robert hear Steady Roll at Katy Red's and/or the Waterfront Club while Robert was in the area. In fact, Robert may have heard Lonnie and his brother playing together at those clubs, since Lonnie was back in St. Louis around that time (see chapter 7). My review, in chapter 5, of Lonnie's 1928 hit record "Crowing Rooster Blues" notes how Robert Johnson also took a key line from that Lonnie J song and made it a keynote line in Robert's own "Steady Rollin' Man," which offers a bit more circumstantial basis for that speculation.

29. Thanks to blues researcher-writer Chris Smith for information on this and other blues lyrics issues. Priscilla Stewart's July 1925 side "Going to the Nation" was apparently the first to use that line, "the sun, it will shine in my door some day," on record, but the line may have been in circulation among blues singers for while. It was also used in one of the all-time great blues songs, "Trouble in Mind," written by Richard M. Jones and first recorded by "Chippie" Hill on February 23, 1926, a little over a month after Lonnie's recording. Lonnie's increasing prominence probably gave its use a good boost, though the popularity of "Trouble in Mind" ultimately gave it a bigger boost.

30. See e.g., Roy Carr, *A Century of Jazz* (New York: Queens Museum of Art, 1994), 23.

31. Paul Oliver, *Conversation with the Blues*, 2nd ed. (Cambridge, UK: Cambridge University Press, 1997), 107.

32. Martin Williams, *Jazz Masters of New Orleans* (New York: Macmillan, 1967), 153–155.

33. B. B. King, *Blues All Around Me* (New York: Avon Books, 1996), 123.

34. Gunther Schuller, *Early Jazz* (New York: Oxford University Press, 1968), 109.

35. Tony Russell, "The Guitar Breaks Through" in Charles Alexander, ed., *Masters of Jazz Guitar* (London: Balafon Books, 1999), 7.

36. Geoffrey C. Ward and Ken Burns, *Jazz: A History of America's Music* (New York: Alfred A. Knopf, 2000), 1–2.

37. Brian Harker, *Louis Armstrong's Hot Five and Hot Seven Recordings* (New York: Oxford University Press, 2011), 109–110.

38. Schuller, *Early Jazz*, 89.

39. Norm Cohen, *Long Steel Rail*, 2nd ed. (Urbana: University of Illinois Press, 2000), 437.

40. Dan Lambert, "From Blues to Jazz Guitar," in James Sallis, ed., *The Guitar in Jazz* (Lincoln: University of Nebraska Press, 1996), 37–38.

41. Frank Driggs and Harris Lewine, *Black Beauty, White Heat: A Pictorial History of Classic Jazz, 1920–1950* (New York: Da Capo Press, 1997).
42. Interview with Dean Alger, July 8, 2004. Although Henry did not specify the model number of the Gibson he described, the L5 best fits the description and timing.
43. David Evans, "High Water Everywhere," in Robert Springer, ed., *Nobody Knows Where the Blues Come From* (Jackson: University Press of Mississippi, 2006), 23.
44. Technically, Bessie's song was apparently written in direct response to flooding of one of the tributaries of the Mississippi, which occurred during the first half of that full, rolling disaster that went on for months.
45. E-mail from Chris Smith, 1 May 2010.
46. Hank Reineke, *Ramblin' Jack Elliott: The Never-Ending Highway* (Lanham, MD: Scarecrow Press, 2010), 88, 86 respectively.
47. Mark Thomas, "I'm a Roaming Rambler," *Jazz Quarterly* 2, no. 4 (1945).
48. "Blues Archive Interview: B. B. King," with William Ferris and others, *Living Blues*, No. 68, p. 13.
49. Jas Obrecht, "Lonnie Johnson" in Stefan Grossman, *Master of Country Blues Guitar, Featuring Lonnie Johnson* (New York: Warner Bros. Publications, 1993), 5.
50. Elijah Wald, *Escaping the Delta: Robert Johnson and the Invention of the Blues* (New York: Amistad, 2004), 175.
51. James B. Dalton, "The Guitar Style of Lonnie Johnson," *Blues Review Quarterly*, no. 11 (1993): 48–49.
52. Dan Lambert, "From Blues to Jazz Guitar" in Sallis, ed., *The Guitar in Jazz*, 38.
53. Dan Lambert in Sallis, ed., *The Guitar in Jazz*, 38, 40.
54. Lenny Carlson, *Away Down in the Alley*, 81.
55. The film, *Nothin' But the Blues*, was made after his back-to-the-roots album, *From the Cradle*, came out. The film is hard to find (if I remember correctly, I videotaped it off the A&E cable channel in 1994).
56. Dean Alger interview with B. B. King March 23, 2005, Minneapolis.
57. "Blues Archive Interview: B. B. King," *Living Blues*, no. 68, 1985.

## Notes to Chapter 5

1. Interview with B. B. King by Dean Alger, Minneapolis, March 23, 2005.
2. Sept. 18, 2003 issue, p. 61.
3. Elijah Wald, *Escaping the Delta: Robert Johnson and the Invention of the Blues* (New York: Amistad/HarperCollins, 2004), 174.
4. 1960 Paul Oliver interview, as per the following reference note.
5. Audio files in two parts made from original tapes from Paul Oliver interview with Lonnie Johnson on July 17, 1960, in Philadelphia. This material is from Part 2, starting at 3:15 minutes.
6. Audio files in two parts made from original tapes from Paul Oliver interview with Lonnie Johnson on July 17, 1960, in Philadelphia. This material is from Part 1, starting at 1:25 minutes.
7. Sheldon Harris, *Blues Who's Who* (New York: Da Capo Press, 1979/1981), 279.
8. W. Royal Stokes, *The Jazz Scene* (New York: Oxford University Press, 1991), 38–39.
9. Little Brother Montgomery interview from May 29, 1958, Hogan Jazz Archive, Tulane University, Reel 1, Track 1 (p. 5 of transcript).
10. Thanks to Richard Shurman for pointing out these influences.

11. Chris Smith liner notes for *Lonnie Johnson: Complete Recorded Works, Volume 4*, Document Records (DOCD-5066).

12. David Evans, "High Water Everywhere," in Robert Springer, ed., *Nobody Knows Where the Blues Come From* (Jackson: University Press of Mississippi, 2006), 51.

13. Paul Oliver interview with Lonnie, 1960, Part 2, at about 11 minutes.

14. Dan Lambert, "From Blues to Jazz Guitar" in James Sallis, ed., *The Guitar in Jazz* (Lincoln: University of Nebraska Press, 1996), 38.

15. Paul Oliver 1960 interview, Part 1 at about 4:50 minutes in audio file.

16. See the photo on page 99 of Lawrence Cohn, *Nothing But the Blues* (New York: Abbeville Press, 1993).

17. Quoted in Lawrence Levine, *Black Culture and Black Consciousness* (New York: Oxford University Press, 1977), 234.

18. See Levine, *Black Culture and Black Consciousness*, 234.

19. From liner notes for *Tampa Red: The Guitar Wizard*, Columbia Records, Roots & Blues series.

20. William Russell and Stephen W. Smith, "New Orleans Music" in Frederick Ramsey, Jr., and Charles Edward Smith, *Jazzmen* (New York: Harcourt, Brace and Co., 1939), 13.

21. Quote in liner notes to volume 6 of the *Document Complete Clara Smith Recordings* CD.

22. Tony Russell, "The Guitar Breaks Through," in Charles Alexander, *Masters of Jazz Guitar* (London: Belafon Books, 1999), 8.

23. Posted Nov. 14, 2004, Pre-War Blues Group online.

24. Lenny Carlson, *Away Down in the Alley: The Great Blues Guitar of Lonnie Johnson* (Pacific, MO: Mel Bay Publications), 125.

25. "Lonnie Johnson Talks to Valerie Wilmer," *Jazz Monthly*, December 1963.

26. "We rehearsed . . .": "Lonnie Johnson Talks to Valerie Wilmer, *Jazz Monthly*, December 1963. Eddie's role: James Sallis, "Eddie Lang" in James Sallis, ed., *The Guitar in Jazz*, 28.

27. Carlson, *Away Down in the Alley*, 125.

28. Stephen Calt, Woody Mann, John Miller, liner notes for *Pioneers of Jazz Guitar*, Yazoo CD #1057.

29. Geoffrey Hindley, ed., *The Larousse Encyclopedia of Music* (Secaucus, NJ: Chartwell Books, 1971), Glossary of Technical Terms, 546.

30. *Away Down in the Alley*, 181.

31. *Away Down in the Alley*, 141.

32. *Away Down in the Alley*, 158; and Carlson added further explanation in e-mailed communications with the author on, August 31, 2011, which I've woven into the material from *Away Down in the Alley*.

33. James Sallis, ed., *The Guitar in Jazz*, 28.

34. Tony Russell, "The Guitar Breaks Through," in Charles Alexander, *Masters of Jazz Guitar*, 7.

35. Nat Shapiro and Nat Hentoff, *Hear Me Talkin' to Ya: The Story of Jazz as Told By the Men Who Made It* (New York: Dover Publications, 1955/1966), 271–272.

36. *Early Jazz* (New York: Oxford University Press, 1968), 109.

37. Quoted in Gary Giddins, *Satchmo: The Genius of Louis Armstrong* (New York: Da Capo Press, 1988/2001), 53; Gunther Schuller, *Early Jazz*, 7.

38. James Sallis, "Eddie Lang," in James Sallis, ed., *The Guitar in Jazz*, 28, 29. On Lang's problem with swinging: James Sallis, *The Guitar Players* (Lincoln: University of Nebraska Press, 1982), 74. "Trip from Naples . . .": Richard Hadlock, *Jazz Masters of the Twenties* (New York: Collier Books, 1965), 248; "Johnson's contagious effect on . . .": Steve Calt liner notes for *Eddie Lang: Jazz Guitar Virtuoso*, Yazoo CD #1059.

39. Paul Oliver 1960 interview, Part 2, at 3:15 minutes, and at 12:03.

40. Mark Humphrey, "Bright Lights, Big City: Urban Blues," in Lawrence Cohn, ed., *Nothing But the Blues*, 157.

41. Paul Oliver 1960 interview, Part 2, at 4:00.

42. Stefan Grossman, "Introduction" to Grossman, *Masters of Country Blues Guitar, Featuring Lonnie Johnson* (New York: Warner Bros. Publications, 1993), 4; James B. Dalton, "The Guitar Style of Lonnie Johnson," *Blues Revue Quarterly*, no. 11 (1993): 48.

43. "Mississippi John Hurt" by Jas Obrecht, obtained 8/20/06 from *www.mindspring. com/-dennist.mjhjas.htm*. Richard Spotswood article in *Blues Unlimited* 4, August 1963.

44. Elmore Theater: ad in *Pittsburgh Courier*, October 16, 1929. Royal Theater: "Timely Topics" column by Salem Tutt Whitney, *Chicago Defender*, October 19, 1929. 81 Theater: "Midnight Steppers Score in Southland," *Pittsburgh Courier*, February 1, 1930.

45. Dean Alger interview with B. B. King, March 23, 2005, Minneapolis.

46. Sheldon Harris, *Blues Who's Who*, 279.

47. E-mail fron Larry Cohn on March 12, 2004, and further exchanges on September 1, 2009. Cohn said Hammond was not explicit about directly hearing the show, just noting its existence to Cohn; but the latter said, from the way Hammond talked about it, it is a fair assumption he had heard the show.

48. Adam Gussow, *Seems Like Murder Here: Southern Violence and the Blues Tradition* (Chicago: University of Chicago Press, 2002), 45, 30.

49. James Sallis, *The Guitar Players*, 51.

50. Dean Alger interview with Jack Wilkins, July 21, 2004, at the New Birdland jazz club, New York City.

51. Jas Obrecht, ed., *Blues Guitar* (San Francisco: Miller Freeman Books, 1993), 21.

52. John Hammond relayed to me by Lawrence Cohn, with whom he worked at Columbia Records.

53. Wald, *Escaping the Delta*, 174.

54. James Sallis, *The Guitar Players*, 37–38. Also on the influence on T-Bone Walker: Helen Oakley Dance, *Stormy Monday: The T-Bone Walker Story* (New York: Da Capo Press, 1987), 2.

55. James Sallis, *The Guitar Players*, 37.

56. Dean Alger interview with Wilkins, July 21, 2004, New Birdland jazz club, New York City.

57. Bill Wyman with Richard Havers, *Bill Wyman's Blues Odyssey* (London: Dorling Kindersley, 2001), 106.

58. See, for example, Peter Broadbent, *Charlie Christian* (UK: Ashley Mark Publishing, 2003), 42.

59. Chris Albertson chapter on Lonnie Johnson in Peter Welding and Tony Byron, *Bluesland*.

60. For a very interesting book on Django, see Michael Dregni, *Django: The Life and Music of a Gypsy Legend* (New York: Oxford University Press, 2004). On Charlie Christian, see, for example, Bill Simon, "Charlie Christian" in James Sallis, ed., *The Guitar in Jazz*; and Dave Gelly, "Charlie Christian" in Charles Alexander, *Masters of Jazz Guitar*.

61. "Lonnie Johnson Talks to Valerie Wilmer," *Jazz Monthly*, December 1963.

62. *Early Jazz*, 109–110.

63. Jas Obrecht, "John Hammond," in *Blues Guitar*, 64.

## Notes to Chapter 6

1. Paul Oliver interview with Lonnie, 1960, audio file, Part 1.

2. "Alhambra Theater" entertainment article/notice, plus ad for the theater, *New York Age*, November 21, 1931.

3. Robert M. W. Dixon and John Godrich, "Recording the Blues," part 3 of Paul Oliver, et al., *Yonder Come the Blues* (1970; repr., Cambridge, UK: Cambridge University Press, 2001), 295.

4. Joe Mosbrook, *Cleveland Jazz History* (Cleveland: Northeast Cleveland Jazz Society, 2003), 122. An advertisement in the *Cleveland Call and Post* issue of April 7, 1934 said: "Majestic Hotel—opens the—HEAT WAVE BAR . . ." (page 6). That suggests it was just opening; but a Cleveland writer cautioned me that the management may have run that notice of the renamed club for weeks, possibly even for months. (He cited an example of another announcement of a "New" club opening that ran for months or almost a year.) It is also *possible* that Lonnie mis-remembered the club name from when he was back in Cleveland playing gigs in other clubs in 1947, but that seems less likely.

5. Joe Mosbrook, *Cleveland Jazz History*, 122.

6. An e-mail of September 29, 2009, from Cleveland jazz historian Joe Mosbrook informed me of the start time for Tatum on WTAM. Also: "Art Tatum Broadcasts Nightly Over WTAM," *Cleveland Call and Post*, March 17, 1934, p. 6.

7. Paul Oliver interview with Lonnie, 1960, audio Part 2.

8. James Lester, *Too Marvelous for Words: The Life and Genius of Art Tatum* (New York: Oxford University Press, 1994), 61.

9. Duke Ellington, *Music Is My Mistress* (New York: Da Capo, 1973), 169.

10. Descriptions of Val's are from Joe Mosbrook, *Cleveland Jazz History*, 24, 29–31; and James Lester, *Too Marvelous for Words: The Life and Genius of Art Tatum*, 61–64.

11. Dan Morgenstern, *Living with Jazz* (New York: Pantheon Books, 2004), 303.

12. Duke Ellington, *Music Is My Mistress*, 170.

13. Count Basie, as told to Albert Murray, *The Autobiography of Count Basie* (1985; repr. with Introduction by Dan Morgenstern, New York: Da Capo Press, 2002), 140.

14. Joe Mosbrook, *Cleveland Jazz History*, 24.

15. Dean Alger interview with Bernard Strassberg, New York City, July 16, 2004.

16. James Lester, *Too Marvelous for Words: The Life and Genius of Art Tatum*, 72.

17. See narrative in Maurice Waller and Anthony Calabrese, *Fats Waller* (New York: Schirmer Books, 1977), 106–110.

18. "In her own words . . . Interview with Mary Lou Williams," *Melody Maker*, April through June 1954 issues (multi-part article). Accessed 9/23/09 at *www.ratical.org/Lwilliams/Mmiview1954.html.*

19. "Wylie Avenue" columns by John L. Clark in *The Pittsburgh Courier*, September 30, 1933 and October 21, 1933.

20. Reported (without specific dates) in Mark Thomas, "I'm a Roamin' Rambler," *Jazz Quarterly* 2, no. 4 (ca. 1945).

21. Peter Guralnick, *The Listener's Guide to Blues* (New York: Quarto Books, 1982).

22. "Masters of Louisiana Music: Lonnie Johnson," *OffBeat* ("New Orleans and Louisiana's Music Magazine"), June 2001, p. 22. Other source: Frank Hoffman, ed., *Encyclopedia of Recorded Sound*, 2nd ed. (New York: Routledge, 2005), in entry titled "Johnson, Lonnie."

23. Stephen Calt liner notes for the album, *Mr. Johnson's Blues*, Mamlish Records.

24. Mike Rowe, *Chicago Breakdown* (New York: Drake Publishers, 1975), 17.

25. Paul Oliver interview with Lonnie, as transcribed in *Conversation with the Blues*, 2nd ed. (Cambridge, UK: Cambridge University Press, 1997), 145.

26. Quotes and descriptions from 1967 Moe Asch interview with Lonnie, and from Oliver, *Conversation with the Blues*, 2nd ed., p. 145.

27. St. Louis Public Library website: *www.slpl.lib.mo.us/libsrc/ghf0402p5.htm* ("Gateway Family Historian" section).

28. Willie Dixon and Don Snowden, *I Am the Blues: The Willie Dixon Story* (London: Quartet Books, 1995), 60–61.

29. Giles Oakley, *The Devil's Music: A History of the Blues*, 2nd ed.(New York: Da Capo, 1997), 176. Other note of Lonnie's influence on Tampa Red and Big Bill Broonzy: Bill Wyman with Richard Havers, *Bill Wyman's Blues Odyssey* (London: Dorling Kindersley, 2001), 161, 316. But surprisingly, the recent book on Broonzy does not offer any material on the Lonnie J-Broonzy musical relation: Bob Riesman, *I Feel So Good: The Life and Times of Big Bill Broonzy* (Chicago: University of Chicago Press, 2011).

30. Mike Rowe, *Chicago Breakdown*, 41.

31. Sonny Boy Williamson quotes: Robert Santelli, *The Big Book of the Blues* (New York: Penguin, 1993), 455.

32. Steven C. Tracy, *Going to Cincinnati: A History of the Blues in the Queen City* (Urbana: University of Illinois Press, 1993), 120, 152–153.

33. From the Library of Congress, "American Life Histories: Manuscripts from the Federal Writers' Project, 1936–1940 [Jazz Music (Chicago)]"; the specific report is titled "Chicago Folkstuff."

34. Brian Priestley, "Soloists of the Swing Era" in Charles Alexander, ed., *Masters of Jazz Guitar* (London: Belafon Books, 1999), 20.

35. Chet Atkins with Bill Neely, *Country Gentleman* (Chicago: Henry Regnery Co., 1974), 135.

36. 1960 Paul Oliver interview with Lonnie, audio file part 2. Larry Gara, *The Baby Dodds Story as Told to Larry Gara* (Baton Rouge: Louisiana State University Press, 1992), xvii. Information on the Three Deuces also comes from my interview with Myra Taylor on July 6, 2004, in Kansas City.

37. Dean Alger interview with Myra Taylor, July 6, 2004, Kansas City.

38. In fall 1940, Winona Short was added; and jazz/cabaret singer Mae Alix joined Hobbs and Lonnie's trio, as one of the "revues" from various clubs performing for a big benefit show on December 13, 1940, which was "to create a Perpetual Community Service Fund" for Chicago (the show and fund effort were backed by Mayor Kelley and two aldermen).

39. Originally published in *Jazz Review*, Max Jones and Albert McCarthy, eds. (London: Jazz Music Books, 1945). Reprinted in *Blues & Rhythm*, no. 156 (February 2001): 18–19.

40. The information on those developments is from club advertisements and photos with captions (probably supplied by the club for publicity purposes) in the *Chicago Defender* Black newspaper in these issues (in order of mention in the paragraph): Photo with caption, March 16, 1940, p. 11; July 13, 1940, p. 11; August 3, 1940, p. 6 (Brass Rail); September 28, 1940, p. 13 (Winona Short); November 30, 1940, p. 11 (Fats Waller-musicians benefit); September 27, 1941, photo with caption on p. 12, and September 19, 1942, p. 9 (*Defender* banquet); December 13, 1941, p. 11 (Perpetual Community Service Fund benefit); December 12, 1942, p. 13 (last ad for appearance at "Square's Lounge").

41. Robert Santelli, *The Big Book of Blues: A Biographical Encyclopedia* (New York: Penguin, 1993), 385.

42. See Paul Garon, *The Devil's Son-In-Law: The Story of Peetie Wheatstraw and His Songs* (Chicago: Charles H. Kerr, 2003), 80.

43. Jazz and popular guitarist George Barnes recorded with an electric as early as March 1938. Country music guitarist Leon McAuliffe evidently recorded "Steel Guitar Rag" using a specially rigged electrified steel acoustic guitar in September 1936. Eddie Durham started experimenting with some form of electric amplification of guitars before the '38 session; in fact, he actually

recorded "Hittin' the Bottle" with one of those experimental electric guitar arrangements in September 1935. And there was an experimental electric guitar effort on a recording in 1935 by guitarist Bob Dunn with the pioneering "Western Swing" country music band, Milton Brown and His Musical Brownies. Leonard Feather, "The Guitar in Jazz" in James Sallis, ed., *The Guitar in Jazz* (Lincoln: University of Nebraska Press, 1996), 4. There is a live recording with Christian at a club in Minneapolis from September 21, 1939. Just below is a full discussion of the pioneering development and uses of electric guitars. On Barnes: Charles Alexander, ed., *Masters of Jazz Guitar*, 20. On early country guitarists' use of electric guitars: Bill C. Malone, *Country Music U.S.A*, rev. ed. (Austin: University of Texas Press, 1985), 157–158.

44. The guitar accompaniment is not at all like Lonnie's other accompaniment work, including the 1938 accompaniment of Wheatstraw just reviewed. Further, it's odd that these recordings for Decca, whom Lonnie was also recording for in the late 1930s, would have placed his guitar so far in the background as to be hard to hear; in fact, it makes no sense to do so with such a significant figure in "race records." Additionally, the playing is weak, simple, and unimaginative, whereas the previous year's recordings for Decca by Lonnie feature very strong, articulate, creative guitar work, which he continued in new sessions just six weeks after those alleged September '39 Wheatstraw recordings.

45. See photos and a little history in Tony Bacon, *The Ultimate Guitar Book* (New York: Knopf, 1992), 54–55.

46. If you are interested in more on the early development of the Gibson electric guitars, see A. R. Duchossoir, *Gibson Electrics: The Classic Years* (Milwaukee: Hal Leonard, 1998), 13–16.

47. For more details and a photo of "the Log," see Tony Bacon, *The Ultimate Guitar Book*, 58–63, and A. R. Duchossoir, *Gibson Electrics: The Classic Years*, 40–46.

48. Duchossoir, *Gibson Electrics*, 41.

49. Quoted in liner notes by Neil Slaven for *Blues Complete*, a Westside CD compilation of early 1950s recordings by Lonnie and others from Jubilee and Rama Records.

50. Thanks—again—to Chris Smith for this music history.

51. Dean Alger interview with Marl Young (by phone), May 25, 2005.

52. "T-Bone Blues: T-Bone Walker's Story in His Own Words," *Record Changer*, October 1947.

53. The photo was/is reprinted in a few places, one having been a special album of Lonnie's 1946 recordings for DISC Records, which included three ten-inch 78 records. New Orleans Wanderers concert/jam session reported in John T. Schenck, "Chicago Breakdown," *Jazz Record*, June 1947, p. 11. Lonnie with jazz session: "Jazz Aces at Twin Terrace," *Chicago Defender*, October 18, 1947, p. 27.

54. Bruce Cook, *Listen to the Blues* (New York: Scribners, 1973), 7–8.

55. Paul Oliver, *Conversation with the Blues*, 2nd ed (Cambridge, UK: Cambridge University Press, 1997), 153.

56. Lonnie's Chicago Musicians' Union Membership Record Card is available in a file in the blues archive in the Harold Washington Public Library of Chicago. Dean Alger interview by phone with Roberta Barrett, March 21, 2005.

57. See, e.g., Robert M. W. Dixon and John Godrich, "Recording the Blues," Vol. 3 in *Yonder Come the Blues* (Paul Oliver listed as first author for full volume) (1970; repr., Cambridge: Cambridge University Press, 2001), 323.

### Notes to Chapter 7

1. Mark A. Humphrey, "Bright Lights, Big City: Urban Blues," in Lawrence Cohn, ed., *Nothing But The Blues* (New York: Abbeville Press, 1993), 159.

2. Buddy Holly's favorite guitarist: Bruce Cook, *Listen to the Blues* (New York: Scribners, 1973), 176. Holly's drummer quote: John Goldrosen and John Beecher, *Remembering Buddy: The Definitive Biography of Buddy Holly* (New York: Penguin Books, 1987), 41. Chuck Berry,. *Chuck Berry: The Autobiography* (New York: Harmony Books, 1987), 25.

3. See Robert Palmer, *Rock & Roll: An Unruly History* (New York: Harmony Books, 1995), 18–23, 6–7.

4. "Tomorrow Night" was composed by Sam Coslow and Will Grosz and was originally recorded by band leader Horace Heidt in 1939.

5. B. B. King with David Ritz, *Blues All Around Me: The Autobiography of B. B. King* (New York: Avon Books, 1996), 23.

6. Dean Alger interviews with Buddy Guy (by phone) on February 11, 2005, and with Robert Lockwood, Jr., in his home in Cleveland on October 28, 2005.

7. Peter Guralnick, *Last Train to Memphis: The Rise of Elvis Presley* (Boston: Little, Brown, 1994), 76.

8. Information from advertisements in *New York Age*, June 20, 1948, p. 6; and *New York Amsterdam News*, July 24, 1948, p. 24, and July 31, 1948, p. 5

9. Liner notes by Jean Buzelin for *Lonnie Johnson: The Rhythm & Blues Years, Vol. 2, 1947–1952*, Blues Collection CD.

10. Liner notes by Colin Escott for "The King Records R & B Box Set," p. 7.

11. Max Jones, "The Men Who Make The Blues," *Melody Maker*, 30 August 1969, p. 12.

12. Quoted in Steven C. Tracy, *Going to Cincinnati: A History of the Blues in the Queen City* (Urbana: University of Illinois Press, 1993), 120–121.

13. Cliff Radel, "King-Sized Dreams," *Cincinnati Enquirer*, November 6, 1994, p. G1.

14. Steven Tracy, *Going to Cincinnati*, 122–123.

15. Transcript of an interview Gary Fortine conducted with Frank Payne, April 16, 1988.

16. *Cleveland Call and Post*, October 21, 1951 and succeeding weeks.

17. Steve Voce, "The Return of Lonnie Johnson," *Jazz Journal* 16, no. 5 (May 1963).

18. Available on *Talking Guitar Blues: The Very Best of Lonnie Donegan*, Sequel Records/ Castle Music.

19. Liner notes by Roger Dopson for double CD album, *Lonnie Donegan: Talking Guitar Blues, the Very Best of . . .* (Castle Music/ Sequel Records). Marc Shapiro, *Behind Sad Eyes: The Life of George Harrison* (New York: St. Martin's Press, 2003), 21. For Harrison's own reflections on Donegan and skiffle music, see Dan Forte, "George Harrison," in the November 1987 *Guitar Player* magazine.

20. See *www.bls.gov/data/inflation_calculator.htm*.

21. Lonnie's royalty check: Stated in "Lonnie Johnson Talks to Valerie Wilmer," *Jazz Monthly*, December 1963. Material regarding the house and debt: Gary Fortine, "Lonnie Johnson in Cincinnati," *78 Quarterly*, Vol. 10, 1999.

22. Liner notes by David B. Bitten for "Blues by Lonnie Johnson" album, Prestige/Bluesville.

23. "Elvis is King" in Lorraine Glennon, ed., *Our Times, The Ilustrated History of the 20th Century* (Atlanta: Turner Publishing, 1995), 412. Dylan: Carl Perkins and David McGee, *Go, Cat, Go: The Life and Times of Carl Perkins* (New York: Hyperion, 1996), 319.

24. Brian Ward, *Just My Soul Responding: Rhythm and Blues, Black Consciousness, and Race Relations* (Berkeley: University of California Press, 1998), 226–227.

25. Robert Palmer, *Rock & Roll: An Unruly History*, 19–20.

26. Brian Ward, *Just My Soul Responding*, 232.

27. Printed as the Foreword in the Berlin Jazz Festival program booklet. See: *http://www. downbeat.com/default.asp?sect=news&subsect=news_detail&nid=1652.*

## Notes to Chapter 8

1. Liner notes by David B. Bitten for *Blues by Lonnie Johnson*, Prestige/Bluesville album.
2. "Interview with Chris Albertson" by Dimitri Zhukov at *http://home.nestor.minsk.by/jazz/interviews/chrisalbertson.html* (accessed 5/3/04).
3. Dean Alger interview with Chris Albertson in his New York City apartment, July 15, 2004.
4. Robert Cantwell, *When We Were Good: The Folk Revival* (Cambridge, MA: Harvard University Press, 1996), 351.
5. See Robert Gordon, *Can't Be Satisfied: The Life and Times of Muddy Waters* (Boston: Little, Brown, 2002), 23, etc. Also see Daniel Beaumont, *Preachin' the Blues: The Life and Times of Son House* (New York: Oxford University Press, 2011).
6. Message to the author, 30 June 2004.
7. Elijah Wald, *Escaping the Delta: Robert Johnson and the Invention of the Blues* (New York: Amistad/HarperCollins, 2004), 220–221.
8. Material from Chris Albertson liner notes for *Blues and Ballads: Lonnie Johnson with Elmer Snowden*, and from Alger interview with Albertson, 2004.
9. E-mail message from Hal Singer's wife, Arlette, relaying Hal's message, 18 August, 2012.
10. Joe Nick Patoski, *Willie Nelson: An Epic Life* (Boston: Little, Brown, 2008), 113; Bill C. Malone, *Country Music U.S.A.* (Austin: University of Texas Press, 1985), 303.
11. Alger interview with Albertson, 2004.
12. For example, in a poignant personal letter to Strassberg dated November 28, 1961, Lonnie said: "I never thought Peter would do this to me, Bernie. I am hurt to the bottom of my heart. You had to take money out of your pocket to loan me bus fair [*sic*]." Strikingly, the particular focus of his complaints this time was his performance with Duke Ellington in Town Hall New York, for which he says he got not a dime?!
Interview by Dean Alger with Bernie Strassberg, New York City, July 16, 2004.
13. Collins George, "Guitarist Lonnie Johnson—Saw Birth of Blues," *Detroit Free Press*, November 6, 1961, p. 30; Mark Thomas, "I'm a Roamin' Rambler," *Jazz Quarterly* 2, no. 4 (1945): 21.
14. "Ellington's Band in Program Here," *New York Times*, November 23, 1961.
15. Advertisement in *The Village Voice*, March 11, 1960, p. 8.
16. Chris Smith liner notes for *Lonnie Johnson: Complete Recorded Works 1937 to June 1947*, Volume 2, Document Records. Alger interview with Strassberg, 2004; Lyn Foersterling, "A Note on Lonnie Johnson," *Jazz Review*, Max Jones and Albert McCarthy, eds. (London: Jazz Music Books, 1945), 7–8.
17. Chris Albertson liner notes for *Blues and Ballads: Lonnie Johnson with Elmer Snowden*.
18. Derrick Stewart-Baxter, "Blues Package—1963," *Jazz Journal*, December 1963; Paul Oliver, "American Blues Festival," *Jazz Monthly*, December 1963.
19. From Interview with Val Wilmer, published in *Jazz Monthly*, December 1963.
20. Willie Dixon and Don Snowden, *I Am the Blues: The Willie Dixon Story* (London: Quartet Books, 1995), 130, 132.


## Notes to Chapter 9

1. The McHarg quote and the quip (from Patrick Scott) about Charles Gall, originally from Scotland, are from the liner notes to the CD, *Lonnie Johnson: Stompin' at the Penny*. . . .
2. McHarg quote and press quotes: Jim McHarg, "Lonnie Johnson," *Coda*, December/January 1965/1966, p. 3.
3. Jim McHarg liner note for the album, *Lonnie Johnson: Stompin' at the Penny with Jim McHarg's Metro Stompers*, Columbia Legacy, Roots and Blues series CD.

4. Phone talk with Ken Whiteley (from Toronto) on July 17, 2011, and e-mail from him on July 15.

5. Jim McHarg, "Lonnie Johnson," *Coda*, December/January 1965/1966, p. 2.

6. The tale of Roberta's meeting with Lonnie and a good deal of the information that follows is from phone interviews with Roberta Barrett on March 21, 2005 and April 4, 2005.

7. Patrick Scott, "Yorkville No Place for Lonnie Johnson," *Toronto Globe and Mail*, May 26, 1965.

8. Mark Miller, *Way Down That Lonesome Road: Lonnie Johnson in Toronto, 1965–1970* (Toronto: The Mercury Press & Teksteditions, 2011).

9. Jim McHarg, "Lonnie Johnson," *Coda*, p. 3.

10. For a good review of the story of Folkways Records, see Richard Carlin, *World of Sound: The Story of Smithsonian/Folkways* (New York: Collins/HarperCollins Books and Smithsonian Books, 2008).

11. From interviews with Richard Flohil, January 16, 2005 (by phone), and with B. B. King, March 23, 2004, Minneapolis.

12. B. B. King with Dick Waterman, *The B. B. King Treasures: Photos, Mementos and Music from B. B. King's Collection* (New York: Bulfinch Press, 2005), 120.

13. Dean Alger interview with B. B. King on March 23, 2005, Minneapolis.

14. "Living Blues Interview: Lowell Fulson," *Living Blues* 2, no. 5 (summer 1971): 20. Liner notes for CD, *The Very Best of Albert King*, Rhino Records "Blues Masters" series, p. 3.

15. Michael Dregni, *Django: The Life and Music of a Gypsy Legend* (New York: Oxford University Press, 2004), 53–54. Tony Russell, "The Guitar Breaks Through" in Charles Alexander, *Masters of Jazz Guitar* (London: Balafon Books, 1999), 7.

16. Dan Lambert, "Django's Blues" in James Sallis, ed., *The Guitar in Jazz* (Lincoln: University of Nebraska Press, 1996), 71.

17. Material and quote from Peter Broadbent, *Charlie Christian*, 2nd ed (UK: Ashley Mark Publishing Co., 2003), 42. On influence of Django, see, for example,the testimony of guitarist Mary Osborne and another quoted in James Sallis, *The Guitar Players* (1982; repr., Lincoln: University of Nebraska Press, 1994), 104–105.

18. From Chris Albertson chapter on Lonnie Johnson in Peter Welding and Tony Byron, *Bluesland* (New York: Dutton Adult, 1991).

19. On the electric guitar as a "new instrument . . .": Dave Gelly, "Charlie Christian" in Charles Alexander, *Masters of Jazz Guitar*, pp. 32-33. For the other points and the second quote in the paragraph, see Gelly, "Charlie Christian" in *Masters of Jazz Guitar*, and "Charlie's Guitar: Charlie Christian" in James Sallis, *The Guitar Players*.

20. Robert Santelli, *The Big Book of Blues: A Biographical Encyclopedia* (New York: Penguin Books, 1993), 423–424. O'Neals' interview with Walker: "Living Blues Interview: T-Bone Walker," by Jim O'Neal and Amy O'Neal, *Living Blues*, no. 11, Winter 1972–1973. Buddy Tate tale/quote: Chapter 5, p. 116.

21. Mark A. Humphrey, "Bright Lights, Big City: Urban Blues" in Lawrence Cohn, ed., *Nothing But the Blues* (New York: Abbeville Press, 1993), 175.

22. Maurice J. Summerfield, *The Jazz Guitar*, 3rd ed. (Newcastle, UK: Ashley Mark Publishing, 1993), 75.

23. Letter from Val Wilmer, July 3, 2013, with quotes and information from interviews with Caton, London 1990–1999, and telephone interviews and Pete Chilver, January 2, 1992 and November 19, 2000.

24. On Tillman, Carl Perkins, etc., see Carl Perkins and David McGee, *Go, Cat, Go!: The Life and Times of Carl Perkins* (New York: Hyperion, 1996), 22–24; Bill C. Malone, *Country Music U.S.A.*, rev. ed. (Austin: University of Texas Press, 1985), 170–172.

25. Chet Atkins and Michael Cochran, *Chet Atkins: Me and My Guitars*,(Milwaukee: Hal Leonard, 2003), 169.

26. Foreword by Eric Clapton for Richard Chapman, *Guitar: Music, History, Players* (New York: Dorling Kindersley, 2000), 6; Buddy Holly citation from chapter 8, p. 269.

27. Clapton, on camera, in *Nothin' But the Blues* film by Martin Scorsese (about 55 minutes into the film). I video-taped this off a cable channel (either VH1 or A&E) in the early 1990s. It apparently is available on DVD, but is hard to find.

28. Clapton studied Mayall's record collection: John Milward, *Crossroads: How the Blues Shaped Rock 'N' Roll (And Rock Saved the Blues)* (Boston: Northeastern University Press, 2013), 43. Mayall "inspired by . . . Lonnie Johnson:" Interview with Mayall, *Guitar Player* magazine, February 2010.

29. Dan Forte, "George Harrison," *Guitar Player*, November 1987.

30. Steven Roby, ed., *Hendrix on Hendrix: Interviews and Encounters with Jimi Hendrix* (Chicago: Chicago Review Press, 2012), 266.

31. Charles Shaar Murray, *Crosstown Traffic: Jimi Hendrix and the Rock 'n' Roll Revolution* (New York: St. Martin's Press, 1989), 8.

32. Bloomfield observation: Murray, *Crosstown Traffic*, 84. Also see Steven Roby and Brad Schreiber, *Becoming Jimi Hendrix* (Boston: Da Capo Press, 2010), 6.

33. See pages 34–36 in Roby and Schreiber, *Becoming Jimi Hendrix*. Further on the B. B. King influence, see Murray, *Crosstown Traffic*, 141.

34. Quoted in Craig Werner, *A Change Is Gonna Come*, 142.

35. *Experience Jimi Hendrix*, MCA/Experience Hendrix/Reelin' in the Years video (2001); the acoustic blues is "Hear My Train A-Comin'."

36. Lenny Carlson, *Away Down in the Alley: The Great Blues Guitar of Lonnie Johnson* (New York: Warner Bros. Publications, 1993), 5 (second paragraph).

37. Tony Palmer, *Julian Bream: A Life on the Road* (New York: Franklin Watts, 1983), 53.

38. See, for example, Norman Weinstein, *Carlos Santana: A Biography* (Santa Barbara, CA: ABC-CLIO/Greenwood Press, 2009), especially 9–11.

39. Gregg Allman with Alan Light, *My Cross to Bear* (New York: William Morrow, 2012).

40. Quoted in B. B. King with Dick Waterman, *The B. B. King Treasures*, 144.

41. Randy Poe, *Skydog: The Duane Allman Story*, 109. On musicians, the South and impacts on the race issue, also see the interesting discussion in Mark Kemp, *Dixie Lullaby: A Story of Music, Race, and New Beginnings in a New South* (New York: Free Press, 2004).

42. Steve Waksman, *Instrument of Desire: The Electric Guitar and the Shaping of Musical Experience* (Cambridge, MA: Harvard University Press, 1999), 2.

43. This and much of the following information is from the interviews with Roberta Barrett on March 21, 2005, and April 4, 2005; interview with Chris Albertson in his apartment in New York City on July 15, 2004; phone interview with Richard Flohil on January 16, 2005, and subsequent e-mails provided further information.

44. Brownie McGhee, "Brownie McGhee Remembers Lonnie Johnson," originally published in *Living Blues* magazine in 1970, reprinted in *Guitar Player* magazine, November 1981, pp. 70–71.

45. Buddy Guy with David Ritz, *When I Left Home: My Story* (Boston: Da Capo Press, 2012), 211.

46. Buddy Guy with David Ritz, *When I Left Home*, 211–212.

47. Information from Danny L. Reed, "Lonnie Johnson; Groundbreaking Soloist When Recording Was Young," *Guitar Player*, November 1981, pp. 69–70.

48. James Agee, Walker Evans, *Let Us Now Praise Famous Men* (Boston: Houghton Mifflin, 1988).

49. Ralph Ellison with Robert O'Meally, ed., *Living With Music: Ralph Ellison's Jazz Writings* (New York: The Modern Library, 2002), 48, 79–81. *Let Us Now Praise Famous Men*, 313, "race records," 255.

50. Jas Obrecht, *Rollin' and Tumblin': The Postwar Blues Guitarists* (San Francisco: Miller Freeman Books, 2000), 300.

51. Statement, on camera, in video documentary *Satchmo: Louis Armstrong*, Columbia Music Video Enterprises, 1989; on my VHS tape this statement is at 1:10:20.

52. Bill Milkowski, "Six String Rapport: Jim Hall and Mike Stern," in James Sallis, ed., *The Guitar in Jazz*, 172.

53. Grossman quote from "Introduction" in Stefan Grossman, *Masters of Country Blues Guitar, Featuring Lonnie Johnson* (New York: Warner Bros. Publications, 1993), 3; Spivey quote from Jas Obrecht, "Lonnie Johnson" in Grossman, *Masters of Country Blues Guitar, Featuring Lonnie Johnson*, 11.

54. Jas Obrecht, "B. B. King and John Lee Hooker" (article originally published 1983) as included in Richard Kostelanetz, *The B. B. King Reader* (Milwaukee: Hal Leonard, 2005), 95.

55. Alain Locke, *The New Negro* (New York: Atheneum, 1968), 209.

56. Gunther Schuller, *Early Jazz* (New York: Oxford University Press, 1968), 109.

57. Quoted in entry on "Lonnie Johnson/Eddie Lang" in "101 Forgotten Greats and Unsung Heroes," *Guitar Player* magazine, February 1, 2007.

58. Terry Teachout, *Pops: A Life of Louis Armstrong* (Boston: Houghton Mifflin Harcourt, 2009).

59. Matt Blackett and staff, "The 50 Greatest Guitar Tones of All Time," in Michael Molenda, ed., *The Guitar Player Book* (New York: Backbeat Books, 2007), 185.

60. Terry Teachout, *Pops,* 144.

61. Quoted in Terry Teachout, *Pops,* p. 377.

62. James B. Dalton, "The Guitar Style of Lonnie Johnson," in *Blues Revue Quarterly*, no. 11, 1993, p. 49.

63. Quoted in Terry Teachout, *Pops,* p. 192.

64. Terry Teachout, *Pops,* p. 141.

65. Brian Harker, *Louis Armstrong's Hot Five and Hot Seven Recordings* (New York: Oxford University Press, 2011), 10-11.

66. See page 96 in chapter 4.

67. Ted Gioia, *The History of Jazz* (New York: Oxford University Press, 1997), 60.

68. Michael Cogswell, *Louis Armstrong: The Offstage Story of Satchmo* (Portland, OR: Collectors Press, 2003), 185.

69. Michiko Kakutani, "Trumpeter Who Gave New Voice to His Age," *New York Times*, November 24, 2009, pp. C1, C8.

70. Nat Shapiro and Nat Hentoff, *Hear Me Talkin' to Ya* (New York: Dover Publications, 1966), 272.

71. Harvey G. Cohen, *Duke Ellington's America* (Chicago: University of Chicago Press, 2010), 575.

## Appendix II Notes

1. William Broonzy's story as told to Yannick Bruynoghe, *Big Bill Blues* (New York: Da Capo Press, 1992), 15 (Introduction).

2. Leroi Jones/Amiri Baraka, *Blues People*, x, xii.

3. Sidney Bechet, *Treat It Gentle* (New York: Da Capo Press, 1978 (1960)), 30, 46–48.

4. Quoted in Randall Sandke, *Where the Dark and the Light Folks Meet: Race and the Mythology, Politics, and Business of Jazz* (Lanham, MD: Scarecrow Press, 2010), 7.

5. Houston A. Baker, Jr., *Modernism and the Harlem Renaissance* (Chicago: University of Chicago Press, 1987).

6. Giles Oakley, *The Devil's Music: A History of the Blues*, 2nd ed. (New York: Da Capo Press, 1997), 97.

7. *John Hammond on Record: An Autobiography*, with Irving Townsend (New York: Penguin Books, 1981), 68.

8. Terry Teachout, *Pops: A Life of Louis Armstrong* (Boston: Houghton Mifflin Harcourt, 2009), 224. Dan Morgenstern, "Portrait of the Artist as a Young Man," in Dan Morgenstern, *Living with Jazz: A Reader*, Sheldon Meyer, ed. (New York : Pantheon, 2004), 39.

9. On this see Raymond Arsenault, *The Sound of Freedom: Marian Anderson, The Lincoln Memorial, and the Concert That Awakened America* (New York: Bloomsbury Press, 2009).

10. Richard Severo, "Norman Granz, Who Took Jazz Out of Smoky Clubs and Put It in Concert Halls, Dies at 83," *New York Times*, November 27, 2001, p. A19. Also see Tad Hershorn, *Norman Granz: The Man Who Used Jazz for Justice* (Berkeley: University of California Press, 2011). On Café Society see Barney Josephson with Terry Trilling-Josephson, *Café Society: The Wrong Place for the Right People* (Urbana: University of Illinois Press, 2009); quote from Dan Morgenstern Foreword, p. xi.

11. Terry Teachout, *Pops,* 283.

12. Stanley Crouch, "Earl and the Duke," *The New Yorker*, January 15, 1996.

13. *Satchmo the Great*: "Louis Armstrong: The Films" in Marc Miller, *Louis Armstrong: A Cultural Legacy* (New York: Queens Museum of Art in Association with University of Washington Press, 1994), p. 175. The photo of Bernstein and Armstrong can be seen on p. 140; the *New Yorker* editorial cartoon is shown on p. 88.

14. A photo of the painting can be seen on page 46 in Marc Miller, *Louis Armstrong: A Cultural Legacy*. It is in the Chicago Institute of Art.

15. Bowie's statement was made in the documentary *Satchmo* (Columbia Music Video Enterprises, 1989), written by Gary Giddins.

16. Harvey G. Cohen, *Duke Ellington's America* (Chicago: University of Chicago Press, 2010), 3.

17. Sadly, this excellent jazz website is now offline.

18. Gary Giddins, *Bing Crosby: A Pocketful of Dreams: The Early Years, 1903–1940* (Boston: Little, Brown, 2001), 139.

19. "Generational effect" quote from Robert S. Erikson and Kent L. Tedin, *American Public Opinion*, 7th ed. (New York: Pearson-Longman, 2005), 136. The "Contemporary youth then . . ." quote is from James Youniss, Jeffrey McLellan, Yang Su, and Miranda Yates, "The Role of Community Service in Identity Development . . . ," *Journal of Adolescent Research* 14, no. 2 (1999): 248–261. The summary of that youth culture pattern and the quote on generational change on interracial marriage are from Peter Levine, *The Future of Democracy: Developing the Next Generation of American Citizens* (Medford, MA: Tufts University Press/ University Press of Massachusetts, 2007), 75, 86.

20. Mark Kemp, *Dixie Lullaby: A Story of Music, Race, and New Beginnings in a New South* (New York: Free Press, 2009), xiii. Gregg Allman with Alan Light, *My Cross to Bear* (New York: William Morrow, 2012), 100.

21. William Barlow, *Looking Up at Down: The Emergence of Blues Culture* (Philadelphia: Temple University Press, 1989), 4–6.

22. Arnold Shaw, *Honkers and Shouters: The Golden Age of Rhythm & Blues* (New York: Collier Books, 1978), 182. B. B. King with David Ritz, *Blues All Around Me: The Autobiography of B. B. King* (New York: Avon Books, 1996), 123.

23. Milt Hinton, David Berger, and Holly Maxson, *The Jazz Photographs of Milt Hinton* (San Francisco: Pomegranate Artbooks, 1991), 118.

24. October 14, 1991, issue.

25. For a good discussion of this, noting most of the key expressions on the issue, see Gene Lees, *Cats of Any Color: Jazz, Black and White* (New York: Oxford University Press, 1994), 225–237.

26. Quoted in Kevin Phinney, *Souled American* (New York: Billboard Books, 2005), 154.

27. Richard Sudhalter, *Lost Chords: White Musicians and Their Contributions to Jazz, 1915–1945* (New York: Oxford University Press, 1999), xvii.

28. Charley Gerard, *Jazz in Black and White: Race, Culture, and Identity in the Jazz Community* (Westport, CT: Praeger Publishers, 2001), 147.

29. Leroi Jones, *Blues People*, quotes on pages 219 and 230–231 successively.

30. *www.deanalger.com*

31. Gene Lees, *Cats of Any Color*, 187.

32. See pages 190–191.

33. Quoted in Lees, *Cats of Any Color*, 240.

34. Gene Lees, *You Can't Steal a Gift* (Lincoln: University of Nebraska Press, 2001), xvii.

35. Tad Hershorn, *Norman Granz: The Man Who Used Jazz for Justice* (Berkeley: University of California Press, 2011), 164–165.

36. Dizzy Gillespie with Al Fraser, *To Be or Not . . . to Bop: Memoirs, Dizzy Gillespie* (New York: Doubleday, 1979), 287.

37. Nat Shapiro and Nat Hentoff, *Hear Me Talkin' to Ya: The Story of Jazz as Told by the Men Who Made It* (New York: Dover Publications, 1955), 252.

38. *Satchmo* documentary film on video (Columbia Music Video Enterprises, 1989), starting about 52 minutes into the VHS tape version (available on DVD).

39. "Most successful recording artist: *www.bingcrosby.com*, "biography" page. ". . . things Bing learned from Louis": Gary Giddens, *Bing Crosby: A Pocketful of Dreams: The Early Years, 1903–1940* (Boston: Little, Brown, 2001), 230–31.

40. "Though his part was small," etc.: Gary Giddens, *Bing Crosby . . . The Early Years*, 419–420.

41. Quotes from Barry Mazor, *Meeting Jimmie Rodgers* (New York: Oxford University Press, 2009), 58, 46.

42. *The Best of the Johnny Cash TV Show, 1969–1971* (Columbia-CMV).

# Bibliography

## About Lonnie Johnson

Briggs, Keith. "Sam You Can't Do That To Me" *Blues and Rhythm*, March 1987. "Reappraisal" of Lonnie Johnson's musical career.

Carlson, Lenny. *Away Down in the Alley: The Great Blues Guitar of Lonnie Johnson*. Pacific, MO: Mel Bay Publications, 1993. Contains transcriptions and analyses of Johnson's recordings.

Grossman, Stefan. with Jas Obrecht. *Masters of Country Blues Guitar: Featuring Lonnie Johnson*. Miami: Warner Bros. Publications, 1993. Contains transcriptions of key Johnson songs. "Country Blues" is just the series name that Grossman established.

James, Steve. "Mr. Johnson's Blues," *Acoustic Guitar* 41 (May 1996): 52–60.

Oliver, Paul. *Conversation with the Blues*. 2nd ed. Cambridge, UK: Cambridge University Press, 1997. Includes several conversation/interview segments with Lonnie Johnson.

Voce, Steve. "The Return of Lonnie Johnson" in *Jazz Journal* (British periodical), May 1963.

Welding, Pete. "The First Jazz Guitarist Who Could Solo: Lonnie Johnson" in *Guitar World*, November 1984.

Welding, Peter and Tony Byron, eds. *Bluesland: Portraits of Thirteen Major American Blues Masters*. New York: Dutton, 1991. Has a chapter on Lonnie Johnson by Chris Albertson.

## About Other Principal Music Figures in the Book

Armstrong, Louis. *Satchmo*. 1954. Reprint with new introduction by Dan Morgenstern, New York: Da Capo Press, 1986.

Giddins, Gary. *Satchmo: The Genius of Louis Armstrong*. Cambridge, MA: Da Capo Press, 2001.

King, B. B. *Blues All Around Me: The Autobiography of B. B. King*. New York: Avon, 1996.

King, B. B., with Dick Waterman. *The B. B. King Treasures: Photos, Mementos and Music from the B. B. King Collection*. New York: The Bulfinch Press, 2005.

Miller, Marc H., ed. *Louis Armstrong: A Cultural Legacy*. New York: Queens Museum of Art, with University of Washington Press, 1994.

Teachout, Terry. *Pops: A Life of Louis Armstrong*. Boston: Houghton Mifflin Harcourt, 2009.

## About Guitarists

Alexander, Charles. *Masters of Jazz Guitar: The Story of the Players and Their Music*. London: Balafon Books/ Outline Press, 1999.

Atkins, Chet. *Me and My Guitars*. Milwaukee: Hal Leonard, 2003. Has beautiful photos of Atkins' guitars, besides text.

Berry, Chuck. *Chuck Berry: The Autobiography*. New York: Harmony Books, 1987.

Broadbent, Peter. *Charlie Christian: Solo Flight—The Seminal Electric Guitarist.* 2nd ed. Blaydon on Tyne, UK: Ashley Mark Publishing, 2003.

Chapman, Richard. Foreword by Eric Clapton. *Guitar: Music, History, Players.* London: Dorling Kindersley, 2000. Includes good, concise sections on classical and flamenco guitar, as well as on popular music guitarists.

Dance, Helen Oakley. *Stormy Monday: The T-Bone Walker Story.* Reprint, New York: Da Capo Press, 1987, originally published by Louisiana State University Press.

Dregni, Michael. *Django: The Life and Music of a Gypsy Legend.* New York: Oxford University Press, 2004.

Gustavson, Kent. *Blind But Now I See: The Biography of Music Legend Doc Watson.* Tulsa, OK: Blooming Twig Books-Sumach Red Books, 2012. New edition coming soon.

Guy, Buddy, with David Ritz. *When I Left Home: My Story.* Boston: Da Capo Press, 2012.

Murray, Charles Shaar. *Crosstown Traffic: Jimi Hendrix and the Rock 'n' Roll Revolution.* New York: St. Martin's Press, 1989.

Obrecht, Jas, ed. *Blues Guitar.* San Francisco: Miller Freeman, 1993. Consists of articles from *Guitar Player* magazine.

Obrecht, Jas, ed. *Rollin' and Tumblin': The Postwar Blues Guitarists.* San Francisco: Miller Freeman Books, 2000.

O'Neal, Jim, and Amy O'Neal. "Living Blues interview: T-Bone Walker." *Living Blues,* no. 11, Winter 1972–1973.

Poe, Randy. *Skydog: The Duane Allman Story.* New York: Backbeat Books, 2008.

Roberty, Marc. *Slowhand: The Life and Music of Eric Clapton.* New York: Crown Trade Paperbacks, 1993.

Roby, Steven and Brad Schreiber. *Becoming Jimi Hendrix.* Boston: Da Capo Press, 2010.

Sallis, James. *The Guitar Players.* Lincoln: University of Nebraska Press, 1994. Includes a chapter on "Mr. Johnson's Blues: Lonnie Johnson."

Sallis, James, ed. *The Guitar in Jazz: An Anthology.* Lincoln: University of Nebraska Press, 1996. Includes chapters by Dan Lambert, "From Blues to Jazz Guitar," and Richard Lieberson, "The Jazz Guitar Duet: A Fifty-Year History," that discuss Lonnie Johnson's music.

Summerfield, Maurice J. *The Jazz Guitar: Its Evolution, Its Players and Personalities Since 1900.* 3rd ed. Newcastle upon Tyne, UK: Ashley Mark Publishing, 1993.

## About Guitars

Bacon, Tony. *The Ultimate Guitar Book.* New York: Alfred A. Knopf, 1992.

Brookes, Tim. *Guitar: An American Life.* New York: Grove Press, 2005.

Carter, Walter. *Gibson Guitars: 100 Years of an American Icon.* Nashville: Gibson Publishing Co., 1994.

Grunfeld, Frederick V. *The Art and Times of the Guitar.* New York: The Macmillan Company, 1969.

St. John, Allen. *Clapton's Guitar: Watching Wayne Henderson Build the Perfect Instrument.* New York: Free Press, 2005.

Shaw, Robert, and Peter Szego. *Inventing the American Guitar: The Pre-Civil War Innovations of C. F. Martin and His Contemporaries*. Milwaukee: Hall Leonard Books, 2013.

Waksman, Steve. *Instruments of Desire: The Electric Guitar and the Shaping of Musical Experience*. Cambridge, MA: Harvard University Press, 1999.

Washburn, Jim, and Richard Johnston. Foreword by Stephen Stills. *Martin Guitars: An Illustrated Celebration of America's Premier Guitarmaker*. Pleasantville, NY: Reader's Digest Books, 2002.

## Blues History

Albertson, Chris. *Bessie*. Rev. ed. New Haven: Yale University Press, 2003.

Broonzy, Big Bill, with Yannick Bruynoghe. *Big Bill Blues*. 1955. Reprint, New York: Da Capo Press 1992.

Charters, Sam. *The Bluesmakers*. New York: Da Capo, 1991. Originally published as *The Bluesmen* I & II, 1967, 1977.

Cohn, Lawrence, ed. Introduction by B. B. King. *Nothing But the Blues*. New York: Abbeville Press, 1993.

Cook, Bruce. *Listen to the Blues*. New York: Scribners, 1973.

Davis, Francis. "Blues Walking Like a Man: The Complicated Legacy of Robert Johnson," *The Atlantic Monthly*, April 1991. Includes discussion of Lonnie Johnson's influence on Robert.

Davis, Francis. *The History of the Blues*. New York: Hyperion, 1995.

Dixon, Willie, and Don Snowden. *I Am the Blues*. London: Quartet Books, 1989.

Guralnick, Peter. *Searching for Robert Johnson*. New York: Plume-Penguin, 1989.

Handy, W. C. *Father of the Blues*. 1941. Reprint, New York: Da Capo Press, 1991.

Keil, Charles. *Urban Blues*. Chicago: University of Chicago Press, 1966.

Lomax, Alan. *The Land Where the Blues Began*. New York: Delta-Dell, 1993.

Murray, Albert. *Stomping the Blues*. New York: Da Capo, 1976. An interesting personal perspective on the nature of blues and jazz and their broader significance.

Oliver, Paul. *The Story of the Blues*. Rev. ed. Boston: Northeastern University Press, 1997.

Oliver, Paul, et al. *Yonder Come the Blues*. Cambridge, UK: Cambridge University Press, 2001. Contains sections originally published as separate books: "Savanah Syncopators" by Paul Oliver; "Black, Whites and Blues" by Tony Russell; and "Recording the Blues" by Robert M. W. Dixon and John Godrich.

Palmer, Robert. *Deep Blues*. New York: Penguin Books, 1982.

Russell, Tony. *The Blues: From Robert Johnson to Robert Cray*. New York: Schirmer Books, 1997.

Titon, Jeff. *Early Downhome Blues*. Urbana: University of Illinois Press, 1977.

Townsend, Henry, as told to Bill Greensmith. *A Blues Life*. Urbana: University of Illinois Press, 1999.

Wald, Elijah. *Escaping the Delta: Robert Johnson and the Invention of the Blues*. New York, Amistad-HarperCollins, 2004.

## Jazz History

Bechet, Sidney. *Treat It Gentle*. 1960. Reprint, New York: Da Capo Press, 1978.

Berendt, Joachim-Ernst, and Gunther Huesmann. *The Jazz Book: From Ragtime to the 21st Century*. 7th ed. Westport, CT: Lawrence Hill Books, 2009.

Blesh, Rudi. *Shining Trumpets: A History of Jazz*. 2nd ed. 1958. Reprint, New York: Da Capo Press, 1976.

Brothers, Thomas. *Louis Armstrong's New Orleans*. New York: Norton, 2006.

Charters, Samuel. *A Trumpet Around the Corner: The Story of New Orleans Jazz*. Jackson: University Press of Mississippi, 2008.

Collier, James Lincoln. *The Making of Jazz*. New York: Delta-Dell, 1978.

Driggs, Frank and Harris Lewine. *Black Beauty, White Heat: A Pictorial History of Classic Jazz*. 1982. Reprint, New York: Da Capo Press, 1996.

Cohen, Harvey C. *Duke Ellington's America*. Chicago: University of Chicago Press, 2010.

Foster, Pops, with Tom Stoddard. *The Autobiography of a New Orleans Jazzman*. Berkeley: University of California Press, 1971.

Gioia, Ted. *The History of Jazz*. New York: Oxford University Press, 1997.

Giddins, Gary. *Visions of Jazz*. New York: Oxford University Press, 1998.

Hasse, John Edward. *Beyond Category: The Life and Genius of Duke Ellington*. 1993. Reprint, London: Omnibus Press, 1995.

Kenney, William. *Jazz on the River*. New York: Oxford University Press, 1993.

Shapiro, Nat and Nat Hentoff, eds. *Hear Me Talkin' to Ya: The Story of Jazz as Told by the Men Who Made It*. 1955. Reprint, New York: Dover Publications, 1966.

Stearns, Marshall. *The Story of Jazz*. 1958. Reprint, New York: Oxford University Press, 1970.

Teachout, Terry. *Duke: A Life of Duke Ellington*. New York: Gotham Books, 2013.

Ward, Jeffrey C., and Ken Burns. *Jazz: A History of America's Music*. New York: Alfred A. Knopf, 2000.

## On New Orleans (Nonfiction and Fiction)

Barker, Danny. *Buddy Bolden and the Last Days of Storyville*. New York: Continuum, 2001. Barker was a top rhythm guitarist in jazz, born in New Orleans.

Campanella, Richard and Maria Campanella. *New Orleans Then and Now*. Gretna, LA: Pelican Publishing, 1999. Contains a fine collection of photos, etc., on the Crescent City in earlier years and the 1990s.

Fulmer, David. *Chasing the Devil's Tail; Rampart Street; Jass*. New York: Harcourt, Inc., 2003, 2005, 2006. These are three mystery novels that wonderfully evoke the look, feel and music of New Orleans around 1900.

Marquis, Donald M. *In Search of Buddy Bolden: First Man of Jazz*. Rev. ed. Baton Rouge: Louisiana State University Press, 2005.

Rose, Al, and Edmond Souchon. *New Orleans Jazz: A Family Album*. Baton Rouge: Louisiana University Press, 1967. A wonderful album of brief descriptions of many New Orleans jazz and pre-jazz musicians, with many photos.

Rose, Al. *Storyville, New Orleans: Being an Authentic, Illustrated Account of the Notorious Red-Light District.* Tuscaloosa: The University of Alabama Press, 1974.

Sublette, Ned. *The World that Made New Orleans: From Spanish Silver to Congo Square.* Rev. Ed. Chicago: Chicago Review Press, 2009.

## African-American History, and Culture

Franklin, John Hope. *From Slavery to Freedom.* 3rd ed., New York: Vintage, 1967.

Levine, Lawrence. *Black Culture and Black Consciousness.* New York: Oxford University Press, 1977.

Nielson, David G. *Black Ethos: Northern Urban Negro Life and Thought, 1890-1930.* Westport, Connecticut: Greenwood Press, 1977.

## Music and Race and Civil Rights

Arsenault, Raymond. *The Sound of Freedom, the Lincoln Memorial, and the Concert That Awakened America.* New York: Bloomsbury Press, 2009.

Barlow, William. *Looking Up at Down: The Emergence of Blues Culture.* Philadelphia: Temple University Press, 1989.

Ellison, Ralph. *Living With Music: Ralph Ellison's Jazz Writings.* New York: The Modern Library, 2002.

Gerard, Charley. *Jazz in Black and White: Race, Culture, and Identity in the Jazz Community.* Westport, CT: Praeger Publishers, 2001.

Guralnick, Peter. *Sweet Soul Music: Rhythm and Blues and the Southern Dream of Freedom.* New York: HarperCollins, 1986.

Jones, LeRoi (later: Amiri Baraka). *Blues People: The Negro Experience in White America and the Music That Developed from It.* New York: Morrow Quill Paperbacks, 1963.

Josephson, Barney, with Terry Trilling-Josephson. *Café Society: The Wrong Place for the Right People.* Urbana: University of Illinois Press, 2009.

Kemp, Mark. *Dixie Lullaby: A Story of Music, Race, and New Beginnings in a New South.* New York: Free Press, 2004.

Lees, Gene. *Cats of Any Color: Jazz, Black and White.* New York: Oxford University Press, 1994.

Oakley, Giles. *The Devil's Music: A History of the Blues.* New York: Da Capo Press, 1997. This good blues history also has a rich broader theme on African-American sociology and the impact of music on society.

Pomerance, Alan. *Repeal of the Blues: How Black Entertainers Influenced Civil Rights.* New York: Citadel Press-Carol Publishing, 1988

Sandke, Randall. *Where the Dark and the Light Folks Meet: Race and the Mythology, Politics, and Business of Jazz.* Lanham, MD: Scarecrow Press, 2010.

Sidran, Ben. *Black Talk: How The Music of Black America Created a Radical Alternative to the Values of Western Literary Tradition.* New York: Holt, Rinehart and Winston, 1971.

Stewart, Jeffrey C., ed. *Paul Robeson: Citizen and Artist.* New Brunswick, NJ: Rutgers University Press and The Paul Robeson Cultural Center, 1998.

Szwed, John. *Crossovers: Essays on Race, Music, and American Culture*. Philadelphia: University of Pennsylvania Press, 2005.

Von Eschen, Penny M. *Satchmo Blows Up the World: Jazz Ambassadors Play the Cold War*. Cambridge, MA: Harvard University Press, 2004.

Ward, Brian. *Just My Soul Responding: Rhythm and Blues, Black Consciousness, and Race Relations*. Berkeley: University of California Press, 1998.

Werner, Craig. *A Change Is Gonna Come: Music, Race and the Soul of America*. New York: Plume Books-Penguin, 1999. New edition from University of Michigan Press.

### African-American Music in General

Courlander, Harold. *Negro Folk Music*. 1963. Reprint, New York: Dover Publications, 1992.

Floyd, Samuel, Jr. *The Power of Black Music*. New York: Oxford University Press, 1995.

Southern, Eileen. *The Music of Black Americans*, 2nd ed. New York: Norton, 1983.

### Other Musical Genres, Miscellaneous

Dylan, Bob. *Chronicles, Volume 1*. New York: Simon & Schuster, 2004.

Guralnick, Peter. *Last Train to Memphis: The Rise of Elvis Presley*. Boston: Little, Brown, 1994.

Malone, Bill C. *Country Music U.S.A.* Rev. ed., Austin: University of Texas Press, 1985.

Palmer, Robert. *Rock and Roll: An Unruly History*. New York: Harmony Books-Crown Publishers, 1995.

Schicke, C. A. *Revolution in Sound: A Biography of the Recording Industry*. Boston: Little, Brown, 1974.

### Modern Society, Music and Modern Art

Appel, Alfred, Jr.. *Jazz Modernism: From Ellington and Armstrong to Matisse and Joyce*. New Haven, CT: Yale University Press, 2004.

Carney, Court. *Cuttin' Up: How Early Jazz Got America's Ear*. Lawrence: University Press of Kansas, 2009.

Crunden, Robert M. *Body and Soul: The Making of American Modernism*. New York: Basic Books, 2000.

Ogren, Kathy J. *The Jazz Revolution: Twenties America and the Meaning of Jazz*. New York: Oxford University Press, 1989.

Shaw, Arnold. *The Jazz Age: Popular Music in the 1920s*. New York: Oxford University Press, 1987.

# Subject Index

# Song Index